The Morenci Marines

The Morenci Marines

A Tale of Small Town America and the Vietnam War

Kyle Longley

 University Press of Kansas

Published by the University Press of Kansas (Lawrence, Kansas
66045), which was organized by the Kansas Board of Regents
and is operated and funded by Emporia State University, Fort
Hays State University, Kansas State University, Pittsburg
State University, the University of Kansas, and Wichita State
University

Library of Congress Cataloging-in-Publication Data
Longley, Kyle.
The Morenci marines : a tale of small town America and the
Vietnam War / Kyle Longley.
pages   cm.—(Modern war studies)
Includes bibliographical references and index.
ISBN 978-0-7006-1934-4 (hardback)
1. Vietnam War, 1961–1975—Biography. 2. Vietnam War,
1961–1975—Veterans—United States—Biography. 3. United
States. Marine Corps—Biography. 4. Marines—Arizona—
Morenci—Biography. 5. Morenci (Ariz.)—Biography. I. Title.
DS557.5.L66   2013
959.704'30922—dc23
[B]
2013021887

British Library Cataloguing-in-Publication Data is available.

Printed in the United States of America

10 9 8 7 6 5 4 3 2 1

The paper used in this publication is recycled and contains
30 percent postconsumer waste. It is acid free and meets the
minimum requirements of the American National Standard
for Permanence of Paper for Printed Library Materials Z39.48-
1992.

To my great friends
Irving and Barbara Rousso and Helen Osif

and my beautiful wife, Maria

Contents

Preface and Acknowledgments

On a warm desert morning on April 30, 2000, I walked out of my house and to the sidewalk to pick up the Sunday *Arizona Republic*. Little did I know that I soon would embark on a long journey of research and writing.

That day, Betty Reid wrote a story, nearly two full pages long, about a band of brothers, most of them recent graduates of Morenci High School, who had headed to Marine boot camp on July 4, 1966. Within two and a half years, six of the nine died in combat in Vietnam. The newspaper piece articulated well the sorrow of the three who survived as well as the community. As I read the story, I fixated on its importance and how much more probably existed to it.

After reading the piece, I cut it out and filed it away. I already had a number of projects under way on topics ranging from US–Latin American relations to a biography of a prominent antiwar Tennessee senator. Still, I wanted to write a longer version of that *Arizona Republic* article.

Slowly, I began amassing materials and doing some interviews. Even then, I realized that I needed to know more about the experiences of Americans who served in the front lines in Vietnam. Although several good surveys existed, they largely did not cover people like the nine young men from the Southwest. I backtracked and wrote another book, a macrostory on Vietnam combat soldiers entitled *Grunts: The American Combat Soldier in Vietnam*. Once that work was completed in 2008, I dived headfirst into this book.

Though I wrote four other books in the past decade, this story was the one that I woke up thinking about each morning and the one on my mind when I fell asleep. It consumed me, all elements of it. I wanted to understand why the nine marched off to war, even as it became increasingly unpopular. I sought to better comprehend how the community shaped them. I needed to better determine how their friendship played out, both in life and in death. Many more questions arose as I pushed forward, a process that never proceeded fast enough for me or others. Still, after years of hard work, the final product came together.

There are many people to thank for sacrificing their time to assist me. George Herring, my doctoral adviser and a dean of the historians of the Vietnam War, read chapters and provided insightful feedback. He remains the single most important intellectual influence in my life as well as a good friend who never anticipated the frequent phone calls and correspondence that would come years after he sent me out into the academic world.

The same dedication to this book also came from one of my favorite people in the world: Vicki Ruiz. She provided encouragement throughout, from writing grants to finishing the work. During her time at Arizona State University and then at University of California–Irvine, she took time out of her busy schedule to talk with me not only about this project but also about her own work, which strongly shaped my focus on topics related to race and gender. She remains a valued friend and colleague.

Another instrumental person in this process has been my close friend and mentor Shirley Eoff at Angelo State University. She provided me wonderful editorial support throughout, reading and correcting every grammatical misstep. She also proved a great sounding board for many of the ideas as well as the structure of the book. I truly have benefited from her expert editorial skills and guidance.

Others have devoted their time and expertise to this project. Good friends from my days at the University of Kentucky have been invaluable, including Steve Wrinn, Bob Brigham, Nick Sarantakes, and Col. John Shaw. The same is true for colleagues at Arizona State University, among them Ed Escobar, Gayle Gullett, Matt Garcia, Keith Miller, Carlos Vélez-Ibáñez, Phil Vandermeer, Catherine O'Donnell, Rachel Fuchs, Andrew Barnes, Chouki El-Hamel, Don Critchlow, and Linda Sargent Wood. I have also had some wonderful students, both graduate and undergraduate, who served as sources of intellectual stimulation, including Col. Tim Cochran, Jean-Marie Stevens, Blake Jones, James Holeman, Jon Flashnick, Sabrina Thomas, Carlos Lopez, Ali Rund, Dylan Crane, Michael Minerva, and Seth Pate. A special thanks goes to my former dean, Quentin Wheeler, who has been a great proponent and friend. Finally, archivist Chris Marin and Arizona historian extraordinaire Marshall Trimble (as well as his songwriting partner Pete Willman) gave me guidance on uncovering materials and provided insights into living in an Arizona mining community.

I have been blessed with being a member of a wonderful community of scholars. Many friends inspire me with their own work and camaraderie, such as Mitch Lerner, Andrew Preston, Jason Parker, Jason Colby, Ron Milam, Dustin Walcher, David Schmitz, Richard Immerman, David Anderson, Andy Fry, Carol Adams, Seth Jacobs, Bob McMahon, Laura Belmonte, Jim Seikmeier, Brian Delay, Ann Heiss, Peter Hahn, Tom Zeiler, Kathryn Statler, Alan McPherson, Max Friedman, Jeremy Kuzmarov, Anne Foster, Ken Osgood, Brad Coleman, Andy Johns, Elizabeth Cobbs, Michael Schaller, Terry Anderson, Molly Wood, Walter LaFeber, Thomas Paterson, Michael Hogan, Scott Laderman, Marilyn Young, Marc Selverstone, Lien Hang-Nguyen, Thomas Schwartz, Emily Rosenberg, David Snyder, Brian Ethridge, Fred Logevall, and Jeff Engel. Other influential colleagues include David Wrobel, Janet Fineman, Peter Blodgett, Lorena Oropeza, Tom Turley, Al Camarillo, Barbara Molony, Al Hurtado, Andy Kirk, Carl Abbott, David Igler, Kevin Leonard, David Johnson, and Susan Schmid.

In addition, I have been blessed with a great working relationship with people at the University of Texas–Austin, particularly at the Strauss Center at the LBJ School of Public Affairs. Adm. Bobby Inman, Frank Gavin, Will Inboden, Kate Weaver, Jeremi Suri, Celeste Ward Gventer, Mark Lawrence, Jackie Jones, and Bill Brands have provided strong support and intellectual development over the past few years.

Many others assisted the project by reading parts of the manuscript or developing concepts that I employed in the work, including Doug Brinkley, Allan Millett, Mike Parrish, Karl Jacoby, John Bodnar, Katherine Benton-Cohen, Kelly Lytle-Hernandez, Kristin Hass, Chip Dawson, Brian Linn, John McManus, and Irwin Gellman. I must also thank agent E. J. McCarthy. Though we did not complete the project together, he proved an invaluable resource and refined the presentation. Others played a role, including Andy Wiest, who read the manuscript and had significant insights on improving it.

A number of people in the US military, past and present, have helped shape this project, including Col. Tim Geraghty, Col. Ed Boyd, Col. Gian Gentile, Col. Kevin Farrell, Col. Greg Daddis, Col. Jorge Silveira, Maj.

Andrew Forney, Tim Day, David White, and Bill Gordon. They have been vital resources, through both conversations and their works. A special thanks goes to my friend Adm. Jim Stavridis, currently supreme allied commander, Europe. We have spent a great deal of time talking about the war and its history and literature, as he remains one of the most voracious readers I know. He proved a prized source on many levels.

Others along the way have been very helpful, particularly people working at numerous archives throughout the country. Ken Williams at the Marine Corps Archives in Quantico, Virginia, deserves special recognition. In addition, Steve Maxner and the staff at the Texas Tech Vietnam Center were especially helpful at making available useful oral histories. Finally, the amazing people at the Lyndon B. Johnson Library assisted me in gathering materials and have been advocates for this project, in particular Mark Updegrove, Marge Campbell Morton, and Tina Houston.

Of course, some of the most important contributors to this work have been the people with deep roots in southeastern Arizona. The Garcia, Draper, Cranford, Cisneros, and Sorrelman families have been especially helpful. Many others, including Sherry and Arnold Carbajal, Ernest Calderon, Oscar and Manny Urrea, Mike and Steve Guzzo, Walter Mares, William Senne, Cathy and Patti Naccarati, Gerald Hunt, Russ Gillespie, Larry Kenan, Armando Rameriz, Robert Martinez, Art Montez, Carol Navarette, Don Hoffman, and so many more, took time to help push this project forward. I thoroughly have enjoyed getting to know them, and I have valued their hospitality.

I also want to thank a series of friends I have made over the past decade as I worked in the President's Enrichment Program (PEP). They include Kathy Simon, Peter and Regina Bidstrup, Dan and Anne Donahoe, Bernard and Carolyn Garrett, David Low, Bob and Rona Rosenthal, Mikki and Stanley Weithorn, Jay Simon, Susie Lavenson, Joel and Ruth Griesman, Tom Taradash, Suzanne Parelman, George Scheer, Merv and Lorraine Lakin, Dick and Olga Seiler, Tom and Sandy Allen, Fred Salmon, Bernie Goldman, Alan and Joan Cohen, Jay and Kathleen Witkin, Bill and Linda Orr, Don and Betty Wilson, Arnold and Anita Brenner, Fran Manley, Jean and Jim Meenaghan, Janis Lyon, and Harriett Friedland, as well as many others (I am sorry I could not name everyone). A special thanks goes to Sally and Hunter Moore, who have been especially supportive. These individuals, along with numerous others, have been good friends and have given me some excellent teaching experiences.

Others within the President's Enrichment Program have become remarkable friends, and I dedicate this book to them. I first met Irving and Barbara Rousso and Barbara's mother, Helen Osif, a decade ago in the first seminar I ever taught. They have attended class after class, usually sitting in the front row. Though Irving often pointed out his lack of academic training, I learned quickly that he was one of the smartest people I know. More important, we have spent much time together outside the classroom, sharing meals and great stories. Each of these three people represents the best of what our country produces, hardworking and generous individuals. I have so thoroughly enjoyed our time together.

I also owe a special thanks to Dick and Alice "Dinky" Snell, who have buttressed my work with a generous fund with which to do research and attend conferences. For nearly a decade, they have been there for me, as both benefactors and friends. I thank them for being such good supporters, and this book has benefited significantly from their patronage.

Finally, I have many family and friends to thank for their encouragement and assistance along the way, including my parents, Joe and Chan, who have nurtured me over the past forty-nine years. They supported my passion for history, and my father especially served as a great role model of what an educator should and could be. He also remains the toughest editor I have. The same goes for my best friend, Dwayne Goetzel, and his wife, Dawn, who have been wonderful comrades, always willing to listen to me and provide words of encouragement; they often keep me humble, as well, and remind me of my origins.

Of all my friends and family, the closest person to me remains my wife, Maria, the other person to whom I dedicate this book. The daughter of an academic, she knew the drill when we married. She carried a heavy burden through the endless hours of my disappearances to research and write. She also endured my constant talking about the project and provided encouragement during the times when roadblocks seemed insurmountable. Often, people ask how I am so productive, and I respond that it is because of her.

Maria also provided coverage for me as I had to take time away from my two young sons, Sean and Drew. Both are the truest pleasures of my life, and they watched me sit at the computer working away for hours.

Sean frequently asked me questions about the Vietnam War, even going as far as to read a good survey to try to understand the subject. He is a remarkably smart and gifted child. Along with Sean, Drew proved my best distraction from the work. He is one of the most lovable kids in the world and could easily pull me away to play. In the end, writing this book was a group project, with Maria providing the emotional support and the boys the needed diversions from heavy topics. I truly love them.

I want to recognize the role of the people at the University Press of Kansas. Mike Briggs maintained an interest in my topic from the first time we discussed it. I settled on the press because of its wonderful reputation for publishing the best in military history and also because of the great recommendations from many friends who had worked with Mike. The production staff, led by Kelly Chrisman Jacques, has put in many hours in copyediting, gathering and editing photos, and so many other tasks. Others, including Rebecca Murray Schuler and Susan Schott, also made substantial contributions to the project. I truly appreciate them, as well as Joan Sherman, who copyedited the work. The press has been so supportive of this book, and I am sincerely grateful for that.

In conclusion, I add one more thank you. I recognize God for giving me the talent and character to produce this book. Many prayers have been said over it, ranging from those asking for wisdom to tell the story well to those asking for the perseverance to see it to the end. We sometimes take things for granted that are part of the grand plan, including all the friends made before and during a long-term project, all put there for a reason. Throughout, I have felt the guiding force of God's presence on this book. Without it, nothing would have ever been produced.

The Morenci
Marines

Introduction
A Small Town and the Vietnam War

For weeks in June 1983, tensions had been building in the copper-mining town of Morenci, Arizona, paralleling the rising temperatures in the desert. Since the last major strike in 1967, threats of work stoppages had arisen every three years when negotiations on contracts began. Occasionally, stoppages happened, though they tended to be very short as the company planned for maintenance, and families built their vacations around the anticipated breaks.

This time, however, the stakes were higher because the Phelps Dodge (PD) Company appeared emboldened by the antiunionism of the Reagan administration, which already had crushed the Air Traffic Controllers Union. In their New York high-rise offices, the executives had listened carefully as analysts from the Wharton Business School and others mapped out a strategy to destroy the miners' union and turn back years of gains by the workers. The negotiations with the Morenci workers would conclude a grand battle for supremacy. In the past, company officials had always avoided hiring scabs and had shut down the mine during negotiations, but now, PD leaders issued ominous warnings about their plans to fire strikers and hire replacements.[1]

At midnight on June 30, workers walked off their jobs at the massive open-pit mine, accompanied by their colleagues from the smelter that operated in the shadow of the nearly always fuming smokestacks. "PD will flex its muscles. We'll flex ours. PD'll make a few claims, crunch a few numbers, cut a few deals, and then we'll settle. Everyone will be back at work in a few weeks," one worker proclaimed. Not everyone agreed. "We're going to lose this one. The best thing is if the union accepts what

1

they can so they can hold the union here and keep us together," another responded, adding, "too many souls owed to the company store."[2]

This work stoppage lasted much longer than anyone anticipated. Both sides dug in their heels, the workers listening to their union leaders' promises of victory even as the PD executives prepared for the long haul, secure in their plan to destroy the opposition. The stoppage would bear more of a resemblance to the nine-month stalemate of 1967 and 1968, when many of the men now manning the picket lines had been serving in Vietnam. This time around, however, no prolabor politician resided in the White House, nor had fifty thousand workers walked away from their jobs simultaneously in solidarity with their union brothers. Instead, management decided to take on one small group in isolated southeastern Arizona.

That fateful day, three men stood with their union brothers. Joe Sorrelman, Leroy Cisneros, and Mike Cranford had been in the military in 1967 during the last long standoff. No longer teenage Marines, they now had families and bills to pay. Yet they refused to abandon their friends. Joe told one person, "I couldn't betray the other people in the union." Mike added, "We wouldn't let one of the group fall out [in Vietnam]. And that's where it all starts. That's where your unionism goes back to."[3]

For the three men, the strike constituted just another part of a journey they began together seventeen years earlier when they joined six other friends—Stan King, Bobby Dale Draper, Van Whitmer, Larry West, Robert Moncayo, and Clive Garcia, Jr.—in making a fateful decision. In March 1966, these sons of miners and smelter workers chose to volunteer for the Marine Corps, and on July 4, 1966, they boarded a bus for San Diego. They stuck together in boot camp, helping each other endure the rigors. Then, at various junctures, each headed to Vietnam. Unfortunately, only Joe, Leroy, and Mike returned. The others died in combat between August 1967 and November 1969. Ultimately, their story received national attention, and the group became known as the Morenci Nine.

That critical day in June 1983, the survivors had to wonder what it might have been like with their friends standing alongside them. Mike and Larry had been good buddies since elementary school, and Larry would never have deserted his friend. The pugnacious Clive would have been a vocal leader, denouncing anyone crossing the picket line. Another natural leader and the son of a longtime smelter worker, Stan would have towered above everyone at 6'5" and been a dominating presence. Few doubted that the quiet and introspective Robert would have stood with his friends and family, an extremely loyal soldier.

But others in Morenci would not stay strong. Though Bobby Dale would never have left behind his childhood friends just for a job, some of his fellow Mormons chose to cross the picket line in 1983.[4] Van, who shared Bobby Dale's faith, might have joined his friends as well, although his family's roots in Morenci were not as deep as those of the others and he may not have been there at the time of the strike. Nonetheless, there would have been other veterans, all joined together by their shared experiences of the military and Vietnam. A larger presence would have strengthened the resolve of the three friends.

Unfortunately, events years earlier had tragically changed the trajectory of the lives of six members of the Morenci Nine—young men who never aged a day in the minds of their friends. Now, the community's losses would only be compounded as the town divided when PD began firing workers and replacing them with scabs and individuals who deserted the union. The environment became a powder keg, with threats made against those who betrayed their friends and crossed the picket lines. In response, Governor Bruce Babbitt ordered the Arizona National Guard, complete with snipers and armored vehicles, to occupy the camp. Ultimately, guardsmen attacked the strikers with tear gas and clubs. Yet despite the pressures, Joe, Mike, and Leroy stood firm for more than a year before joining many of the displaced workers in a massive exodus from Morenci, with only Mike ever returning to live in the area again.

In the end, PD emerged victorious after three years, destroying the power of the union and forever changing labor relations in Morenci. The mining camp, one that had experienced momentous turmoil throughout its existence, never fully recovered from the divisions caused by the 1983 strike. It was a sad chapter in a rich history of vibrant community, one that too often had been replicated in other mining and industrial towns across the country.

Some may question whether the story of nine young men and their decision to join the Marine Corps in July 1966 really deserves much attention. The answer is unequivocally yes. Though it has unique characteristics, the tale of the Morenci Nine has several significant commonalities with the stories of many others who fought in Vietnam. Their narrative spotlights a generation of young adults who joined the military during the tumultuous 1960s and informs people not familiar with the period about the often hard choices that were made, many with long-term consequences.

During the Vietnam War, young men from across the country joined in large numbers, pushed forward by patriotism, the draft, and declining economic opportunities. Many came from small towns, especially those who joined the Army and Marines and comprised the frontline combat troops. Many had just graduated from high school and were the sons of farmers, miners, industrial workers, tradespeople, or lower-middle-class clerical and government workers.[5] Although the demographics changed over time with the ending of deferments and the implementation of the lottery system, the Morenci Nine in 1966 represented a significant number of the American combat soldiers who fought in Southeast Asia.

In particular, the Nine reflected a demographic of the Southwest, where Mexican Americans and Native Americans constituted a sizable part of the population. People east of the Mississippi typically viewed race relations through the lens of a black-white dichotomy, but in the Southwest and the Mountain West, the racial dynamics were far more complex and fluid. And throughout the region, many Mexican Americans and Native Americans joined the US military, particularly the branches that funneled large numbers of soldiers into the fighting in Vietnam. Among the names of the casualties from the area extending from Oklahoma to Southern California and from Arizona and New Mexico up to Idaho, Mexican American surnames appear frequently. Thus, the story of the Morenci Nine in many ways reflected the realities of the Southwest regarding military service.

Finally, the Morenci story was replicated across the country in various small towns and urban industrial communities that experienced a significant clustering of deaths. In Bardstown, Kentucky, for example, the activation of a National Guard unit and its deployment to Vietnam ultimately led to a considerable number of deaths.[6] Beallsville, Ohio, lost 6 young men out of a population of just 475.[7] In some cases, even large cities experienced a concentration of deaths. Thomas Edison High School in Philadelphia had 54 graduates die in Vietnam. The disproportionate death rates—and the lost potential they represented—often arose from patriotic idealism, youthful feelings of invincibility, and a lack of economic opportunities.[8]

The blood sacrifice made in Vietnam was uneven for small towns and working-class and lower-middle-class communities. They experienced death on a much greater scale compared to areas of affluence or communities with strong antiwar cultures. Many factors played out in this regard—the bad luck of being in the wrong place at the wrong time; the timing of service, since more Americans died in 1968 and 1969 than in the other years combined; and a host of other dynamics. However, certain common factors, including the draft and socioeconomic background, fostered a concentration of deaths in some sectors of the country.

Yet there are also unique characteristics in the story of the Morenci Nine that make it especially compelling. The young men came from a segregated mining camp completely dominated by a major corporation, PD. The company controlled all aspects of life, telling people where they could live and with whom and managing all facets of the community, down to the schools and the security forces. It provided health care along with all utilities and even a company store where people shopped. Being such a small, insular community created a distinct political culture that shaped the decisions people made about joining the military during the Vietnam era, as well as how people dealt with the losses the war brought.

Furthermore, the fact that the nine young men all headed to the front lines in Vietnam also ensured a relatively distinctive experience for the group. Most of the more than eight million Americans who served in the military during that era never neared the shores of Vietnam. And of the more than two million men who did serve in Vietnam, the majority never fought in the rice paddies or jungles on the front lines. At the most, only 20 percent drew the difficult task of humping through the harsh environment in search of the enemy. The Morenci Nine all received that assignment, as did many others from small towns across the United States, demonstrating an uneven distribution of the most dangerous duties in the Vietnam War.

The clustering of deaths among the Morenci Nine was unusual as well. The odds of dying in Vietnam in combat were less than 10 percent. Thus, based on probabilities, in a group of nine only one person should have died. However, 66 percent of the Morenci Nine died in Vietnam, five within an eight-month period. Something similar happened often in World War II due to the fact that many communities had National Guard units mobilized and deployed throughout the world, but this was much less frequent in Vietnam. Consequently, the Morenci case study provides insights into how families and friends and, to a larger degree, the small and tight-knit community dealt with the staggering losses they sustained.

This project was exceptionally challenging to construct. My earlier work focused on prominent politicians such as José Figueres and Senator Albert Gore, Sr.[9] In each prior study, I had a multitude of sources to consult in archives, public documents, letters, and published oral histories. If anything, I had too much to review rather than too little, and that forced me to make many choices on what to include.

However, in this book, the materials were sparse, and I needed to capture much of the detail through legwork—for instance, by conducting a large number of personal interviews. In addition, I devoted significant time and energy to tracking down people with primary materials, including letters, photographs, and videos that provided vital insights into the personal lives of the Morenci Nine. There was no central depository to aid the process, no easy way to glean materials for relevance. The project proved a challenge on many levels.

One of the most difficult aspects of re-creating the story of the Morenci Nine involved capturing the voices of the dead.[10] The book is uneven in certain ways, but it was never my intent to honor the lives of some more than others. It just worked out that the primary materials and other sources privileged some, especially the living, because their voices were present. At times, family members refused to talk about their relatives due to the great sadness that it caused. Others gladly provided letters and access to numerous people who wanted to talk and who provided in-depth information. It was not by choice but by circumstance that the imbalance occurred, and it naturally shaped the narrative.

When available materials were redundant, the timing of the person's service in Vietnam influenced the story. For example, I described in detail Joe Sorrelman's experiences in a frontline combat unit as opposed to those of Robert Moncayo or Van Whitmer. Joe went first, and it would have been unnecessarily repetitive to describe everyday life in a frontline rifle company more than once. In addition, because Van was in country just forty-three days before he died and Robert just eighteen, only a limited amount of information existed for these two soldiers. Again, my goal was not to privilege one over the other or diminish the importance of either; rather, access, timing, and the demands of the narrative structure dictated the relative attention given to individual actors in the compelling drama at the heart of this book.

In addition, the types of materials that the study relied upon to build the story contained inherent challenges. Historians who use oral history understand the obstacles that exist in employing such materials. The narratives are often compiled many years after the events they describe. In that time, memories fade and details disappear. Furthermore, the events become viewed through filters reshaped to protect a memory or promote a particular perspective that bears either positively or negatively on the subject.[11]

In the case of Morenci, several issues highlight this reality. For example, what people did during the 1983 strike, whether standing with the union or acting as scabs, colors the way in which they view their community and how it evolved. Thus, the fact that the three surviving members of the Morenci Nine stood strong with their union brothers might affect their own memories of the events of 1983 or those of others.

Race can also play a role. Some Anglos promote an idealistic view of Morenci, recalling that even though segregated by the company, it really had few racial problems. But some Mexican Americans contest that portrayal, pointing to a repressive environment that often became apparent only after they left the camp and discovered different realities in other settings. In both visions, the perspective of the individual has been shaped over time by his or her own experiences, clouding views of the past.

Even when presented with letters written by the Morenci Nine, I recognized the limitations of such primary materials. While in combat, the young men frequently censored the words they wrote for the consumption of their parents, friends, and other loved ones. They worried about disclosing too much to their worried mothers and fathers about the dangers they faced. Others withheld information about their extracurricular activities for the obvious reasons. Consequently, the letters only provide a part of the story, a story that I often struggled to corroborate through other official sources.

Despite the obstacles, enough materials surfaced to create an in-depth study of the Morenci Nine. The story that follows is a moving depiction of an intrepid community composed of hardworking people who made an uneven blood sacrifice during the Vietnam War. They rarely questioned the conflict, even after the war ended. Yet ambivalence developed over the losses they endured. Some questioned why so many of Morenci's sons died, and they expressed their sorrow. Simultaneously, few could fully accept that the young men died in vain, as radical opponents of the war would have people believe. An inherent tension remains even today as the questions linger—a tension that is unlikely to be resolved in the near future.

1
Life in a Small Town
The Culture of
Morenci, Arizona

In late September 1904, several members of the Sisters of Charity and others from the New York Foundling Hospital, accompanied by more than fifty orphans, gathered at Grand Central Station in New York City. The young children, ages three to six and most of Irish or Irish American descent, waited anxiously to board a train to take them to the territories of New Mexico and Arizona. The orphans were about to embark on a great adventure, one that ultimately would lead many to their new homes in southeastern Arizona and the town of Clifton and the mining camp of Morenci.[1]

After a week traveling to different locales to deposit children, the sisters and their staff arrived at the Clifton Train Station, just in the shadows of the lavender and gray mountains of the northern Sonoran Desert where prospectors had discovered valuable copper deposits in the late nineteenth century. Up the hills to the northwest a couple of miles lay Morenci, Clifton's sister town. There, smelters belched out thick white smoke that reached high into the sky. Morenci's miners toiled underground in extremely dangerous conditions, laboring in long shifts; many others slaved feeding the blast furnaces of the smelter. An abundance of work existed—but only for the hardy souls willing to risk their lives to harvest the copper.

At the train depot, a group of people waited for the arrival of the orphans. In the crowd stood expectant parents, all approved as upstanding Catholics by Father Constant Mandin, the local priest and recent immigrant from France. The women, many darker-complexioned Mexican Americans, looked anxiously at the new arrivals. Meanwhile, Anglo women congregated, drawn by the curiosity of the orphan train. Several became enamored of the little light-skinned children, and anger flared when they watched them being assigned to Mexican American parents from both Clifton and Morenci.

After the crowd dispersed, the Anglo women gathered together and began complaining about the fact that the Mexicans claimed the children. Rumors began circulating that the Mexicans had bought the children. And many of the Anglo women began to perpetuate the negative stereotypes of Mexicans as immoral, lazy, and drunken individuals who would endanger the orphans. Soon, a group of these women began pressuring their husbands and law enforcement officials to act to protect the children.

When local officials hesitated, arguing that they needed to follow the law and work through the courts, a vigilante justice prevailed. Many Anglos held animosities toward the Mexican Americans, particularly for the role they played in the 1903 strike ultimately dispersed by the US military. The Anglos also secured the blessing of the Phelps Dodge (PD) mining boss, Charles Mills, whom Mexicans called the *patrón* or *mayordomo*. He held the true power in the area, far more than even the local government representatives. In fact, in Morenci, the people had no city council, mayor, police chief, or any other officials. Mills embodied all three branches of government, and his word often constituted the law.

In a driving rainstorm on October 2, 1904, bands of armed Anglos, aided by some PD officials, spread out over Clifton and Morenci to round up the orphans. They appeared at the homes of the Mexicans armed with Winchester rifles and shotguns, beating on front doors with the ends of their guns to wake the occupants. Sleepy inhabitants cautiously opened the doors to find the well-armed Anglos demanding the children. Only in one case did a Mexican vigorously refuse to comply, but after a heated argument, even he relented. Ultimately, the vigilantes gathered with their wives at a local hotel and distributed the children to relatively prosperous Anglo families to raise as their own. Their work done with the complicity of Mills and the acquiescence of local officials, the vigilantes helped families start lives with their new children while many of the Mexicans, women in particular, grieved over their losses.

Representatives from the Catholic Church immediately complained about the kidnappings. The sisters from the Foundling Hospital contacted their superiors, who began legal proceedings to have the orphans returned to the Mexican American Catholic families. In January 1905, several children from Greenlee County, along with their parents, gathered at the Territorial Supreme Court in downtown Phoenix for a trial to determine who should keep the children. Journalists flocked to the courthouse to cover the case. Strangely absent from the subsequent coverage were Mexican Americans' opinions in the affidavits and interviews that flowed from the proceedings. Fearing Anglo reprisals, they avoided both Phoenix and the publicity. Ultimately, with great fanfare, the Arizona Supreme Court upheld the seizures and the adoptions by the Anglos. The parents returned home in triumph with their children in their arms, heartily greeted by a large crowd at the Clifton Train Station.

One final obstacle remained, for the Foundling Hospital appealed the Arizona verdict to the US Supreme Court. But the high court proved equally unsympathetic. Justice William R. Day wrote in support of the Arizona decision, stressing that "the child in question is a white, Caucasian child . . . abandoned . . . to the keeping of a Mexican Indian, whose name is unknown to the respondent, but one . . . by reason of his race, mode of living, habits and education, unfit to have the custody, care and education of the child."[2] Thus ended the efforts to return the children to their Mexican American and Catholic guardians. The children became part of the local Anglo community.

The episode highlights several important characteristics in the history of Morenci and the region. First, the geographic isolation allowed the dominant Anglo socioeconomic groups, often in collaboration with PD officials, to become the law unto themselves. The Anglo vigilantes who kidnapped the orphans feared no retribution. A clear racial and class differentiation existed, which the company supported and sustained, partly to divide the labor force. Though some things changed by the 1960s, in many ways the community structures of the early twentieth century still existed as the Morenci Nine reached draft age in the mid-1960s.

*   *   *

Like the social constructions of the area, the landscape of Greenlee County differed little in the mid-1960s from that of the early twentieth century, apart from the large open-pit mine that created a huge gash in the countryside and began swallowing the land in the 1930s. Located in southeastern Arizona, only about 20 miles from the New Mexico border and 60 miles from Silver City, Morenci rests where the Sonoran Desert ascends into the Apache Sitgreaves Forest, whose peaks ultimately reach over 11,000 feet. In the foothills lies Morenci (latitude 33.078 N and longitude '109.364), over 4,700 feet in elevation. Clifton sits down a thousand feet in the shadow of the peaks of the San Francisco Mountains, and the San Francisco River runs through the town and south toward the Gila River.

The environment that produced the Morenci Nine remains a dry (14 inches of rain in an average year), wild, and sometimes dangerous place. Author Barbara Kingsolver has observed that "everything in the desert is poisonous or thorned,"[3] which is certainly true in Morenci, where creatures with fangs and razor-sharp teeth fill the canyons to the south. Deer and bighorn sheep populate the northern forest, and everywhere, jagged edges protrude from rocks and boulders, threatening all passersby. On paths, loose rocks and red dirt may look stable but can quickly loosen and send people tumbling down steep embankments.

The vegetation is equally inhospitable. Waist-high cacti (including the prickly pear variety) blend in with low-lying, often brown and gray scrub brush. The master of these plains is not the saguaro cactus that visitors view to the west around Phoenix and Tucson but the ocotillo. In many ways, this cactus represents the environment of southeastern Arizona, especially in the hills of the red clay canyons of northern Greenlee County.

The ocotillo resembles an octopus with its head buried in the ground and its tentacles extending stiffly upward into the air, sometimes reaching 10 to 15 feet. For most of the year, its tall, thin, and rigid limbs remain gray, and sharp, thick thorns protrude from the vines, cutting the flesh of the unfortunate person who stumbles into them. During the infrequent rainy periods, however, the plant becomes green and has beautiful orange and red flowers (ovates) sprouting atop the vines. Only robust plants such

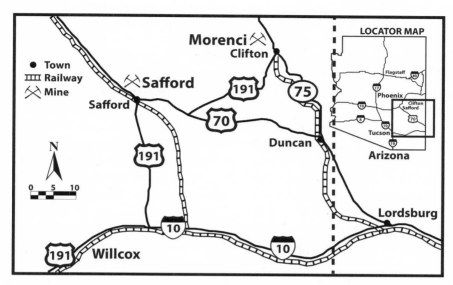

Regional map of southeast Arizona. (Map courtesy of Freeport-McMoRan.)

as the ocotillo survive in the harsh climate of the region, and much the same can be said of the people in this area.

The untamed wildness and rugged environment create a magical and alluring land that appeals to such hardy souls. To the south of Morenci, canyons cut through the red soil, and shallow rivers, such as the San Francisco and Gila, meander through them. Relatively fertile farmland sits farther to the southeast in the Duncan area, where Mormon farmers flourished and large ranches were established, including the Lazy B Ranch owned by Harry Day, father of the future Supreme Court justice Sandra Day O'Connor.[4] To the north are millions of acres of national forest complete with tall pine and aspen trees, flowing streams filled with fish, cold-water lakes, and beautiful meadows that provide a welcome escape from the stifling summer heat. Outdoor enthusiasts love the area for hunting, fishing, and camping, as well as for the beautiful sunrises and sunsets and amazing vistas where one can see for many miles without detecting any real signs of human civilization.

The landscape and environment created a tough and prideful people steeped in western concepts of hard work, self-sufficiency, and rugged individualism. These people lived in relative isolation, far from the creature comforts that many identified with fast-paced city living, such as fancy restaurants and high culture. Males in the area traditionally led an industrial life but often envisioned themselves as outdoorsmen and hence in some ways as heirs to the frontiersmen. They enjoyed guns and hunting and a rambunctious lifestyle characterized by heavy drinking and hard-fought athletic competition on football fields, wrestling mats, and baseball diamonds. When combined with the type of work done by most in the mines and smelters, the personal character of the men in particular seemed well suited for military service, especially for the most physically demanding jobs in the military, including infantryman.

Although the natural environment helped shape perceptions of people and their place in the grand scheme of the world, a major factor that molded people in Morenci remained the mining companies. In the late nineteenth century, the promise of gold and silver attracted people from all over the world to the Arizona Territory. But the more sustainable prize became copper. Throughout the southern half of Arizona, extending from Bisbee and Douglas to Ajo and Jerome, copper became king. In the process, the Morenci-Clifton area became one the biggest producers in the world at a time when the demand for copper skyrocketed with the mass development of electrical power.

In southeastern Arizona, American entrepreneurs and settlers faced numerous obstacles and many hardships. The Apache tribes of the region resisted fiercely but ultimately signed a peace treaty that opened up the new territory, although periodic raiding by leaders such as Geronimo continued into the 1880s. The desert climate and starkness also proved daunting, although the promise of work and the possibility of making a fortune continued to draw robust souls into the area.

These included the Metcalf brothers, James and Robert, who in 1872 discovered copper outcroppings near present-day Morenci and established the Longfellow and Metcalf Mines. Investors began pouring in money to develop the abundant copper deposits, and they provided funds for building a railroad track to the nearest major line, located 60 miles away in Lordsburg, New Mexico. Over time, enterprising individuals such as

James Colquhoun developed a leeching process that allowed for easier extraction of the minerals, and others built smelters that processed the ore. Miners and workers—Anglos, European immigrants, and Mexicans—rushed into the community of Morenci (named after a small town in Michigan). And with them came problems of lawlessness, disease, and a certain degree of anarchy. Nonetheless, by the turn of the twentieth century, several different companies had produced millions of pounds of copper and reaped huge profits.[5]

For Morenci, one company ultimately emerged as the principal force—the Phelps Dodge Company. The New York City–based corporation, working through its agents in the southwest territories, among them James Douglas, created a mining empire. In 1895, Douglas traveled to Morenci, where he quickly built up the existing operation and bought out competitors.[6] For more than one hundred years, PD completely dominated Morenci. The massive enterprise became one of the largest in the world, moving from underground mining to a huge open-pit operation in 1937. One observer noted that by the early twentieth century, Morenci had become "a formal, legal company town, the provincial capital of a private kingdom."[7]

Life in the company town differed from that experienced by the vast majority of Americans. Mining camps such as Morenci existed all over Arizona, Colorado, and Montana and also in the coalfields of Pennsylvania, Kentucky, and West Virginia. But the complete dominance exerted by PD separated the Morenci camp from other towns, even mining communities such as Globe and Bisbee, which still maintained some autonomy from PD. Democracy existed in Morenci only in a few forums such as the school board, but in reality, PD's officials often superseded those organizations.[8]

Most mining camps resembled a corporate socialist state.[9] The company provided the housing for workers, usually in dwellings that were the same color and size and offered the same amenities. In Morenci, these homes perched on the terraces that climbed from the center of town up the red clay hills. Most had two or three bedrooms, and they rarely exceeded 700 square feet in size. Company officials assigned the homes by seniority and race. Until 1969, PD segregated the town into sections, with Anglos living in several locations, Mexican Americans housed in New Town and Plantsite, and Native Americans occupying Tent City in the shadow of the always billowing smokestack that reached several hundred feet into the sky.[10] Managers and other prominent members of the company, such as doctors, had larger homes, typically located on promontories overlooking the camps, a practice even continued today in new Morenci, where the elite live on what the workers call Snob Hill.

The starkness of the Morenci camp struck many people as they moved into the community or when they visited, even as late as the 1960s. One Irish priest assigned to the local parish in 1962, Eugene O'Carroll, remembered walking out of his house on the first day and then writing his mother, "I'm in a shanty in an old shantytown."[11] Another person traveling to Morenci observed that the town and the belching smelter constituted quite a sight: "The Dantesque image obtained—sulfur, slag, glaring heat, perpetual subterranean fires, roasted landscape . . . seem to fulfill the abomination of desolation of scripture."[12] Morenci took on an even more surreal appearance when the smoke of the smelter blew north into the center of town, leaving it blanketed in what one person described as like the wisp of white smoke produced by a firecracker exploded on a still night, except this wisp engulfed the entire camp.[13]

In Morenci, PD designed the town around the large Longfellow Inn and the Morenci Hall, the latter with its three full stories and archways and large verandas overlooking the camp. Church steeples dotted the landscape, representing all the major denominations, particularly southern ones such as the Baptists and Methodists, although the Catholic Church remained the largest because of its substantial, predominantly Mexican American congregation. Schools also were part of the landscape, figuring prominently in the life of the town. The three-story, white high school built in 1949 stood near the middle of town. A large football field up the hill hosted many events, including baseball games in the spring. Built on an old slag dump, the field forced teams to kick their extra points and field goals on one end because the other end dropped off a hundred feet to the highway below and no one wanted to chase an errant ball.[14]

Also in the center of town was the massive PD Mercantile Store, made largely of limestone and locally quarried red granite. Called one of the finest department stores in all of Arizona at the turn of the twentieth century, it provided the workers with lots of their necessities. Many laborers and their families bought on credit, with the company debiting their paychecks for the purchases or extending loans to those in need,

The old town with the smelter in the background from the 1960s. (Photo courtesy of Marshall Rice.)

Parts of Old Morenci in 1969. (Photo reprinted with the permission of the Arizona Republic.*)*

The old football field built into the side of a hill. (Photo courtesy of Marshall Rice.)

albeit often at relatively high interest rates. For many, the situation clearly fit with the 1950s country song by "Tennessee" Ernie Ford and its famous chorus: "You load sixteen tons, and what do you get? Another day older and deeper in debt. Saint Peter, don't you call me, 'cause I can't go; I owe my soul to the company store."[15] No competition existed unless one traveled down to smaller stores in Clifton or made the long trip to bigger establishments in Safford or Silver City.

The lack of competition extended into all areas of material life. PD owned the water, electric, and gas companies. The company debited the workers' paychecks for their utilities fees and pocketed the profits. Some private enterprises existed, such as the gasoline station and a few restaurants that rented space from the company. Still, PD owned all land and buildings in the camp and even regulated the local cemetery as well as the whorehouse, which operated through the 1950s until a scandal involving an underage prostitute forced its closure.[16]

The company's control of public space meant that little individual space existed. In turn, an artificial conformity developed, enforced by PD policy on everything from the color of houses to how people kept their yards. The company also controlled public spaces such as the libraries, swimming pools, and a few parks. Local law enforcement officials were company security personnel who enforced local edicts passed down by PD officials.[17] Workers understood that divergence from established norms and resistance would result in removal from their jobs and the community, as no one lived in the camp without the permission of PD. Thus, a fairly snug noose hung around everyone's neck, not truly apparent until the person tried to stray too far from the community standards—ones often dictated by company officials.

Workers traded away individual liberties for significant material benefits. When compared with many of their fellow citizens in the small towns of the Southwest, such as Clifton, Duncan, Lordsburg, and Alpine, and especially when compared with people on the reservations, the PD workers and their families had relatively cheap housing, guaranteed medical and dental care, good schools for their children, and comparatively high wages. They took pride in working in an important industry, especially during times of national emergency when copper was a valuable commodity. Yet they often resented working so hard (twenty-six days on and two off through the 1960s) and making massive profits for stockholders on the East Coast. This situation created an often ambivalent relationship between labor and management, one that sometimes erupted into open hostilities.

Labor-management struggles often played a central role in the human relationships of Morenci, and worker strikes constituted one of the few overt acts of resistance to PD hegemony. Morenci's long history of strikes dated back to 1903 when workers, led by Mexican labor organizers, walked out to protest the reduction of hours by the company, particularly after learning that white workers had received wage increases to compensate for their diminished hours. Company officials, relying on territorial guardsmen and federal troops, arrested the leaders and effectively dispersed the agitators, a process aided by huge floods that killed more than fifty people.[18]

A little more than a decade later, the miners again walked off the job but with very different results. In September 1915, Morenci miners left their worksites to demand better wages and recognition of their union, the Western Federation of Miners (WFM). But this time, the workers found a strong ally in the person of former miner and then governor of Arizona George W. P. Hunt. Determined to prevent the murder of workers, as happened in April 1914 in Ludlow, Colorado, Hunt traveled to the area and personally interceded.[19]

This time around, the state government favored the workers despite vocal denunciations by the PD-owned or PD-influenced press. Hunt ordered the National Guard to keep strikebreakers out of town and praised those "who had the temerity to stand up for their rights." Eventually, buoyed by rising copper prices from World War I, PD acceded to the demands of labor and increased wages and recognized the union. However, its officials learned from the action, and later, after Hunt had lost an election by a mere thirty votes, they took a much harder line and forcibly deported striking Bisbee workers, the majority of them Mexican Americans, into the deserts of New Mexico.[20]

Labor unrest always hung over the mines, although during the 1920s the government clearly favored businesses over labor, a process aided by the first Red Scare. In the 1930s, the Great Depression devastated everything, including the mines. PD closed the Morenci operation for nearly five years. But the switch to the open-pit mine in 1937 and the onset of World War II ushered in a new era of prosperity. Vocal workers wanted to share in the wealth, resulting in the founding of a new local chapter of the International Union of Mine, Mill, and Smelter Workers, Local 616. In 1946, with membership growing as the open-pit mine continued to expand, labor leaders led a strike that lasted 107 days. Mexican Americans, many of them World War II veterans, pressured PD for better health care and, just as significant, equal wages for everyone regardless of race. For nearly twenty years, the labor strife would simmer but not boil over in Morenci. But as eight members of the Morenci Nine readied to graduate from high school in 1966, the union spirit persisted and antagonisms brewed just below the surface and threatened to erupt.[21]

The 1946 strike reflected another important reality in Morenci: an imposed division of people by race. Throughout American history, people have been separated by race. In the South and North, the division was generally between African Americans and Anglos, with pockets of Latinos in places such as Chicago and New York City. Racial divides also existed between Native Americans and Anglos in states such as North Dakota, Utah, and Montana. In the Southwest, the division typically revolved around Mexican Americans and Anglos as well as Native Americans, although exceptions existed in the major urban areas of Los Angeles and San Diego, where African Americans settled in large numbers during the various migrations of the twentieth century.

In the Southwest, discrimination against Mexican Americans often paralleled that suffered by African Americans in the South. Morenci proved no different from other parts of the Southwest in this regard, as many of the people who settled there came from regions with strict rules of racial separation. Frequently, these people merely shifted their negative perceptions of African Americans to Mexican Americans and Native Americans. In particular, they viewed Mexicans as lazy, shiftless, and untrustworthy, as well as alien in important cultural ways, such as language, food, and religion. Many Anglos embraced notions of superiority, helping mask their own insecurities about their place in the world as laborers.[22]

PD managers and their policies aggravated existing tensions, creating divisions and undermining class solidarity. Company officials justified their actions (such as providing segregated housing) by claiming that they respected existing social traditions and thereby prevented troubles that would stem from a mixing of the races. Nonetheless, keeping the races apart—a process also aided by the division of the community along religious and cultural lines—made the job of divide and conquer in relation to worker concerns much easier.

Many established institutions reinforced the system, even without being officially segregated. Schools in particular stood out in this regard. The Morenci schools had very few Mexican American or Native American teachers; in fact, only one Mexican American worked in a high school classroom in 1966, and there were not many more throughout the entire school district—despite the student body being nearly 50 percent Mexican American or Native American. Some, though not all, of the Anglo teachers and townspeople showed contempt for the Mexican American culture in particular. In fact, students caught speaking Spanish at school often received corporal punishment, a practice that was replicated across the Southwest for many years.[23]

Some Anglo educators advocated for Mexican American students, but other teachers and administrators typically funneled prominent Anglos, especially those from management and professional families, toward college while pushing Mexican Americans and working-class whites toward trade or technical occupations. One example from the 1960s underscores the point quite clearly. Nellie Calderón was the mother of a bright Mexican American fifth-grader, Ernest. His teacher encouraged her to stop pushing him toward college and instead to focus on getting him into a useful trade. Insulted, the mother refused to comply, and to make a point in later years, she sent graduation announcements to that teacher when her son finished eighth grade, high school, Northern Arizona University (NAU), and the University of Arizona (UA) Law School. Ernest later became president of the State Bar of Arizona and then president of the Arizona Board of Regents.[24] Yet as a schoolboy, he had to overcome obstacles because of the prejudices that persisted in Morenci during the 1960s.

Some Anglos in the town downplayed the persistence of racism, but in fact, discrimination often extended beyond the educational and housing systems and into social settings. By the 1960s, children tended to be less prejudiced than their parents, but they nevertheless had to deal with the results of the racist attitudes of the older generation. At times, this applied to romantic interactions. For example, one young woman's father characterized the Mexican boys in Morenci as notorious womanizers and told her that he would kill her if he caught her involved romantically with a Mexican. Her family also told her never to ride down Gila Street where many Mexicans lived, out of fear for her safety.[25] Yet some of the young people went behind their parents' backs and dated across racial lines, although usually in secret and with a fear of retribution.

Despite the racism, both overt and subtle, most of the young people interacted well in groups such as the Boy Scouts and on athletic teams. And even though the company and their parents (both the Anglos and the Mexican Americans) pushed for separation, the kids proved less likely to divide and frequently interacted within groups such as the cowboys, the jocks, and the nerds. Still, significant wedges existed at many levels, and most of the kids admitted that even if they ran around together during the day, they separated and returned home to their own communities at night. PD's artificial racial construct, combined with existing sensibilities, played a significant role in shaping life in the mining camp.

*   *   *

In 1960s Morenci, teenage boys like the Morenci Nine thought little about the issues of race, labor-management relations, or the strange hold PD had on them and their families. Instead, like many adolescents across the country, they devoted their energies to sports and hunting, trucks and girls, and trying to graduate from high school. Some thought about going to college and about the widening war in Vietnam, but most concentrated on their everyday lives. If the Morenci Nine thought about the long term, their concerns related more to following in their fathers' footsteps in the mines or local jobs, rather than international relations.

But even though the Morenci Nine paid little attention to their environment and its effects, their hometown fundamentally shaped their lives. The education system (strongly affected by race and class) along with the absence of a tradition of attending college in most families helped ensure that the majority of Morenci's male graduates in the class of 1966 did not consider escaping the draft with a college deferment. Most knew deep down that they lived on borrowed time until the selective service system nabbed them. Consequently, many decided to be proactive and make the choice of service on their own terms rather than have it dictated to them. The Morenci Nine understood the situation and accepted its inevitability. Rarely did they look beyond to the root causes of their predicament.

The type of work performed by their fathers also guaranteed that military recruiters would come calling. The sons of miners were tough, hardworking, and skilled hunters and outdoorsmen, and as a result, military recruiters prized them, particularly for the infantry-focused Army and Marines. Moreover, many of their fathers and other relatives had marched off to serve during World War II and in the Cold War. The boys likely had much in common with Vietnam veteran Tim O'Brien, who described his own evolution as a soldier in powerful terms: "I grew out of one war and into another. . . . I was the offspring of the great campaign against the tyrants of the 1940s, one explosion in the Baby Boom, one of the millions come to replace those who had just died. My bawling came with the first throaty note of a new army in spawning."[26] And for the Morenci boys, being in a working-class environment meant that the recruiters would court them with well-rehearsed, tried-and-true methods designed to pique their interest.

The sense of community, fundamentally shaped by PD and its enforced conformity, also helped determine how the Morenci Nine responded to calls to join the military, whether they realized it or not. Unlike millions of others in college towns, upper-middle-class suburbs, and other antiwar enclaves across the country, the Nine never openly questioned the system that pushed them toward military service. During the Cold War years, union members, especially those who already had their loyalty questioned because of their ethnicity, sought to demonstrate their Americanness in a time of conflict. Furthermore, the education system of Cold War America enshrined patriotism as a core value, and community forums such as the editorial pages of Morenci's local newspaper, the *Copper Era,* reinforced conformity to American ideals.[27] Even company officials buttressed that message, especially in order to shut down criticism of PD, a need that had been clearly demonstrated in the 1951 workers' strike against Empire Zinc in nearby Bayard, New Mexico.[28] Thus, on both a conscious and a subconscious level, the young men of Morenci thought about military service and what it meant to them and their families and friends in terms of what constituted real American patriotism.

Finally, having grown up in a working-class setting, these young men weighed the long-term benefits of military service, beyond the travel and adventure promised by recruiters. Knowing about the mundaneness of the work miners did, about the recurring need for assistance during hard times, and about the isolation miners experienced, the Morenci boys saw the benefits of belonging to the fraternity of veterans. They would gain access to groups such as the American Legion and the Veterans of Foreign Wars (VFW), both prized memberships in social organizations that would help break the monotony of a miner's everyday life. Military service would also give them entry into a brotherhood respected by the community, in recognition of their service to the nation. Lastly, they considered the material benefits that came with access to the Veterans' Affairs Department and other assistance programs provided by the government. In a small town, all of these factors meant a great deal—even for youths who normally did not look all that far into the future.

Despite the uniqueness of its physical setting, Morenci in many ways resembled thousands of other small towns across the country that contributed large numbers of troops for the American effort in Vietnam. The most common element among these towns was the political culture, derived from the national level but with local variations. In Morenci, though labor and racial strife often divided people, the community never wavered in its patriotism. Even the angriest worker who would denounce the PD leaders as brutally exploitative never viewed the American political system as anything but the finest system possible, particularly during the Cold War years. As a result, the mines, farms, industrial centers, and other small communities of the nation, including urban ethnic enclaves, produced a steady stream of infantrymen for the US military during the Vietnam War.

2

Semper Fi Boys
The Morenci Nine Join the US Marine Corps

Throughout the third week of November 1965, the people in Morenci prepared for the annual gridiron battle with the hated Clifton Trojans. Everywhere—in store windows, at school, in front yards—signs appeared supporting the Wildcats. Youngsters attached streamers of black and red to car radio antennas and poles, and shoe-polish slogans of "Beat the Trojans" or "Go Morenci" adorned windshields and storefront windows. The Clifton-Morenci football game sparked more enthusiasm and passion than almost any other event of the year in Greenlee County.

On Thursday evening, a large group gathered between the school and the local swimming pool. Cheerleaders, clad in skirts and sweaters of black and red with pom-poms rustling, exhorted the crowd with shouts under the yellow glow of a large bonfire whose flames threw large shadows on the red canyon walls; embers rose into the sky, a burnt offering to the god of football. The young warriors, decked out in their letter jackets (complete with stripes to let people know how many years they had been on varsity and patches signifying their awards), stood around the bonfire as coaches Truman Williamson and Vernon Friedli whipped the crowd into a frenzy with promises of victory over the Trojans. On the next day, the young men would enter the field of battle, hoping to return home as conquering heroes with the cherished Copper Ingot Trophy.[1]

On the night of the game, a long stream of car lights illuminated the path down the old Highway 666. The drive from Morenci to Clifton and the football field near the banks of the San Francisco River took only a few minutes, but for the excited fans, it was too long. All types of cars and trucks, carrying exuberant, sometimes partly intoxicated football fans, headed down the narrow road on the brisk mid-November evening. This particular night, the segregation of the company town ended momentarily as Mexican Americans, Anglos, Native Americans, and African Americans mingled, brought together by their love of football and their hatred of Clifton. Only those toiling away in the mines or the smelter stayed away, as the rest marched off to watch the struggle to determine who would retain bragging rights for the next year.

A group of young men already had made the trek on a yellow bus. They waited anxiously in the small, dank, smelly locker room to take the field of battle against the Trojans. The intense Bobby Dale Draper, a solid, muscular mass of humanity topped by short-cropped blond hair, slid on his shoulder pads, further magnifying his broad shoulders. The team captain and all-state linebacker, Draper passionately played the game. People described him as a teddy bear off the field but a monster on it, a guy who sometimes hit the opponent so hard that even Morenci fans felt sorry for the enemy.[2]

Sitting alone not far from Bobby Dale, Joe Sorrelman lost himself in thoughts about the game. He had dark-black hair and a dark complexion and was one of the few Native Americans on the team. His mother and father spoke no English, retaining only their Navajo language, but they supported his efforts to play a game they never really understood. The backup quarterback, he rarely raised his voice and remained calm and composed during the heat of the battle.

Other colleagues sat around Joe, including the short and powerfully built Leroy Cisneros and Clive Garcia, Jr., both of whom flanked Draper on the offensive line to drive gaping holes in the opponent's line. With the exception of Draper, none appeared imposing, but everyone knew that the rugged mining kids always fought hard and never quit, even when faced with bigger and faster opponents. They often willed themselves to victory by their sheer toughness and tenacity.

Outside the locker room, people from both towns congregated, first in the parking lots where many consumed liquor from flasks and bottles, at times offering some to underage drinkers. A few banded together to take bets on the game, although most of the wagering had already been laid down over the preceding weeks.[3] Others hooted and hollered as they saw friends or coworkers. The whole scene, built around the public spectacle of football, had a carnival-like quality, although an intense one on this night when no friendships or family ties outweighed those of community and loyalty to one's team.

It is likely that the 6'5", 230-pound, red-headed Stan King stood out in the crowd, having made the trip from Tucson and the University of Arizona (UA) to watch the game. Only two years earlier as an all-state tackle, he had led Morenci to a 19-to-18 victory over its archrival. During the game, Morenci had punched over a touchdown behind his solid blocking, and at the bottom of the pile, a Clifton player bit him. Enraged, the quick-tempered King jumped up and started flailing away, cursing his tormentor.[4] Tonight, however, he watched from the sideline, remembering the glory days when he and his friends of the Morenci High School (MHS) class of 1964 reigned supreme.

Besides the players on the field warming up under the glow of the stadium lights as the sun set over the red rock hills to the west, others from the class of 1966 waited for the annual battle. The handsome Robert Moncayo had played football, but because he had started school late, he could not participate as a senior. When he walked by, girls from both Morenci and Clifton giggled and swooned in his presence.

Elsewhere, the tall, lanky Larry West, whom everyone knew from his work at the local Foster Simms's Texaco Station, joined his fellow self-described "kicker" buddy Mike Cranford and Mike's girlfriend, Joyce Hulsey, who had graduated a year earlier. Both of the boys wore cowboy boots and jeans and had reputations as hell-raisers, and everyone knew that the annual game always provided a great opportunity for trouble.

Van Whitmer probably sat in the crowd, as always seemingly lost within it. Neither a jock nor a kicker, Whitmer was shy and unassuming. In fact, few people really knew that much about him, and when he did connect with others, he did so awkwardly. But that night, he joined the people of Morenci in yelling for their Wildcats.

Like almost all the battles between the Trojans and the Wildcats, the game remained close and hard-fought well into the fourth quarter. Cheerleaders grabbed their megaphones to rev up the crowd from the opening kickoff, and the energy remained high throughout the contest, with more than a few obscenities launched against the opponents.

A defensive struggle ensued as both sides labored to score. A reporter covering the game wrote that "sparked by some artful running by halfback Robin Archer, and the determined driving of fullback Ronnie Sartin, the Wildcats out clawed the Trojans." With Bobby Dale, Leroy, and Clive opening holes for the two running backs, the Wildcats scored two touchdowns, the first right before halftime and the second with only two minutes and forty seconds left in the third quarter. A ferocious defense led by Draper swarmed the Trojans, allowing only one touchdown in the fourth quarter. After the final gun sounded, the Wildcats walked away victorious by a score of 13 to 6.[5]

Several of the exhausted victors grabbed the Copper Ingot, really nothing more than a huge, rectangular, solid-copper slab on a small stand, and hoisted it into the air. They marched around the Clifton field with the trophy held aloft, basking in the glow of the lights that illuminated the field, which lay near the red clay cliffs. Everyone on their side reveled in the joy of defeating the enemy, a victory they would relish for another year. No one could know that a year later, nine of the young men on the field and in the crowd that night would be far from their beloved home of Morenci in the hills of southeastern Arizona and one step closer to their ultimate destination, the Republic of Vietnam.

On a warm and sunny day in March 1966, Marine sergeant Earl Peterson left his recruiting office in Globe, Arizona. Dressed in his formal blue uniform, he jumped in his big black Cadillac convertible for the two-hour trip to Morenci. His mission had a new urgency. On March 7, Secretary of Defense Robert McNamara, anticipating significant manpower requirements for the expanding war in Vietnam, had requested a dramatic increase in the size of the Marine Corps, boosting it to 278,184 by June 30, 1967. This expansion would make the force even larger than at the height of the Korean War.[6]

Peterson passed through the rolling hills of the Apache Reservation, noting the vibrant hues of the wildflowers in full bloom after the abundant rains of the previous fall. After more than an hour, he left the reservation and went through the small towns of Thatcher and Safford, places rarely as rich in recruits as the mining towns that lay ahead. Barreling down Highway 191, he turned north on Highway 666. After half an hour traveling through the hills and climbing toward the mountains, he took the switchback up the road that led to the center of Morenci. Finally, he arrived at the high school parking lot, located in front of the three-story white building nestled in the middle of the mining camp. He gathered his materials and marched into the school, carrying himself stiff and erect to make a good first impression. Checking in at the front office, he asked school officials to help him round up young men with an interest in joining the greatest fighting force on earth.

The school administrators snapped to attention when Peterson entered the office, for they knew the drill well. During World War II, recruiters had found lots of volunteers in Morenci, many of whom were the fathers, uncles, and cousins of the class of 1966. The process had continued after Korea when the lure of adventure and the push of the draft led many young men to meet with the recruiters of all the branches but especially the Army and Marines, which placed a high value on the sons of miners. Now, as had happened many times before, several school staffers headed to the classrooms to find males with a possible interest in the Marine Corps.

As the administrators dispersed to gather students, the matronly Helen Arnold stood at the front of her senior English class. She held a stack of papers, a surprise for her students. Unprepared students groaned as they realized that she had a pop quiz waiting for them. Suddenly, someone knocked on the classroom door, and Mrs. Arnold ambled across the room to confer with that individual. After a short discussion, she announced that anyone who wanted to talk to the Marine recruiter could skip the quiz. At that, a blur of blue jeans and flannel shirts scurried toward the door, nearly trampling the teacher. Some boys grabbed their award-decorated letter jackets before rushing away from the momentary pain of a quiz and headlong toward their destiny.[7]

Sergeant Peterson soon had a captive audience. Standing tall, he began the refrain of all Marine recruiters, declaring that the Marine Corps only desired the best and the toughest of men, completely dedicated to becoming members of an elite fighting force. He told tales of how the Marines had fought bravely in every major American war, often being the first into battle on the shores of the nation's enemies. Skilled at his job and equipped with painstakingly gathered research and data on what appealed to young American males in 1966, he guaranteed the students

not only a chance to prove their manhood but also an opportunity to see the world—a wonderful lure to those in the room, for many had rarely traveled more than a few hundred miles from their hometown. He even promised them an opportunity to serve in an all-Arizona platoon.[8]

As the day unfolded, the potential recruit pool grew when word spread that Cranford, West, Moncayo, Sorrelman, and Garcia had decided to sign up together. Peterson continued to hold court at the local restaurant, the Copper Kettle, where more young people arrived and listened to him tell about his own experiences and those of other brave Marines such as Lewis "Chesty" Puller. Among those listening were Larry Cisneros, Van Whitmer, and finally Bobby Dale, whom Coach Williamson had tried in vain to talk out of heading over to hear Peterson's pitch. Several of Bobby Dale's friends had taunted him: "Come on, Draper, you're gutless. Let's go join the Marines." He could not ignore the challenge.[9]

Within a short time, a ninth young man, Stan King, who came home from the University of Arizona, joined his fellow Morenci Wildcats and committed to the Marine Corps.[10] Many times in the past, recruiters from all branches of the US military found that Morenci and other Arizona towns such as Douglas, Bisbee, Jerome, Superior, and Ajo were rich mines, both figuratively and literally. Now, Peterson had made quite a haul: he likely filled a major part of his monthly quota that day. He knew his superiors would be happy, making his long trip back to Globe a more pleasant drive.

The nine who volunteered that day in March 1966 constituted a cross section of the working class in Morenci, both socially and culturally. Stan King was the oldest, a 1964 graduate of Morenci High School. Like his father, Glenn, a smelter worker, King intimidated people physically, standing well over 6 feet tall and weighing more than 200 pounds. With a light complexion and red hair cut short to prevent it from curling, King stood out in most crowds, towering above almost everyone else. A dominating presence, he commanded respect, and when he spoke, people listened. He was a talented athlete and lettered in football, basketball, and baseball, winning honors as an all-Arizona tackle in football. Tough as nails and prone to anger quickly, he fought all comers when challenged. According to his mother, he was an extremely "strong-willed" young man.[11]

Stan loved playing practical jokes, even going so far as to place Icy Hot in the jockstraps of his teammates on one occasion. Another time, he and his friend Gary Isaacs played a prank on their girlfriends, Priscilla and Carol Richardson. They took them to the cemetery at Ward Canyon, where kids loved to go to drink and make out. As they parked, Stan and Gary pretended to get into a fight. During the struggle, Stan reached over and retrieved a realistic-looking toy gun from the glove compartment. He pretended to fire it at Gary, who squirted some ketchup packets on himself just as the gun sounded. "That's what he gets," Stan yelled as he jumped into the car and sped off, with the hysterical young women screaming at him from the back seat. Heading down the road, kicking up the red dirt, he burst out giggling. Furious, the girls yelled at him as they returned to pick up the miraculously healed Gary.[12]

Besides being athletic and fun loving, Stan was also extremely intelligent. Throughout high school, he succeeded academically, especially when motivated and focused. Yet he never pushed too hard for fear of being labeled an egghead by his fellow jocks. He even refused induction into the National Honor Society for that very reason. His athletic and academic skills won him an appointment to the US Coast Guard Academy in New London, Connecticut, which the high school principal proudly announced to the community on graduation day. Unfortunately, shortly afterward, Stan failed his physical because of his poor eyesight, and the academy rescinded its offer.[13] Devastated, he coped poorly with the rejection and settled on attending the University of Arizona in Tucson, only 160 miles from home.

During his two years at the UA, he studied engineering but struggled for the most part. Tucson, though small by comparison to Los Angeles or New York City, dwarfed Morenci. In fact, the university alone had four times more people—twenty thousand in 1965—than his entire hometown. Stan found it hard to adjust to the city and the many distractions it offered in the form of parties and sports.[14] A friend swore that during a football game between the UA and Arizona State University (ASU), its bitter rival, a fight broke out when an ASU player went into the stands after some hecklers—and Stan, with his red hair and height causing him to stand out, apparently joined the melee, all caught on television.[15]

In his second year, Stan lost even more focus. He had started dating Donna Bradford, daughter of the MHS superintendent, and impulsively, he decided to surprise her in Flagstaff, where she was studying at Northern Arizona University. After making the four-hour trip through the mountains and canyons from Tucson to NAU, he found her and offered an engagement ring, but she refused his offer. Heartbroken, he moped around, becoming even less interested in school. He hated putting a financial strain on his parents due to his college costs, and the classes he attended provided little inspiration. By March 1966, as one friend observed, Stan staggered toward the Marine Corps, joining his younger colleagues from home.[16]

The irony of Stan's situation was that he had the magic ticket for avoiding military service in the mid-1960s—a college deferment. Each year, the draft board pushed his file to the side and focused on those graduating from high school, including members of the class of 1966. Across the country, people in situations like Stan's fought to maintain their status as college students in order to avoid the military, particularly as events unfolded in 1966 with a massive escalation of hostilities and an expansion of the American presence in South Vietnam. Yet Stan marched headlong into the Marine Corps, breaking with many of the people of his generation.

A different set of conditions propelled Robert Moncayo into the Marines. He was the second oldest of the Morenci Nine, behind Stan, and a member of the MHS class of 1966. However, he had started school a couple of years late, as his family experienced a number of hardships. Robert's father deserted the family early on, leaving his mother to struggle to make ends meet in the harsh conditions of the mining area, where women had few economic opportunities. Ultimately, she married Louis Freniza, a powerfully built smelter worker.

The family resided in New Town, the old Mexican American part of town where some of the poorest people lived. Robert had a large extended family that relied heavily on hunting in the northern forest for food. His mother and others tended small gardens to give the family fresh vegetables and herbs. The threat of a strike and the often crushing levels of debt accumulated by people at the company store kept his family and many others living on the margins. In one case, some of his relatives even rustled a cow, butchered it, and distributed the meat before local law enforcement could uncover the perpetrators.[17]

Despite the relative poverty he endured, Robert had some advantages. Extremely handsome, with high cheekbones, dark-black hair, and penetrating coal-colored eyes, he looked like something of a cross between Ricardo Montalban and Tyrone Power. Slim, wiry, and athletic, he fit well into local stereotypes that asserted Clifton had the prettiest girls but Morenci had the best-looking guys. The girls in both towns loved him, and most guys envied him. One friend described him as a "lady's man"; Leroy called him a "lover boy."[18]

Despite being handsome, he lacked the conceit that often accompanied good looks. Everyone emphasized his pleasant personality. Typically, he had a smile on his face, and he loved having a good time, especially dancing at the Morenci Club or the Catholic Youth Organization in Clifton.[19] One aunt stressed that he rarely spoke ill of anyone and that he loved caring for animals and the infirmed, having a tenderness and compassion for everyone.[20]

Of all the Morenci boys who enlisted in the Marines that March day, Robert seemed the most unlikely fit. But the quiet and sensitive young man had few options as he graduated from high school. Lacking the grades or money to go to college, he believed the military would offer him a temporary reprieve from life in Morenci. Like so many other males in his generation who could not meet the requirements for a draft deferment due to health or other concerns, he was pushed toward military service by a lack of opportunities. The power of peer pressure and the prospect of adventure ultimately helped drive him away from family and home and into the Marines just as the Vietnam War escalated.

Another Mexican American, Leroy Cisneros, joined Robert that fateful March day in signing up for the Marine Corps. Leroy lived in Plantsite (Site 3) on Mimosa Street, south of the smelter and a couple of miles from the center of old Morenci. The company congregated many of the Mexican Americans in the southern shadow of the smokestack. Some people characterized the area as Tortilla Flats, since gringos passing through often commented on the smells of tortillas, green chilies, and beans in the air there. Some even exchanged their sandwiches for burritos.[21]

Site 3 produced some of the toughest kids in the area. They often played football together in the rough copper tailings, making shoulder pads with towels and electrical tape and using cardboard for knee pads. Many went without helmets as they crashed into each other and prepared for the day when they would play for the Morenci Wildcats. Their toughness led their coaches to comment that it was "the hot chili peppers that gave them some piss and vinegar." Their mischievousness landed many in the office of the junior high principal, Byron McGough, who did not hesitate to administer corporal punishment. He liked to say, "The Site 3 guys have some hard butts."[22]

Leroy was not really one of the troublemakers, but he remembered being part of the Site 3 group. In search of work during World War II, his family had moved to Morenci from the farming community of Manassa, Colorado, home of Jack Dempsey.[23] Being short (no more than 5'5") but solidly built and weighing about 150 pounds, with dark eyes and complexion, Leroy stayed in the background compared to Stan and other boys of bigger stature. One person described him as "kind of quiet" and someone who worked hard, especially on the football field.[24] Another characterized him as reserved and claimed to have never seen him angry.[25]

Nonetheless, Leroy could take care of himself when he went to Clifton to "stir up a hornet's nest."[26] In one hilarious instance, he played to the stereotype of a tough Mexican. That day, Leroy and Robert started shoving each other in gym class, with Leroy yelling that Robert had stolen his girlfriend, Betty Trujillo. In loud voices, they agreed to meet by the swimming pool after school to settle the affair. They staged the whole event, building on it throughout the day. More than a hundred people arrived after school to watch the fight. Tensely, the two boys circled each other, pretended to throw a few punches, and then abruptly shook hands. They had a lot of fun at the expense of their friends.[27] In most ways, Leroy fit well into the stereotype of the Morenci kids, being hard-nosed and tenacious, the type of kid who led a girl from a rival school near Tucson to observe after a football game, "They are so little and they beat us."[28]

Leroy was the consummate team player on the field and longed for a challenge after high school. His family had a good reputation, so he could have easily found a job in the mines, but at eighteen and without any firm commitments to fulfill, he saw in the Marines an opportunity for adventure beyond southeast Arizona. Like most of his colleagues, he lacked the grades or the mentoring to pursue a college degree and, with it, a student deferment. So he followed a long line of mining kids right into the military, in a rite of passage performed by many before and after him from Greenlee County.

Whereas Leroy was comparatively shy and unassuming, Clive Garcia, Jr., was anything but reserved. He too lived in Site 3 on Gila Street, not far from Leroy. About 5'8" tall, Clive weighed a solid 180 pounds and had a thick neck and broad shoulders. A handsome young man, he had piercing eyes, jet-black hair, and a relatively dark complexion that turned even darker when exposed to the sun. His parents met after Clive, Sr., mustered out of the US Army after World War II and went to work in the mine. One day, he ended up at the Phelps Dodge hospital, where his future wife, Julia, worked. A friend told her to go see the good-looking man, but he left before she could visit. Not long after, though, Julia's father escorted her to an event where Clive, Sr., asked her to dance. They fell in love and married shortly thereafter, on November 16, 1946. Ten months later, Julia gave birth to Clive, on September 17, 1947.[29]

The Garcias had a large extended family around Morenci, and on pay-days, the relatives often gathered for a barbecue. Fights repeatedly broke out between the cousins, as Clive proved his toughness and martial abilities early on. Like so many others, he loved to hunt, along with his younger brothers. One time, Clive and his brother Danny went hunting on the Frisco River. On a particularly dark night, they encountered something with glowing red eyes out on an old bridge. They shot repeatedly at the target, but it never budged. Scared, they retreated to the safety of their home on Gila Street.[30]

Family was always a central feature in Clive's life. He loved his brothers, Danny and Marty, and often gave them unsolicited advice. He had a close bond with his mother, an extremely religious woman who taught classes at the local Catholic Church. He also stayed close to his father, a vibrant, striking man who worked many different jobs in the mine, from the track crew to the powder gang. Finally, his much younger sister, Kathy, was the apple of Clive's eye. He doted on her long after leaving for the Marines. He even directed that if something ever happened to him, his parents should use his life insurance to pay for his funeral and then put the rest away to underwrite Kathy's college education.[31]

In high school, Clive devoted himself to becoming a good football player. Vern Friedli, who coached football and taught physical education, nicknamed Clive and his buddies the "animal farm." A strong and tough-minded kid, Clive stood out, and one classmate recalled that on the football field, "Clive was the cheerleader. Always yelling to motivate."[32] He was also a practical joker, even locking Coach Friedli in the gym office after a practice.[33] He was full of life and exuded the grit and confidence that made him an attractive recruit for the armed services.

Of all the guys in the group, Clive most fit the image of the "gung ho" Marine who would represent himself and his family well in the service, possibly one day becoming the commandant of the Marine Corps according to Leroy.[34] He had few aspirations of going to college, and in fact, he had the mentality of a military lifer. Never one to avoid a fight and hard as nails, he was already a skilled marksman and outdoorsman. When Sergeant Peterson came looking for a few good men, people pointed him in Clive Garcia's direction. The young man marched proudly toward the Marine Corps, following the example set by his father, an infantryman in the famed Bushmaster Regiment in World War II.

The Mexican American boys constituted the largest racial minority among the Morenci Nine, but Joe Sorrelman represented the local Native American community, which also produced a large number of soldiers for the front lines in Vietnam.

During the Great Depression, at the urging of family members, Joe's father had migrated from the Navajo Reservation to Morenci to work in the mine. More and more people had started leaving the reservation for jobs in mines and other employment in the area, bringing home much-needed cash and goods to help the struggling community. At first, Joe's father labored during the winter and returned to the reservation farm for the harvest season, seeking to find a way to support the family while maintaining many of the tribal traditions. During the prosperous period of World War II, however, the family decided to settle permanently in Morenci.[35]

Joe was the youngest of eight children who survived (five others passed away early in life). He lived in a multicultural world where neither his mother nor his father spoke English. His mother wore traditional Navajo dress, with long skirts and cotton blouses of beautiful, bright colors, and she often cooked customary Navajo meals. His father, a peyote medicine man, worked hard to sustain Joe's ties to his culture. As Joe later observed, "When I went to school it was the white man's culture. When I came home it was the Navajo culture." Nonetheless, his parents bought a television for their son, and sometimes he sat and translated the dialogue for them. All around him, other aspects of the dominant culture also shaped him.[36]

Joe lived in Tent City, the area where Phelps Dodge segregated the Native Americans, mostly Apaches and Navajos. At the entrance to this area, someone posted signs with derogatory wording, including "Warning: Scalping Party Ahead" and "No White Man Allowed." In the shadow of the smokestack and overlooking the Bunker Hill Cemetery, Tent City housed Joe and his friends, among them fellow Navajos Earl Begay and Guy Todacheeny. They often went out together and maintained a close relationship for years.

In junior high, Joe became close friends with Larry West and Mike Cranford, sharing a love of riding horses and hunting in the hills south of town and the forest to the north. Cranford and Sorrelman liked to double-date with their girlfriends, Joyce Hulsey and Virginia Hollyway, whom they ultimately married. Joe also became more involved with Leroy Cisneros, Clive Garcia, Robert Moncayo, and others when he joined the Catholic Church as a teenager. Thus, much of his life entailed moving between the Anglo, Mexican, and Native American worlds as he learned to navigate the complexities of society in the mining camp.[37]

Almost everyone liked Joe, the relatively short, dark-eyed, black-haired backup quarterback at Morenci High. Quiet and humble but a fierce competitor, he exuded a confidence that calmed those around him. One person observed that when he spoke his piece, people listened. Another noted his special talent in art, especially in working with wood and metal.[38] He was a popular figure among many groups at the high school—the Native Americans, the kickers, the jocks, and more. He moved between many different people and cultures with an ease that often evaded others.

Never a great student, Joe nonetheless dreamed of attending college. But he had few role models to encourage that dream and few financial resources to pursue a degree, so he thought the Marines would offer his best chance of bettering himself. He did have role models in that regard, in the form of a brother who had served in World War II and a brother-in-law and uncle who had been code talkers, the latter having been wounded at Iwo Jima.[39] When the recruiter promised that he and his high school friends could stay together as a cohort in the service, Joe fell right in line with the others and marched off to the Marine Corps.

*   *   *

Two of Joe's good friends, Mike Cranford and Larry West, represented another segment of the public culture of Morenci and the Southwest: they were "kickers" (or cowboys). As a kicker, Mike belonged to a subgroup that identified strongly with the cowboy myths of the Southwest and existed across a swath of land from Texas and Oklahoma to California. Kickers donned boots and jeans, carried themselves with a swagger that challenged authority, and proudly wore the title of hell-raisers. Living the imagined life of the cowboy, complete with guns, horses, and women, as well as modern additions such as Chevy or Ford trucks, kickers also loved country-and-western music and the messages that it carried about rugged individualism and toughness.

As an adolescent, Mike's father had worked as a ranch hand at the sprawling Lazy B Ranch outside Duncan, owned by the family of future Supreme Court justice Sandra Day O'Connor.[40] At some point, a foreman told the fifteen-year-old Cranford that ranching was too hard a life and encouraged him to move on. The boy left but traveled only a short distance to Morenci, where he worked at the PD store until he was old enough to transfer into the mines. After serving in the US Navy as a landing-boat driver delivering Marines to beachheads in the Pacific, he returned home and started a family.[41]

Like most of the group, Mike spent his entire life in Morenci. Tall and thin, with sandy blond hair, he loved riding horses and hunting. On a number of occasions, he and Larry took a friend's greyhounds out into the Frisco River basin. They jumped into Larry's '62 pickup at night, carrying a big spotlight to scour the land and locate jackrabbits. Once they found some, they turned the fleet-footed greyhounds loose to chase them until they tired out or caught the varmints. Sometimes, they just shot the rabbits and threw them in the back of the truck to feed to their animals.[42]

Like many kickers throughout the Southwest, Mike frequently rebelled against authority in school and elsewhere. Though he emphasized that he could run faster than all the jocks, he preferred to chase girls. He and his friends often went to the horse corrals south of Plantsite or up to a picnic area on the Coronado Trail to drink beers and park.[43] His dreams revolved not around going to college but marrying Joyce, settling down and working for PD, and then raising a family in Greenlee County, never far from his horses or the sprawling countryside he loved. Serving in the Marines would be merely an interlude, a rite of passage, in the life that he envisioned for himself.

Larry was one of Mike's best friends and shared his passions. Everyone knew the 6-foot-tall Larry because he worked at Foster Simms's Texaco Station pumping gas. He loved to hang out there, along with Mike and Joe, to work on his blue-and-white pickup, a six-cylinder with a huge front grill that made it look like it had a giant grin. Larry enjoyed hot-rodding around the area with his friends. Happy-go-lucky and rarely concerned about much more than his truck and having fun, Larry "didn't seem to pay too much attention to anything that was going on with himself," according to Joe, and he always appeared disheveled: "You could put tailored clothes on him . . . and he would still be unkempt."[44]

Like many young men, Larry just moved along with his group, searching for something to do with his time and rarely appearing to plan more than a few hours ahead. One person even described him as a James Dean type— "not wild, but [he] carried himself as a tough guy."[45] Like Mike and Joe, he enjoyed spending time with his horses and hunting in the canyons and mountains, drinking beer, and partying with his friends. When Sergeant Peterson came along, he discovered someone willing to listen to his stories of adventure and opportunity, although in many ways, Larry found the Marine Corps stifling and regimented. Nonetheless, he cherished his friends, so when the chance arose, he readily signed up with his buddies.

The cheerful, fun-loving Larry was a dramatic contrast to the most intense and driven of the Morenci Nine, Bobby Dale Draper. A solid 190 pounds and 5'9" in height, with blond hair worn in a short crew cut, Bobby had a thick neck, big shoulders, and large, tree-trunk legs supporting his stout frame. His family had moved to Morenci in 1953 when he had barely turned four, his father leaving the coal mines in southeastern Oklahoma to work for PD as a track laborer. A few years later, Mormon missionaries converted the family, and they entered the small but very tight-knit Latter-day Saints (LDS) community in the area, which provided substantial assistance to members, especially during strikes and lockouts.[46]

An excellent athlete and well respected in the community, Bobby Dale epitomized the ideal young American male. Through hard work and perseverance, he became an Explorer Scout, and he continued participating in the Boy Scouts until he entered the Marines. On the football field, he especially distinguished himself. Strikingly agile for his size, he was a strong blocker and tackler. Intense, he set a high standard for himself and often proved to be his own worst critic. Once, while playing against Bisbee, he recovered a fumble and ran it back more than 90 yards for what appeared to be a game-winning touchdown. But the referees called the play back, and Morenci lost. Afterward, a distraught Bobby Dale refused to leave the bus while his teammates ate dinner. Instead, he just paced up and down the old yellow vehicle, angry and inconsolable. Eventually, his efforts on the field earned him all-state honors, and a number of colleges talked to him about playing for them, including the University of Colorado and the University of Hawaii, though none extended a formal offer.[47]

Despite being known for his ferociousness on the field, Bobby Dale was a sensitive, thoughtful person off the gridiron. When he shot his first deer and went to inspect his prize, he broke down crying and never killed another one.[48] A Morenci local characterized him as a "good Mormon [kid]," a respectful, hardworking young man whom others admired and respected for setting a good example. For instance, while he was playing basketball down at the Mormon activity center in Clifton, a friend, Ricky Melton, used some profanity. Bobby Dale promptly decked him with a strong right hand, castigating him for cursing in a church.[49]

To many in the community, it seemed that Bobby Dale had more opportunities than his friends for going on to college or getting a well-paying job after high school. As a result, when the Marine recruiter arrived in March 1966, Coach Williamson pulled aside several of the young men, including Joe, and asked them to try to talk Bobby Dale out of joining. Along with Bobby Dale's father, the coach really believed that the boy could go to college and possibly play football. They knew he had a strong work ethic that could ensure success on the field and in the classroom. Nonetheless, Bobby Dale made his decision and remained adamant about joining his friends as they enlisted in the Marine Corps.[50]

Another young LDS member, Van Whitmer, would be part of the Morenci Nine as well. Not imposing and lacking Bobby Dale's athleticism and visibility, Van blended into the crowd in Morenci. Joe and others who remembered him described Van as "real quiet," a person who "didn't call much attention to himself." Most people in the town acknowledged that they did not know him well. When he tried to interact, he often did so awkwardly, and some recalled only his propensity for making mistakes. For example, one day Van and other Boy Scouts helped load some Christmas trees into a truck. The scoutmaster told the young men not to throw them in trunk first. Van did not listen, launching a tree into the bed with the trunk facing forward and breaking out the truck's back window.[51]

Unlike the self-described kickers Larry and Mike, Van was a country boy, more like a farmer who associated with people in Duncan rather than the miners and the cowboys. He lacked roots in Morenci, although he was active in the local Mormon ward. In fact, his family had moved around some and left for Safford soon after he joined the Marines. As a country boy, he often wore different clothes than the kickers and loved to attend square dances as a member of the Greenlee County Promenaders Square Dance Club. However, he also enjoyed hunting and fishing, and he was a natural outdoorsman who killed his first deer at twelve. He worked on the Wiltbank Ranch at times, helping with the cattle, and labored part-time for Joe Spear at the American Service Station, where he developed some mechanical skills. Yet he never really found a place among his peers.[52]

For Van, it appears that he simply wanted to belong to something when Sergeant Peterson showed up in March 1966.[53] Though not really close friends with any of the group, he faced the same challenge they did in terms of limited opportunity, and he, too, had a desire for adventure. When given a chance to be part of an organization that people respected, he jumped at it. The Marines really never distinguished between the jocks and kickers and country boys. They wanted willing recruits seeking a test, young men with hunting and outdoor skills. And Van fit the profile of the young people Marine recruiters concentrated on when they visited the small towns of America. He needed something, anything, to identify with at a tough time in his life, when so many decisions were barreling toward him as he graduated from high school.

By the end of that day in March 1966, Sergeant Peterson had snared eight young men, with another on the way in the not-too-distant future. Although they had different backgrounds, the new recruits shared their hometown and experiences living there, comprising a cross section of the working class in the mining camp. Across the country, recruiters visited similar communities searching for young men who were skilled hunters and outdoorsmen and anxious to break the monotony of their everyday lives. And in the small towns and working-class industrial communities and suburbs of the nation (though not the elitist prep schools and high schools in affluent parts of urban areas), the Marines rarely had any trouble finding recruits, especially in the early stages of the Vietnam War. To be sure, the Morenci Nine had some unique experiences related to living in a segregated mining camp, but in many ways they represented the generation of young Americans in the 1960s that provided the majority of the infantrymen in Vietnam.[54]

Because eight of the nine had not yet finished school, they chose a 120-day delayed entry program. In the meantime, they traveled to Phoenix to take their tests and physicals. They endured poking and prodding by doctors as well as a battery of mental tests. Joe originally failed the aptitude exam, but the group banded together and asked for him to be given another chance, and Joe passed.[55] By the end of the day, they emerged from the testing center ready to enjoy the big city.

They stayed in downtown Phoenix at the 1920s-era San Carlos Hotel at the intersection of Monroe Street and Central Avenue, ironically not far from the downtown gathering area known as Copper Square. The Renaissance–inspired, seven-story hotel had hosted Hollywood dignitaries such as Clark Gable, Mae West, Jean Harlow, and Spencer Tracy, people drawn to its air-conditioned rooms before they became a common commodity. However, by the mid-1960s, the hotel's clientele had changed after major resorts in Scottsdale and elsewhere pulled more visitors away from the downtown area. Despite having seen its glory days, the San Carlos was still a nice place, especially when compared to the accommodations back home in Morenci at the Longfellow Inn.

The San Carlos had a central location not far from the bars and restaurants of downtown Phoenix, a bustling metropolis that made life in Morenci seem like it moved in slow motion. After completing their exams, the young men enjoyed the local nightlife. They proudly boasted about their impending service in the US Marines, and despite being underage, they conned people into buying them drinks. After several hours, the raucous group decided to retreat to their quarters. Several stumbled back to the hotel and their rooms on the sixth floor, where they decided that bombarding local pedestrians with ice cubes would provide good sport. Somehow, during the night, a mattress ended up in the third-floor sundeck swimming pool. They trashed one of the rooms so badly that it looked like they had thrown a grenade into it and then run.[56]

The next day, their Marine hosts received a report from the staff at the San Carlos about the previous night's activities. The young men had a glimpse into their future as the Marines launched into a verbal assault on their new recruits. They had embarrassed the Marine Corps and caused a financial loss due to the cleaning and repairs that had to be made in their room. The dressing-down ended with a threat of being thrown into the brig even before they officially entered the service. Finally, the Marines packed the boys up and put them on the bus for the long ride back to Morenci, some suffering through the hot day with severe hangovers.[57]

Not long after, in late May, more than one hundred members of the class of 1966 crowded into the high school gym for graduation. Dressed in their long gowns, the graduates waited anxiously for a school official to call their names. Then they marched across the gym and took their diplomas in front of proud parents and other relatives, who later crammed into their small houses to celebrate the milestone. Many of the graduates still did not know what their next step would be, but eight of them did. Within a short period of time, they would turn in their caps and gowns for fatigues and rifles. For them and for tens of thousands of their peers across the country in 1966, this rite of passage was on the near horizon.

While they awaited their journey to boot camp, the nine recruits, including Stan King who joined his younger colleagues after leaving the University of Arizona, enjoyed their last days at home. Sometimes, they found trouble in the process. One night, for instance, Joe, Mike, Bobby Dale, Larry, and another friend, Ricky Melton, jumped in a pickup and headed south toward the Gila River. Using 22 rifles and pistols, they spotlighted and killed more than fifty jackrabbits. Unwilling just to leave the bloody carcasses for the desert predators, the group decided to speed through Clifton and throw the dead animals up on the buildings and onto the sidewalks on Main Street.[58] Next, they barreled up the hill toward their homes, stopping at Morenci High School to toss some rabbits on the balcony of the building. They also took time to run one of the dead animals up the flagpole as a final defiant act. Then they sped away and headed toward the swimming pool. They jumped the fence and decided to take a dip on the hot June evening. Once finished, they tied some rocks to a few more jackrabbits and threw them into the deep end of the pool, where the bloody animals polluted the pristine waters.[59]

The next day, infuriated PD officials discovered the vandalism. They had to drain the pool and clean it, costing several hundred dollars. After that, they started a manhunt for the boys seen in a blue-and-white GMC pickup who had sped through town the night before. The company had eyes and ears everywhere, so it did not take long to track down the perpetrators. Fortunately for Mike, he had gone on vacation with Joyce's family, so he escaped punishment. Ultimately, company officials confiscated the boys' guns and read them the riot act. They decided not to throw them in jail because they would soon receive their just due—Marine boot camp.[60]

After their final prank, the group had only a short time before shipping out. They put their affairs in order, packed away their clothes, and said good-bye to their family and friends. Though apprehensive, most looked forward to the challenge, not really understanding what lay ahead even after listening to all the veterans talk about their own experiences in boot camp, usually embellished a bit to scare the young men. Simultaneously nervous and excited, each wondered how he would fare. Yet unlike many other recruits across the country that summer, they would start the journey in the company of lifelong friends. They could not know, of course, that in the end, only three from their group would return alive.[61]

3

The Creation
of a Warrior in
Cold War America
The Push-Pull Factors in
the Decision to Join

The young men from Morenci had a common background with a Minnesota veteran named Tim O'Brien, who wrote that his generation arose during a time when Americans basked in the glory of the victory over the fascists in World War II. "I was bred with haste and dispatch and careless muscle-flexing of a nation giving bridle to its own good fortune and success," he concluded, "I was fed by the spoils of 1945 victory."[1]

Why would so many young American men, more than eight million during the Vietnam conflict, march into the armed services? Like O'Brien, the recruits from Morenci constituted the first wave of the baby boom, born right after World War II—the age-group that comprised the majority of those fighting in Vietnam. The world these young people faced differed greatly from that their fathers had encountered two decades earlier. After 1945, the United States assumed leadership of the Western world in the fight against the perceived international Communist conspiracy spearheaded by the Soviet Union. As a result, several major push factors existed in the lives of young males when they turned eighteen and became eligible for the draft in the Cold War era.

During the Cold War, one marine observed, "the draft was a deadly serious sword of Damocles that hung over the head of every healthy boy in America."[2] Though the majority of their generation avoided military service thanks to the liberal deferment system in place at the time, the draft pushed forward the young men from Morenci, for they refused to put their lives on hold while waiting for the randomness of the selective service system to determine when they left civilian life and what branch of service they joined.

The draft had a strong local component. According to the selective service system, each local draft board was to consist of "friends and neighbors of the registrant it classifies." Members of the board had the "responsibility to determine who is to serve the nation in the Armed Forces and who is to serve in industry, agriculture, and other deferred classifications."[3] By 1966, a total of 4,087 local boards existed, each composed of at least three members and typically five. Usually, one paid staff member handled paperwork and collaborated with others, including medical advisers and appeal agents. The community agencies ranged in size from one in Colorado that administered twenty-seven registrants to another in Los Angeles that had more than fifty-four thousand potential draftees.[4]

The Greenlee County draft board had its headquarters in Clifton and met in Virgil Waters's Mobil station, as he was the board's director. Like similar organizations all over the country, the system relied on volunteers, although the Greenlee County board employed a part-time staffer to update the records. They met periodically and evaluated the files of local youths, determining classifications and moving some toward the dreaded 1-A classification. Then they talked with the individuals who sought deferments for educational, medical, occupational, or family reasons and classified them accordingly.[5] Needless to say, Greenlee County funneled more than its fair share into the military via the draft during the Vietnam War because fewer young men in the area attended colleges or held jobs that justified deferments.

The draft provided a powerful push for many young men in the county. Oscar Urrea, Morenci High School class of 1966, provided a cautionary tale for others. After graduating, he went to study at the University of California–Los Angeles (UCLA) near family in Southern California. One semester, he decided to take some time off from his studies to work. Urrea knew he would lose his draft deferment but decided to take his chances, thinking that being in Los Angeles would help him buy time until he could start the next semester and regain his status. Within three weeks, however, a notice of induction landed in his mailbox. The gamble had failed, and he soon became a member of the 101st Airborne, ultimately joining his brothers serving in Vietnam.[6]

Hearing about such experiences shaped the perspectives of the Morenci Nine. Larry West summed up the feelings of many within the group when he told his mother, "I don't see any need of sitting around waiting to be drafted. Why not just go and get it over with?"[7] With educational deferments out of the question for most, Larry's words reflected the sentiments of the others. As Mike Cranford put it, "Larry was like us. He had no future. He wasn't going to go to school. He just barely got through [high] school [and] was working at a service station."[8]

Numerous surveys have investigated the effect of the draft, even for those who volunteered like the Morenci Nine. In 1964, 40 percent of all volunteers admitted that fear of the draft motivated their enlistment; the number increased to 50 percent after 1965.[9] In Senate Armed Services Committee hearings as the war escalated in 1967, it was noted that the annual report by the selective service system for 1966 found that 1,090,000 enlisted in the service. Of that number, the military drafted 345,000, and another 380,700 joined voluntarily after receiving preinduction notices. The overall numbers fail to include others who sought better military assignments in the Air Force or Navy to try to reduce their chances of having to serve on the front lines in Vietnam. Nevertheless, more than two-thirds were either draftees or draft-induced enlistees as the Vietnam War intensified.[10]

The draft could also affect the type of service selected by volunteers. The Navy and the Air Force typically, albeit not always, ensured fewer dangers and provided training in more marketable postservice skills than the Marines or Army. As a result, many young men flocked to these branches during the war, which meant the Navy and Air Force rarely had any problem filling their manpower needs until much later in the conflict.

On the other extreme, some people volunteered for more dangerous duties because of the draft. One Marine, Phil Ball, wrote, "I figured that the Army was going to draft me anyway, so I might as well join the

Marines; at least that way, I would have something to be proud of. The Army was looked upon as the worst bunch of misfits, but the Marines were tough misfits, and they had the elite reputation of being the best in the world."[11] Another Marine admitted joining because "I'd rather be over there with motivated people, people who've got their shit together, as opposed to being in a paddy with a bunch of zeroes who don't even want to be there."[12]

The same was true for some in the Morenci Nine. Joe Sorrelman later discussed why the group joined the Marines rather than the Army, despite concerted efforts by recruiters for the latter branch. He stressed, "We only had heard about the Army where you had a lot of draftees and at that time the draft system was still in and a lot of guys didn't want to go. I always wanted to go with somebody that wanted to be there and wanted to be an all volunteer kind of thing."[13] Such a perspective, however, increased the likelihood of seeing frontline combat in Vietnam.

The selective service system pushed many young men into the military—some as draftees, others as draft-induced volunteers—during the Cold War and especially during the Vietnam War, when manpower needs increased exponentially. The draft thus was a powerful coercive tool for a generation of young males, particularly those without access to the deferments that existed for the sons of white-collar managers who filled college classrooms or others such as the farmers' sons in certain regions whose draft boards classified them as vital to the production of goods necessary for the national defense.

Of course, eccentricities existed in many areas. In eastern Arizona, for example, some draft boards granted deferments for Mormons who headed off on mission trips when they graduated from high school; then, upon returning, these individuals often married at once in order to secure a family deferral. It all depended on the local interpretations and priorities. However, the Morenci Nine had few options as draft quotas increased, and when their time came to deal with the draft, they took a proactive approach.

Given the large number of men who volunteered to serve in that era, whether draft induced or not, there must be some other explanations beyond the draft to illuminate how the country and its leaders conditioned

young males for military service. As noted, there were ways to avoid service through deferments or, in extreme cases, through fleeing to Canada
or other foreign lands. But most young men answered the call when it
came, even if reluctantly, and marched off to war. To understand why,
one must comprehend the conditions at play in Cold War America that
influenced these men, particularly in places such as Morenci and many
other small communities where young people rarely openly questioned
the assumptions on which their service rested.

Frequently, military recruiters wrapped the messages they delivered in
the cloak of patriotism and duty, building on prevalent attitudes about
service to one's country. A reporter for the *Eastern Arizona Courier* wrote
in March 1969, at the height of the conflict in Southeast Asia, that for
people in Morenci and Clifton "their community peculiarity is national
patriotism. Not to infer that other towns have shirked their duties, and
regardless of the sociological factors involved, the plain fact is the young
men of Clifton and Morenci have enlisted into the military service at a
fantastic rate."[14]

The broad, amorphous idea of patriotism was rooted in long-standing
traditions in US society. One historian observes that during the Vietnam
War, a "national political culture" existed that was "a product of thousands
of small and not-so-small ideas" that flourished "in the collective wisdom
of the agencies and departments of government, of the players in the
political parties, of the press, the president." The culture evolved "so that
future decisions have precedent, probably several."[15]

Many layers formed the political culture of the 1950s and 1960s, among
them hero worship of veterans such as John Kennedy and Audie Murphy;
the constant indoctrination in schools and churches about the dangers
of communism; national holidays honoring those who had served in the
military; and a popular culture that praised the sacrifice of the warrior,
primarily of the World War II generation.

Though often national in scope, the ideas trickled down to the regional
and local levels, where they assumed unique characteristics depending
on the particular social, economic, cultural, and political systems in play.
The local context helped clarify some of the differences between those
who joined and those who more actively sought to escape service. Smaller
working-class communities in rural areas and the ethnic enclaves and
lower-middle-class neighborhoods in large urban or suburban communities

had comparatively distinct community standards, ones largely shaped by issues of money and influence. The anonymity of life in larger cities as well as the effect of living in like-minded communities that opposed the war—typically more middle-class and upper-middle-class areas in cities such as Berkeley, California, and Madison, Wisconsin, or the borough of Manhattan in New York—also explained variations. But above all, the prevailing concepts of patriotism affected the decisions of the millions of young men who came of draft age during the Vietnam War.

Many veterans understood the pressures that pushed them into the military, although they may not always have comprehended all elements of those forces until they reflected later. Living most of his childhood on the plains of Minnesota in the small town of Worthington, the "Turkey Capital of the World," Vietnam veteran Tim O'Brien internalized Middle America's view of being a citizen. He earned a degree in political science at Macalester College, served as student body president, and became an antiwar protestor. However, when his draft notice arrived after graduation, he answered it. He explained this apparent anomaly by noting that "piled on top of this was the town, my family, my teachers, a whole history of the prairie. Like magnets, these things pulled in one direction or the other, almost physical forces weighting the problem, so that, in the end, it was less reason and more gravity that was the final influence."[16]

Southeastern Arizona differed little from the small towns in Minnesota or, for that matter, towns such as Wartburg, Tennessee, and Beallsville, Ohio, all of which sent large numbers of men into the war and also experienced significant losses. As O'Brien observed, the gravity of the local cultures, when blended with the larger national one, pushed the young men forward, many without any firm understanding of the pressures. Mike Cranford summed it up well: "We were small-town people, we still believed in mom and apple pie. It was part of my duty as a man, growing up, to join the service. They didn't have to draft us. It was part of what we were supposed to do."[17]

If patriotism was the amorphous concept that often explained the decision to volunteer or report when the draft notice arrived, what were the concrete foundations of that idea? One significant factor was the social construction of manhood in America, particularly the version that evolved in the post–World War II years.[18] Though other issues, such as class, clearly played a part, the young man's perception of masculinity in relation to military service helps explain differences in individuals' responses.

Author Graham Dawson argues that "masculinities are lived out in the flesh, but fashioned in the imagination," which creates a "range of possible selves" that individuals then choose in order to construct their lives around the narratives of their experiences.[19] In America during the 1950s and early 1960s, the social construction of masculinity revolved primarily around male members of the family, the community, and a strong set of national standards perpetuated in the educational system and the media. The closer a young man was to the source of modeling (for example, his father or an uncle), the more likely that his perceptions of masculinity corresponded to reality. Conversely, the more remote the source of modeling was (say, the movies or political folklore), the more likely that his construction lacked grounding in actual events and time. In the latter case, this often led to more of the individual's lifestyle being "fashioned in the imagination" rather than actuality, which later contributed to a significant questioning of masculine myths among some combat veterans.

In many cases, the young men who comprised the majority of the frontline troops (outside the officer corps) in Vietnam came from local cultures that measured men by their physical rather than their intellectual skills, especially in working-class, lower-middle-class, and agricultural communities.[20] Physically demanding sports provided arenas in which to demonstrate manliness, as did the type of work that a person performed, whether in mines, fields, or factories or in other labor-intensive jobs. Muscle and stamina marked the measure of the man, not his ability to add numbers or write essays. In such communities, physical prowess signified a good potential breadwinner and differentiated the young men from one another.[21]

For many individuals from such communities, masculine differentiation even influenced their choice of military branch. The Marine Corps ranked highest in terms of toughness and challenges, and the Navy and Air Force lay at the other end of the spectrum. The Army fell in between, with the infantryman regarded as the highest echelon and additional value attributed to those choosing specialized training such as Special Forces or Airborne. At the low end were jobs such as clerical worker. For many, demonstrating courage in the face of extreme danger was the ultimate test in continuing the grand traditions of their national heroes and forefathers.

Multiple levels of the masculine conception appealed to young men during the Vietnam era, even those who had reservations about the war. These included the influence of fathers and other male family members; the impact of other masculine role models in the community and at the national level; the imprint of institutions such as the Boy Scouts; and the effect of media such as movies, television, books, and music. All these reinforced virile beliefs regarding service, especially in the face of the Communist threat, and helped push many young people into the military.

The most important role models were the fathers and other male family members. The veterans of World War II and Korea constituted a large percentage of the fathers and uncles of the Vietnam-era soldiers. Thus, the baby boomers learned only about the "good war" and, tangentially, Korea in the context of the Cold War. Though their family members sometimes warned about the horrors of war, they also regaled the impressionable youths with stories of bravery and sacrifice for their country. Many shared the attitude of an army veteran who stated that those who avoided fighting in World War II regretted missing the seminal event of their generation. "I was the perfect age to participate in Vietnam," he added, "and I didn't want to miss it, good or bad. I wanted to be part of it, to understand what it was."[22]

The presence of multiple male role models exerted pressure on the Vietnam generation to replicate their family members' military service. One historian has observed that in American history, "veterans compared the younger generation's easy life with the heroic sacrifices and hardship of the war generation. Could the sons be equal to their fathers? Would they have a like opportunity to test their manly worth in the fires of war?"[23] Such feelings ran strong in the 1950s and early 1960s for the Vietnam generation, including the Morenci Nine, especially as the dark cloud of fear regarding Communist domination hovered over the United States.

Several of the fathers of the Nine had served in World War II. Clive Garcia's father joined early, as did many others from the Morenci mines. During the war, he served with the Bushmasters, the 158th Regimental Combat Team of the Arizona National Guard called into federal service in 1941 and deployed first to guard the Panama Canal before joining the

US Sixth Army in the South Pacific in 1943. A rifleman, Clive Sr. fought in the brutal jungle campaigns in New Guinea and the Philippines. His unit received numerous commendations, and he earned a Bronze Star for his role in capturing a massive Japanese gun emplacement. Occasionally, he showed his sons the medals and decorations, reminding them of his time in the war to save the world from fascism.[24]

Mike Cranford's father joined the Navy. He deployed to the South Pacific, where he performed the hazardous duty of driving landing craft to disembark Marines under the intense fire of the Japanese defenders. During the latter stages of the war, he watched a kamikaze pilot slam into his ship, being so close that he could see the young man's face clearly as he made his final dive.[25] Leroy's father also served, although he never left the States.[26]

Some fathers did not enter the military due to age (Bobby Dale's father was too young and Joe's father too old), but other family members reinforced the sense of duty via service. Joe remembered how his uncle and brother-in-law served as code talkers during World War II—the specially trained Navajo translators who became local and eventually international heroes for their bravery in the South Pacific. His relatives rarely talked about their experiences except to say that combat horrified them, but Joe admitted that he occasionally looked at the pictures they had taken in places such as Tarawa and Iwo Jima. At other times, he would examine their medals and citations, which "always fascinated" him.[27]

The attitudes expressed by male family members had an effect on local youth. Oscar Urrea noted that his father talked about how his ancestors had fought, originally for Mexico and later the United States, including those who served during World War II. His parents constantly reminded him of the family heritage of service, which was a powerful push factor when it came time for him and his brothers to make a decision on joining when called upon.[28]

Another Greenlee County veteran, Steve Guzzo, summed up well why he and others enlisted when he noted that his forefathers had gone into the military, that he himself believed "I can do anything that anyone can do," and that upon returning home he wanted to be able "to look anyone in the eye because I had served my country."[29] Guzzo and other Morenci veterans knew that military service guaranteed respectability in their family and the community.

*   *   *

Morenci provided many other role models for its young men when it came to military service. One Morenci Vietnam veteran remembered listening to World War II veterans swapping stories about their experiences in the good war at the barbershop. And at football games in Morenci, members of the American Legion, some dressed in their old uniforms, marched to the 50-yard line before the game started, presented the American flag during the playing of the "Star-Spangled Banner," and then left the field in unison. This simple ritual exemplified the high visibility that veterans retained in the community, no matter their social or economic position.[30]

In addition, the community recognized the heroism of the veterans, especially on special days such as Memorial Day, the Fourth of July, and Veterans Day. People designed and constructed memorials on these occasions, and the festivities were usually capped by parades featuring the veterans, many wearing their uniforms and medals. (One Vietnam veteran from Morenci described the camp as being "engulfed with old veterans.")[31] In small but powerfully symbolic ways, these activities reminded young men of their duty and of the recognition and respect that came with it, even for the worker in the lowest-level job in the community.

Among the veterans, some of the most influential outside of the family were teachers and coaches. In an era when teachers commanded respect and society reinforced their value within an established hierarchy, they often exerted a powerful hold over their charges. This was especially true in junior and senior high schools, where male faculty members held more positions. Like the fathers of the young men, significant numbers of these educators had fought in World War II or Korea. Also, as with most family members or perhaps even more so, the sense of the Cold War mission to protect the country from the Communist threat permeated teachers' psyches. As one veteran noted, "Our teachers told us that we were fighting communism and that was the thing we had to do. So all through high school I was in favor of the war."[32]

Coaches also significantly influenced the young men. Unlike teachers, who typically saw the students just once a day, coaches often interacted with them for three to four hours at a stretch on the practice field and on long trips for games. And the sheer nature of sports, especially the extremely physical ones such as football, basketball, and wrestling, embodied concepts that were central to military life, among them endurance, team cohesion, obedience, and toughness. Even the language of a game like football incorporated military metaphors ("ramming through the line" and "containing the opposition"), and these kinds of metaphors were readily used by Presidents Lyndon Johnson and Richard Nixon when describing the war in Vietnam.[33] As Robert Kennedy noted of the sport's character-building effects, "Except for war, there is nothing in American life—nothing—which trains a boy better for life than football."[34]

Several of the teachers and coaches in Morenci appeared quite prominently in the memories of the men who served in Vietnam. They included Coach Vern Friedli, who often talked about military service with the boys in his physical education classes and on his sports teams. A relatively recent graduate of the University of Arizona, Friedli looked the part of a military man. An imposing physical figure, complete with a tight crew cut, he had served in the military, and some of the impressionable youths in town believed he had been in the Special Forces.[35] Hard-nosed in gym class and on the football field, the young assistant coach made a favorable impression with his toughness and commanding presence. At one point, Friedli gave Leroy a book entitled *Road to Glory*, which retold stories of the Marine Corps and its heroism.[36] Other teachers and coaches, such as science teacher Joseph Galusky, talked about their military service as well. According to one of the veterans who had been in his class, Galusky emphasized on many occasions that "you slobs better not take off for a foreign country."[37]

Beyond the local masculine role models, national forces also helped shape young Americans into fighting men. Throughout the country, the political culture, strongly influenced by the Cold War, bombarded young men on a daily basis with messages about their duty to their country, especially in the face of the Communist menace that threatened to destroy their way of life and enslave their families. Many institutions as well as individuals stressed these ideas, including the Boy Scouts, political organizations, Hollywood, and the churches.

In Morenci, the Boy Scouts stood out as a particularly significant institution, reinforcing the principles of the national political culture. Founded in 1912 to accomplish, as one historian notes, the introduction of "coddled boys to the wilderness, to competition, to hardy play and strenuous virtue," the Boy Scouts indoctrinated young men with all-American values and had adults leaders "intervening to provide 'boyish' experiences so that boys would not lose touch with the sources of manhood."[38] Designed to buttress respect for God and country and create a generation of men skilled in the outdoors, the Boy Scouts grew quickly throughout the country. As the historian observes, "They were founded and run by adults with adult concerns in mind, and they placed a heavy emphasis on subordination of the boy to his larger group."[39]

During the 1950s, the number of Boy Scouts increased astronomically as the baby boomers, including the Morenci Nine, matured. In 1950, there were just over 2 million, but the number soared to 3.7 million in 1960 and 4.6 million in 1970.[40] The emphasis on duty and service to God and country played out in many scouting rituals, such as learning how to properly display the flag. Meetings concentrated on the traditional American history, often incorporating idealized versions of Native Americans. Local troops emphasized physical activities and competition to win merit badges and move into leadership positions, and in many ways, this paralleled military structures. At the core were adult males, many of them veterans, trying to pass on a view of a strong America to a new generation of potential warriors.[41] Almost all of the Morenci Nine participated in scouting, as the small mining camp had at least seven scout troops (with at least twenty-five boys per troop) during the 1950s and 1960s, including Bobby Dale who became an Explorer Scout and remained active in the organization until he left for the Marines.[42]

The impact of the Boy Scouts on young men who fought in Vietnam permeated many Greenlee County veterans' stories. One recalled his experiences in scouting and how they were similar to military service. His group of eleven- and twelve-year–old scouts encompassed most of the Morenci Nine, and they went on campouts where they separated into platoons and played army. They frequently marched 10 miles along the creeks and through the mountains of southeastern Arizona. During the summers, they went to camp, where they hiked, fished, and practiced firing rifles, something that they often did at home in an old abandoned building under the supervision of scout leaders. The parallels to military training would be obvious to this individual when he joined the 101st Airborne in 1969.[43]

Likewise, an Eagle Scout and Vietnam veteran helicopter pilot from Morenci characterized the Boy Scouts as a "paramilitary organization" and remembered being taught how to put on the uniform properly, to stand at attention and salute, and to march. His troop took special trips to Army and Air Force bases, such as Williams Field in the Phoenix area where they played on the flight simulators. When he reached Eagle Scout status at sixteen, he received a prize of a two-week cruise aboard a Navy ship in the Pacific, which included a port call in Acapulco, Mexico. For him, the similarities between the Boy Scouts and the military were readily apparent.[44]

Millions of youngsters received this kind of indoctrination through the Boy Scouts during the 1950s and 1960s. The organization focused on making American males stronger in the face of both internal threats (that is, becoming emasculated by urban lifestyles and the affluence of the 1950s) and external threats that challenged the values of God and country (primarily communism). Participation in scouting constituted a rite of passage for many boys, few of whom were teenagers. It reinforced concepts of duty and service, making it easier for armed service recruiters and the draft system to move young men into the military, even during the more tumultuous period of the late 1960s.

The Boy Scouts blended local and national influences and provided nonfamilial male role models, many with military experience, for the youngsters in Morenci. However, in 1950s and 1960s America, there were numerous male role models far beyond Greenlee County, models who fundamentally shaped the Vietnam generation. When the warrior ethos of the Cold War period reached its zenith before the disillusionment of Vietnam, the country had many real and imagined war heroes on which young men could pattern their own service. Popular culture blended with politics and vice versa. And in an age of uncertainty in the 1950s, Americans typically found comfort in their leaders, such as President Dwight Eisenhower, a former Army general. World War II and the Cold War dramatically reinvigorated the nation as a society that worshipped its war heroes.

Perhaps no one shaped the Vietnam generation more than John Kennedy, who exuded self-confidence, virility, and patriotic fervor.[45] His life sparked numerous books and the popular movie *PT-109* in 1963, and Catholicism added another layer of allure for the many young Americans who shared his faith. The vibrancy of Kennedy, despite private battles with health problems and addictions, influenced a generation of Americans, who responded to his inaugural address in January 1961: "Let every nation know, whether it wishes us well or ill, that we shall pay any price, bear any burden, meet any hardship, support any friend, oppose any foe, in order to assure the survival and the success of liberty." The address concluded with the words that resonated long and far: "Ask not what your country can do for you—ask what you can do for your country."[46]

Examples of the Kennedy mystique shaping volunteers and draftees alike can be found in many Vietnam veterans' recollections. One remembered that he joined the Army with an eye toward Special Forces in part because of "the fact that you've got a catholic guy that's going to be president. He's ex-military. It just seemed like everything was jelling. I had been thinking seriously about enlisting. It was not too long after that, that I just decided that now's the time."[47] Another veteran, Philip Caputo, wrote that "war is always attractive to young men who know nothing about it, but we had also been seduced into uniform by Kennedy's challenge to 'ask what you can do for your country' and by the missionary idealism he had awakened in us."[48] Many of the young men, including the Morenci Nine, shared the vision of the president and what he represented, especially Catholics and union members, who saw him as an ally.

Movies also played a role in building the national political culture that molded contemporary thought, especially in relation to gender roles. In nearly every community in the United States, theaters were central sources of entertainment, even after the advent of television. An entire generation shared a love of movies and the break that they provided from the monotony of everyday life. A steady diet of war movies such as *Halls of Montezuma*, *Battle Cry*, *Pork Chop Hill*, and *The Longest Day* shaped perceptions of honor and duty. Film emerged as a major source of social conditioning.[49]

For example, young men flocked to movies such as *To Hell and Back* (1955), the life story of Audie Murphy, who, like many of them, had come from very modest beginnings. Murphy would become the most decorated US soldier in World War II. From there, he became a movie star, and everyone knew his story, although most did not know about his battles with alcohol and nightmares caused by the war. A Marine veteran remembered that he never forgot about Murphy in *To Hell and Back* and the final scene where he jumped on a burning tank and sprayed the Germans with machine-gun fire. He called it the "greatest movie I ever saw in my life."[50] Murphy's story especially affected people like the Morenci Nine, whether consciously or not. They saw military service as a possible vehicle to the kind of life enjoyed by the young Texan who rose from extremely humble origins to become a national hero and movie star.

Murphy was a real-life everyday hero, but the figure most often glorified in war films of the period (as well as westerns) was John Wayne. For many of the Vietnam generation, he represented the ultimate example of masculinity, a man of imposing stature, swagger, and outspokenness. These characteristics translated into a commanding on-screen presence that combined bravado with misogyny and the willingness to bravely challenge all odds. For many young men of the period, Wayne became their imagined ideal of manhood, especially in relation to military service through films such as the *Sands of Iwo Jima*, *The Flying Tigers*, *In Harm's Way*, and later *The Green Berets*. Of course, all this occurred despite the fact that Wayne actually avoided service during World War II, and his sons who came of age during Vietnam never served in the military either.[51]

The Marine recruiters, like their counterparts in the other branches, knew what buttons to push with the impressionable youths they courted. Thus, as Joe Sorrelman recalled, the recruiter in Morenci promised a chance to "test our manliness."[52] Recruiters for the Marine Corps played on existing images of heroes in American society, many promoted by the media (such as Murphy) as well as cultural icons (such as Wayne). In fact, no other branch had done more since World War II to promote itself through the use of persuasive images in movies and the building of impressive monuments, among them the massive structure in Arlington Cemetery depicting the Marines raising the US flag over Iwo Jima (which had a strong Arizona connection via Ira Hayes, one of the soldiers memorialized in the statue).[53] A Morenci Vietnam veteran noted that the Morenci Nine "were gung ho John Wayne boys."[54] And Coach Friedli stressed, "They believed what they read on the posters. They believed you were something special if you were a marine. That recruiting sergeant did a helluva job."[55] The movies and other elements of the Cold War political culture clearly reinforced the existing perceptions of masculinity.

The social constructions of masculinity shaped many young men's decisions to join the military, but for several of the Morenci Nine, other factors—often grafted onto concepts of masculinity—also played a part in the decisionmaking. For many minorities in the United States, including some of the Nine, race had a significant role and added to the complexity of making the choice to join. Frequently, commonalities existed among minorities regarding military service, especially economic push factors, since minorities typically constituted a sizable portion of America's working and lower middle classes. Further, members of minority groups often had a strong sense that they needed to prove their loyalty to the country. Others inherited strong warrior traditions dating back for centuries. For Latinos and Native Americans in the Southwest, serving in the Vietnam War therefore presented noteworthy challenges, on the one hand, and clear opportunities, on the other.

Latinos, especially Mexican Americans, served in large numbers in combat units in Vietnam.[56] Author Victor Martínez observes that they "fought for reasons that were ill-defined, often confusing, but for the most part devoid of any cogent understanding of the political and economic forces at play which took them from [the United States to Indochina]."[57] But whether or not they understood completely, especially on the conscious level, their choices were informed by many factors.

The numerous World War II and Korean veterans in the Mexican American community who had distinguished themselves and established a legacy of service affected the decisions made by the younger generation. Many young Mexican Americans were intensely patriotic and wanted to prove themselves to their Anglo counterparts, much like African Americans did. As one Mexican American veteran from Bakersfield, California, stated, "I enlisted a couple of years after high school. At the time I was young and innocent and I was under the impression that enlisting was the All-American thing to do."[58] Another Mexican American veteran noted, "I was gonna get drafted so I went ahead and volunteered. It was part of trying to be an American and patriotic and the whole romantic notion of war. When we got to Vietnam, we wanted to prove that we really were Americans. Even now I think we Chicano guys want to prove how patriotic we were."[59]

Leroy Cisneros, Clive Garcia, and Robert Moncayo all carried such sentiments, whether consciously or subconsciously, into the decision-making process. Concepts of masculinity were, of course, present in the Anglo community as well, but the machismo ethic further reinforced the idea of military service as a venue for proving manhood. In Morenci, with so many Mexican American veterans from World War II and Korea, the pressures to demonstrate one's masculinity were real and pervasive. And for the young men of the community, one major way to respond was to enlist in the military.[60]

In addition, the racial dynamics of a search for equality in citizenship, both politically and economically, played a key role. When large numbers of Mexican American servicemen returned to Morenci from World War II and demanded equality in the workplace, especially during the successful strike in 1946, the value of military service in one's personal and professional life was enhanced.[61] Therefore, many young Mexican Americans in the mining camp followed in their fathers' footsteps and entered the military when they turned eighteen or soon after.

Native Americans in Morenci and throughout the region, Joe Sorrelman among them, also volunteered in numbers out of proportion to their overall population, and they suffered significant casualties and often performed with valor in Vietnam. Yet Joe and others encountered significant obstacles in gaining recognition for their contributions.[62] One observer noted, "The deep impression made upon American minds by the Indian struggle against the white man in the last century has made the contemporary Indian somewhat invisible compared to their ancestors."[63]

Geographic considerations also contributed to this situation. Most Native Americans lived in sparsely populated areas of the American West or blended into large urban areas where their ethnic identity became confused with that of other groups, including Latinos. Then, too, surnames made it difficult to identify Native American individuals, and problems of classifications existed because some Native tribes did not receive official government recognition.

Despite such challenges, a significant percentage of Native Americans joined the military during the Vietnam War for many reasons. Historian

Tom Holm argues the postwar surveys indicate that for many, "military service was part of an honorable family and/or tribal tradition. They wanted to be warriors—to protect their land and their people. And, in the tribal tradition of reciprocity, they wanted to gain respect from other Native Americans."[64]

Many examples illustrate the impact of these various influences. One Native American veteran noted, "A lot of us Indians were living with our tribal archetypes as being warriors. We had a purpose."[65] In the comparatively large Native American community in Morenci, the warrior culture had deep roots among the Apaches and Navajos. The Apaches had role models in Geronimo and Cochise, who valiantly fought the US military in the latter half of the nineteenth century, often in the lands around their homes. In the case of the Navajos, a long tradition of military service existed in oral histories and in modern examples such as the code talkers, who became famous for their exploits in the South Pacific during World War II.[66]

Joe, along with many of his friends, including Earl Begay and Guy Todacheeny, carried the images and ideals of past service into their decision to join. The fact that his uncles and other family members had been code talkers clearly fascinated Joe and sparked his imagination about what he could accomplish as a soldier. Other compelling factors, such as the economic opportunities and the adventure military service provided, as well as the acceleration of an assimilation process, also contributed to Joe's decision-making process. But the actions of his ancestors clearly pushed him forward.

Gender and racial factors were significant, but other cultural forces were influential as well, including religion.[67] Joe, Leroy, Clive, and Robert all belonged to the Catholic Church, which had a special place relative to the Vietnam War. The virulently anti-Communist Catholic Church often denounced the Soviet Union, a process accelerated by the Soviets' subjugation of countries with large Catholic populations, such as Poland, after World War II.

In French Indochina, the Catholic Church had occupied a prominent position. With the Viet Minh's defeat of the French in 1954, American Catholics became even more involved in the region, particularly Cardinal Francis Spellman, head of the massive New York Diocese. Assisted by prominent senators such as Mike Mansfield (D-MT) and John F. Kennedy (D-MA), Spellman supported the faithful Catholic leader Ngo Dinh Diem, who became the leader of South Vietnam. Working with the American Friends of Vietnam, the Catholic Relief Services, and other similar groups, the Catholic Church played a substantial role in South Vietnam.[68]

Even after the assassination of Diem in 1963, Catholics remained a backbone of the US support for South Vietnam. In 1965, while visiting troops there, Cardinal Spellman told them that the struggle was a "war for civilization." He added, "Through valor and dedication of our men and women in the armed forces, we will soon have a victory for which all of us are praying." In conclusion, he stressed that "[anything] less than victory is inconceivable."[69]

With such backing by the hierarchy of the Catholic Church and only limited dissent, most Catholics in the United States, especially those in the working class, remained strong supporters of the war.[70] This apparently proved particularly true among the smaller farming, mining, and rural communities as well as in ethnic enclaves across the country. The young men in these areas heard priests in the pulpits denounce communism, and papal speeches and church literature delivered ominous warnings about the dangers of the atheistic Communists. As one veteran noted, "It was better to fight Communism there in Vietnam than our back yard. . . . We had to be the Legions of God. We were doing it for our faith." Another veteran recalled, "We were inculcated with a strong anti-communist bias by the nuns and priests. . . . By the time I was nine or ten, I firmly believed that Joseph Stalin was the incarnation of evil and that the United States was locked in a death struggle with the Soviet Union."[71]

In the end, the Catholic Church was pivotal in promoting the dominant message circulating in Cold War America, and the young Catholic men in Morenci knew that their duty included defending the church against the atheistic Communists. This attitude blended well with the political culture of the time, and particularly in a small community where few people tolerated dissent, especially in 1966, when the majority of Americans clearly supported President Johnson and the crusade in South Vietnam.

The Catholic Church may have constituted the cornerstone of US support for South Vietnam, but denominations such as the Baptist Church, to which Stan and Larry belonged, took an equally strong stance against communism, and though more decentralized, evangelical denominations, particularly in the South and the Mountain West, strongly supported the war effort.[72] Early on, in December 1966, the prominent evangelical Billy Graham toured Vietnam and condemned those clergy who were urging a pullout in Southeast Asia, stressing, "Communism has to be stopped somewhere whether in Hanoi or on the West Coast. The President believes it should be stopped in Vietnam."[73] The message, much like the one emanating from Catholic leaders, was clear: young men needed to take up arms to protect America's freedoms, especially the freedom of religion that the atheistic Communists threatened.

Others shared the convictions of the Catholics and Baptists. In Morenci, the small Mormon community also held the line against communism, especially its active members and young men such as Bobby Dale Draper and Van Whitmer. However, Mormon leaders often reflected an ambivalence toward the Vietnam War (and war in general), and many Mormons used their missions as a way to avoid the draft until they returned and married or moved into industries including agriculture or colleges that guaranteed deferments. Young men often employed the opportunities in other Mormon communities throughout eastern Arizona, and they were open to young Mormons in Morenci as well.[74]

The fact that Bobby Dale and Van joined their comrades in enlisting reflected the other side of the coin. Their action might, in part, be attributed to the Mormons' efforts to fit into mainstream American society and overcome the suspicions of their secretive practices as well as their legacy of polygamy, practiced among traditional Mormons through the 1890s. In addition, some in the Mormon leadership became rabid anti-Communists after World War II and emphasized the need for LDS members to participate in the war against communism.[75] Led by prominent church leader Ezra Taft Benson, who served as secretary of agriculture under Eisenhower, and others including Cleon Skousen, many Mormons became zealous anti-Communists and strove to emphasize their patriotism and underscore that they were 100 percent American.[76] The Mormon commitment to the fight against communism arose in many areas, military and otherwise, during the Vietnam era and depended on individual communities and family connections. In Morenci, many young Mormon males joined the armed services.

Religion was a vital part of life in the small mining camp. It provided identification and solidarity and carried with it responsibilities, among them the obligation to reinforce acceptable behavior. This included military service in the defense of religious freedom in the Cold War period. Daily, whether at church or in church publications, young men in Morenci and throughout the country received the call to move onward as Christian soldiers, to be the tip of the spear in defending their nation on the front lines in South Vietnam. This impulse related less to spirituality and more to another powerful influence in their lives, the common political narrative of the time about the dangers of communism and their duty to stop its spread. Religion was not an overt push factor like the draft, but it combined with many other factors to form a central element of the cultural landscape that shaped perspectives on military service.

In addition, practical, everyday reasons existed for joining the military. For some, service held the promise of government programs to finance college and technical training, something most of the Morenci Nine desperately needed. Equally important, it gained them entrance into the brotherhood of veterans (or at least it should have) through organizations such as the VFW and American Legion. In the mining camp, the prospect of having support in times of need or social activities at the local halls on weekend nights provided a strong incentive for doing one's time in the military. Thus, military service became an investment in the future for many of the young men, for they knew they would most likely otherwise live out their days in the mines without enjoying such benefits.

Whatever the promises of rewards or the pressures from social, cultural, and political institutions, the Morenci Nine ultimately had few options other than to march off to war in 1966. Each of the individuals made his choice, determined by a series of complex factors. It was a decision partly molded by the local community, by the national political culture, by socioeconomic position, and by race and gender. A multitude of factors contributed to how young men like the Nine dealt with the draft and volunteering, and for many of them, the choice to enlist was the seminal decision of their young lives. They expected to be welcomed home as heroes, but unfortunately, things did not work out that way for veterans of the Vietnam War.

4

Eight Weeks in Hell and Beyond

The Morenci Nine Become Marines

On Independence Day 1966, people all across the United States prepared for the holiday. Red, white, and blue streamers flew everywhere, along with American flags on front lawns and public buildings. Mothers arose early and started baking apple pies, while fathers put beer on ice and began prepping for the big barbecues. Kids scurried about town, some already in their swimsuits as they headed for the pools or local rivers. Boy Scouts prepared for parades, dressing up in their uniforms to accompany the large groups of veterans who wore their uniforms and medals to march down main street. It was the most patriotic time of the year, and most Americans in 1966 looked forward to a day of revelry capped by firework displays in the warm summer evening skies.

Not everyone woke up and prepared for celebrations that Fourth of July in Morenci. People in the mining town usually enjoyed the holiday—participating in eating contests, coin dives in the recently cleaned company pool, and other festivities. But this day, instead of driving to the store to buy food and drinks for the partying, a large group gathered at Foster Simms's Texaco Station, as the bright yellow sun rose over the red canyon peaks. There, nine young Marine volunteers, the youngest seventeen and the oldest twenty, clustered with families and friends. Mothers and sisters, tears flowing down their cheeks, hugged their young sons and brothers. The more stoic fathers stood back a bit and ultimately extended their hands for a final handshake before the recruits' adventure began. Then, most of the young men boarded a small white bus for the short trip to Safford, where a larger one awaited them for the extended trip to Phoenix and a return visit to the San Carlos Hotel before taking off on the final leg to San Diego.

Across the country that day, thousands of other young Americans embarked on similar journeys, jumping on board buses, trains, and planes and generally missing the nation's celebration of its independence. Many had received orders from Uncle Sam to report for duty; others had volunteered like the Morenci Nine. They headed for boot camps in San Diego or on Parris Island or basic training at Fort Bliss or Fort Benning and the start of a new life as soldiers in the US military.

The Morenci Nine stopped for the night in Phoenix. The young men carefully avoided the youthful indiscretions that nearly led to their incarceration during their earlier stay at the San Carlos. The mood differed, as well, as a mix of anxiety and excitement permeated the group. Many of their fathers, uncles, and teachers had followed similar paths in earlier years, and each young man wondered about what lay ahead. Would he endure the rigors of boot camp? How well would he fare in the harsh training? Was he man enough to become an elite warrior? Would he make his parents and community proud? Was he one step closer to the rapidly expanding war in Vietnam?

A couple of the recruits slept soundly that night, knowing it would be their last chance for a good night's sleep for at least two months; others tossed and turned in anticipation. A few likely did not sleep at all, dealing with a combination of anxiety and fear. The night went by quickly, and soon they headed toward the bus depot and the final stage of their journey.

The long bus ride to San Diego across the desert allowed them more time to think. The barren land outside the windows provided little distraction, for there was not much to see except their own reflections. Several slept, and others stared into the distance, especially the particularly introspective ones such as Bobby Dale and Robert. It was the last time that they would really have a chance to think on their own, apart from the lonely nights when they would stare at the bunk above them or the ceiling, wondering what they had gotten themselves into this time.

* * *

Once the bus arrived in the much more temperate climate of San Diego, some 40 degrees cooler than Phoenix, the group of young men bounded down the steps and waited and watched. Leroy had been given the duty of carrying the orders and was told to call a particular number once they arrived to secure transportation to the Marine Corps Recruiting Depot (MCRD). He received a jolt when the person who picked up the phone called him a "fag." "Go to the corner and stand at attention," the Marine ordered, "and wait for someone to pick you up."[1]

Leroy, looking a bit shocked, reported back to his comrades. Awkwardly, the nine stood at attention at the street corner, providing quite a sight for locals and tourists passing by. Soon, a big olive-drab truck arrived. Leroy ran to jump in the front while the others piled in the back. The driver told Leroy, in some colorful profanities, to join his friends in the rear. He then sped off with his quarry for the short drive to the base and the start of boot camp. The passengers had little time for the initial shock to wear off.[2]

The wide-eyed Morenci boys, many leaving their families for the first time in their relatively short lives, watched as the truck passed through the gate at the MCRD on that fateful day, Tuesday, July 5, 1966. They had no real chance to take in the scenery, for the truck stopped and a group of drill instructors (DIs), dressed in khaki uniforms with broad-brimmed Smokey the Bear hats, immediately swarmed the recruits like angry bees. They yelled, "You faggots, get out of the truck. Get the fuck out!" They grabbed those leaping down and flung several to the ground. "Move! Move! Move! You maggots, what is wrong with you? Goddamnit, get your asses over there," they screamed, pulling and kicking those who hesitated.[3]

Before long, the instructors herded them toward the yellow footprints painted on the ground, heels in, toes out. "Put your feet there, you assholes. Damn it, just stand on the footprint," the instructors yelled. The shell-shocked Morenci boys, caught in the summer sun of San Diego, ran to do what the instructors ordered. They looked at each other for support, but the instructors jumped in, asking, "What the fuck are you looking at? Keep your eyes forward." They grabbed the young recruits, pulling back their shoulders and kicking them in their butts to push their groins forward. With little room in front or behind, in what became a familiar formation known as "asshole to bellybutton," the young men stood and waited for others to arrive.[4] Like tens of thousands before and many more after, the new Marines never forgot their initial introduction into the military.

Once everyone gathered, some from as far away as Cincinnati, the instructors marched the young men off for processing. The motley group tried but failed to keep cadence, leading to more pushing, screaming, and shoving by the instructors. "What is wrong with you? You can't even walk, how are you going to be Marines?" they shrieked. The instructors hurled loud insults when the young recruits responded, "Sir, yes, sir." "Say it like you've got a set, you worthless cunts!" became the common refrain as the instructors bull-rushed the recruits and continued the fusillade of insults and profanities.

The young men, many in blue jeans and short-sleeved shirts, tried to follow the directions, but no one satisfied the instructors, who continued their verbal and sometimes physical assaults. Inside one of the buildings, they heard the command, "Undress." With the fear of God already in them, they rushed to do as told, but some waited too long and had the instructors zero in on them. Once they had stripped down, they marched through a line where they deposited their clothes and discarded personal items such as watches amid taunts, "You're on Marine time now." They took showers to wipe off the "civilian scuz" and then received their uniforms, footlockers, and other accessories, almost all olive-drab except for the black boots.[5]

Again, the instructors tore into the recruits, screaming, "You slime, you worthless pieces of shit," grabbing them and herding them like cattle toward the barbershop. There, they stood in line waiting their turn. The barber quickly removed Mike's wavy blond hair and Stan's short red crop. Clive's dark-black mane followed, as did Robert's and Leroy's, leading one person to note, "That's the first dehumanizing thing, so you all look alike."[6]

For hours, the instructors continued the routine that they had down to a fine art. Running the recruits all over the camp, sometimes only in their underwear and socks, the DIs continued the assault, beginning the process of stripping them of their individualism and of any vestiges of the outside world. At one point, they stopped in a building with a long set of phones on the wall. The recruits received orders to proceed to the phones, one by one, and call home. When someone picked up, they would simply say, for example: "This is Recruit Whitmer. I have arrived safely in San

Diego. Please do not send any food or bulky items to me in the mail. I will contact you in 3 to 5 days by postcard with my new address. Thank you for your support. Goodbye for now." The call constituted a final farewell to the outside world.[7]

It was a severe shock for many as, once they finished the dressing and shearing, the drill instructors led the recruits to their Quonset huts, which looked like replicas from the popular show of the time *Gomer Pyle, USMC*. Yet the similarities to the television show ended immediately, for no bumbling Gunnery Sergeant Carter existed. The drill instructors continued their profanity-laced assaults on the new arrivals, questioning the manhood and family origins of the recruits as they ran them from one place to another. The harassment lasted long into the night, when the exhausted and overwhelmed young men finally climbed into their bunks. Then, the drill instructors told them to shut their mouths and lie at attention. Many collapsed in the beds and likely shared the thought of a fellow Marine who concluded, "I ain't going to make it to Vietnam. I'm going to die right here in San Diego."[8]

As promised, the Morenci boys stayed together in Training Platoon 1055, B Company, First Battalion. Seventy-nine recruits started boot camp, many from Arizona and Texas. The group reflected the general composition of recruits in 1966, the majority coming from working-class and lower-middle-class backgrounds; they were the sons of miners, farmers, grocery store clerks, and industrial workers, with only a few, such as Stan, having any college education. They were young, typically between eighteen and nineteen years old. Racially, they mirrored some of the demographic trends of the time, with four African Americans (actually far below the average in the US military then), eight Latinos, and one Native American. The Morenci boys provided a significant segment of the diversity.

The next day set the tone for the following two to three weeks of boot camp. At 0330 (3:30 a.m.), long before the sun rose, the drill instructors, led by Sgt. J. A. Roche, entered the barracks. After waiting a moment in the dark room, they pounced, turning the lights on and off and screaming for the recruits to get up. Their charges jumped out of the racks in their boxer shorts and T-shirts. Some moved slowly, exhausted after being run ragged the previous day. Sgt. B. L. Purcell and Sgt. M. G. Hewitt joined

Roche in rousting out those who dallied. "You pussies gonna sleep all day?" the instructors screamed. "Get your asses out of them fart sacks."[9] The young men scrambled, many falling out of the top bunks as they rushed to reach the floor. The drill instructors went up and down the barracks berating their charges for their sloppiness, poor posture, and a host of other deficiencies.

Then, the fun started. After about ten minutes to go to the head, clean up, and put on shorts, T-shirts, and sneakers, the Marines lined up. Endless sit-ups, push-ups, jumping jacks, leg lifts, and squat thrusts followed. Many of the young men struggled under the strain, exacerbated by taunts of "You pussy. You cannot even do a few push-ups." Others yelled, "What's wrong with you? You will never be a Marine."

Large guys such as Bobby Dale and Stan found their arms strained to lift their huge frames, which only led to more attacks on their manhood. "Get off the ground and up, get off the ground and up," rang through the room. Over time, sweat dampened the floors as the men tried hard to follow the cadence of "up, down, up, down." Then they would roll over and begin doing sit-ups until their stomach muscles burned and they could not lift their heads off the ground. The instructors jumped again: "What's wrong with you? Do another, for God's sake. You don't belong in the Marine Corps."

Good and tired, some of the recruits gasped for breath. Others were ready to collapse. Nonetheless, the men dressed quickly, made up their racks, cleaned their areas, and began running into the darkness in formation, something they would do over and over again in the weeks ahead. The cool San Diego air slapped their faces as they exited their quarters, and the harassment continued from the DIs who pushed and prodded the stragglers, yelling, "Why the hell can't you keep up?" The recruit's standard view became the back of a comrade's head, with only a short distance separating the two men. Suddenly, the world had become a much smaller place.

The long runs, mile after mile, often in predawn darkness, proved torturous for many, especially Bobby Dale and other heavier-set recruits whose bodies were built for strength and power, not endurance and stamina. Others, such as Stan, who had been away at college and partying too much, struggled as well. Stan's large barrel chest heaved as he tried to catch his wind, particularly as some of the shorter, leaner, and more fleet-

Clive (center) waiting in line while at boot camp in summer 1966. (Photo courtesy of US Marine Corps.)

footed recruits pushed the pace. For many, aching legs began feeling like concrete blocks as they lifted them off the ground, laboring to continue to go forward while their lungs burned from the cool morning air.[10] The Parris Island Marines, facing the stifling heat and humidity of South Carolina, liked to characterize the San Diego soldiers as Hollywood Marines because of the more favorable weather and location of their camp. But the West Coast recruits endured their own brand of hell.

To break the boredom and keep their minds off the pain as they ran, the recruits learned chants such as: "If I die in a combat zone / Bag my body and send it home / Pin my medals on my chest / Tell mom I did my best." Another went: "My granddaddy was an old Marine / Meanest man you ever seen / He ate steaks twelve inches thick / Picked his teeth with a guidon stick."[11] Loud voices singing these chants broke the predawn slumber as San Diegoans awoke, although the Marines had already been up and on the go for hours.

If not running, the young recruits marched in formation for hours at a time around camp or on trails and roads crisscrossing the base, and later, heavy packs and weapons were added to their load. "Left-right-left, left-right-left," rang out endlessly, only punctuated by comments such as "Your other right, sweetheart." When someone screwed up badly, the drill instructor yelled, "Everyone hit the deck," and the push-ups started until the men's arms ached and sometimes their hands bled. Then it was back up and "left-right-left, left-right-left" once again, hour after hour.[12] Often, the marching was mind numbing. One Marine commented, "I do not know which was worse, the monotony or the effort—the monotony of putting one foot in front of the other hour after hour" or the effort of keeping the right interval with the man in front. He concluded after such marches that the "sense of the Marine Corps experience . . . was pain."[13]

The Marine recruits could brag that they did more before 8:00 a.m. than normal people did by noon, but even they needed to eat. Meals proved an interesting experience and featured the same regimentation as the training exercises. The DIs marched the recruits to the mess hall, where a sign hung over the entrance, "Take All You Want but Eat All You Take." There they sidestepped through the chow line looking straight ahead, trays held out in front as they waited to be served. Next, the young men moved along to the tables, where everyone stood with their chairs pushed back until the seats filled. Once that was done, a drill instructor yelled, "Ready seats." At that, they all tried to hit the chairs simultaneously. If they did not succeed, they continued the exercise, with the drill instructor repeating, "Getup! Getup! Not fast enough." Eventually, everyone did it to the instructor's satisfaction, and at that point, the DI yelled, "Eat."[14]

When not engaged in physical training or eating, the recruits attended classes to learn rudimentary military information about topics such as weapons, basic tactics, and the traditions and history of the Marine Corps. The latter included tales about the heroes such as Smedley Butler and Chesty Puller, the highly decorated officer from the Banana Wars, World War II, and Korea. Such lore helped create the esprit de corps so valued by the Marines. Drill instructors required the members of Platoon 1055 to repeat after them each night, "Goodnight Chesty Puller wherever you are." Though most entered boot camp not knowing who Puller was, they quickly learned and appreciated the tales of his heroism. The intense learning the recruits endured led Clive to emphasize in a letter, "They work us harder than the average college student. But there's a reason. We are learning how to kill, while the college student is learning how to live."[15]

The Marine Corps regulated all aspects of life during the day, including when to clean up, dress, eat, go to the bathroom (the ass must be wiped front to back), and even the occasional few minutes allotted for a smoke break. This ensured regimentation and conformity, two of the major goals for boot camp. One recruit observed that he felt like there was an "invisible noose around my neck which doesn't tighten or isn't noticed unless I try to move."[16] The goal of boot camp remained the same throughout: take individuals and mold seventy-nine men into one group. Each Marine was to be a man who "would be physically fit, perfectly disciplined, an outstanding sharpshooter, and trained to kill. . . . The Marine Corps was about killing and following orders."[17]

More physical training and running followed classes, as there was no rest—more running, marching, jumping jacks, push-ups, squats, and sit-ups, always more. When the recruits tired, they did extra exercises. The first phase of boot camp sought to create men at the peak of their physical condition, instilled with pride in being able to push themselves beyond what they had thought possible.[18]

The constant haranguing of the drill instructors, the physical exercise, the mental strain of trying to react when ordered, and the steep learning curve all contributed to the recruits' exhaustion by the end of the day. Usually around 2100, the drill instructors entered the barracks and yelled, "Prepare to mount." The recruits snapped into position near their racks. "Mount," the call went out. All recruits tried to hit the bunks quickly, assuming a rigid attention position. "Get out of those goddamn racks you goddamn shit maggots," might be heard. Everyone scurried down and waited for the command to ring out again, "Mount." This went on until the DIs were satisfied.[19] At last, lights went out, and some fell asleep immediately. Others looked up—at the bottom of the bunk above them or at the ceiling—and wondered for the umpteenth time: What had they gotten themselves into? Would they really make it?

Despite the pressure and exhaustion, Clive wrote home after a couple of days in camp, reporting that "they work us long and hard but we can take

Platoon 1055, Boot Camp, MCRD, San Diego, California, July 1966 (Photo provided by Oscar Urrea from the personal belongings of Robert Moncayo.)

it." He added that they only had one break, a time to go to Mass, where he marveled at the sound of a thousand Marines singing in unison. He talked about the fact that they had walked into boot camp as boys but would emerge as men. Still, he admitted, he was "feeling sore, tired, homesick," and he lamented, "I wish in a way I was going to college I mean like everybody else but somebody has to be here and I don't like being second but that's why we're here."[20]

In Platoon 1055, Sergeant Roche originally commanded training. However, one recruit described him as often appearing drunk and being overweight and "way-way out of shape." He never joined the platoon on their runs or marches, and one day when he tried to show the recruits the proper way to do a pull-up, he could not do even one himself.[21] Roche would not last long.

One morning about a week into training, the dynamics changed significantly with the arrival of a new senior drill instructor. That fateful day, Sgt. R. A. Bowser, the archetypal Marine DI, marched onto the scene. Standing 6'4" tall with a square jaw and broad shoulders, Sergeant Bowser towered over most everyone in the platoon except for a couple such as Stan who could look eye to eye with him. (Of course, no one ever dared to do that unless so ordered, fearing some type of harangue such as "Are you eye fucking me, you faggot?" or "Are you looking at me like you love me, you sorry queer?") Sergeant Bowser always appeared pissed off. As one of the recruits noted, "Every time an airplane would take off from the San Diego Airport, Bowser would stare at the plane, mumble something, and then lay into us as if it was our fault the plane took off."[22]

The new sergeant liked to chew Copenhagen snuff. The dark-brown juice produced by the combination of saliva and tobacco often found its way onto the faces of the recruits, as Bowser bragged that he liked to spit out his words and see where they would splatter. Frequently, he grew frustrated with those who could not keep up or who failed to march in cadence. When that happened, he charged the offender and proceeded to stand only inches from his ear, yelling and cursing, "You goofy looking maggot. Why can't you do the simplest thing?" Out of fear, the young man dared not flinch. When Bowser moved on to another victim, the young man was left with dark snuff juice in his ear, but he inevitably waited until the sergeant could not see before he cleared out the ear canal.[23]

Sergeant Bowser and his colleagues were tough as nails across the board, often punishing the entire group for the transgressions of an individual. When someone screwed up, the platoon dropped into push-up position with hands and toes on the deck, staying in the stance for as long as fifteen minutes, an especially difficult chore after a long day of physical training. In other cases, such as for those violating the prohibition against talking after lights-out, the DIs stormed into the room and ordered everyone to the ground, where they had to grunt like pigs until the instructors decided they had had enough. Clive acknowledged that "at first it was funny but now it hurt. I don't like it."[24]

One of the worst punishments occurred when Sergeant Bowser ordered the recruits to the sandpit, where they sank ankle deep into the sand while doing physical training in full gear with their rifles. Everyone walked out determined not to repeat the mistake that caused the detour to the pit.[25]

Even when Sergeant Bowser appeared to soften a bit, he continued to keep his recruits on their toes. In one case, he took them to see the movie

Hud, starring Paul Newman as an unscrupulous, amoral, and rebellious young man challenging the system and especially his overbearing father. Several of the recruits recognized the irony relating to their current condition. The young men expected to receive individual servings of popcorn and soft drinks. Instead, Bowser brought only a few sodas and a few bags of popcorn, which he distributed among the seventy-nine members of the platoon. Unfortunately for them, Sergeant Bowser lacked the supernatural ability of another man who fed five thousand years before in a faraway land. So the recruits went home hungry and thirsty and pissed off, although the movie gave them a nice change of pace for a couple of hours. [26]

Sergeant Bowser and the other drill instructors could also administer devastating individual punishments. One day, Tom Pierson, who had become a friend of Bobby Dale, received a package. A colleague who had survived boot camp had told him that the keys to success were "don't get noticed [and] don't get care packages in the mail." But another friend who had moved on to Camp Pendleton played a nasty trick on him and sent him a box containing a small toy police car. Upon its arrival, Sergeant Bowser ordered everyone to march to the "grinder" (a major parade ground) for some exercise. There he ordered Pierson to the front and told him to start duckwalking (bending at the knees and squatting and walking), all the while pushing the toy car the length of the grinder (several hundred yards) as he made siren noises. Pierson later remarked that the grinder never appeared longer than it did that day and that, unfortunately, from "that day forward the DIs knew my name," which proved "not a good thing."[27]

Such actions had an effect. Early on, Clive wrote his parents and begged his mother never to send anything other than letters to him. "If you get anything to eat they make you eat it fast while working hard," he wrote, "and then you drink a canteen of hot, hot water." Clive told of a friend who began convulsing so violently that he had to be hospitalized when forced to endure that punishment.[28]

Changes in training began to unfold in boot camp after a few weeks, as the recruits began running the obstacle course, a 225-yard-long field with lumber obstructions looking like old telephone poles positioned in various configurations. The drill instructors also added new regimens, including more hand-to-hand combat as well as rifle training. When the young men moved into weapons, they had a new and constructive focus. As one observer noted, "For the first time, the recruit feels that he is being given something useful to do, that he is acquiring a skill that is of some interest and value." He added that the young man faced proficiency tests with the rifle and when he passed, "suddenly, he is no longer a worthless human being; he has a worthwhile skill for which he's rewarded by a lessening of harassment." When achievement combined with a calculated reduction of emotional stress, the recruit began to believe that he would survive after all, and he experienced a sense of pride in his accomplishments.[29]

The Morenci boys particularly enjoyed the rifle range. They had been around guns all their lives, hunting in the forest and canyons for deer and rabbits. Unlike many of their city-bred comrades, they had used larger rifles for deer or elk hunting, weapons that resembled the M-14 they fired in training. Clive bragged to his father that he now slept with his rifle, adding, "I feel naked without it." He even named the nearly 4-foot-long, 11-pound weapon that fired a 7.62mm bullet. "I can hit anything I can see at 1,000 yards," he crowed to his father.[30] Every Marine was a rifleman, and the Marine Corps particularly prized prowess with the weapon. The Morenci boys had a special gift for the rifle and enjoyed showing off their talents.

Along with the new training opportunities came changes in the drill instructors' tactics. Though a tendency to marginalize "unsats" (people deemed unsatisfactory in performance) persisted, the goal of unit cohesiveness and teamwork—a building of esprit de corps—became even more important as boot camp continued. When a comrade faltered during the long hikes or runs, one veteran remembered, "somebody would take his rifle, somebody would take his pack, and two other people would take his arms, and you always bring your fellow Marine along because we're a unit."[31]

The Morenci boys already had an esprit de corps, which paid dividends on long marches and during exhausting physical training. The larger, more muscular Bobby Dale sometimes failed to keep up, lacking the stamina and endurance of Joe, Leroy, Robert, and others. Unlike back home on the football field, he often stumbled along and made mistakes. "Pig," the drill instructors called him. A couple of them zeroed in on him for some reason. It may have been because he was an Explorer Scout or because of his religion, for at least one DI questioned whether a Mormon could kill. For whatever reason, Bobby Dale faced extra harassment.[32]

In one instance, the group had to sound out encouragement to Bobby Dale after he mistakenly called his M-14 a gun rather than a rifle, a major faux pas. As the platoon marched, Bobby Dale, his lips and nose coated with white zinc to prevent a deep sunburn, circled his comrades with his weapon held high, repeating the line, "This is my rifle, this is my gun [grabbing his crotch]. One is for shooting, the other for fun."[33] Throughout their training, he and others received encouragement from their Morenci buddies; as Clive wrote to his father, on the 6-mile marches, "I always wind up carrying somebody's pack because he falls back. You know dad Marines never leave a Marine behind."[34]

The exhaustion from the constant physical and mental strain made the nights hard for many recruits. Sleep deprivation added to the challenges. Some slept soundly, but living right near the end of the San Diego airport—where the loud roar of turbine and jet engines filled the air as planes landed and departed, often late into the night and early in the morning—made sleeping difficult. For some, the nights constituted the only downtime they had, the only hours when drill instructors were not yelling at them. Many remained homesick and lonely, for most were teenagers away from home for the first time and adjusting to the demands of becoming soldiers in an extremely stressful environment. Some even thought about the potential threat looming over the western horizon in a far-off place called Vietnam.

Clive wrote that over time, the DIs lightened up on being quiet during lights-out. Many recruits horsed around, practicing hand-to-hand combat that often sent someone to the sick bay with a gash. Others played poker, although not Clive: "I work too hard for my money to lose it." He observed, "Sure its [sic] wild and rough but we like it like that."[35]

Clive and his friends had the advantage of having friendly and familiar faces nearby. He wrote his parents that at night, the guys talked about Morenci. "When we get a letter," he added, "you can tell because our marching improves and no one fights." At another time, he told about how much everyone liked to talk about the food and fun they had in Morenci, laughing over the good old days of hunting, fishing, playing sports, and chasing girls. Yet he lamented that after all the laughing died down, each man still found himself alone in his thoughts. He added, "I thank God I joined with my friends when I did. I don't know what I'd do without them."[36]

Throughout boot camp, violence was omnipresent, both in the controlled atmosphere on the training grounds and elsewhere. When the mental and physical pressures, mixed with high doses of testosterone, reached a fever pitch, fights erupted. In one case, Joe got into it with a Texan named Armando Fuentes. It started over a silly thing, when Fuentes took Joe's assigned job. Fearing that the drill instructors would find him just standing around, the normally quiet Joe began verbally sparring with the Texan; as Joe later noted, by that point in their training, "you could fly off the handle at anything just to get release of some tension." A melee erupted as fists flew and the two recruits grabbed each other fiercely, tangling up in a blur of olive-green uniforms while their comrades gathered around. The fight ultimately ended when Joe repeatedly rammed Fuentes's head into a footlocker. When the drill instructors arrived to investigate, neither man turned the other in, and instead, they said they had both slipped and gave assorted other stories. Joe acknowledged that the DIs did not believe them, but deep down, the drill instructors knew such things happened—and personally, they liked the aggressiveness the recruits demonstrated.[37]

At some point, Clive received guard duty in one of the barracks. He complained that fights broke out all the time and that he had to turn in people. One night, armed with a billy club and an unloaded rifle, he tried to separate two sparring recruits. They attacked him instead. He disengaged and waited in a corner and then jumped one, taking the club and repeatedly striking his antagonist. When he was finished, he called another guard, who escorted the man to the sergeant on duty. Clive recalled that the recruit would have gone to the brig except that "they took one look at him and sayed [sic] that he's had enough and let him go." He also observed that from then on, the big monster hated him but stepped aside when he approached. He even concluded, "Maybe I'll ask [sic] to go to M.P. school." It proved a prophetic insight.[38]

The violence, the homesickness, and the psychological strain could have devastating results for some recruits, something the young men from

Morenci saw up close and personal. In one case, a young man from another platoon had been pushed too hard and cracked. Extremely depressed, he took out an extra round at the rifle range, placed his rifle under his chin, and pulled the trigger. He died immediately. Clive reported, "You can still find brains and flesh on the walls where it happened."[39]

Most of the Morenci boys handled the pressures well, especially the former athletes, who were already familiar with physical demands and the psychological strain of being yelled at by coaches. They also relied on each other for encouragement and support. However, Van struggled, and some in the group feared that he might become a boot camp casualty. Despite being near the familiar faces from home, he remained an outsider in many ways.[40]

His penchant for sometimes screwing up made him a target of the drill instructors as well as others. Once, at mealtime, he cut through the line of another platoon, a cardinal sin. Members of that platoon began kicking and punching him. Immediately, the Morenci boys jumped into the skirmish, followed by other platoon mates who savored a fight with a rival group. Eventually, the instructors broke it up, and Van emerged relatively unscathed. Everyone stood and waited for the punishment, but Sergeant Bowser and the others merely congratulated the men for defending a fellow Marine.[41]

The routine especially seemed to wear on Van, who had not participated that much in organized sports. He remained socially awkward in the boot camp environment, and though he had the Morenci connection, he lacked the deep relationships experienced by the others, who belonged to either the jock or the kicker group. At one point, the strain threatened to push him over the edge, and he told a couple of the Morenci guys that he might jump the fence and leave. The thought horrified his colleagues. They had developed a reputation as a group, and the desertion of one would have tarnished the image of all. They pulled him aside, promised him support, and then threatened bodily harm if he deserted. That proved enough of a deterrent, along with his own deep sense of pride in not wanting to embarrass himself or his family.[42]

Having comrades from back home certainly paid dividends, but it could also cause problems due to expectations and connections. For example, Stan became a squad leader of a group that included Larry, who was notoriously unkempt. Stan was responsible for making sure everyone

Larry at boot camp. (Photo courtesy of the US Marine Corps.)

in his group performed up to expectations. When they failed, the drill instructors took it out on him, both physically and psychologically, during visits to their quarters. Several times, Stan clashed with Larry after he reported with buttons out of place on his uniform or without having shaved properly. And tensions sometimes exploded into confrontations as the towering Stan, with his red hair and accompanying temper, confronted Larry to demand better. In the end, however, Larry continued to march to his own drummer throughout boot camp, regardless of the consequences.[43]

Despite the occasional bumps in the road, the eight weeks of training (an abbreviated term due to the manpower requirements) went fairly quickly for the Morenci recruits, and graduation appeared on the horizon. Toward the end of boot camp, Sergeant Bowser gathered the platoon to announce each man's MOS (Military Occupational Specialty). Some of the recruits anxiously sought the designation 0311, or rifleman. They wanted to be

grunts, and the Marine Corps obliged. Some received alternative des-
ignations, among them Stan, who headed off to train as an engineer, and
Mike, who received orders for communications school.[44]

On the day of the announcements, Sergeant Bowser had a few choice
words for those who avoided the 0311 assignments. For instance, he
growled at a person designated as a combat engineer, "Good, you get to
step on a fuckin mine in Vietnam."[45] But the majority of the men took
their assignments in stride, as they at least knew their next step—although
a few worried about moving ever closer to South Vietnam.

After receiving their assignments, the Morenci Nine prepared for
graduation. Yet an obstacle arose that threatened to keep everyone from
celebrating together. A short time before graduation, Joe developed a
severe case of athlete's foot that caused him so much pain and aggravation
that he had to go to the infirmary for several days. As a result, the Marines
talked about delaying his graduation. The other eight banded together
and pleaded for him to be allowed to make up the time he had missed.
Ultimately, the Marines relented, and he completed training with his
eight friends.[46]

Finally, on September 6, the Morenci Nine and their comrades in
Platoon 1055 finished boot camp. They excitedly prepared for the
ceremony marking the end of hell and induction into the fraternity of the
Marine Corps. Many of the recruits, including the Morenci boys, looked
forward to seeing their parents and friends for the first time in more than
two months. A caravan of cars from Morenci had trekked across the desert
to San Diego to be with the group on their special day, making it much
easier for the Morenci boys to get out of the racks that Tuesday morning.

The sun shone brightly on the recruits as they gathered at the grinder.
When their time came, members of Platoon 1055 proudly marched across
the parade ground in front of their families and friends. Sergeant Bowser
and the other drill instructors shouted orders and cadence as the group
flawlessly responded, a far cry from the motley crew that had struggled
to assemble only two months before. Then, the young men stood at
attention in formation as several Marine officers congratulated them on
their accomplishments and offered some words of wisdom. The Morenci
boys looked forward, but many anxiously sneaked peeks to find their loved
ones in the crowd. They listened to the speakers but retained little as their
thoughts drifted to the parties afterward and the first real taste of freedom
out of the reach of Sergeant Bowser.[47]

The group (minus Van Whitmer) pose with the standard bearer at the end of boot camp graduation in September 1966. (Photo courtesy of Leroy Cisneros.)

At the end of the ceremony, the young men dashed toward their loved ones, who had congregated at the bottom of the stands where they had watched the event. The Morenci boys hugged and kissed their mothers and girlfriends, shook the hands of their fathers and friends, and breathed a collective sigh of relief. Then they proudly stood in the bright sunlight in their pressed uniforms, posing for numerous pictures with their Morenci brothers, arms slung over each other's shoulders. The cameras captured the memory of the local heroes who now had taken a major step in joining an elite fighting force. In short order, the group dispersed to various locations in San Diego (and ultimately, for a few, in Tijuana) to enjoy the local nightlife and blow off some of the steam that had been building for nearly two months.[48]

Graduation from boot camp left an indelible mark on the young men in Platoon 1055 as well as many others of the Vietnam generation. One Marine acknowledged, "[When] I came out I was convinced that I could beat anybody in the world. I didn't have enough sense to be afraid of anything. I didn't question why or how to do something, I just did it."[49] Another veteran recalled, "Boot camp was a bitch, but you came out feeling good and looking good. . . . You felt you could kick anybody's ass and that all the girls would just jump all over you."[50] The Morenci Nine shared such feelings, which, when combined with a youthful belief in their immortality, made them walk taller and with more swagger than at any other time in their lives. They stood ready to take on the world, and for several, that opportunity would present itself very quickly.

Once they completed boot camp, the Morenci Nine dispersed in several different directions, although Leroy, Clive, Larry, Bobby Dale, Van, and Joe stayed together and took a short jaunt up the road to Camp Pendleton for ITR (Infantry Training Regiment). Stan and Robert headed to Advanced Individual Training (AIT) to focus on their specialties. And Mike received a very short reprieve, traveling home on a brief leave so that he could marry his high school sweetheart, Joyce, at the Mormon temple in Thatcher, the sister city of Safford and about 50 miles from Morenci. After a short honeymoon, he headed away for the first time without his Morenci buddies for training in communications.[51]

Those who headed to Camp Pendleton built on the process begun in boot camp. With the war in Vietnam heating up, they faced an accelerated training schedule. Heavy doses of physical training continued; Leroy remembered the struggles of running up and down between the peaks to the west of the base, breathing hard and straining with the heavy packs.[52] Instructors taught them more about firing weapons, principally the M-14 (most would not fire the new regulation M-16 until they reached Vietnam, especially in the early stages of the war). Bayonet and hand-to-hand training continued as the newly minted Marines learned advanced techniques. Trainees also spent time in the classroom, assimilating knowledge of warfare and tactics. The intense training further confirmed the recognition that they had moved one step closer to combat in Vietnam.

A major transition in ITR included the firing of specialized weapons. Recruits often received instruction in how to use the 50-caliber machine gun and other automatic weapons, how to lay claymore mines and other antipersonnel ordnance, and sometimes how to operate more advanced weapons such as flame-throwers and rocket launchers. They also learned about equipment such as mortars. The ongoing development of their weapons capabilities further increased their confidence and led them to feel more and more like professional soldiers.

However, the specter of Vietnam loomed larger and larger in sunny Southern California. Some of the instructors now had combat experience, a few even carrying the wounds of battle, and during training exercises, they frequently yelled at their charges, "Doing that will get you killed in Vietnam." The recruits also spent time in the field on maneuvers and training, sometimes in mock Vietnamese villages where Asian American troops dressed as Vietnamese peasants in order to provide an approximated combat experience and prepare them for the real thing once they landed in Vietnam. One Marine noted that such actions "gave you a basic idea of the villages and stuff but of course they couldn't portray the . . . fear, they couldn't portray of course going into an actual village with people in it and having them stare at you and hate you and things of that nature."[53]

As the training unfolded, Clive wrote his parents that he would be doing all kinds of challenging things, "like going through mine fields at night and the mines really blow up. Only their [*sic*] not strong enough to hurt you."[54] He wrote that it was hot during the day but that at night temperatures plummeted, forcing the Marines to don jackets and gloves. Out in the field on maneuvers, he said, they ate well, but he added that "this place has a lot of rattlesnakes too." At one point, he told them, he fell into quicksand, sinking in the muck up to his waist. To add insult to injury, the enemy found him, shot him, then put him down as a prisoner of war (POW), before using a rope to drag him out of the sand. "Boy that was sure fun," he told his parents.[55]

Unlike the long, grueling boot camp experience, the advanced training only lasted a few weeks, and there were no major celebrations as it ended. Uncle Sam needed Marines for posts throughout the world but especially in Vietnam, where a massive buildup was under way by the time they graduated from AIT. Fierce fighting with the Vietcong and regulars of the North Vietnamese Army (NVA) raged throughout the country as the enemy decided to meet the American escalation with an escalation of its own. By December 1966, more than four hundred and fifty thousand American troops would be stationed in Vietnam, including several members of the Morenci Nine.[56]

Leroy, Larry, and Bobby Dale on leave in Morenci right before shipping out to South Vietnam in late 1966. (Photo courtesy of Leroy Cisneros.)

*   *   *

By the end of October, the group had completed their advanced training and earned some leave time. They climbed on a bus and headed home to enjoy some rest and relaxation for a couple of weeks before reporting back and boarding a troopship bound for South Vietnam in December. One night, Bobby Dale, Larry, Joe, Leroy, and Clive gathered together at the Garcia home. Bobby Dale had bragged that he could handle the hot Mexican food that Julia Garcia could cook. Clive made sure to instruct his mother to make it extra hot for his buddy.[57]

When the time came, they all sat down at the small table as Bobby Dale began digging into the potent mix of chilies and other spices. His pale face turned red, and he began sweating profusely. He reached for a glass of water, gulped it furiously, and then drank more and even more, trying to extinguish the burning sensation in his mouth and throat. All around him, particularly among the Mexican American kids, loud roars of laughter erupted. The gringo had not handled the hot Mexican food very well at all. His friends loved to tell the story afterward.[58]

The young men said their final farewells to their families, knowing the next stop in their whirlwind year was South Vietnam, where the war continued to escalate, something they all knew from television and newspaper reports. They already felt a little out of place in their town now that they had donned their Marine uniforms, and they clearly shared a different life from those of their own age who either worked in the mine or had been lucky enough to head to college. The distance between them and the majority of their generation had only begun to develop. By the time these soldiers finished the next year of their lives, the chasm would be closer to the Grand Canyon that lay northwest of their beloved hometown.

5

The First Wave Hits Vietnam
Leroy Cisneros, Recon

On the twentieth-fifth anniversary of the attack on Pearl Harbor, Joe, Larry, Bobby Dale, and Leroy threw their packs over their shoulders and walked up the gangplank of the USS *General Gaffey*. The Admiral W. S. Benson–class transport had been in service many years, ferrying troops across the Pacific during World War II and the Korean War and now Vietnam. On this particular day, more than four thousand Marines, complemented by a crew exceeding 350, joined the Morenci boys for the voyage to Da Nang in the Republic of Vietnam.

Soon, the four friends moved below decks and stored their gear. For nearly three weeks, this ship would be their home—a 608-foot-long, 75-foot-wide, floating mass of men crammed together like sardines. In the vast expanse of the Pacific, it constituted only a tiny fraction of the world, but for this group of men, it would comprise their whole universe.[1]

As they left the harbor, some of the Morenci boys stood on deck and looked back at the California shore. As the ship gained steam and moved out to sea, they watched the brownish, hazy landscape fade into the distance as an ocean of blue engulfed them, a dramatic contrast to their beloved Greenlee County. Only a few weeks earlier, they had hiked around the copper canyons and pine forests of their home, enjoying the short leave before embarking on this great adventure.

Apart from the faces of the childhood friends standing beside them on the ship, only the twin smokestacks of the vessel, belching smoke just like

90

the smelter back in Morenci, reminded them of home. Everything else appeared foreign as they left America's shores for the first time, knowing that at least thirteen months would pass before their return. And through those months, the longing for the red clay canyons and pine-topped mountains of Greenlee County never dissipated.

When the four friends descended into the bowels of the ship, a foul stench greeted them. Few of the Marines on board had ever left dry land, so seasickness plagued many as the ship plowed through the seemingly endless ocean. The unpleasant smell of vomit blended with the odor of the shared heads and the smell of thousands of perspiring Marines, creating a nauseating aroma that sickened even the hardiest soul.

In the belly of the ship, the four made their way to the bunks, stacked four high in small rooms. Uncomfortable, with only a few inches separating a person lying down and the bunk overhead, the accommodations brought claustrophobia to many of the young men, most of whom were only a few months removed from their own beds at home. Lying in their bunks, the boys from Morenci daydreamed of better times back home. The eighteen- and nineteen-year-olds also thought a lot about the future, the dangers of combat, and even death.[2]

During the three-week, bargain-basement cruise, Larry, Bobby Dale, Joe, and Leroy bonded further. When not in the bunks and without much to do to pass the time, they tried to keep each other's spirits up with conversations about home. The lanky, pimply-faced Larry talked about his '62 Chevy pickup that they filled with dead jackrabbits while spotlighting in the southern red canyons or about how he and Joe rode their horses along the beautiful trails in the northern forest. Bobby Dale recounted stories about how he had knocked the snot out of some Clifton football player or how Joe had made the winning throw in a big game. All laughed at the tall tales.

At other times, they wondered about Mike, Clive, Robert, Stan, and Van and where these friends were while they themselves floated in the Pacific Ocean. They shared visions of the big parties they planned to throw at the Morenci Club when they made it home. All were teenagers embarking on an adventure much like several of their fathers and other male relatives had done twenty years earlier during World War II.[3]

Underneath the lighthearted bantering and storytelling, they knew that they faced a serious challenge—one that filled them with trepidation. For them and for everyone on the boat, death loomed as a real possibility, especially since reports had increased about the number of Americans dying in Vietnam. Nearly four hundred Americans died in November 1966.

Once as the four friends sat around reminiscing, someone brought up the topic of what to do with the $10,000 life insurance policy that each had been guaranteed by the US government. For a while, they kidded around, considering the idea that each should sign his policy over to one of his buddies—something of a macabre death lottery. "What would you do with $10,000?" they asked one another, and some talked about the cars they would buy, the trips they would take, and a host of other possibilities, such as parties of epic proportions at the Morenci Club. Then reality set in: they were talking about benefiting from the death of a friend, even if jokingly. In the end, they decided that their parents needed the money more, especially since talks of a PD lockout had begun to surface.[4]

For weeks, the *General Gaffey* plodded through the Pacific waters, never making more than 19 knots an hour. Bobby Dale complained about the boredom being broken only by a movie at night, adding, "I don't care too much for these ships, all they do is bob up and down all day long—everyday."[5] Tempers flared, exacerbated by simmering racial animosities. Some of the Marines whiled away their days with gambling; others spent time reading or writing letters to their families and girlfriends.

Leroy and Bobby Dale received some relief when officers ordered them to assist the Merchant Marine crew in the galley. In the bustling dining hall, they served desserts and salads, having helped prepare the foods beforehand. Though this was a dreaded duty for most of the troops, it turned into a good one for them. Leroy marveled at the mass of humanity passing by as he served up the food: there were a few old, grizzled veterans, but the majority were, like him, fresh-faced teenagers on their way to war. Because of this duty, he and Bobby Dale escaped from the lower decks of the ship and ate well, even enjoying time with civilian colleagues who lounged in their own television room. Leroy also found that time went faster, as the work took his mind off Vietnam.[6]

One adventure broke the monotony for everyone on board. When the *General Gaffey* docked in Okinawa, the ship's commander granted permission for the Marines to disembark and enjoy a few hours on solid ground in the local bars at White Beach. He made a colossal mistake.

Long-simmering tempers flared under the influence of alcohol. Race played a big factor in the fights that broke out. As Joe, Larry, Bobby Dale, and Leroy walked down a street, they saw six African Americans pummeling a big white guy, kicking and punching him until they split his head open. The wounded Marine lay on the ground bleeding, but they bypassed the spectacle, not wanting to take on another man's problem.[7]

Instead, they stopped at a dingy bar, one of many that serviced the US military. They ordered some beers and talked about how much they enjoyed being on dry ground. Suddenly, some tough-looking Puerto Rican Marines burst in. They bunched together and demanded to know Leroy's location. Exiting the bathroom, Leroy saw his friends squared off against his fellow Marines. Some jawing began as the Puerto Ricans chastised him for hanging out with whites. Leroy countered with a few colorful insults and told them to back off. Then the pushing and shoving started, quickly developing into a full-fledged melee. Fists, elbows, and feet flew along with bottles as a flurry of green uniforms entangled. The tough Morenci boys never backed down from a fracas, for it was all for one and one for all, no matter the color of the skin. Ultimately, warnings of MPs approaching sent everyone scurrying.[8]

After a few hours, all the Marines regrouped at the *General Gaffey*. MPs had rounded up stragglers, usually those either too drunk or too hurt to report back under their own steam. Marines limped up the gangplank, complete with black eyes, cuts, and scratches, among them the Morenci boys and their Puerto Rican counterparts. Some wore slings, and others struggled to climb back aboard their home away from home. Disgusted, the commander went on the public address system and dressed down the Marines. He understood that shore leave usually entailed rambunctious behavior, but he hated the racial strife. Despite the fact that the Marines bragged they only saw green, Americans in 1966 rarely lived up to that ideal, except on the front lines, where everyone had to cooperate to survive.[9]

Once all the troops returned, the ship headed south toward Da Nang. Christmas Day came amid sweltering heat and humidity as the ship plowed through the South China Sea, but few people seemed to give the holiday much thought. Only a year before, the Morenci boys had been with their families in their small company homes, with festive decorations and presents underneath the Christmas trees. This year, they saw few reminders of the holiday, only a sea of blue and a growing, aggravated mass of young men headed toward war, not thinking much about peace on earth.

As the ship cut its way through the South China Sea, officers began distributing packets to the young Marines. Inside, the men found their assignments. Larry and Bobby Dale opened theirs and learned they would be headed toward rifle companies, Bobby Dale in the Da Nang area and Larry north toward the demilitarized zone (DMZ) near the base of Con Thien. Joe landed what many people characterized as a cushy duty just south of Da Nang at Chu Lai, guarding the large air base.[10]

As Leroy opened his orders and read them, his face flushed as if he had just received a death sentence. When his friends queried him, he gave a one-word reply: "Recon." Everyone on board the *General Gaffey* knew that Recon was the most dangerous job in the entire Marines Corps. Leroy seemed shaken, apparently gripped by a sense of dread and uncertainty. Though he clearly had received no formal Recon training, he should have been honored because Recon got its choice of replacements.[11] Still, Joe observed, it seemed Leroy felt, "'I am going to give you guys my last goodbyes right now.'"[12]

Finally, late on the night of December 27, the *General Gaffey* anchored in Da Nang harbor. The young Marines awoke the next morning and clambered up to look toward the shore for some indication of what to expect. Leroy and others joined their comrades on the top deck and scanned the docks and the port. Everywhere they looked they saw stacked sandbags and Marines running around carrying weapons and wearing flak jackets. Off in the distance, they heard the sounds of American artillery and machine guns firing at enemy targets. They had entered a war zone, not an imagined one with music in the background and the promise of romance in the future but an altogether real one. Leroy admitted being "scared to shit."[13]

Unlike some of their family members during World War II, the Marines of the *General Gaffey* did not charge ashore into the face of machine-gun fire and explosions of enemy artillery. Instead, they disembarked without weapons and boarded olive-green government-issue trucks for dispersal throughout the operating area. Some eventually would board planes for flights north to the heavy fighting near the DMZ, and others just took short rides to their camps ringing Da Nang.

Leroy Cisneros's boot camp portrait. (Photo courtesy of the US Marine Corps.)

Despite the early morning hour, the hot, humid air engulfed them, weighing them down with a clammy feeling that they rarely escaped during their foray into Southeast Asia. The Vietnamese sun would add to the misery; it beat down on the Americans and sucked the moisture out of their pores, making many a grunt feel like a fish thrown out of the water and onto the shore to bake.[14] Fortunately, coming over on a ship had allowed them to acclimatize somewhat. Many of the soldiers who followed in the months ahead did not have that advantage. Those guys stood one day in the cool air of San Francisco or Los Angeles and twenty-four hours later landed by airplane and entered a blast oven, not unlike the heat the smelter exuded back home, except that the air contained more liquid. For the Morenci boys and most others, they had never experienced anything quite like it.[15]

On that hot, humid day in late December 1966, Leroy walked down the gangplank of the *General Gaffey*, threw his bag in the back of a big green truck, and jumped in with four other recently arrived Marines. As they pulled away, he looked back one more time toward the huge troopship where he had just left Bobby Dale, Joe, and Larry. Sitting in the back of the bouncing truck as it sped away, he felt sick to his stomach, knowing that his last immediate tie to Morenci had just been severed. Everywhere he looked, people scurried about as if in perpetual motion. Yet in the midst of the organized chaos, the eighteen-year-old Leroy felt all alone, plopped down into a war zone in a strange land thousands of miles from home. He looked around for something, anything to make him feel better, but nothing helped.[16]

The drive to Camp Reasoner took a while, and Leroy absorbed his new environment. Back in San Diego, signs of the Christmas season had been on full display when he embarked on his adventure. In Da Nang, no visible symbols of the season of peace existed; there were only signs of war, as US troops with flak jackets and rifles shuffled all around. In the distance, he could hear the firing of artillery. Overhead, silver jets streamed through the sky, taking off and landing at the huge air base, and helicopters swarmed around like overgrown gnats. The sheer volume of the activity overwhelmed the five newcomers in the back of the truck, but what amazed Leroy most was the massive number of Marines and other soldiers congregated just off the road in one area. Pointing to the group, the driver told them that Bob Hope had come to put on a show. They kept on driving, though, so the young Marines could only dream about seeing the sexy Joey Heatherton and sultry Carroll Baker, who performed with Hope.[17]

As the truck made its way down the road and away from the coast, Leroy marveled at the lushness of the countryside. The truck rumbled through a few small villages and zipped by rice paddies. Everywhere he looked, he saw Vietnamese clad in black pajamas. Stateside, his instructors had talked about how the enemy wore black pajamas, but here, people in the garb walked around nonchalantly with no Americans appearing too concerned. At one point, a woman just dropped her pants and defecated near the road in clear view of the passing Marines.[18]

Not long after, they passed through the ramshackle Dog Patch section of Da Nang where young women ran out of bordellos, yelling and flashing the young men. As Leroy attempted to process everything, the stench of diesel exhaust mixed with the heavy smell of the garbage and natural fertilizer of the paddies to flood his nostrils with strange, unpleasant odors. It was such an alien land for the teenager from southeastern Arizona, and the exotic setting only reinforced his sense of loneliness.[19]

Arriving at Camp Reasoner, the five replacements—also known as the new "meat" or the "fucking new guys" (FNGs)—dismounted and looked around, waiting for someone to greet them. As Leroy lingered, the sun beat down on him, starting the process of darkening his already brown skin and draining the moisture from his body. Leroy knew about the sun that baked a man in the nearly 5,000-foot elevation of Morenci, especially in August when guys wore full pads for two-a-days during football camp, but this sun was different. Even at sea level, the sun showed no mercy and allied with the humidity to deplete the body. Perspiration oozed from Leroy's pores, soaking his uniform.[20]

For a moment, Leroy reflected on his assignment and how scared he had been since opening his orders a few days earlier. Of the four Morenci arrivals from the Pacific crossing, he clearly walked into the most dangerous duty, joining a group whose motto was "Swift, Silent, Deadly." Working in small groups of five to seven men, Recon troops went deep into enemy territory on missions that often lasted at least a week. Members traveled light and had orders to follow the "3 Fs"—"Find 'em, fix 'em, and fuck 'em over."[21] They usually avoided combat because, as one Marine noted, "we were too large to hide, too few to fight."[22]

Their mission differed significantly from most others, as their commanders wanted them to locate the enemy and then allow larger units to sweep the area. Officers also relied heavily on Recon for intelligence to acquire targets for US aircraft and artillery, so the soldiers became, in essence, their eyes and ears. If fighting erupted, Recon troops often tried to disengage to save ammunition and continue their mission. Deep inside enemy territory, they always ran the risk of being overrun and annihilated.

Within a short time, a Marine sergeant met up with the new arrivals to give them their unit assignments; Leroy joined Charlie Company of the First Recon Battalion of the First Marine Division. The sergeant then ordered Leroy to follow him, and as they walked through the camp, the young Marine received a quick orientation. "Over there is the enlisted men's mess," the sergeant said as he pointed to a green building with a tin roof, and "over there is Wynn Hall, the enlisted men's club." Leroy looked and saw nothing more than a small building with a thatched roof, with some chairs and tables under it. The sergeant noted other important locations, including the latrine—an eight-seat outhouse—and the showers, whose typically cold water descended from a tank a couple of hundred feet up the hill.[23]

The final destination was Leroy's new quarters. They began climbing to his lodging, bounding up the pathway toward a wooden hooch with a tin roof and screened windows. Looking at it from a distance, Leroy could have envisioned it as a rustic resort villa on a Caribbean island, but this was Vietnam and a war zone. At the entrance to the hooch, he climbed a few steps and then barged his way through the screen door to see ten cots lined up, with assorted gear on the ground. The accommodations were spartan, but they had wood floors extending several feet off the ground, something he learned to appreciate during the monsoon season. Later, when Leroy talked with Bobby Dale and learned that he lived out in the bush for weeks and in a tent or bunker while at base, he realized just how good he had it at Camp Reasoner.[24]

Leroy had little time to adjust to his new job, receiving only some remedial additional training on weapons such as the M-79 grenade launcher and specialized instruction on how to call in artillery. He made new friends, including Sgt. Robert Rudd and LCpl. Eddie Simmons, who took Leroy under their wing. Over ten-cent, ice-cold beers in Wynn Hall, he listened as they dispensed wisdom on how to survive. "Keep your eyes open" and "take nothing for granted," they instructed him, and "always ask questions about what to do." Despite the slight buzz from the beer, Leroy gobbled up the wisdom, for he remained scared to death. His lack of Recon training worried him, as did the fear that he might die early from inexperience or, worse, that he might cost the lives of his fellow Marines.[25]

A couple of his new buddies also warned him to stay away from Tex, a burned-out Recon veteran who had seen one too many missions. As Leroy went about his duties, he always looked around for Tex, carefully staying out of his path. One night, as he sat on his cot just wasting time, the big Texan burst into the hooch, screaming, "I can't take it anymore, I can't take it anymore." In his hands, he gripped a grenade. Frozen in place, Leroy watched as Tex pulled the pin and tossed it toward him. Instinctively, he jumped up and fled out the back of the hooch, diving into the bushes. He waited for the boom, but it never came. Then he heard the laughter of his comrades standing out back, looking at the terrified new guy.[26]

Such pranks helped ease some of the tensions, but Leroy remained a terrified teenager. He often questioned his decision to join the Marines and thought about being in Morenci in the safe confines of his little home. A lot of whys crossed his mind during his downtime. All he could do was wait to learn on the job, which was not necessarily a desirable way to go forward. Eight months removed from his high school graduation and armed with only basic and minimal advanced training, he had a lot to learn—everything from how to secure grenades properly to how to keep his weapon clean in the muck of Vietnam. He proved a willing pupil: fear constituted a great motivating factor.

Within a short period, Leroy found himself assigned to a mission. His unit prepared for a couple of days for insertion into enemy territory, having chosen an area down the hill from their hooches to work on maneuvers. The sergeant walked the group through drills, practicing marching intervals and learning the standard operating procedures for patrolling. These included the hand signals for stopping, moving forward, circling back, and so on, for Recon took its mantra of silence very seriously. Noises carried in the jungle, and the enemy listened. The group perspired under the intense Da Nang sun, but the young Morenci Marine paid close attention, much more so than the salty veterans who saw such practices as a waste of time and energy. They had been there, done that.[27]

The night before Leroy's first mission, the lieutenant leading the patrol called his unit together and outlined their landing zone (LZ), route, and goals. A scared Leroy realized that the time had come to test his mettle. Apprehensively, he walked back to his hooch to pack. On his bunk, he laid out his 782 gear, a frameless backpack. Several of the veterans helped him with the choices he had to make, including how much ammunition and how many C rations to carry, along with a poncho, a weapon-cleaning kit, and extra socks. Rookies always wanted to carry more, but the veterans told him to travel light. After repacking several times, Leroy bedded down but found sleep elusive amid the rising anxiety of the upcoming mission. How would he perform in battle? Were all the stories about the dangers of the jungle real? Most important, would he die tomorrow?[28]

The next morning, he skipped breakfast, afraid that he could not hold it down. Decked out in his green utility uniform and wearing the boots

H-34 Helicopter that carried Leroy and others into the field. (Photo courtesy of the Draper family.)

he had had since boot camp, he gathered with his comrades near the dirt landing pad built out of a rice paddy at the base of the hill. On the horizon and out of the fog, lumbering helicopters appeared, followed by the whomp-whomp-whomp sound of the rotors as they prepared to touch down and pick up their cargo.[29]

Leroy looked around at his fellow Marines and the Navy corpsman assigned to accompany them, all with their weapons and gear at their sides. The men trotted toward the single-rotor H-34s, which one Marine described as looking like "giant, heavy bodied gnat[s]."[30] Leroy stared for a moment at the swirling rotor above his head, remembering to bend slightly so as not to be knocked down, his relatively diminutive 5'5" frame paying dividends in this case. Watching the flurry of Marines head toward the choppers and into the bellies of the aircraft, he instinctively followed despite never having been in a helicopter. He plopped down on a canvas seat and tried desperately to hide his fear, worried that everyone around him could only see a scared and unsure teenager.[31]

The flight to the landing zone did not last long, less than a half hour. Leroy tried not to show his nervousness, his face covered in blackened camouflage and partially hidden by the visor of his patrol hat, but he felt that everyone was looking at the new guy and wondering how he would measure up. The helicopters, flanked by gunships, climbed to several thousand feet to avoid the small-arms fire of the enemy. As they beat a path toward the LZ, much of the countryside below looked like a checkerboard, but the rice paddies were outlined by tree lines and mountains rising upward, interspersed with canopy jungle that looked impenetrable from above. A few small hamlets with a handful of thatched roofs appeared below, reminding the Marines that civilians, not just the enemy, occupied the territory.

Throughout the approach, a knot remained in Leroy's stomach; his throat dried up, and it became hard to swallow. But he looked around at the veterans and found some solace. Despite their darkened faces, he could make out the features of many of them, some of whom already had completed multiple missions. They appeared relatively calm, which slightly reassured him.[32]

Leroy's head jerked up when he heard the lieutenant yell, "Lock and load!" His hands tightly gripped his canvas seat as the helicopter began a relatively quick and steep descent into the LZ and the gunships and an F-4 Phantom jet fighter went in to provide covering fire. As he would often do during his tour, Leroy prayed as the helicopter touched down. Then, the doors swung open amid the thumping sound of the rotors beating down the tall grass outside. Leroy heard the command to "Go, go, go!" and took off with his gear and rifle in hand, jumping onto the soft, marshy ground. Looking around, he saw his team heading toward a tree line, so he instinctively sprinted to stay up. His heart pounded as he ran across the field and toward the safety of the trees. Quickly, the helicopters flew away, disappearing on the horizon. A quiet settled over the area, the only sounds being those of the jungle and the heavy-breathing Marines. They seemed to be very much alone in an immense jungle.[33]

Silence, apart from the natural noises of the jungle, became Leroy's constant companion in the bush. During his first mission, he followed his comrade in front, rarely seeing more than his back and not knowing what lay ahead, to the side, or behind. The only sounds were the soldiers' strained breathing and the soft clanking of gear.

But before long—and throughout most of the forty missions he participated in during his tour in Vietnam—Leroy was not a follower but a trailblazer. By his third mission, he took over the dangerous position of point man, part by assignment and part by choice. He wanted to lead, to have the responsibility and demonstrate his mettle to his comrades and his officers. Morenci guys were tough, and he would prove it.[34] A certain irony existed. Less than eighty years earlier, US Cavalry scouts traversed the area around Morenci in search of elusive Chiricahua Apaches, who relied on guerrilla tactics to harass Anglo settlers and soldiers. At one point, Geronimo even ended up in the jail in Clifton. Now, Leroy found himself searching for an elusive enemy in harsh conditions, just like the Cavalry scouts years before in Arizona.

After the intense adrenaline rush of the landing on his mission, Leroy joined his lieutenant as he led the patrol, along with the radio telephone operator (RTO). The teenager watched as the officer pulled out his compass and map to pinpoint their location, something not always easy to do depending on the terrain and visibility. Soon, the lieutenant had plotted the course and set the ultimate goal: establishing a defensible position by nightfall. Once done, he hand-signaled Leroy on where to proceed. The young Marine then took his position a few meters out in front of the patrol and began the hike.[35]

At first, Leroy struggled during the long, arduous marches of the missions, slipping and sliding in the mud until he stole some jungle boots from a supply depot. Certain tasks proved harder than others. Sometimes, he cut his way through the green elephant grass that extended 10 to 12 feet in the air. Though similar to the mature cornfields back home, elephant grass grew much higher and thicker. Everyone hated it, but it provided cover in enemy territory.

When ordered forward, Leroy would stare momentarily at the seemingly impenetrable maze of interconnected, long green leaves, much like the gangly and intertwined ocotillos around Morenci. Then, he would take out his machete to slash at the long-armed, towering natural foe. It fought back, its serrated, razor-edged leaves cutting exposed skin, leaving multiple cuts on his hands and arms and small trickles of blood flowing downward. Walking became exhausting, and it was hard to focus as sweat flowed off his forehead, burning his eyes and soaking his uniform. Painfully putting one foot in front of the other, his legs burned from the constant exertion

Leroy at an abandoned French plantation in South Vietnam during a patrol. (Photo courtesy of Leroy Cisneros.)

in the muck and felt heavier and heavier. His arm and wrist also ached from the overhead swings needed to hack the grass. Gasping for air in the heat and humidity, his lungs constricted as if in a vise. At times, he felt he could not go any farther, but he had to keep moving.[36]

Whether battling through the elephant grass or trekking up slick and muddy slopes, Leroy moved forward slowly and deliberately. Haste ensured dead Marines. His eyes scanned the dense foliage, often straining in the canopy jungle because only slivers of light made it to the floor. He frequently looked down toward the brown and black mud, searching for trip wires and mines or other forms of enemy booby traps. Every few minutes, he stopped and listened for anything abnormal. The sudden sound of birds flying off, a crack of a branch, a voice in the distance, or the smell of cigarette smoke sent Leroy and his unit scurrying for cover. Besides silence, the constant companion of the Marine Recon members was fear.[37]

Like a scout of the old West, Leroy became a skilled tracker. Walking through the jungle, paths would suddenly appear in the midst of thick foliage. Immediately, his fist flew up, indicating that those behind should stop. Carefully, he would peer onto the trail, looking for any signs of recent activity such as fresh sandal tracks or a wide path indicating the enemy used it often. If all was clear, the lieutenant would decide whether to expose the unit by crossing it or to just simply mark it on the map and proceed parallel to or away from it. At other times, Leroy came upon a stream. Into the water he looked. If he found it muddy, that indicated someone had crossed it recently, and his comrades went on high alert. Leroy developed a sixth sense about the enemy's presence, knowing full well that NVA and Vietcong counterreconnaissance teams patrolled the jungles looking for him and his friends. It was a deadly game of cat and mouse.[38]

In the combat zone, the Marines had to be alert not only for the VC and NVA but also for the natural enemies present in the jungle. Some slithered underfoot, such as king cobras and Malayan pit vipers, all swift, silent, and deadly. In southeastern Arizona, the venomous rattlesnakes at least warned you before striking, but not the snakes in Vietnam.[39] When Leroy sat down, ants and other hostile creatures crawled over his hands or up his legs, biting ferociously, as if they were small enemy foot soldiers sent out to torment the Marines. Their airborne allies, malaria-carrying mosquitoes, always swarmed in squadrons in search of blood, whereas

Leroy patrolling in the bush during a mission. (Photo courtesy of Leroy Cisneros.)

leeches laid ambushes in the murky waters or simply fell from the trees onto the men.[40] There was no relief from the natural enemies, and bloody stains on the uniforms of troops returning from a mission were often attributable to the bites of the native fauna rather than enemy bullets.

Even the elements tormented Leroy and his comrades. The beating sun combined with the intense humidity extracted a heavy toll, leaving the Marines overheated and dehydrated. Yet a moment later, the skies might open and a deluge might descend as the heavens emptied water onto the Marines. Their thin ponchos provided minimal shelter in a downpour, so when the rains stopped, the men just continued on in their soaked uniforms, now heavier from the added moisture. They faced the further indignity of having to sit and lie in the mud, sometimes 6 inches deep. Leroy and his comrades went from being near heat exhaustion to shivering through a brutal night, not able to warm up with fires or anything else that might disclose their position. Cold and drenched replaced hot and thirsty. Either way, they were miserable.[41]

Typically enduring such hostile conditions for a week at a time, Leroy and his small group slogged on through the jungle. Rarely speaking a word except in a hushed whisper and under the constant strain of being deep in enemy territory, Recon members trudged forward during the day, often traversing less than 1,000 meters on their marches. As the sun set, they settled into a defensible position, laying out small claymore mines on approaches to their site and working out escape routes should the enemy happen upon them. Finally, they sat down and, for the first time in the day, had more than a few minutes to unwind—to the extent that they could in a jungle where the enemy controlled the terrain.[42]

While in the small encampment as dusk descended on the jungle, Leroy looked around at his comrades, faces that changed frequently due to rotations and losses. All were young; the lieutenant, often the old man of the group, was rarely more than a recent college graduate. He watched as some drank the precious water that they rationed from the beginning, hoping to avoid having to drop iodine water-purifying pills into the canteens. Others opened C rations, ravenously devouring the parts that they liked and discarding the others, all the while dreaming of the steak, beer, and chocolate milk back at Camp Reasoner. Some took off their boots and socks, rolled up their pants, and searched for leeches, pouring the regulation bug juice on the bloodsuckers to dislodge them.[43]

As darkness descended, Leroy watched the lieutenant take his final bearings with his compass and map, and then he handed the coordinates to the RTO to transmit to headquarters: no one wanted US artillery intended for the elusive enemy landing in their encampment. The light disappeared quickly in the jungle, rarely providing vistas such as the beautiful and exotic sunrises on the beach in Da Nang or sunsets to the west as one perched on a hillside.[44]

Once darkness fell, each person buried himself in his own thoughts, so unlike back in camp when the young men loudly shared stories of home and girlfriends or bragged about their sexual conquests while slamming beers at Wynn Hall. Some took watch while the others slept. The only sounds were those of the jungle and maybe the occasional artillery round going off in the distance. Often, the darkness was so thick that the Marines could not even see their buddies a few feet away. Everyone hunkered down for a long night, praying for some momentary peace.[45]

Nighttime proved the hardest for the homesick teenager from Morenci. Leroy sat under his poncho trying to stay dry, staring into the dark, lost in his thoughts. Occasionally, he looked upward for some sign of the stars or moon to break the piercing darkness of the canopy jungle. The setting was such a contrast to Greenlee County and its open skies where thousands of stars sparkled in the night, the only other illumination coming from the smokestack of the smelter and the haze of lights in the always working deep-mining pit.[46]

During the night, his thoughts drifted to the red clay hills of Morenci. He fondly remembered standing in the cold waters of the Frisco and Gila Rivers on hot summer days, jumping around and splashing for hours with his friends and family. Exhausted, everyone emerged from the water to enjoy picnics spread on blankets, complete with their favorite foods, including watermelon cooled in the waters of the river. Leroy's visions shifted to the thick stands of majestic ponderosa pines in the north, extending into the blue skies amid green meadows and running streams that emptied into small, crystal-clear lakes. He could feel the cool breezes flowing through the forest, chilling him to the bone—a marked contrast to where he lay that night. Then he fondly recalled joining Bobby Dale and other friends sitting in the back of Larry's 1962 Chevy pickup. The guy in the passenger seat held the spotlight out the window while Leroy and the others waited for a jackrabbit to appear. He thought about lifting his 22 rifle and firing at the elusive creatures, followed by the crackle of multiple guns, each guy claiming to have bagged the quarry. Those were very different days and much happier ones, and remembering them helped him get through the night in Vietnam.[47]

But bad feelings also could permeate his thoughts on those dark nights. Most of all, he worried about his family, especially during the lockout by PD that started midway through his tour. He closed his eyes and envisioned his mother and father sitting at the small table in the kitchen and sifting through a stack of bills as only the small income of the strike fund flowed into the family coffers. Morenci must have been a ghost town in some ways by then, for people, particularly fathers, went off in search of other jobs to supplement incomes until the strike ended. He sent money home, but was it enough? What the hell was he doing in Vietnam while they struggled back home? At that point, he wished he could have been there to do more.[48]

Other thoughts jolted him and increased his sense of anxiety. He wondered about Bobby Dale, Joe, and Larry and about his older brother, Ted, who had arrived in Vietnam a few months after he did. Were they safe? Were they buried as deeply as he was in the war? Even as he looked back at all the good times he had shared with his friends, he also worried about them. Would they ever again have the same fun together in their beloved Greenlee County? "What the hell am I doing here?" he asked himself repeatedly during the lulls. In fact, he often wondered if he would survive. He prayed that he would, but all around him he saw death; he had lost several good friends and comrades. Nothing appeared certain for the teenager who had already seen more death and danger than most people would experience in a lifetime.[49]

Despite the myriad thoughts swirling in his head, exhaustion eventually won the day. Leroy fell to sleep amid the hum of mosquitoes and sometimes the howl of monkeys in the dark jungle world of a strange land so far from the wide skies and rugged hills of Greenlee County.

The next day, the routine started again. Sleep-deprived, hungry, and thirsty, Leroy and his comrades gathered together and awaited their instructions from the lieutenant. Leroy took his position out front after receiving his directions. The drudgery of any grunt, whether in a frontline rifle company or Recon, was the boredom of doing the same thing over and over again, in this case heading into the jungle and another full day of pain from battling the local pests, exhaustion, and the tension of not knowing what lay around the corner. Yet many welcomed the boredom, for it beat the heck out of the alternative.[50]

Most veterans remembered spending much of their time in Vietnam walking around in search of an elusive enemy. But what vividly stuck in their minds were those moments when they trudged along and then suddenly all hell broke lose, the times when the mundane ended and the extraordinary descended.

Although Recon troops sought to avoid the fight, they sometimes failed. One day, Leroy walked ahead in the area known as Happy Valley (because you were happy to leave it), his M-14 ready as he scanned ahead. Moving slowly and deliberately, he looked and listened for signs of the enemy. That day, however, he noticed nothing suspicious and actually walked right past a group laid out in an L-shaped ambush. Suddenly, to his horror, he heard the click of a grenade being armed. Loud explosions ripped the jungle, with a boom followed by the tat-tat-tat of enemy machine guns and small-arms fire. The terror of combat descended on the small corner of Vietnam where Leroy lay, right in the middle of the calamity.[51]

Instinctively, he hit the dirt when he heard the click of the grenade, rolling away from where he thought it would land. He hugged the ground but eventually looked up. Terrified, he searched vainly for the hidden enemy. Looking across the grass and dense foliage, he saw bright flashes of enemy gunfire lighting the day. There were no faces, only dark shadows in the underbrush.[52]

Amid the incessant pow-pow-pow of the enemy AK-47s, he heard cries behind him: "Corpsman!" "Corpsman!" Two of his colleagues had died instantly in the first volley. The shaken lieutenant yelled out the unit's call sign and coordinates on the radio, frantically screaming for support. Terrified of being overrun, the Marines had no clue what they had encountered and feared the worst. For what seemed like forever, Leroy stayed low and fired at the nearly invisible enemy only yards away.[53]

All over the battlefield, the muffled sounds of exploding grenades mixed with machine-gun and rifle fire. The smell of gunpowder and freshly turned dirt filled Leroy's nostrils. Being out front, he drew an inordinate amount of the fire. His colleagues tried to crawl forward to support him and deal with the dead and wounded. All around him, he heard bullets whizzing by, some landing close and splattering him with mud and muck. On three separate occasions, enemy grenades fell near him. Panicked, he rolled away from them as furiously as he could, going in the opposite direction of where he thought they had fallen: "That's all I could do," Leroy later stated. "I didn't want to die."[54]

Though it was over in a matter of minutes, the firefight seemed to last an eternity. In an instant, his life literally flashed in front of him, just like what they showed in movies right before someone died. He saw Morenci through the eyes of a child and then a teenager. There were his family and friends, the smelter tower, the high school, his old girlfriends, and many other people and locations. Then, in the midst of the pandemonium, he began praying, "Please God, please God, if you get me out of this, I will go to church every Sunday, I promise."[55]

Almost as soon as he finished his prayer, the enemy forces began to disappear as death rained down on them, the first sign being the whistling sounds of artillery shells screaming to earth. The tree line where some of the heaviest enemy fire had been concentrated abruptly exploded when shells launched from some far-off firebase hit their targets. Leroy lifted his eyes to see huge plumes of black smoke rising as the rounds split trees like toothpicks and lifted mounds of dirt high into the sky.

"Get up and follow me," yelled the lieutenant. Leroy looked behind to see him and the others struggling with their equipment and the bodies of their dead colleagues. As the American artillery continued to bombard the enemy, he lifted himself off the ground and ran toward his comrades. Instinctively, he took over as point again, following the directions of the lieutenant, who barked orders on where to head. They took off running into the dense jungle.[56]

When the unit finally stopped to catch a breath and take stock of their situation, Leroy tried to gather himself. What had probably been only ten minutes of combat seemed infinitely longer. Slightly doubled over, he felt his heart pounding in his chest as if trying to escape his body, and his head throbbed. Dropping his pack, he reached down to pull out his canteen, hoping the water would quench his thirst and maybe even calm his nerves. As he tried to open it, his hands shook uncontrollably from the adrenaline surging through his body, making the task much more difficult than normal.[57]

Slowly, Leroy regained his senses and focused on his surroundings as they gathered near the lieutenant and waited for orders. A terrible reality set in as he looked down and saw the two Marines who had been killed in the engagement, both wrapped in ponchos. Only minutes before, they had been alive and healthy—young men in the prime of life. Leroy's mind flashed back to eating meals with them in camp, swimming together in the South China Sea, and talking endlessly about their lives back home over beers. Now they were gone, victims of a violent and quick end.

A knot in his stomach and tightness in his chest settled in as he realized that it could have easily been him lying there lifeless, thousands of miles from home. Feelings of guilt began to seep into his mind. What could he have done differently to avoid the ambush? Why had he survived and his two friends not? But he had little time to mourn or to think about the loss. That would come later.[58]

Stealth constituted Recon's greatest weapon, but the enemy now knew their approximate position. Down two men and slowed by the need to carry the bodies with them, they could afford even less than usual to stand and fight. Fortunately for them, the enemy lost their trail, and they safely made it to an extrication point not too far away. Leroy had grabbed one of the ends of a poncho with his dead friend in it as they moved forward. When they arrived at the landing zone, he kept his grip on the slick poncho, trotting across the field toward the helicopter, whose blades beat down the tall grass. It was a heavy burden on many levels. After he jumped into the helicopter, Leroy had more time to reflect on just how lucky he had been to survive. Would his luck hold out the next time? Such were his thoughts as he collapsed into the canvas seat.[59]

There were many other chances for the death angel to visit Leroy during his thirteen-month tour. More than forty times he trekked into enemy territory. In one case, while on a patrol deep in the heart of the enemy's territory, he marched forward slowly and deliberately when he came upon a stream. He laid his rifle on a boulder and took out his canteen to refill it. As he crouched down, out of the corner of his eye he saw something moving upstream from him. Abruptly, four enemy soldiers emerged out of the brush and began crossing the narrow waterway. Without his rifle, which was several meters away on a rock, he froze and prayed. The soldiers just kept moving onto the other bank and then disappeared into the jungle. Again, a prayer had been answered.[60]

After that narrow escape, the enemy located Leroy and his comrades four times during that day, firing some scattered shots over their heads and sending the Recon group scurrying for cover. The enemy soon disengaged, however, apparently worried that the Americans would call down an artillery barrage or bombs from above. Fortunately, the enemy failed to call in more experienced troops, who would have laid out ambushes. By the end of the day, with their location narrowed down and surprise surrendered, the Recon commanders decided to not push the luck of the unit. They extricated them from the zone to try again another day.[61]

Such danger clearly imprinted itself on Leroy's mind, but the memories that lasted longer related to the death that he saw in Vietnam. He lost a number of friends along the way, but one death stood out in particular.

Leroy and the other young Marines absorbed many physical hardships and moved on, but the psychological hardships proved more lasting. Losing a friend was the worst combat experience they encountered. Because of the small size of Recon units, especially strong relationships developed among members of each group regardless of their disparate backgrounds. A lot of the time, the men sat around and talked about home and their families, and before long, each knew the most intimate details of the others' lives. This made losing a comrade hard, particularly since it also reminded the young survivors of their own mortality.[62]

One of the most painful experiences for Leroy occurred when his friend Eddie Simmons died on patrol just days before he was to ship out for the States. At the time, Leroy had taken off for some rest and recreation (R & R) at China Beach. Eddie's death hurt horribly even though Leroy was not present for the actual event. Some guilt crept in, too, for he felt that if he had been there, maybe he could have made a difference. The fact that Eddie only had a few days left in country made his death seem even worse.[63]

Halfway through his tour, Leroy experienced an equally traumatic and profound loss. A new, twenty-five-year-old lieutenant straight out of The Basic School (TBS), Larry Stone, joined his group. Stone came from the Nevada town of Yerington, which was even smaller than Morenci. He

Leroy posing for a photo during Bobby Dale's visit to Camp Reasoner in late July 1967. (Photo courtesy of the Draper family.)

had attended Nevada State University before joining the Marine Corps and had been described by one classmate as very affable, a member of the university's baseball team who dated all the most beautiful women at the Henderson campus. Leroy described him as "gung ho" and a solid soldier who developed a good relationship with his men, including his young point man from Morenci.[64]

On May 20, 1967, Stone, Leroy, and eight other Marines and a Navy corpsman—code-named Recon Team Dreadful—landed on the east slope of Hill 1210, about 8 kilometers northwest of Dai Loc. After an uneventful couple of days that included finding where B-52 bombers had leveled an area, the mission turned deadly on May 22. While on point, Leroy spotted several Vietnamese near three small bamboo-and-thatch huts around a bend in a river. He held up everyone and called for Stone, who worked his way forward. After conferring, the lieutenant ordered two men into the first hut. Finding it empty but locating a tunnel inside, the Marines moved on to the next one. There, Stone spotted a VC inside. Positioning two of his patrol to flank the structure, he threw three grenades inside and started toward the third hut.[65]

Someone saw two additional VC nearing the huts and shot them. All hell broke loose as Stone headed forward. Gunfire erupted, and he fell mortally wounded.[66] Under intense enemy fire, Leroy scrambled forward and retrieved the lieutenant. The bullets had made only small holes on entering his body, but when Leroy turned him over, he found huge gaping wounds where the bullets had exited; blood spurted out around the muscle ripped apart by the projectiles. Leroy vainly shoved bandages in to stop the bleeding and slapped the lieutenant, trying to keep him awake. As the red fluid soaked the mud, Stone died in Leroy's arms.[67]

Leroy would remember forever the image of the lieutenant's lifeless body being hoisted by a sling at a hastily selected landing zone not far from where he perished. In the immediate aftermath of the event, the team stayed in the field for two more days, which meant Leroy had little time to stop and think about the loss.[68] However, when he returned to Camp Reasoner and had some quiet moments, the loss hit him hard. Why did death come to such a good man in such a violent manner? Would he himself be next? What was the meaning of it all? He also thought about the unhappy family in Nevada who would now be without their son for Memorial Day, which came only a few days after his death. It was a lot for a nineteen-year-old to process.[69]

Despite the dangers, Leroy survived more than forty missions and finally received orders for home. In late November 1967, his commanders stopped assigning him to missions, as it was feared that short-timers would become too cautious in the bush and put their comrades at risk. Leroy's initial orders called for a December 21 departure so he would not miss another Christmas at home. However, when that day came, his flight was canceled. Unlike the flights back home, they could not just bump someone to make a place for him. Thus, he spent Christmas at Camp Reasoner and did some work around the base while he waited.[70]

Finally, on January 4, 1968, he took a truck to the Da Nang airport. Looking out across the landscape, he realized how much everything had changed since he had arrived more than one year before. No longer did he marvel at the people working in rice paddies with their water buffalo or the Vietnamese in black pajamas walking up the road. All this had become his new world.[71]

His thoughts wandered to Greenlee County with its barren red clay hills and the streets leading to his home. In his mind, those images were real but distant, and they stood in marked contrast to everything around him at that moment. Memories of sleeping on a real mattress with sheets and the smell of beans and fried potatoes coming from the kitchen flooded into his head. Within a couple of days, the dreams that he had held onto so tightly would become reality.[72]

At the airport, he waited in his short-sleeved khaki uniform on the tarmac, grasping his orders and ticket and battling the nervousness of never having flown on an airplane. In a short time, a huge white plane taxied down the runway, with the easily recognizable Pan Am symbol on the tail. Grunts watching them take off frequently characterized the planes as freedom birds. Leroy observed a group of officers deplane, followed by a bunch of fresh-faced kids in clean uniforms. He thought to himself, "Ah, the stories that I could tell," but he had neither the time nor the breath to waste on the kids. They would not listen anyway.[73]

Meanwhile, a crowd of excited and anxious GIs formed a line and waited to board the plane. Leroy had cleaned up before departure, but he recognized the smells of the jungle on these men, for several reeked, obviously just out of the bush. As so often happened over the past year, the sun beat down on Leroy and the humidity continued to sap his strength, but this time, he cared little about the discomfort. In less than twenty-four hours, he would be stateside. Shortly, everyone started to climb up the stairs of the plane. At the top, pretty flight attendants in pressed uniforms, with short blue skirts, white blouses, and light blue hats, greeted them, "Welcome aboard. We are glad to have you flying with us today." For Leroy and many others, they were some of the first non-Asian women they had seen in a year.[74]

Leroy shuffled toward the back of the plane, finding a place and plopping down onto the soft seat cushion. He noticed that everything appeared so clean and neat, all the way down to the attendants' uniforms—quite a contrast to his surroundings for the last thirteen months. In a few minutes, everyone took their seats, anxiously anticipating the departure from Vietnam. The flight attendants made their way up and down the aisles, handing out pillows and blankets to the soldiers, some of whom looked like they had not slept soundly in a long time. Finally, everyone heard what they had been waiting for from the pilot, "Stewardesses, make preparations for takeoff."

The plane taxied and began hurtling down the runway of the massive military base. Leroy felt himself pushed deeper into the seat as the aircraft picked up speed. Out the window, he watched the landscape flash by as the plane made its way up into the blue skies. As it climbed, "the greatest damn feeling" in the world enveloped him. Others spontaneously started clapping and yelling, and Leroy joined in the chorus that continued for several minutes. It was like a New Year's Eve party with the dropping of the ball at midnight. All around him, hundreds of his comrades shared in the celebration. Leroy thought to himself: "I made it. I'm going home!"[75]

The Pan Am jetliner raced across the Pacific, buoyed partly by the spirits of its jubilant passengers. Leroy slowly melted into his seat and relaxed. Only the hum of the jet engines and the voices of his comrades disturbed his peace, apart from the occasional visit by a pretty flight attendant to serve a meal or drink. Around him, he looked at the faces of the other GIs, many puffing away on their cigarettes. Most were young, some bore visible battle scars, and more than a few appeared distant, lost in their thoughts.[76]

He joined them in reflecting on the past and future. Recalling the smells of his mom's cooking caused his mouth to water, and thoughts of hugging his parents in the small house on Mimosa Street led him to tear up a bit. But then some morose feelings seeped in as well. Feelings of guilt about leaving behind his friends in Vietnam engulfed him. They had been his family for a year, and he worried about them. Images of his dead comrades surfaced, including his good friend Eddie, who had died on his last patrol, and Lieutenant Stone, who had passed away in his arms. Once more, questions flooded his mind. Why had he survived and ended up on a plane bound for America, when his dead friends had traveled in the cargo bay in coffins? Again, feelings of loneliness consumed him, just like when he landed in Vietnam, even when surrounded by hundreds of his fellow GIs.[77]

Only short fuel stops interrupted the long flight. After nearly fifteen hours cooped up in the plane, the passengers became increasingly restless. At long last, the pilot announced, "We have just crossed into the United States." Shouts of joy once more filled the plane. Within a short time, Leroy's spirits soared when he spotted the bright lights of San Francisco in the distance and then the Golden Gate Bridge and Alcatraz in the harbor. Thirteen months had passed since he had leaned over the edge of the *General Gaffey* to say good-bye to the United States. He was a naive kid back then. Now, a battle-hardened Recon veteran readied to set foot once again on American soil.[78]

An elated Leroy bounded down the steps of the airplane at Travis Air Force Base just outside San Francisco. Hundreds of other young GIs followed, some kneeling to the ground to kiss the tarmac. He shivered in the cold, damp January air of Northern California, his thin, short-sleeved uniform providing little protection from the chill. It had been a long time since he had been so cold. In the distance, he saw a few protestors, the ones that all the GIs complained about in Vietnam and that *Stars and Stripes* warned would spit on them when they returned home. Leroy avoided them and instead moved off to find out about the next flight to Phoenix as he transferred over to the San Francisco Airport. Arriving at the airport terminal with his gear, still shaking in the chilly Bay Area climate, he found a bar and sat down to order a beer.[79]

Though a battle-tested Marine, Leroy still looked quite young. A waitress approached him and asked, "Are you twenty-one?" Leroy just stared back, surprised by the question. No one had asked him his age while in Vietnam. She repeated the question, "Are you twenty-one?" In fact, he had another nine months to go before reaching that milestone, so he finally responded, "No." The waitress brought him a soft drink instead of the beer. While sipping on the drink, he pondered the irony of being able to fight and die for the country but not down a beer. The next morning, he boarded another plane, this time headed to Phoenix and closer to home.

The flight from San Francisco took only a couple of hours. Leroy finally found himself in the desert environment that he loved so much. A warm January sun beat down on him as he exited the terminal in Phoenix. The humidity that had surrounded him for a year was suddenly absent, and the air was wonderfully dry and crisp.[80]

Decked out in his khaki marine uniform, he jumped into a cab to get over to the bus depot in downtown Phoenix. Again, he headed to a bar to wait for the next bus to Safford. This time, he found a much warmer atmosphere, albeit in a dingy tavern. The waitress happily asked, "What do you want?" Like before, he responded, "A beer." Unlike before, she did not hesitate for a moment but quickly returned with a bottle. Not far away, a couple of guys made eye contact with the Marine, and they started exchanging war stories. They bought him a couple more beers and thanked him for his service. After a long conversation and a few shared laughs, they escorted him out the door and toward his bus. At long last, Leroy felt at home.[81]

He hopped onto the bus for the four-hour trip to Safford. It seemed to take forever, since the bus stopped in each little town from Mesa to Globe. When it finally reached Safford, he hurried down the steps, then looked up at the imposing Mount Graham towering 12,000 feet in the air to the south. He gazed northeast toward Morenci, only 20 miles away as the crow flies. The red clay mountains rose out of the desert floor, causing his heart to race as he realized how close he was to home.[82]

Entering the bus station, he searched for a phone. No one waited for him with banners or rushed across the floor to hug him. He had wanted to keep his arrival a surprise, so he had not let anyone know that he would be home that day. Picking up the phone, he deposited the money and called his sister, who lived not too far away. For thirty minutes, he tried vainly to convince her that he really was in Safford. She thought it was a joke and initially refused to traipse over to pick up someone who had not even bothered to let anyone know he was on his way. Finally, after much cajoling and pleading, she agreed to pick him up.[83]

On the 45-mile drive, first going east on Highway 70 and then north up Highway 666, Leroy looked out the window at the barren lands dominated by the dormant scrub brush, cacti, and occasional ocotillo. Everything was brown, pale yellow, or copper red, all framed by a beautiful clear blue sky. A cool January breeze swept across the landscape, not too cold but enough to chill him, as his blood felt thinned out from a year in Southeast Asia. What a contrast to the lush green landscapes of Vietnam, where only days before he had stood and baked in the intense sun and sweated in the humid coastal breeze. Now, he found himself so close to home and everything that he had dreamed about for a year.[84]

His sister made small talk, mainly about the family and Morenci, but Leroy was lost in his own thoughts for most of the trip. His excitement grew as they made it to the three-way stop right across from the large drive-in theater where he had spent many evenings. It only increased as they descended into the valley that surrounded Clifton, passing by the high school and football field where only a couple of years before he had waged battle with his friends Bobby Dale and Joe—although that term now carried a very different meaning. Some Christmas decorations still hung as they passed through the small town and began the ascent up the hill. Then they drove into Morenci, which itself was in flux as Phelps Dodge buried the old town under the mine and resettled its occupants to the south. Everywhere he looked, construction people were at work re-creating a town. Things had clearly changed since he last saw Morenci more than thirteen months before.[85]

But some things had stayed the same. As Leroy and his sister neared their family home at 123 Mimosa Street, he asked her to stop and let him walk the last block so he could surprise his mom and dad. The young Marine, with his pack swung over his shoulder, made his way down the street where he had spent so many hours playing with friends and riding his bike. He had dreamed of this day for more than a year, and he could hardly keep himself from breaking into a full-out sprint.[86]

As he walked through the gate in the middle of the waist-high chain-link fence, he could hear his parents talking through the screen door of the house. His father walked to the door at the sound of his knock.

Leroy asked through the screen, "Is Leroy home?"

His father replied, "No, he is in Vietnam."

Then his father's eyes focused on the young man on his doorstep. The door flew open, and father and son embraced. Leroy cried tears of joy, overwhelmed by the flood of emotions at returning home. It had been a whirlwind eighteen months, much as the Marine recruiter had promised. Like other young Vietnam veterans returning home that January all across the country, Leroy had lived a lifetime compared to many others of his generation. He did not know, however, that things in Vietnam had just started to heat up for the rest of the Morenci Nine.[87]

Leroy never returned to Vietnam. He landed duty at the Marine base in Yuma, only five hours from home. The Marines offered him promotions to consider returning to Vietnam, but he refused. He would say a couple of years after completing his tour, "I was lucky, really lucky. Sometimes, didn't know how lucky I was."[88] Ultimately, he mustered out ten months early on his four-year contract, in 1969.[89] He had made it, although during that time in Yuma, it became abundantly clear to him through the misfortune of others how truly fortunate he had been during his time in Vietnam.

6

The Miraculous Journey
Joe Sorrelman in Vietnam

On the same day that Leroy had headed off on the short ride over to Camp Reasoner in December 1966, Joe Sorrelman stood on the deck of the *General Gaffey* and prepared for his own departure. Unlike his uncles, who had waded ashore under enemy fire on the Pacific islands during World War II, Joe walked down the gangplank to reach the shore, his heavy pack thrown over his shoulder. Signs of war surrounded him: stacks of sandbags protected installations, and Marines scurried around in flak jackets, carrying rifles. In the distance, the sound of artillery firing broke through the clamor of the bustling docks. Unlike what his uncle experienced at Tarawa, no enemy awaited Joe at the edge of the water, ready to cut down Americans. Instead, he encountered only lines of trucks dispersing fresh-faced young Marines to units all around Da Nang and beyond. He headed away from his friends and toward an uncertain future with the First Marine Air Division at Chu Lai.

The quiet and contemplative Joe had spent a lot of time on the *General Gaffey* reflecting on his journey. Excitement combined with trepidation, something that he had tried to assuage even before leaving Arizona. Although he was not especially tied to his Navajo culture like his parents, he had asked permission to travel to the reservation in northeast Arizona for a traditional Blessingway Ceremony, designed to prepare young men for the trauma of combat. The ritual extolled the good in life, including its beauty, harmony, and order, all of which the warrior would leave behind

*Joe Sorrelman's boot camp
portrait. (Photo courtesy of
the US Marine Corps.)*

for the chaos and destruction of war. The ceremony sought to reinforce a positive outcome for the young man about to enter a difficult stage of life.[1]

All night long at the ceremony, Joe listened to the chanting of the medicine man and tribal elders. They sang of the hogan, the traditional Navajo home and locus for order in life. Other verses of traditional songs spoke of the lands of their ancestors, the sacred columns of the universe, and the sky and mountain corner posts of the traditional Navajo lands that extended over large portions of the Southwest. Joe struggled to follow the chants and prayers, and when it came time for him to recite his verses, his mother rose and repeated the required phrases.[2]

The ceremony provided some solace, even tying Joe a little more closely to the beloved lands of the Southwest. But like so many teenage Americans landing on the shores of Vietnam in 1966, he still dealt with fear. Joe knew that the next thirteen months of his life revolved around the humid and lush world of Vietnam, not the mountains and desert of his homeland. The fact that an unseen enemy awaited in the strange environment only added to the apprehension he felt.

Joe jumped into the back of a big truck for the ride over to the massive air base at Da Nang. As the lumbering vehicle wove its way through town, he watched the frenetic activity. All around him, the hustle and bustle of soldiers blended with the dashing about of the Vietnamese as they took care of their business. No one seemed to notice him or the other new arrivals perched in the bed of the truck, their eyes wide open at being dropped into the middle of a war zone in an alien land. One veteran summed up the feeling of many Americans like Joe when he observed, "I felt like Alice stepping through the looking glass."[3]

Within a short time, Joe arrived at the sprawling air base, where he received orders to jump on a C-130 for the 60-mile jaunt over to Chu Lai. Boarding a plane for the first time in his life, he anxiously walked up the ramp and into the gigantic aircraft. When he had received his orders on the *General Gaffey* to join the First Marine Air Division, everyone congratulated him for landing a cushy duty compared to those received by Leroy in Recon or Bobby Dale and Larry, who headed to the heart of the fighting in rifle companies. Now, as he sat in the cargo plane and waited to take off, he hoped that the reports regarding his duty were correct.[4]

Joe flew in the belly of the large plane, not knowing anyone or even what to expect once he reached his final destination. When they landed in the darkness on that late December day in 1966, he remembered, "it was drizzling, it was cold. Everything was real still, eerie."[5] It was a feeling that proved fleeting once the sun rose and the heat and humidity enveloped him.

The next day, Joe awoke to life on the edge of one of the largest airports in Southeast Asia. Bordered on the east by the South China Sea, Chu Lai was a massive conglomeration of long runways and buildings constructed in 1965 to ease the congestion at Da Nang. Towers, bunkers, and hangars dotted the sandy landscape, surrounded by fortifications and barbed wire. It was an imposing yet tempting target. The Vietcong had launched a major offensive against the installation in 1965, but the Americans' Operation Starlite in August inflicted heavy casualties on the VC.[6] The enemy operated all around the base but rarely assaulted it, making it a relatively secure location.

Those who told Joe that guarding the air base would be a rather cushy duty proved to be right. Despite all the precipitation—he said that he had "never seen so much rain in all my life"[7]—for nearly six months he lived in a comfortable screened hut complete with cots, radios, and reel-to-reel players. When hungry, he walked over to the mess hall, where he ate his meals at a table, using silverware. During his downtime, he frequently hung out at the enlisted men's club, which served all the cold beers a Marine could afford, or traveled a short distance over to the beach, where he swam in the warm waters. He wrote letters to his girlfriend, Virginia Lee Hollyway, and read those that she sent him, ultimately admitting that "it was like there was no war going on."[8] Only the arrival of the medevacs carrying wounded soldiers and occasionally combat units that briefly stayed at the base before heading into the jungle reminded him that, indeed, people were fighting and dying just a few miles away.[9]

Joe's time at Chu Lai lacked the dangers that he had anticipated. He spent many hours on the perimeter, peering into the dark night to spot signs of a lurking enemy, but few ever materialized. His platoon would leave the base and probe for enemy buildups, but they rarely encountered anyone except the locals. Of course, many of those locals could have been VC, but during the day, they blended into the population that worked the rice paddies and tended animals. At other times, Joe and his comrades ran convoys to various bases, but enemy forces almost never showed themselves. The pace was slow, and for many of the Marines, including Joe, the war did not meet their expectations or match the romantic imagery they had entertained before arriving in country. In the end, they had few chances to put their training to work.[10]

Still, occasional reminders of the conflict going on around them floated into view. For instance, Joe remembered seeing a young grunt recently returned from the field. He had hollow eyes, a boy who obviously had not slept enough and had seen way too much during his time in Vietnam. Skinny to the point of being almost emaciated, the soldier wore boots that had turned nearly white from constant exposure to moisture. His uniform was torn and stained with blood and mud. Such visuals had an effect. Even as Joe acknowledged his own comfortable duty, he thought about his friends Bobby Dale, Leroy, and Larry who had received more intense combat assignments, much like the young grunt had experienced.[11]

The most vivid reminders of the war came when the helicopters brought in the wounded and dead from combat zones. At times, Joe hung out in a bunker not far from the landing zone, and he and his comrades occasionally assisted with the unloading of the incoming helicopters. They rushed across the pad and lifted stretchers, carrying wounded Marines to waiting ambulances for transport to the local trauma units. Blood was everywhere—on the stretchers, the helicopter floors, and the uniforms of the wounded. Its sickly sweet, nauseating smell filled the nostrils, leaving a sensory memory not easily forgotten.[12]

Besides the wounded, Joe sometimes lifted the dead from the helicopters. One case stood out, a young grunt who had his M-1 carbine lying by his side on the stretcher. Looking down on him, Joe noted that his face and hands were ashen and that he looked like he had just fallen asleep. He walked away wondering about the kind of battle the dead man had seen, about his life and why he had died, and about what it might be like someday to face death himself.[13] This was not what nineteen-year-olds thought about stateside, but for many in Vietnam, such thoughts became commonplace, even for a Marine serving in the relatively safe duty of Chu Lai.

The boredom and lack of adventure, coupled with thoughts of the sacrifices being made by his Morenci buddies, ultimately led Joe to request a transfer to the action. First, he sought to become a door gunner on a helicopter, hoping to earn his air wings. When that failed to materialize, he asked for a frontline rifle company. After a few months, the Marines granted him the transfer, desperately needing troops in the northern provinces, where the fighting between US forces and battle-hardened North Vietnamese regulars had escalated in the spring of 1967. With orders in hand, Joe boarded a plane and headed north in late June of that year.

He went from one of the easiest jobs in the Marine Corps in Vietnam to the most dangerous and ended up near Con Thien, the "Hill of Angels." The location was anything but angelic for the Marines who occupied the strategically valuable outpost, only 2 miles from the DMZ. A linchpin of the efforts to create a McNamara Line to prevent North Vietnamese infiltration, Con Thien had an elevation of 158 meters in the reddish-brown clay. It was a great position, offering a full view well into North Vietnam past the Ben Hai River and all the way to Highway 1 and the South China Sea to the east, as well as to major parts of the American sector to the south extending to Cam Lo and Dong Ha. Originally a base for the Army of the Republic of Vietnam (ARVN), the site had been taken over by the Americans in February 1967, only a few months before Joe arrived.[14]

The fighting around Con Thien was some of the most intense of the war. The site became a valuable asset, both symbolically and strategically. Engineers built a massive series of trenches and bunkers into the hillside, stringing lines of barbed wire and placing mines on the best approaches to the main compound. They constructed helicopter pads to provide resupply capability as well as roads linking Con Thien to the other support bases.[15]

The North Vietnamese responded in kind, sending large numbers of troops into the area to probe and harass the Marines and constantly bombarding the hill with heavy artillery from their positions. In the summer of 1967, US commanders feared a full-scale assault on the installation by the NVA, which wanted to create an American Dien Bien Phu in the middle of the increasingly unpopular war.[16]

Joe deplaned at Dong Ha, only a few miles southeast of Con Thien. Immediately, he moved into processing, taking time to pick up some gear, a task that provided a shock. As he gathered new equipment in a shed, all around him were stacks of helmets, web gear, and flak jackets, most caked in dried blood. The macabre sight shook the young Marine, knowing he now headed to where many of the men who had been wearing the gear had fought and bled, with some paying the ultimate price.[17]

That night at Dong Ha, the enemy forces introduced themselves to Joe with a spectacular pyrotechnics show. He heard high, shrill sounds and then shouts of "Incoming! Incoming!" Joe watched as people dived into foxholes and bunkers. Instinctively, he followed, just as enemy artillery rained down on his position. Amid the bright illumination of the enemy shells falling into the American perimeter, he joined others in hugging the ground and staying low to avoid flying shrapnel. To Joe, the incoming shells sounded like a car barreling down a freeway. The ground shook each time one hit nearby, frightening the young Arizonan, who admitted that death from above remained his worst fear. At least with a gunshot, you had a chance to fire back at the enemy.[18]

While hunkered down after the barrage, Joe met a guy heading out of the fighting after receiving his third Purple Heart. As they sat and talked, he told Joe about his wounds. The first had been a sniper shot through the helmet, creasing his head and drawing blood. A far more serious wound followed, again from a sniper. That time, while he was out on patrol, a bullet creased his neck, almost slicing open his throat. Finally, during an artillery attack shrapnel hit his hand and arm, earning him his third Purple Heart and a ticket home. Joe listened intently as the grunt outlined his harrowing near-death experiences. He had seen dead men in the helicopters at Chu Lai, but never had he been this close to it or known that he would be on the front lines himself in mere hours.[19]

When the weather cleared the next day, he took a helicopter over to a site near Con Thien to join his unit, the Third Platoon of Lima Company, Third Battalion, Ninth Marine Regiment. As the helicopter flew over the land, Joe gazed down on the fortifications of Con Thien and the nearby countryside. Everywhere he looked, he saw bunkers surrounded by sandbags, interconnected trenches, strands of barbed wire on the perimeter, and artillery and tanks sprinkled across the base. The spectacle helped him understand that the Marines had truly honored his request to be near the fighting.[20]

Out of sight of the American observers, and unbeknownst to Joe at the time, the enemy had tunneled in all around the base, using the jungle for cover. A few miles to the north across the DMZ in North Vietnam, large artillery pieces fired their huge projectiles at Con Thien and the surrounding bases that protected approaches to it. It was a deadly place, perhaps one of the most lethal on the planet in June 1967.

Joe joined his Marine rifle platoon in 1967 along the DMZ in what the Marines labeled Leatherneck Square. The area extended from Con Thien, east to Gao Linh, south to Dong Ha, across to Cam Lo, and back north to Con Thien. It was approximately 160 square kilometers and constituted the entire world for many young Marines, Joe among them, in the summer of 1967.

Unlike Leroy, who typically spent a limited number of days in the bush before returning to the comforts of Camp Reasoner, Joe rarely knew when he would visit a base camp for a shower, a hot meal, and a little sleep on something other than mud. One Vietnam veteran summed up the feeling of many in the area:

This is hell. Besides killing and maybe being killed there are other things that make life almost unbearable. Leeches that suck our blood, insects of all kinds, snakes, spiders . . . the heat, the rain and mud. The long marches with heavy pack, going two or three weeks without a bath, wearing the same clothes for weeks at a time, not having a place to sit down or even lie down except in six inches of mud.[21]

Unlike Recon units, rifle companies wanted to draw out the enemy and kill as many of the NVA as possible. Joe and his comrades faced a well-trained enemy equipped with artillery and rockets, heavy machine guns, and mortars, making it a formidable foe. Though the NVA forces were often elusive, determined to avoid fighting in the open, they attacked ferociously when the opportunity presented itself. This was a war of extermination, one with few prisoners of war on either side, much like the one Joe's uncles had fought in the Pacific during World War II.

Often during Joe's service in the north, his company headed into the jungle for weeks at a stretch. It was an active period in the Con Thien area. From the time that he landed in June until he left in early September 1967, Joe fought in several major operations, including Buffalo, Hickory II, and Kingfisher.[22] In the field, he survived on little sleep, food, and water. It was a miserable life in the high heat and humidity, all with the added burden of an enemy determined to kill the Marines whether in a pitched battle, in a rain of artillery, with a sniper's bullet, or with a booby trap.[23]

At night, Joe and others in his unit typically spent the time in a foxhole with a buddy, where one person slept for two hours and the other watched for the enemy. They traded positions throughout the night, two hours on, two hours off. When the sun rose, they exited their foxholes, ate some C rations, policed the area, and awaited orders. Upon receiving those commands, the Marines marched through the jungle toward the next location, watching warily for booby traps, snipers, and enemy positions. The officers urged silence, but expecting large groups of men to march silently in sparsely occupied areas was, as Joe later put it, "a joke." Everyone could hear the unit moving, including the enemy.[24]

Searching for an often elusive enemy proved exhausting work. The mud made walking difficult, and the heat and humidity drained the body of liquids. Their green fatigues soaked in sweat, the Marines slogged through the jungle. They occasionally received a resupply of water, but it rarely lasted long. At times, they headed toward a stream, where a few guys from the platoon would sneak away and bring back canteens of water. Joe and his friends threw in the Halazone purification tablets, but being so thirsty, they rarely allowed the pills to dissolve before gulping down the water.[25] Being parched became a way of life for Joe that summer.

Most of the day, the Marines trekked through the jungle. The constant fear of an enemy appearing from nowhere plagued Joe and his comrades. The NVA constructed bunkers and camouflaged them so skillfully that Marines could walk right up on them without knowing. The NVA also burrowed deep into the ground, creating intricate, interconnected complexes that housed hospitals, sleeping quarters, and command centers, some very near US bases. They literally could pop up on Americans, attack, and then disappear into the ground. It was a cat-and-mouse game combined with whack-a-mole in dense jungles and mountains, where Joe and his fellow Marines sought to prevent enemy buildups and to make the mission costly for the North Vietnamese in lives and matériel.[26]

After a long day of humping through the bush, the Marines settled into a defensible position and began the ritual of digging foxholes, setting out claymores, and preparing for a long night of staring into the blackness of the jungle. Joe and his friends then sat down and ate their C rations, the young Arizonan usually hoarding the "beanie weenies." Then they would head into their foxholes accompanied by their constant companions, mud and exhaustion.

Nighttime in the foxhole allowed Joe a lot of time to think. Through the long hours, he wondered about Gina, his family, and his friends, especially Bobby Dale, Larry, and Leroy. And he frequently pondered whether he would make it through the terrible experience. Though exhausted, he had a hard time turning off his mind. One constant thought remained: "What was I thinking when I requested a transfer?" He could have been back at Chu Lai sleeping on a cot, eating hot meals, and not worrying about the NVA suddenly overrunning his position.[27]

Joe spent most of his four months in the jungle during his time in Leatherneck Square, but occasionally, he ended up at the firebase named C-2, which he helped build just northeast of Cam Lo. He later remembered a number of things about the base, including the fact that the outhouse sat at the top of the hill in full view of both the Marines and the enemy. He recalled that when he dug one of his first foxholes, a 10-inch, jet-black scorpion crawled out of the pit, scaring him senseless. At least at C-2, he and his buddies received hot meals and usually an allotment of two hot beers and two sodas, although Joe always traded away the beers for extra pop.[28]

But life at the base camp came with many drawbacks as well. The boredom of being on work details wore on Joe and his fellow Marines. They spent a lot of time loading sandbags with dirt and then stacking them high around the bunkers and trenches. When Joe and his comrades completed that task, they would dig more trenches and foxholes, although Joe's fear of the artillery attacks made that task more bearable. They also sat around a great deal, spending their time cleaning their weapons; Joe especially liked to keep his M-79 grenade launcher in good condition because when in the bush, he rarely had the time or energy to do so.[29] Boredom set in, and the hours passed slowly in the blistering heat, giving a grunt a lot of time to think about his predicament.

Whether trudging through the jungle or guarding C-2, Joe remained a shy young man from southeast Arizona. Still a teenager, he fought in a strange land dramatically different from his beloved homeland. Fear was a constant companion, along with hunger and thirst. The experience was not how he imagined war, and he saw too much death and suffering at a very early age. Tens of thousands of Marines in Leatherneck Square shared his feelings, although each lived in his own world and thought it was unique in some ways.

Joe and his friends spent most of their time searching for an enemy that typically waited in ambush and fought limited engagements, often at night, to prevent the Americans from using their tactical superiority in aircraft and artillery. The boredom experienced over the long days with no contact could change in an instant and morph into a moment of blinding terror when the enemy decided to appear. Engagements were not that frequent, but when they erupted, the ferocity of the fighting seared itself deeply into the memory of the combatants.

One day, Joe found himself on patrol on a ridge deep in a dense jungle. Unexpectedly, the unit's point man turned around and walked back nonchalantly, but Joe and the others instinctively knew something was amiss. As Joe stood by the lieutenant, carrying the M-79, the point man lit a cigarette and appeared to be having just a regular conversation with the officer. Yet his report made the hair on Joe's neck stand up. "Man, I can smell gooks here," he said, "I can really smell them." The lieutenant, trying to appear unconcerned, simply replied: "Okay. Just go back up there, up to your point area and mess around a little bit like you're looking for something and then we will all draw back."[30]

The patrol followed orders and retreated down the hill a little way. Then the lieutenant requested an artillery strike on the tree line where the group had been heading. Enemy troops immediately started running out of the area and straight into the firing of the Americans, who lay waiting to pick them off. The planned enemy ambush turned into a slaughter due to the sixth sense of an experienced point man. Joe later stated, "To me that was one of the most creepy times that really scared me."[31]

For Joe, the worst aspect of the combat experience was his fear of death from above. Throughout his service in the north, he dreaded the enemy artillery, for when it arrived, the grunt had no choice but to burrow into the ground and pray, not able to even see the enemy. It unnerved lots of men, not knowing when shrapnel would rip them apart. The awful sound that preceded an earth-shaking explosion, one that sounded like a car roaring down a freeway, spawned many nightmares. In the south, the enemy troops usually had only mortars or rockets, but in the northern provinces, they fired large projectiles from their huge cannons across the border in North Vietnam. Some of the Marines' fathers had served in Europe during World War II and could identify with the terror of incoming artillery, as it left a terrible memory, one not easily forgotten.

One night while sitting outside, Joe had a close brush with death. Loud screams of "Incoming! Incoming!" pierced the summer night as enemy shells fell on the compound. They exploded with deafening volume, lighting the sky with brilliant flashes of white. Everyone jumped into foxholes, including Joe. As he hugged the ground, he suddenly felt a terrible concussion, one that shook his insides. A loud ringing in his ears accompanied the feeling of a rumbling in the earth. Momentarily dazed, he slowly recovered his senses and began digging into the earth frantically, so much so that his fingers bled. "I didn't know I was bleeding," he recalled. "Talk about scared."[32]

When the shelling stopped, his squad leader and friend from boot camp, a Texan named Jesse Hittson, screamed out, "Joe? Joe?" He exited his own hole and crawled toward Joe with a "crazed look" on his face, trying to find his comrade. As he neared, the Arizonan raised his hand and then poked his head up out of the foxhole. Hittson smiled wryly and then launched into a profanity-laced tirade about how Joe had scared him.[33] Joe, who rarely raised his voice, responded forcefully with his own barrage. "What the hell are you doing trying to crawl toward me? Trying to get a Bronze Star?" After the short exchange, the Texan withdrew to his hole, happy to have found his comrade alive—but not before flipping the bird to him as a final salute.[34]

Joe slowly gathered himself, still recovering from the ringing in his ears and the shaking in his body. "I looked over at the next foxhole, there was a big gouge. I looked at the hole and I looked at myself. I sat there and trembled." The enemy shell had missed him by not more than 10 feet. He had been a fortunate grunt that night, but he worried whether his luck would hold.[35]

Even in the face of death, the absurd found its way onto the battlefield. One day, someone observed an enemy artillery spotter lurking nearby, providing coordinates to NVA artillerymen. Someone ordered Joe to take out his M-79 and send some rounds at the guy. Joe responded immediately, placing a round in the chamber and firing. Joe had been working on the grenade launcher earlier, stuffing it with rags to clean it, and in his haste to fire on the enemy, he had forgotten to remove them. As the projectile flew toward the spotter, so did the rags, blasted into the air like confetti. Everyone laughed, including Joe, who soon regained his composure and fired a few more rounds toward the spotter. The memory of the rags, however, remained with him and his comrades for a long time.[36]

The nearly four months he spent fighting with his fellow Marines in the northernmost part of Quang Tri Province against the well-supplied and motivated NVA shaped Joe's life forever. He carried horrible images in his memory, such as the sight of his dead comrades stacked like wood in the back of trucks after the NVA ambushed their convoy.[37] The young Marine faced death on many occasions, as well as long stretches of boredom, and all the while, he dreamed of home and his girlfriend, Gina. He shared such feelings with his fellow soldiers as they endured much more than the majority of their generation would ever experience.

Fear and death remained constant companions for any American grunt in a front rifle squad in Vietnam. But for Joe, fate intervened and removed him from harm's way before he completed his thirteen-month tour. One day, his platoon headed from C-2 toward Con Thien in trucks when the enemy spotted the convoy and laid down a barrage. Everyone bailed out and ran for cover, Joe jumping into a big bomb crater.[38]

Once the shelling stopped, the lieutenant began going up and down the unit doing a headcount, calling out names and listening for responses. When Joe answered, a chaplain who had been in the hole with the lieutenant blurted out, "I have been looking for you for two weeks." He pulled Joe aside and reported that his older brother had died. The chaplain acknowledged that the funeral had already taken place but added, "If you want to go home that is fine. We will send you home on emergency leave if you want to." Stunned, Joe tried to process everything, including his loss. His mind drifted to his comrades and the need to complete his tour. However, his lieutenant had another perspective. "Get out of here," he ordered. "You have a chance to get out of here, now go take it."[39]

Though he was sad to leave his colleagues, Joe returned to base camp and packed his belongings "in the blink of an eye." But before he could leave, the enemy gave him a going-away party. That night, Joe sat on the perimeter as the NVA probed the base's defenses for weaknesses, and bullets zipped through the pitch-black sky and over his head. All through that long night, fear and sorrow combined with excitement as Joe thought about his older brother but also the fact that in a day or so, he would be home. He slept little, knowing he could rest some other time.[40]

The next morning, he stood anxiously near the helicopter landing pad with his duffel and rifle in hand. He scanned the horizon for the Hueys that he often had watched deliver supplies. So did the enemy. When the copters approached, their propellers making a loud swooshing noise and slowing to land, the enemy artillery opened up with overhead airburst projectiles, trying to bring them down.[41]

Under fire, the helicopters came in hard, bouncing on the ground while their crews hurriedly discarded their supplies before heading skyward again. As the enemy shells exploded overhead, Joe concentrated on getting his timing right. He waited and then began a mad dash across the pad, trying to coordinate his jump properly to catch one of the Hueys. As he ran, the shrapnel from the enemy artillery fell to the earth and peppered him but not with enough force to penetrate the skin. Breathing heavily, he threw his bag and rifle on board and leaped toward the door. He initially missed and landed more on the skid, but he refused to let go as the Huey headed upward. Dangling precariously, only the quick response of the door gunner reaching down to pull him in prevented him from falling back to earth.[42] In the distance, the NVA artillery observer must have thought to himself, this guy really wants to get out of here.

Once firmly ensconced on the Huey, Joe breathed a sigh of relief as the helicopter headed toward Dong Ha. There, he received orders to join another group of Marines standing at the end of a landing strip. After a while, a C-130 came barreling down the runway toward them, the enemy firing furiously as it landed. The pilots, unfazed, headed toward the group, and as the plane approached Joe and the others, its back ramp lowered while the propellers still spun furiously. The Marines scrambled on board, and before the new passengers could even catch their breath, the pilots gunned the engine and headed back up into the air before banking to the south and toward Da Nang.[43]

The flight did not take long, and Joe soon found himself in Da Nang, where he finally showered, cleaned up, and put on some new clothes. On the tarmac, a jet airliner waited for him. He bounded up the steps and into a new world, clean and comfortable. As the plane lifted skyward, like so many grunts before and after he celebrated his last glimpses of Vietnam through the window of a large plane pointed northward. After a short layover in Okinawa, Joe jumped on another plane for the long ride across the Pacific, a very different trip from the one he had taken nine months before as he rode in the belly of the *General Gaffney*. Like countless others, he had changed from a young man into a tough and experienced veteran, having seen some of the most vicious fighting in Vietnam preceding the Tet Offensive. No longer in his green, worn, and tattered fatigues but wearing a freshly pressed khaki uniform, he sank deep into his seat and thought about home as he drifted off to sleep.[44]

Arriving at Travis Air Force Base, Joe stepped off in the cool air of Northern California and wandered into the terminal, where he waited for transfers for further travel to Arizona. There, he noticed some young soldiers readying to take the long flight west across the Pacific, heading into the world that Joe had just left behind. They laughed and joked around, mere teenagers going off to war. They talked tough about how they could not wait to get into combat and kill some "gooks." Joe had seen war, and he thought to himself, "You guys have no idea what's in store for you."[45]

Joe made his way back home, going first to the Gallup, New Mexico, area where his family had resettled after his father retired from PD. After that, he drifted down to Morenci for several days to spend time with Gina and some friends and family, readjusting to life at home. During his leave, he went to a football game, where people looked at him quietly but intently, knowing he had just returned from Vietnam. They all watched the news, and many wanted to ask questions, but they knew that veterans rarely talked about their service, especially someone like the quiet, soft-spoken Joe. He remembered, "It just wasn't the same anymore. It seemed like everybody was kids. It seemed like they were far away. Like I couldn't really relate to them anymore. It kinda felt like a numbness . . . just like I was there but I really wasn't there. My thoughts were back in Vietnam."[46]

During his leave, Joe visited Larry West's mother. As they sat and talked, she took out a recent letter from her son. In it, Larry told her that he thought a lot about Joe because "they are really catching hell up there and I have really been thinking about him and worried about him. I hope he makes it through." Obviously, he did not know that his buddy had already left Vietnam. Joe found it very ironic that Larry worried about him while he sat there in the Wests' living room.[47]

After several weeks, Joe again reported to Camp Pendleton, ready to return to Vietnam to complete his tour. The Marine Corps decided it would be a waste of time to send him back for only a month, knowing that most of that time would have been spent on administrative duty because commanders typically took cautious short-timers out of the bush. Instead, Joe settled into garrison duty, helping train young Marines, many on their way to Vietnam.

A chilling event happened one day as Joe sat down in a different mess hall than the one that he usually frequented while in noncommissioned officer (NCO) school at Camp Mateo. Across the big room and amid the noisy banging of dishes and silverware, he heard someone calling his name. Turning around, he recognized a comrade who had been in the same company with him in Vietnam. They started a conversation, and the other young man told him how lucky he had been. A couple of days after Joe dusted off, his squad walked into an enemy ambush. The enemy poured down a heavy fusillade of bullets on the Marines, and by the end of the engagement, everyone in Joe's squad was either dead or wounded. Once again, it seemed, Joe had narrowly missed the grim reaper, causing him to reflect deeply on what had happened and how Providence had stepped in to save him from death. He realized how fortunate he had been the first time around.[48]

Despite missing the camaraderie of his unit and despite his gut feeling that a job remained for him in Vietnam, Joe resisted the Marines' enticements to return for a second tour. The monotony of the spit and polish of garrison duty wore on his nerves, but unlike others who thumbed their noses at such duty and ended up with a plane ticket to South Vietnam, he was "scared enough not to buck the system." He remained at Pendleton, often going on long marches, shooting different weapons, and heading out on ships for weeks at a time to practice amphibious assaults on California beaches.[49]

However, fate once again almost changed his path. In late January 1968, the VC and NVA launched the massive Tet Offensive all over South Vietnam, pounding American bases throughout the country. The ferocious fighting caught American policymakers and military leaders off guard and required a major counteroffensive. In living rooms across the country, Americans watched on television as US troops fought off assaults on Khe Sanh and then Saigon and Hue. The brutal aftermath of what was often house-to-house fighting raised US casualties significantly, undermined predictions of an American victory, and contributed to the start of a US withdrawal from Vietnam.[50]

In response to the Tet Offensive, the Marine Corps mobilized its forces, locking down Camp Pendleton and ordering the Marines to the grinder, the main parade grounds. Joe and Mike Cranford, who had joined his battalion, mustered with their packs and weapons and waited anxiously, having had little time to say good-bye to their loved ones. Joe listened closely as the commanders started calling off the names of those who would leave. They began with men who had not yet served in Vietnam, thus ensnaring Mike. Then they started going through those who had recently completed a tour. They worked their way down to the men who had been home for nine months, eight months, seven months—and stopped. Joe had arrived home six months earlier, and now he breathed a deep sigh of relief. Never again would he face a real threat of returning to Vietnam.[51]

Joe endured garrison duty for another eighteen months, and then, in September 1969, Cpl. Joe Sorrelman officially separated from the Marine Corps. Like Leroy and Mike, he made it back from Vietnam alive, having dodged death on several occasions. But of course, not everyone in the first wave and those that followed had such good fortune. The grim reaper, it turned out, had different plans for others of the Morenci Nine.

7

The Grim Reaper Descends

Even during the hot, sunny days of July 1967 in Greenlee Country, a proverbial dark cloud hung over Morenci, as storm clouds had been gathering for months. Finally, on July 15, workers marched off their jobs on the orders of the powerful United Steelworkers Union (USW). During the weeks of contract negotiations leading up to the walkout, labor leaders had clashed with the major copper companies, including Phelps Dodge, over a host of issues. Neither side budged, sparking a colossal standoff and resulting in a work stoppage.[1]

Before, local unions had negotiated individually with the companies, but this time, the USW had united groups, including production and refining operations, from across the country. They wanted significant changes in wage systems and better benefits, especially for copper workers. On July 15, Morenci workers joined more than sixty thousand others at seventy-three locations across the country, from California to New Jersey, and walked off the job. Most of the family members of the Morenci Nine stood with the many others whose sons fought in Vietnam and left their jobs to march on the picket lines.[2]

It had been a long time since an extended work stoppage had taken place. However, the unions, buoyed by unprecedented organization and solidarity, stood strong. Frustrated company officials dug their heels in, fearful of looking weak and establishing bad precedents. In particular, they opposed following the pattern of the steel companies with their uniform wages for all stages of production, something not replicated in the copper industry.[3] Instead, PD fought back in the press and in the halls of Congress, using its powerful allies to paint the labor unions as greedy parasites intent on undermining an industry vital to national defense.[4]

With both sides refusing to budge, throughout July and into August the mine remained shut down. Optimistically, many workers had believed that the massive show of force across the country would ensure a quick resolution in their favor. They clearly underestimated the resolve of the copper barons. By early August, the monsoon rains had arrived, and the strike appeared ready to stretch into the fall. People began settling in for the long haul, although no one knew for sure what that meant.[5]

During the strike, most people went on with their daily lives, for the company allowed them to remain in their homes and the company store extended credit. PD also followed earlier patterns and refused to hire replacement workers. Nonetheless, in the small kitchens and living rooms across Morenci, people worried about how long their savings would last. Everyone sought to stretch family budgets supplemented by small union strike checks.

The strike led to significant dislocations. Family members found odd jobs, but with so many unemployed, few opportunities existed. Over time, some began leaving Greenlee County for Tucson and Phoenix and other parts of the state to find work. Doubts began to arise among the workers. Would they eventually lose their company-provided health care or ultimately be thrown out of their homes? How far would they have to go into debt to survive? Would the company eventually fire them? Living in a company town created a dependence known only by a small group of Americans.

The mounting heat and humidity of August paralleled the rising tensions as the strike continued and workers had more time on their hands. People tried to stay busy, but the disruption of normal routines gave individuals, especially fathers and mothers, more time to think about their loved ones in Vietnam. In the Draper, West, and Cisneros households, family members apprehensively read the newspaper and watched the television, seeking to glean any information they could find on their sons' units. Daily, parents scoured the mail, searching for a letter letting them know that their boys were alive.[6] Still, many worried about the sudden appearance of an Army or Marine officer bearing the worst news.

Across the globe in Vietnam, many young men thought about their families and friends in Morenci. When Leroy had a free moment, typically at night, he worried about the hardships caused by the strike.[7] Serving on Guam, Clive expressed similar concerns about his parents, and he often tried to funnel money from his meager paycheck to his family.[8] Their radical counterparts in the United States might have pondered the irony of young men fighting for a system that allowed a major company to brutally exploit their parents, but the Morenci boys had more important things on their minds—mainly, staying alive.

Like Joe and Leroy, Bobby Dale had disembarked the *General Gaffey* in late December 1966, leaving his friends and his last direct ties to home on the dock in Da Nang. Bobby Dale found himself in a rifle company, a duty shared by many Marines during their tours in Vietnam. His unit focused on searching for the elusive enemy, although he encountered more VC than NVA in his sector south of Da Nang. His was a dangerous job carried out in a stifling environment. It entailed long periods of boredom that might be shattered in an instant by the terror of combat. And not infrequently, it involved the loss of comrades.

Bobby Dale Draper's boot camp portrait. (Photo courtesy of the US Marine Corps.)

Bobby Dale settled into his role in his unit of the Second Platoon of Golf Company, Second Battalion, Fifth Marines, though he told his parents early on, "I don't hardly know anybody that I'm with right now so it makes it a little lonely."[9] He spent most of his time either near An Hoa or guarding a coal mine at Nong Son. Upon arriving, he wrote about the constant, soaking rains and emphasized, "Outside there's nothing but mud. You can't walk outside without sinking up to your ankles. It's not the usual type mud either, it's the kind you find in pig pens, real slushy and stinks to high heaven."[10]

Many days, he filled sandbags to pile on bunkers or along trenches at An Hoa. Other days, his unit hunted the VC and NVA in the bush. After his first firefight, Bobby Dale admitted, "I didn't even know what I was shooting at, just a place where we thought they were firing."[11] Not long after, he reported that the VC fired on his unit as they neared a village. "So, we took the village and burned down all the little hooches the people live in," he said rather nonchalantly.[12] He even seemed to develop a rather cavalier attitude about Marines being wounded: "We get casualties every time we go out, but nobody thinks anything about it. It just means that guy gets a little vacation out of the field."[13]

Like Joe and others in frontline rifle companies, Bobby Dale had to deal with the elements as well as boredom. "Socks are real hard to get out here and they are really needed because your feet stay wet all the time," he told his parents when he requested that they send extras.[14] He also suffered due to having a light complexion in the searing Vietnamese sun. Early on, he made a special request for Blistex: "My lips are pretty well sunburned and that's about the only stuff that does any good."[15] Of course, he complained about the local pests: "I couldn't sleep for all the mosquitoes buzzing around. There is enough to drive a guy crazy."[16]

Despite the boredom he discussed at length in his letters home, Bobby Dale participated in several large operations, including Stone, Lanoke, Union, and Calhoun. During such actions, the enemy forces struck back at times, as happened one night when they pounded his base with mortars. "We all had to run outside and jump in the trenches to keep from getting blown away," he related. "Nobody got hurt so it wasn't too bad. Kind of exciting having things blown up all around you."[17]

Sometimes, however, the enemy hit back with devastating results. While returning from Operation Dixie, Bobby Dale rode on an amtrac

Bobby Dale in the field smiling as he poses with friends in the background. (Photo courtesy of the Draper family.)

with more than thirty others. Suddenly, the lumbering vehicle hit a large antitank mine. Smoke and flames filled the vehicle as gasoline and napalm ignited inside the trac. The ringing from the explosions and the sounds of Marines screaming in pain flooded Bobby Dale's ears. He told his parents that he felt himself "start to burn. All I could think of was get off! Get off quick before this thing really goes." He reported seeing "men running around all over the place with their faces, arms, hands, all burnt to heck. The skin was just hanging off of their bodies."[18]

Bobby Dale received second-degree burns from the enemy ordnance and required treatment and rest. He was lucky. Most of his fellow Marines had to be evacuated, and only a couple were ever able to return to their units. He had witnessed a ghastly scene that left some of his comrades forever disfigured, and the images would stay with him.[19]

Bobby Dale barely escaped death on several other occasions, as well. On July 3, a major battle erupted at the coal mine outpost that he regularly guarded. "The VC snuck up the side of the mountain and early yesterday morning they came swarming over the top of the hill," he wrote his parents. The enemy killed thirteen Marines and wounded another forty-three of Company F of the Second Battalion, Fifth Marines, before the Americans counterattacked. "Nobody ever expected to get hit very hard out there. The world is full of surprises," he reported.[20]

His company arrived soon after to replace the decimated unit. Bobby Dale complained about the foul stench filling the air, claiming, "The reason it stinks is because there are dead gooks laying around the hill that we can't get to or can't do anything with, so they are just laying around rotting away."[21]

For nearly nine months, Bobby Dale endured the grunt's life. Sometimes, he seemed to regret his decision to join, stressing to his parents to "tell Kenneth Niel [his teenage brother] to stay out of the service . . . you're better off in school. Like I'm going to be when I get out of the corpse [sic]."[22] Finally, in mid-July 1967, he earned some R & R and headed off to Japan. Like so many others, he chose an exotic destination where a person could sleep on clean sheets, eat delectable meals, and enjoy the nightlife. For the GIs, it was often a surreal experience to be in the jungle in combat one day and in a modern Asian city the next. Most hated to return to Vietnam, including Bobby Dale.

On his way back from R & R, he decided to visit Leroy at Camp Reasoner. Fortunately for Bobby Dale, his friend was not in the jungle on a long patrol. Instead, he found Leroy hanging around camp, and like long-lost brothers, the two bear-hugged when they met. Leroy noticed that Bobby Dale had lost weight, but in the photographs of the two, he was still the fair-skinned bear of a man that he had been at home, clearly dwarfing his smaller friend. As they talked, he admitted being several days late in returning to his unit, but when Leroy asked him if he was worried about that, Bobby Dale simply replied, "What are they going to do? Send me to Vietnam?"[23]

Bobby Dale and Leroy at Camp Reasoner, July 1967. (Photo provided by Leroy Cisneros.)

That night, the two partied into the wee hours, drinking cold beer at the thatch-roofed Wynn Hall, where the enlisted men gathered. Bobby Dale loved the cold beer, calling it "the greatest thing in the world," for frontline units typically received warm beer only. They sat around a table and talked about home, the good times, and their families, although Leroy recalled, "I know we were a lot quieter. There was no more kiddie stuff for us."[24] Nonetheless, they promised to throw the biggest party in the history of the Morenci Hall when they returned to celebrate their good fortune at having survived the experience.[25]

Eventually, they stumbled out into the dark and passed out in a trench before finally dragging themselves back to Leroy's hooch. The next morning, Leroy headed out on another mission, hung over but sobering up quickly as he prepared to board a helicopter. As Bobby Dale lay on his buddy's bunk, they exchanged a "God Bless," then Leroy turned and said, "Don't get shot. We'll have that big party soon."[26]

Bobby Dale returned to his unit and started counting down the days until he completed his thirteen months. On August 2, 1967, Corporal Draper, who had recently turned nineteen, went out on a mission, a relatively routine one doing a road sweep moving north from An Hoa to Phu Lac in the vicinity of AT909481.[27] Bobby Dale and his comrades had made many such sweeps in the past without incident.

On this particular day, however, approximately fifty well-armed Vietcong waited for them, having formed a classic horseshoe ambush to trap the Marines in a cross fire. As the Americans moved along the road, the pow-pow-pow of enemy AK-47s ripped the relative quiet of the countryside. Soon, heavy machine-gun fire joined the chorus and then the loud ripping sound of a 57mm Recoilless Rifle heaving a large cannon projectile toward the group. Chaos ensued as the small cluster of exposed and nearly surrounded Marines faced a larger force firmly entrenched in defensible positions.[28]

Frantically, the Marines fired back at the enemy. Lt. Paul Bertolozzi desperately called for fire support and reinforcements. His commanders originally hesitated, thinking he was exaggerating the threat because the enemy had not been active in the area. Meanwhile, the continued barrage of the VC, well coordinated to lay down a withering cross fire, picked off the Marines one by one. A rapid-response force finally headed out, but when these Marines arrived, the VC had already melted back into the countryside—though not before picking over the bodies for valuables and finishing off each of the wounded with a gunshot to the head. Bobby Dale had been hit three times, in the leg, abdomen, and head.[29]

That day, fourteen men died in a small battle that few would remember apart from the families and friends touched by the short, deadly skirmish along a road snaking through the Vietnamese countryside. Nine people from Bobby Dale's company perished, including Raymond Abbott of Sugar Grove, Pennsylvania; James R. Majors of Clute, Texas; and Glenn McCuaig of Americus, Georgia. Others hailed from industrial centers such as Gary,

Indiana, as well as small towns such as Midwest City, Oklahoma; Garden City, Michigan; and San Lorenzo, California. The dead represented every major region of the country and, disproportionately, smaller towns like Morenci.[30]

In the first week of August 1967, a phone rang in Phoenix at the downtown office of the inspector and instructor for the Marine Reserve. An officer picked the phone up and listened to another Marine identify himself as being with the Marine Casualty Section in Quantico, Virginia. The officer in Arizona knew the drill. The man on the other end of the line would proceed to deliver details on either the death or the wounding of an Arizona Marine. This day, it was the death of Robert Dale Draper of Morenci, Arizona. Only a day before, it had been Donald Robert Elmore of Buckeye, who died in combat in Vietnam on August 1. The officer took down all the information, hung up, and then prepared for the horrible duty of informing the family.

The trip to Buckeye had taken only forty-five minutes, but this time, the officer had to make a four-hour drive to Morenci. It gave him a lot of time to think about what he would say and to reflect on the feelings of those whose lives he was about to completely alter with the news of the death of their family member. He practiced the standard, short refrain: "Mrs. Draper, as a representative of the commandant of the Marine Corps, it is my duty to inform you that your son, Robert Draper, was killed in action on August 2, 1967, in the Republic of South Vietnam in the defense of the United States of America."[31]

The Marine carried paperwork with details on arranging for the arrival of the body and planning a military funeral, together with a host of other materials to assist the family. He knew that he should seek out someone in the community, usually a minister, to accompany him, so he looked over Bobby Dale's information and determined that he would try to locate a Mormon leader. Unfortunately, he and others had been getting a lot of experience in what to do when reporting deaths: US military officials would travel to thirteen different homes in Arizona during August 1967.[32]

On August 2, on the other side of the world from An Hoa, Vietnam, Bobby Dale's mother, Carlene, had an uneasy feeling about him. Her husband, Robert, wanted to spend time with family in Oklahoma, but Carlene dragged her feet. She finally agreed to a short trip to the mountains, but as they packed, a government-issue sedan pulled up in front of their house. Larry Spear, a friend and counselor from the LDS church, exited along with a Marine officer, walked up to the front door, and knocked. Carlene opened the door and immediately asked, "Larry, what's happened?" The two men entered the house as Carlene kept repeating, "What's happened? What's happened?" They waited for a moment, querying about Robert's location. When he appeared from another room, the Marine officer proceeded to tell them that Bobby Dale had been killed in combat in the Quang Nam Province of South Vietnam.[33]

The death of Bobby Dale stunned his family and friends. Only a few weeks before, he had been writing about being in Tokyo on R & R. Once the tragic news arrived, nothing could stop the pain. Some cried until their eyes burned. Others felt a tightness in the chest or a heavy knot in the gut as they tried to process the loss. Images of Bobby Dale flooded their thoughts. For some, the mind stopped functioning fully, for they were not able to cope with losing such a fine young person with so much of his life in front of him. At times, they would just stare into space, the mind having shut down due to the pain. The anguish was worse for certain people and lasted longer. Many tried to stay busy with anything they could think of just to keep from dwelling on the loss.

The family prepared for the arrival of Bobby Dale's body, making plans with the funeral directors of the Lewallen Funeral Home in Clifton. The Marines had promised his return within a week, so relatives traveled to Morenci from all over, some from as far away as Oklahoma. The people in town rallied around the family. Someone brought a camping trailer for family members to stay in, since the small, three-bedroom home in East Plantsite at the corner of Hopi and Reservation Streets had become crowded. Others delivered meals or helped prepare the Mormon ward building in Clifton for the service.[34]

However, Bobby Dale's body did not come as promised, and family members soon had to return home to their jobs.[35] When the body did at last arrive, under the escort of Marine corporal Edward Northcut, people headed down Highway 666 from Morenci and into Clifton to visit the funeral home where Bobby Dale rested.[36] A solemn processional followed, including a number of classmates, many home before the start of the semester at colleges in Tempe, Tucson, and Flagstaff. Less than two years before, Bobby Dale had been playing football at the nearby Clifton football field. And just sixteen months earlier, he had walked across the stage to pick up his high school diploma. This day, however, he lay in a coffin, and the loss of the star football player and respected young man devastated everyone who had known him.

Tears flowed during the viewing for the soldier, who had turned nineteen less than a month before his violent death. As if to share the family's loss, the skies opened and torrential rains fell like heavy tears the night before the funeral. Soon, the San Francisco River began spilling over its banks.[37] The Mormon ward, relatively isolated from the center of Clifton, sat across a small bridge in the shadow of the big hill leading to Morenci. Sometimes during heavy rains, it was cut off, leading Bobby Dale's family to fear the flooding would delay the service.[38]

However, the floodwaters subsided in the morning, just in time for the memorial that began at 10:00 a.m. on a hot and muggy Saturday. People piled in their cars and trucks and drove down the highway to Clifton and the meeting hall where the funeral director had transferred Bobby Dale's body. Miners and their families and friends filled the big room, joined by farmers and ranchers from Duncan's large Mormon community. Death had brought people from all faiths and backgrounds together in Greenlee County.[39]

Bishop Irven Carter led the service, and Armon Williams opened with the invocation. Donna Smith, Sherrie Hatch, and Betty Elmer had traveled from Duncan to provide the music, singing three hymns, "The Lord Is My Shepherd," "Beautiful Isle of Somewhere," and "Hold Thou My Hand." Others from the Mormon community gave a sermon and a reading of the obituary, among them Joe Goodman, a close friend of Bobby Dale from his days in the Boy Scouts. Many of those who gathered shed tears for the loss of such a fine young man who had made a significant impression on family and friends during his short life.[40]

After the service, mourners proceeded to their vehicles and followed the hearse as it crossed the bridge and headed south along Highway 666, passing through Clifton before turning off the Ward Canyon Road toward Bobby Dale's final resting spot. The Clifton Cemetery lay in the shadows of red clay hills carved out by millions of years of erosion, in a quiet spot not too far from town. At the gravesite, Bobby Dale received full military honors. Veterans from the local American Legion Post 28 formed a color guard and fired a final salute to the fallen soldier, and Jim Brooks played "Taps" as a closing tribute. Then they lowered Bobby Dale's body into the red clay soil that he had trekked across most of his life.[41] It was a hard day for the community, one already reeling from the strike. Unfortunately, such sad occasions had become more commonplace in many towns across America during the late summer of 1967.

Not long after, a letter arrived for the family with a return address of the White House. Inside, they found a standardized note from President Lyndon Johnson. "Dear Mr. and Mrs. Draper," it opened, "Mrs. Johnson and I join in expressing our deepest sympathy to you in the loss of your son, Corporal Robert D. Draper." It continued, "Americans throughout our great country are eternally indebted and humbly grateful to your son for his selfless courage in fighting to preserve the ideal of freedom for all men." It concluded, "You are in our prayers at this time of great sorrow."[42] The letter would be replicated 466 times for all the Americans who died along with Bobby Dale in Vietnam during the month of August 1967.[43]

The loss of Bobby Dale, the first of the Morenci Nine to die in combat, devastated his friends. Many remembered exactly how they learned of his death. Mike Cranford, stationed at Camp Pendleton with the Twenty-Eighth Marines, sometimes stayed off base with his wife, Joyce, who had an apartment in San Clemente. One day, they had a bitter fight, and an angry Joyce bolted for a pay phone across the street to call her mother. She returned crying, not in anger but in anguish. "Bobby's dead, Bobby's dead, Bobby's dead," she cried out to Mike.[44]

The death particularly devastated Leroy, who learned about it in a letter sent by his sister. Bobby Dale had been one of the most beloved members of their group, especially to Leroy. "It can't be," he lamented. "He can't be dead. We just talked about throwing a big party in Morenci after 'Nam."[45] He knew about death, having seen it often during his missions. But he had a longer, more intimate relationship with Bobby Dale, having toiled with him in the classroom, on the football field under the scorching Arizona summer sun, and in boot camp and advanced training. Everything changed for Leroy when a huge gaping hole opened in his world with Bobby Dale's death, one that widened as other friends passed away over the next two years.[46]

Larry West's already sour mood clearly worsened when he learned of Bobby Dale's death. In early September, he wrote his parents that Joe had informed him about the loss of their friend. "At first I didn't believe it, but I can't see no reason for him to lie," he wrote. "Damn gooks I hate them like hell. They ought to kill everyone of the slant eyed bastards," he continued angrily. "No one of them better even look at me cross eyed or I [*sic*] kill it same way I'd kill a damn fly. Won't bother me a damn bit, don't care if he's 10 months old or a 100 to me there [*sic*] all the same."[47]

For Clive Garcia, who had been serving on Guam, Vietnam was always first and foremost in his thoughts. When he received news that Bobby Dale had died, he immediately barged into his commander's office and demanded a transfer to the fighting. The surprised officer looked at the angry Marine and barked, "No! You have a job and you need to go cool off!" Then he berated Clive for speaking the way he had to a superior officer, stressing that he better not address him in that manner ever again.[48]

Afterward, Clive angrily wrote his mother, complaining that she had not told him about Bobby Dale's death. He told her to stop worrying so much about him and that he needed to know about everything, even such sad information. "You'll get me angry," he said half-jokingly, "and I'll have to write you a Dear Jane letter to you for being a sorry sort of a mother and I'll hate to write you after all you are very best and most faithful girl." He promised to forgive her, but only this one time. He admitted to being angry at the world for what had happened to his friend and to feeling guilty deep down because he himself had survived. Yet Clive acknowledged that Bobby Dale had "a biger [*sic*] and better football field to play in now."[49]

The anger and resentment caused by the loss of Bobby Dale would linger for the remaining members of the Morenci Nine. Less than a year before, they had been basking in the glow of adoring parents and friends on the parade field in San Diego, celebrating their graduation from boot camp. They had traveled home as a group to spend time with their families before heading out to different assignments. Now, one of them lay in the ground in the red clay hills not far from where they had hunted, fished, and played football against the Trojans. Bobby Dale's death shocked his friends and reminded them of their own mortality, something difficult for any teenager to process. Unfortunately, this was only the beginning.

*   *   *

People had to go on with their lives after Bobby Dale's death, of course, but the strike continued to weigh heavily on the residents of Morenci. The routine of twenty-six days on and two days off for workers had been disrupted. The expected quick victory never materialized, as the union leaders failed to anticipate the resolve of the copper barons. And government pressure to sustain the production of vital war materials slowly developed. Optimism faded as the strike continued, and neither side appeared willing to budge as the monsoon rains ended and the football season reached its midpoint in October.[50]

Bobby Dale's death had a chilling effect on the people of Morenci and others in Greenlee County. Many parents had sons in Vietnam. Daily, they prayed for the safe return of their boys, all the while worrying that they too might receive a visit from a Marine or Army officer bringing horrible news. The reports on national television and in the newspapers showed intense fighting in South Vietnam, including Con Thien as well as VC strongholds around Da Nang. Almost weekly, reports appeared in the *Copper Era* highlighting the actions of soldiers from Greenlee County in Vietnam. It was a tough time for the miners on many levels.[51]

The intensified fighting in the summer of 1967 increased pressure on the Marine Corps and other branches to maintain troop levels in South Vietnam. With Joe stateside by September and Larry and Leroy firmly embedded with their units in Vietnam, the Morenci Nine already were well represented in Southeast Asia. Several more waited in the wings, including Clive in Guam, Robert and Van in Hawaii, and Mike in San Diego. The ninth member of the group, Stan, had held a variety of stateside assignments and thus far had remained firmly ensconced in relatively safe garrison duties. No one knew exactly what the Marine Corps had in mind for each, but Vietnam always loomed on the horizon for those not already there.

Now, the Marines needed more infantrymen because losses in 1967 had jumped, with nearly five hundred killed in action (KIA) a month and many more wounded who could not return to duty. The rotation system also required replacements to fill the ranks. Thus, it became a matter of

Stan King's boot camp portrait.
(Photo courtesy of the US Marine
Corps.)

when, not if, Stan and the others would jump on a troopship or plane and head to Vietnam.

In late September, Stan became the first of the Morenci Nine since the original four to receive orders to ship out to Southeast Asia. The Marines granted him a brief leave, and he returned to Morenci for a short visit. Apprehensive about the future, he gave his family and friends conflicting signals on what he thought would happen. On one hand, he told his family to keep his toothbrush in the medicine cabinet and his clothes in various drawers and closets. Stan seemed to be preparing to return home and wanted everything in good order.[52]

On the other hand, as he prepared to return to Camp Pendleton, he sat up with his mother and talked all night, and one of the central topics he focused on was his burial site. "He had his grave picked out in the Clifton Cemetery," Penny King reported. He wanted his final resting place to be in the shadow of the red clay hills where he and his friends had often gone to park. "He told us dozens of times he wanted to be buried there," his mother remembered. "I don't know what he meant. Just knew what he wanted."[53]

While on leave, Stan also went over to the house of one of his best friends, Gerald Hunt. During the visit, he somewhat jokingly proposed to Gerald's younger sister, Sandy. He told her that he wanted to marry her so that when he died, he could leave his life insurance money to his widow. Sandy and Gerald's mom howled in protest, chastising Stan for talking that way. He just shrugged and responded that he did not think he would be coming back. Gerald acknowledged that his friend liked to tease people, but that day his actions and words indicated a deep-seated fear of what lay ahead.[54]

Stan had shared his fears openly with a number of people. Bobby Dale had done the same, although with only a few. Larry's mom remembered driving with Leroy, Larry, and Bobby Dale to Phoenix to catch the bus to San Diego for boot camp. While Larry bragged about the car he intended to buy, she observed that Bobby Dale sat quietly, not saying anything. When she queried him about what he intended to do with his money when he returned, he simply responded, "I'm not coming back." Reflecting on that moment, she noted, "Oh, that really chilled me when he spoke like that." She asked Larry about it later to see if he was joking, but Larry responded that Bobby Dale had talked that way several times, adding, "No mother, [he's] convinced he's not coming back."[55]

A sense of fatalism seemed to accompany some of the young men as they headed to Vietnam, including Stan, especially as the fighting escalated and the number of deaths climbed in 1967. For many, it was likely a coping mechanism to help them deal with the fear and uncertainty, hoping for the best but preparing for the worst. Although the facts and figures highlighted by the military revealed that the average person serving in Vietnam had a less than one in ten chance of dying, some soldiers dwelled on the fear of being killed or maimed.[56] Others had a more optimistic outlook. Leroy rarely thought about not making it, despite his very dangerous duty. Whether Stan or Bobby Dale really believed that they would die and dwelled upon that prospect is uncertain, but the reality was that they had prepared themselves for death.

After the brief respite at home to put things in order, LCpl. Stan King boarded a plane for Vietnam, arriving on October 13, 1967. The long flight allowed all the soldiers on board to think about their upcoming tour of duty. Some quietly sat in their seats and looked out the window at the vast blue ocean passing beneath, contemplating their past and future. Others acted like rambunctious boys going off to camp, constantly pestering the flight attendants. A few, unable to calm themselves, nervously puffed on cigarettes or ordered drinks to steel the nerves. As one veteran observed, being served meals and alcohol seemed "ridiculous," given that in a short period, most of the passengers would be in a combat zone.[57]

The flight was Stan's first long trip on an airplane, and with his height and broad shoulders, he must have been uncomfortable in the cramped quarters. But after a couple of stops for fuel, the plane finally descended in a steep dive into Da Nang. With hundreds of others, he exited the plane and left behind the last vestiges of his normal life. The pilots and flight attendants quickly dispatched his group and boarded another, composed mostly of battle-weary troops who had completed their thirteen months and were headed home. Stan walked off into a foreign land, slapped in the face by the heat and humidity of Vietnam, a sharp contrast to the cool, crisp weather of October in Southern California. He likely shared the feelings of another grunt, Robert Peterson, who commented that as he deplaned, "I felt like Alice stepping through the looking glass. . . . I knew my life would never be the same from this moment on."[58]

Stan joined H Company of the Second Battalion of the Fifth Marines, working around An Hoa, the same battalion that Bobby Dale had served in until his death only a couple months earlier. He went in as a replacement for those like Bobby Dale who had been killed or those who had completed their tours and returned to the States. He knew no one and probably would have seconded the sentiments of another grunt who arrived in Vietnam: "Each man was on his own. Each man was an island. Each man had to face the future using his own inner strengths and dealing with his own inner weaknesses. I owned plenty of both."[59]

The tall, red-headed Marine from Morenci had a short tour in Vietnam but experienced a great deal. Around An Hoa, the VC and the NVA continued to keep the pressure on the Americans. In response, the Marines took the fight to the enemy in October and November, trying to force them to abandon civilian areas and move into the cover of the western mountains. The brutal fighting took a toll on Stan, who wrote a letter to his brother Sam talking about how he had seen a comrade die from an enemy blast only a few days after arriving. He admitted, "I cry a lot and that helps."[60]

A little more than three weeks into his tour, the battalion launched Operation Essex into Antenna Valley, 6 miles south of An Hoa. The enemy had fortified several villages in the area, surrounding them with interconnected strands of barbed wire, and their engineers had constructed deep caves and bunkers to provide cover against American artillery and aircraft. To approach the foe, American troops had to traverse open rice paddies and head toward the heavily defended positions. In addition, the adversary had fashioned escape routes through the valley and into the mountains. Uprooting the enemy would pose a formidable challenge for the Marines.[61]

On November 6, Stan's company boarded the UH-34 helicopters that looked like huge gnats and flew into Landing Zone Raven in Antenna Valley to commence their operation. Stan and his comrades jumped out of the lumbering craft, reforming into their units and moving out. The NVA allowed the Americans to land unopposed but made a stand near the village of Ap Bon in the northeast part of the valley. Fierce fighting broke out as the Marines approached, the NVA sweeping the rice paddies and open fields with 50-caliber machine guns. Stan and his fellow Marines scurried for cover as the heavy machine guns strafed them. Well-placed mortar rounds fell among the troops, propelling mounds of earth and steel into the sky. Officers and noncoms barked out orders and pushed their men toward the NVA.[62]

The attack against the heavily fortified enemy encampment continued for several hours. Barbed wire and bamboo obstacles stalled the Americans' assaults. In response, Capt. Gene Bowers, commander of H Company, called in artillery and air strikes to break up the enemy concentrations. The bombs and napalm often landed no more than 50 yards from the Marine lines, the deafening explosions ringing in the ears of the young soldiers and the heat searing their faces.[63]

The heavy fighting raged at close range, with the Marines relying on rifle and machine-gun fire as well as grenades to move forward. Reinforcements arrived, but the enemy continued to repulse the Marines with withering fire from concealed positions. Throughout the day, the enemy rained down heavy fire on the Americans, and by dusk, the Marines had advanced only a short distance. They had to create defensive positions for the night. In the dark, the enemy continued to harass them while American AC-130s flew overhead to bombard the NVA, sometimes within 10 meters of the Marine lines. By 0430, however, the enemy forces disengaged and slipped away through their escape routes.[64]

The NVA inflicted heavy casualties on the Americans at Ap Bon. By the end of the first day, sixteen Americans had fallen, including a tall, red-headed Marine from Arizona who had been in country for only three weeks. Many others had been seriously wounded, and the company sustained substantial losses in leadership, including a lieutenant and several sergeants. Throughout that day and into the next, helicopters picked up the wounded as well as the body bags laid out in landing zones. Among them was the body of Stan King, who started his final journey home.[65]

Back in Morenci on November 6, Stan's mother, Penny, woke in the middle of the night. Visibly shaken, she told her husband, Glenn, about her horrible dream. In it, she saw Stan in Vietnam entering a hut, much like the ones often shown on television. "I saw him shot in the heart," she tearfully told Glenn. As he died, Stan cried out, "Mom, Mom." Glenn reassured her that it was just a dream, encouraging her to go back to sleep. However, she carried a bad feeling in her heart for several days.[66]

A few days later, the Marine Corps Reserve Office in Phoenix received a call from the Marine Casualty Division in Quantico. Once again, a staffer took down information about the death of another Arizona soldier. Familiar with the routine, an officer jumped in his car and retraced the route taken just months earlier by someone delivering the same news to the Draper family.

As the government-issue car wound its way through the community, people prayed that it would keep moving. It finally arrived at the King home. The Marine exited, passed through the short chain-linked fence gate, and knocked on the door. No one answered. After a few queries, he tracked down Glenn. The news devastated the burly smelter worker, sending him into a tailspin that would last for a long time. On that day, though, he gathered himself, and accompanied by his close friend Floyd Hoffman, he drove with the officer to the high school where Penny worked in the lunchroom. As soon as Glenn and the Marine walked in, Penny let out a piercing scream. She knew what had happened, admitting forty years later that the memory was "still just as fresh as that day."[67] The officer proceeded with his formal announcement, and the family began the horrible ordeal of acknowledging the death of the eldest son while preparing for his final trip home.

* * *

The cold winds of November replaced the crisp air of fall in Morenci as the leaves in the forest to the north fell with the approach of winter. People had begun planning for Thanksgiving, although many wondered how abundant the dinners would be that year with the strike persisting. Though some grumbled, union leaders and strikers prepared to rally in Tucson to demonstrate solidarity and buoy spirits. But in the King family, Thanksgiving preparations gave way to more pressing matters.[68]

Like the Draper family only three months before, the Kings had to make arrangements for the arrival of their eldest son's body. Family descended on the small community, some from as far away as west Texas, where Glenn and Penny had lived before migrating to Arizona in the 1940s. Relatives piled into the small house and spilled over into those of friends; others found lodging in the small motels in Morenci and Clifton.

Once more, Morenci prepared to bury one of its best-known young men, tragically cut down before he could fulfill his potential. Loved by many, respected by all, Stan lay in the Lewallen Funeral Home parlor where Bobby Dale had lain a short while earlier. And just as happened for Bobby Dale, the miners and their families drove down Highway 666 to the mortuary to view the body. Hundreds passed by the large casket to pay their respects to the fallen warrior and his family. Glenn and Penny, joined by their sons Sam and Doug, tried to stay strong, but the loss was so painful. Only two months earlier, Stan had been with them, walking around and harassing his younger brothers. Now, his lifeless body rested in a coffin only a short distance from his home.

Eleven days after Stan died, family and friends gathered in the early afternoon on Friday, November 17, at the American Baptist Church. A huge crowd packed the church, some forced to stand in aisles overflowing with miners and their families. The organist, Glenna Hunt, who had berated Stan only a couple of months earlier for proposing to her daughter, played as people assembled.[69]

Pastor F. G. Dodson rose and opened the service with a few words and a prayer, followed by a quartet made up of William Conger, Bob Harrison, Wayne Holliday, and Marlin Treadway singing "Nearer My God to Thee" and "I Won't Have to Cross the Jordan Alone."[70] Tears fell for the fallen Marine as the men sang. Stan's body was at the front near his family, his coffin draped with an American flag.[71]

The music concluded, and Pastor Dodson rose to deliver a eulogy invoking many of the concepts that unified the community in accepting the loss of Stan in a violent manner in an increasingly unpopular war. He opened by characterizing war as "a hateful and cruel business" that was "sometimes necessary if a nation is to survive." Highlighting past examples of governments and their "surrender to tyranny" that had cost millions of lives, he then focused on the relationship between citizen and state. "And lest we think that government has nothing to do with religion," he quoted the passage of Matthew 22:21 about giving unto Caesar that which was his and unto God what was God's. "We cannot disassociate ourselves from responsible government, and we honor those whose duty it is to protect it . . . for in honoring him we honor God who ordains government and we honor ourselves as citizens."[72]

Pastor Dodson then shifted the focus, obviously trying to find a way to explain loss to the family and community. In many ways, he zeroed in on the concept of the "good death," one that, though tragic, had a purpose.[73] The pastor underscored that "death is a terrible reality, particularly to one who is so young and who presumably had a much longer life to live." But he pointed out that "some things are worse than death," such as having "nothing of value to die for." He praised Stan for his willingness "to assume such a responsibility" and asked how many in the audience would do so. "To my way of thinking, it is better to die than to live as some appear to be living—an irrational, unrealistic, negative, idle, unpatriotic and uncourageous existence—under the protection of a government which permits all of these privileges." Acknowledging the imperfect union, the pastor nevertheless emphasized that "it is dedicated to human liberty, even of those who, at the moment, appear to be its most bitter foes."[74]

Pastor Dodson concluded by expressing his condolences before praying that the King family "may be comforted in the thought that their son died in the fulfillment of his sincere and sworn duty. Who knows but that his death may mean that millions of others may live a life of usefulness, and if so, he shall in a sense continue to live through them, even as the spirit of the founders of our country live through us." "May the God of peace bring peace, with justice tinged with mercy, to our war-torn, strife-filled, confused world," he stated, adding, "but whatever transpires in the uncertain future before us, may each of us have the courage of young men such as the one whose memory we do now honor."[75]

Pastor Dodson clearly expressed ideas percolating through Morenci and most American communities dealing with the loss of young men at that juncture of the Vietnam War. He acknowledged the sorrow of death but firmly placed it within a common national narrative that contended Stan died defending the liberty of people fighting against Communist tyranny. Courage and duty to country remained central themes, and the pastor clearly differentiated between honorable men such as Stan, on the one hand, and the unpatriotic antiwar activists streaming into the streets of America to challenge authority, on the other. To Dodson and many others, there had to be a noble explanation for the loss. The death could not have been in vain, or else it would be a maddening, inexplicable waste of such a fine person. Publicly and privately, Americans across the country grappled with such issues in November 1967.

After the service, a caravan followed the hearse carrying Stan's body down the hill through Clifton and out the meandering road to the Clifton Cemetery. There, he received the same full military honors that had been given to Bobby Dale. The two friends, linked by one fateful decision made in the spring of 1966, both died from an enemy bullet in a far-off land that neither could have located on a map only a year or so before. In fact, they perished in the same battalion and on ground only miles apart. Now, they lay near each other in the Clifton Cemetery in the shadow of the red cliffs of Ward Canyon.

The pain for the family naturally continued after Stan's burial. Outsiders added to it when, less than two months later, someone took out a subscription to an antiwar paper for the Kings. Penny believed that a local person had done it because the family had just recently changed its address and only someone in Morenci or Clifton would have known that. Soon after, letters started arriving asking the family to speak out against the war. Penny called the local sheriff, Forest Wilkerson, who requested assistance from the Federal Bureau of Investigation (FBI). Agents arrived to gather information. As they left, Penny asked if she would receive communication about the subscription. They simply replied, "No ma'am, you will never know." The family also placed a hold on the newspaper at the local post office, and Doug began screening the mail.[76]

The paper delivery stopped but restarted a couple of years later, around the time when the story of the Morenci Nine received national news coverage in late 1969. Penny wrote an angry letter to the group that published the paper, demanding that they stop sending the trash to her family. Worried that her letter might be too harsh, she asked Sheriff Wilkerson to read it to make sure that she had not crossed any lines. Then, she mailed it. Once more, the materials eventually stopped arriving—but not before reopening some deep wounds.[77]

For many people outside of Morenci, particularly in the antiwar movement, the death of Stan made no sense, and they could not understand the absence of an outcry from the family and community. They found it ironic that Stan had traveled thousands of miles to die fighting for a government that favored the powerful copper barons operating out of their Manhattan skyscrapers. These same men profited handsomely from supplying materials to the country's war machine—even as the young men from Morenci fought overseas and sent their combat pay back to their families to help them make ends meet. Worst of all, people in Morenci paid with the blood of their sons, while the children of wealthy managers and stockholders used draft deferments and family connections to avoid combat. The antiwar activists could never comprehend why the Morenci workers remained loyal to such a brutally exploitative system.

The people in Morenci, however, never publicly challenged the policies of the US government, rarely if ever acknowledging the capitalist system as the root cause of US involvement in Vietnam or government collaboration in their own oppression as workers. In part, their silence related to the dominant political culture of the country and region, but equally as important, small-town people despised the antiwar movement as un-American. They fundamentally detested the atheistic, long-haired hippies of the large urban areas, believing themselves to be heirs to the real America, the type of people who had built the country and remained its backbone in the face of the Communist threat. They took great pride in their patriotism, refusing to publicly question President Johnson and his advisers and why and how they waged the war. That was the way things stood, and nothing would change even as conditions deteriorated after Stan's death.

The wounds for the King family never fully closed. Some of Stan's comrades reached out to them, and later, Penny told a reporter that she had been "awed by the sincerity and dedication" of the young men who had been her son's friends and who visited her after his death. "You know," she said, "when I asked them if they would return to Viet Nam, every one of them replied that they would definitely return if their services were needed." She also kept letters, including one from a Marine friend who talked about where Stan wanted to be buried, despite the fact he had never visited.[78]

Yet moving on proved hard, especially for Glenn, who had a nervous breakdown after Stan's death. Sam and Doug carried a huge burden, living in the shadow of a near-mythical brother whose absence left a hole in the family. The Kings kept Stan's clothes and toiletries in place for a couple of years, just like he had instructed. However, they returned his military outfits when they arrived. They were the wrong size to have been Stan's, and therefore, Penny sent them back so the military could pass them on to those who could use them.[79]

Stan's memory would live on for many years in Morenci, as would Bobby Dale's. And sadly, in the not-too-distant future the same would be true for other members of the Morenci Nine.

8

The Death Angel Returns

The signs of Christmas began to appear not long after Stan's death. Street decorations lined the Chase Creek section of Clifton, and storefronts and windows sported signs of the season. Advertisements for Christmas gifts filled the *Copper Era,* and children scoured catalogs in search of the perfect toy. Churches prepared services for people to celebrate the birth of Christ, and choirs planned special music for the occasion. Some holiday cheer filled the air as the big day approached and the weather cooled.

But at Christmastime in 1967, the smokestack lay dormant, signaling that the strike continued. Few in Morenci had money to celebrate the holiday, since most remained out of work. Only a limited number of households—those whose men had left for other cities—had income flowing in; most survived on savings and the small strike checks they received from the union. All around the mining camp, people worried about making ends meet, especially with credit at the company store dwindling. With no end in sight for the strike, the only things in abundance during this holiday season were fear and uncertainty.

The season was worse for some than for others. In the Draper and King households, one less stocking would be hung and one less chair would be needed at the Christmas table. Sadness shrouded family members and friends when the sense of loss gripped them. In other households, including those of the West and Cisneros families, worries abounded about sons nearing the ends of their tours in Vietnam, for they still lay in harm's way thousands of miles from home. Many others in Morenci, among them the Moncayo, Garcia, and Cranford families, had sons in uniform scattered across the globe, few able to enjoy the holiday with their loved ones. Some feared it might be a long time before they could once again celebrate Christmas together.

The Christmas season passed, and the strike continued, as did the war in Vietnam. As always, Americans followed news of the combat on television and read about it in the papers. They also watched the antiwar movement gaining steam, picking up support from mainstream leaders such as Martin Luther King, Jr., and Senator J. William Fulbright. Protestors from many different backgrounds, including former members of the military, took to the streets in major cities around the country to denounce the ongoing war.[1]

Nonetheless, some believed the optimistic reports of President Johnson and his advisers, hoping for success in the near future. The commander of the US troops in Vietnam, Gen. William Westmoreland, told reporters in November 1967: "We have reached an important point where the end begins to come into view. . . . Whereas in 1965 the enemy was winning, today he is certainly losing."[2] President Johnson visited South Vietnam right before Christmas and defiantly told troops at Cam Ranh Bay that they had ensured the United States "had come from the valleys and the depths of despondency to the heights and the cliffs, where we know now that the enemy can never win."[3] Public support remained in flux, but it rebounded slightly in response to the major public relations campaign conducted by the White House.[4]

Despite the assurances coming from Washington, many Americans continued to closely monitor the war, particularly as a massive battle began in January 1968 around the Marine base of Khe Sanh near the DMZ and the Laotian border. Nearly forty thousand North Vietnamese forces had massed around Khe Sanh, pouring thousands of artillery rounds onto the base. At the same time, they continually probed for weaknesses. Six thousand Marines and South Vietnamese Rangers defended the relatively small base, which could only be resupplied by air. Americans watched the battle unfold on television. US leaders, fearing a repetition of the French defeat at Dien Bien Phu, pounded the NVA with heavy bombing sorties and dispatched reinforcements who fought courageously to hold the base.[5]

While Americans remained fixated on Khe Sanh, the enemy prepared a surprise. In late January, all hell broke loose, shaking the confidence of large numbers of Americans and throwing into the line many of the young men from Morenci who had not served in Vietnam to that point. On January 30, the beginning of the Vietnamese New Year, Vietcong and NVA troops launched simultaneous attacks against American and ARVN forces throughout the country, hitting most of the provincial capitals and major American bases. Caught off guard, US and South Vietnamese troops scrambled to fend off the enemy.[6]

News of the fighting almost instantaneously reached the White House after VC sappers penetrated the outer walls of the US Embassy in Saigon, one of the most heavily fortified compounds in the country. President Johnson and his aides marveled at the scope of the attacks as the chairman of the Joint Chiefs of Staff (JCS), Gen. Earle Wheeler, characterized the offensive as "a very near thing." At a prayer breakfast not long thereafter, the president personally lamented the situation: "The nights are very long. The winds are very chill. Our spirits grow weary and restive as the springtime of man seems farther and farther away."[7]

For weeks after the attack, Americans watched the graphic television coverage of the offensive. The intense fighting in Saigon and Hue provided numerous images of US soldiers locked in a life-and-death struggle with the enemy. In Hue, the enemy seized the ancient Citadel, former home to Vietnamese emperors. Footage of Americans firing furiously from behind walls, many of them wounded and bandaged, reached stateside televisions. Pictures of dead bodies and burned-out buildings in Hue also flooded the airwaves. The images shocked the American public.[8]

They had an immediate impact. Despite being an administration stalwart for years in support of the war, distinguished newscaster Walter Cronkite now asked: "What the hell is going on? I thought we were winning the war." After he made a short trip to Vietnam, he told his viewers that it appeared "more certain than ever that the bloody experience of Vietnam is to end in a stalemate."[9] On hearing of this, President Johnson reportedly said, "If I've lost Cronkite, I've lost Middle America."[10]

Throughout February, American troops and their Vietnamese allies counterattacked and inflicted heavy casualties on the enemy, but they also took substantial losses, with more than five hundred men killed that month and thousands wounded, many seriously. The long, bloody battle in Hue, where the fighting destroyed more than 80 percent of the town and thousands died, continued, as did ferocious fighting around Khe Sanh. More pictures on television showed the graphic reality of the war. More important, a significant credibility gap developed between a large portion of Americans and the Johnson administration. By March 1968, the president's approval ratings for his handling of the war had plummeted, and the nation appeared more divided than ever over the increasingly unpopular war.[11]

The reports from Vietnam paralleled pessimistic news about the labor negotiations at home in Arizona. There, the stalemate extended past Christmas and into February, with neither side willing to compromise. Some union members groused about their leaders, but they refused to break ranks. On the other side, PD and the other copper companies pressured congressional supporters and allies in the media to highlight the damage being done by the union bosses to small businesses throughout the Southwest.

In response to multiple pressures, conservative political leaders in Arizona, among them former governor Paul Fannin, who replaced Barry Goldwater as US senator in 1965, launched a series of attacks on the unions.[12] Fannin took his case to the Johnson administration, charging that the situation threatened local economies and the national defense.[13] In a strongly worded letter to the president, he stressed, "You have the power to put the miners back to work under emergency provision of existing labor law (Taft-Hartley Act). You have the power to breathe economic life back into these communities. I appeal to you to use it."[14]

President Johnson resisted such appeals even as economic pressures mounted. Increased copper imports from Canada and Mexico upset trade balances, and the Defense Department reported higher costs for war materials. In January, Johnson appointed a three-person panel to make recommendations on how to break the impasse.[15] The panel failed, forcing the president to insert himself more fully into the dispute. When Republicans continued to press him to invoke Taft-Hartley, he resisted and told them that he wanted to do everything possible "before ordering men" back to work. "It is one thing to tell men to go to hell and another thing to make them go there," he responded.[16]

Finally, as both sides continued to dig in their heels, Johnson directly intervened. On March 1, day 231 of the strike, he sent a note to all the major players, requesting a meeting at the White House on Monday, March 4, at 4:00 p.m. "I am confident that in light of the urgency of the situation, all concerned will respond to my request in the interest of our nation," the president wrote. One name on the list of attendees was Robert Page, president of Phelps Dodge.[17]

Representatives from both sides honored the president's invitation. When they arrived at the White House that Monday afternoon, they witnessed Johnson demonstrating the traits that had made him an effective leader in the House and Senate. The imposing Texan sauntered in, towering above almost everyone in the room, and launched into a harangue about both sides needing to reach an agreement and to support the "men who fight for all of us half a world away in Vietnam." A Phelps Dodge representative observed, "We were . . . jawboned by the president. He instructed us to begin intensive negotiations in the Executive Office Building where he could keep an eye on us."[18]

The ploy worked, and within a couple of weeks, the *Copper Era* announced in big letters at the top of the front page, "THE COPPER STRIKE IS OVER!" The unions won wage and pension increases, but they had to compromise on companywide contracts and common contract expiration dates. Still, a reporter for the *Copper Era* acknowledged, "on the whole, the members seemed more than pleased with the results, an understatement would be to say the men will be more than glad to see the stack smoking again."[19]

A genuine joy swept the camp as miners and smelter workers returned to work. But it had been a long eight months. Debts had accumulated and families had been separated as men went off in search of work. Even the young soldiers fighting in Vietnam had sent their money home to help. Everyone knew that living in a mining camp entailed enduring the occasional strike, but this one had been longer than normal and more disruptive. It would take years to recover the lost wages, but at least things looked much brighter on the horizon for the majority of the people in Morenci.

Even with the jubilation on the home front, each night people in Morenci watched newscasts that continued to show the heavy fighting in Vietnam in the aftermath of Tet. The parents in Morenci with sons in Southeast Asia held their breaths as the number of American dead kept climbing. Pictures of flag-draped coffins and military funerals became common images on television and in newspapers and magazines. Wounded soldiers, many missing limbs or significantly disfigured, also appeared regularly in the nightly news and on the streets. Even living in isolated southeast Arizona could not shield people from the realities of the expanding war, something the Draper and King families already understood all too well.

The intense fighting directly affected the members of the Morenci Nine who had not yet deployed to Vietnam. In the immediate aftermath of the Tet Offensive, the number of American troops there swelled to more than five hundred and fifty thousand. Those who had not served in country were the first to be mobilized to meet the new manpower requirements, and within a short period, the Marines sent Van, Robert, and Mike into battle. Even Larry, who had shipped home in January after completing his tour, volunteered to return. A great deal of uncertainty gripped the group and the community as many others from Morenci and Clifton headed into harm's way in spring 1968.

As the four members of the Morenci Nine wrapped up their duties in Hawaii and California and headed to Vietnam, the war claimed a political casualty, one that left many in the country wondering about the nation's future. On March 31, President Johnson went on television and shocked Americans by announcing that the country needed more than "partisan divisions that are developing in this political year." "Accordingly," he said, "I shall not seek, and I will not accept, the nomination of my Party for another term as your President." Earlier in the speech, Johnson acknowledged his goal to "deescalate the conflict" in Vietnam by "substantially reducing—the present level of hostilities."[20]

The president kept his promise and dropped out of the race for the Democratic presidential nomination. He also sought to negotiate with the enemy to reduce the hostilities and secure an honorable exit from Vietnam. Meanwhile, the Republican nominee for president, Richard Nixon, told audiences on the campaign trail that he had a secret plan to escape the quagmire in Vietnam. Yet nearly thirty-seven thousand more Americans would die there from early 1968 until the fall of Saigon in 1975, including more than sixteen thousand in 1968—a deadly year for many communities, including Morenci.

Van Whitmer's boot camp portrait. (Photo courtesy of the US Marine Corps.)

*   *   *

Van Whitmer was the first of the Morenci Nine directly affected by Tet. After boot camp, he headed to various garrison duties but repeatedly requested service in Vietnam.[21] Finally, the Marine Corps honored his wish, in response to Tet. Commanders needed fresh troops to fill the gaps caused by all the casualties and to meet the calls for additional troops by General Westmoreland. Van and many others who had not yet served in Vietnam headed overseas as the Marines launched a major counteroffensive against the enemy. Green troops, including Van, poured into Vietnam daily by plane and ship in early March.

Before shipping out, Van had returned home for a quick visit with his family, staying with them in their new home in Safford, where they had moved a short time after he left for the Marines. As he prepared to depart, he announced that he had increased his life insurance policy. His parents protested, telling him to hold on to his money. He simply responded, "Dad, I'm going to pay off this place for you."[22]

Van landed in Vietnam on March 1 in the Central Highlands in Thau Thien Province, the site of some of the heaviest fighting of Tet.

The NVA and VC continued to hold out in some sections of Hue, while their compatriots operated around the old royal capital. Lance Corporal Whitmer joined B Company of the First Battalion, Twenty-Seventh Marines, as a combat engineer.[23]

For six weeks, he trudged around the operating sector near Hue. The zone remained hotly contested by the enemy forces, who returned to relying primarily on ambushes and small engagements after Tet. Only a few days before his death, Van wrote home about the loss of his comrades and, according to his mother, "how he felt God had a purpose for him." On April 13, 1968, while on a patrol not far from Hue, he died at the hands of a skilled enemy marksman. The official Marine casualty report listed his death as the "result of gunshot wound to the head from hostile rifle fire."[24]

As had happened so many times before, the phone rang at the Phoenix office of the inspector and instructor for the Marine Reserve. Another report arrived from the Marine Casualty Section in Quantico, forwarding the name of Alfred Van Whitmer. Once more, an officer headed across the desert, this time going to Safford—one of the first occasions when the Marines visited the larger town lying to the southwest of Morenci with the grim account of a soldier killed in action. The officer located the home of the Whitmer family and shared the sad news about Van's death with his parents. For the third time in only nine months, a member of the Morenci Nine had fallen in combat in Vietnam.

Van left behind many family members, including his parents, one brother, and four sisters, as well as the relatives who traveled to Safford for the funeral, many from Southern California. During their time of sadness, his family received strong support from the LDS community in southeastern Arizona. People from throughout Greenlee County, among them many miner families from up the hill in Morenci, joined the Whitmers at the LDS ward meeting hall in Clifton, where just nine months before Bobby Dale had been eulogized.[25]

After the service, a caravan headed down to the Safford Union Cemetery for the burial on a small hill dotted with cottonwood trees, near the imposing Mount Graham where Van and others had hunted and fished in a forest teeming with deer and rivers overflowing with trout. In the evening, Mount Graham cast a large shadow that enveloped the cemetery and the community, which helped start the process of cooling down the valley floor on hot summer days. It was a beautiful resting spot, and not long after, Van would be joined there by his friend Larry.[26]

Barely twenty-one when he died, Van never aged another day in the minds of those who knew and loved him. An anonymous author summed up the feelings of many regarding Van and others from the Vietnam generation who died in combat: "War drew us from our homeland in the sunlit springtime of our youth. Those who did not come back alive remain in perpetual springtime—forever young—And a part of them is with us always."[27]

Morenci still mourned Van's death when Larry West died in combat on May 17. And only a few weeks later, a Marine officer appeared in town looking for the family of yet another member of the Morenci Nine. This time, he traveled over to New Town and the home of Robert Moncayo. The Marine delivered the news that Robert had been killed on June 18, 1968, just outside Khe Sanh, where a major battle between US forces and the NVA had raged for several months. Robert had been in country only nineteen days.[28]

His journey paralleled that of others in his group who had not shipped out immediately to Vietnam. After finishing his training, he ended up in Hawaii. There, his love of horses (his fellow Marines called him "Cowboy") landed him a job as horse wrangler and guide, typically working with the children and spouses of Marine officers who wanted to ride along the jungle trails and the picturesque Hawaiian beaches. He wrote one friend, "It's just beautiful down here in Hawaii. I know I'll have the best years of my life here." A picture showed him smiling while he sat astride a big black horse, riding along a beach with the surf breaking in the background. Clearly relaxed, he wore jeans, cowboy boots, and a white shirt with the sleeves rolled up.[29]

Robert's love affair with a "beautiful young lady" made his time in Hawaii even more special. In September 1967, he wrote about getting serious with the young woman, who came from a very affluent family. The couple spent a lot of time waterskiing, scuba diving, and going to beach parties as well as to the nightclubs in Honolulu. She took him to several concerts given by various performers, including Ray Charles and the Beach Boys. Several times, they headed out to sea on her family's yacht to host parties, including one for Robert right before he shipped out in May 1968. Life was good for him despite his homesickness and complaints about "inspections and parade." He lamented, "I just can't take all these silly things."[30]

Tet interrupted Robert's life in paradise. In the spring of 1968, he received orders for Vietnam and immediately returned home to pay a visit before heading into combat. He enjoyed seeing family and friends, yet a dark cloud hung over him. Along with most Americans, he watched the daily reports of the death and destruction in Vietnam, and several times, he expressed his fear of imminent death. "My son had a feeling," his mother remembered. "He told me he would not come back alive and not to cry when they brought his body back."[31] Another time, he sat down with his aunt, Elena Sánchez, and tried to put on a happy face, talking about how much he loved the songs "Jeremiah Was a Bullfrog" and "Tequila." At one point, she left the room but returned and found him sobbing. She asked him what was wrong, and he simply replied, "I'm scared," adding, "I am coming back in a box."[32]

Soon thereafter, Robert boarded a plane for Vietnam, arriving in late May 1968. He immediately transferred north to the heavy fighting around Khe Sanh, where he joined the Third Platoon, Mike Company, Third Marine Battalion, Fourth Marine Regiment. In one of his first letters, he talked

Robert Moncayo's boot camp portrait. (Photo courtesy of the US Marine Corps.)

about the "different and hard life . . . the climate is so hot & damp all times. The bush, jungle, is so thick and hard to maneuver." Beyond the environment, he mentioned that the enemy continued to pour in mortar fire at all hours of the night, making sleep nearly impossible. Terribly homesick, he begged for letters to help him pass the time.[33]

Throughout his short tenure in Vietnam, Robert described other hardships and dangers in his letters. In early June, he wrote his cousin, Fidela Archuleta, that "it's real sad and lonely life up here." He talked about being on Hill 471, just a few hundred yards outside the perimeter of the Khe Sanh base. "Right now, it's so peaceful and quiet, cause it's raining outside. But wait until tonight, if it stops raining." When the weather cleared, thousands of NVA troops surrounding the base would probe for weaknesses in order to launch attacks against the Marines. He complained about the terrible heat and humidity in "this damn place."[34]

Nonetheless, he reported learning to "put up with this mixed up life in the service." "It's Hell up here because they are playing the real game and for keeps," he wrote a friend; "it's an awful experience fighting this war and losing a lot of your fellowmen." Stoically, he observed, "That's life and all of us are doing our best to help these people win their freedom. We are paying high, with our lives, but it's for a great cause." Noting that it was "time for our C-ration chow" and then sleep, he concluded, "God bless and write to me as often as you can."[35]

On June 18, Robert's letters stopped. In response to NVA maneuvers, the Marines launched Operation Robin-South just outside Khe Sanh. Robert's unit found itself fighting against the Eighty-Eighth Regiment of the 308th Division of the NVA, which had attacked the Marines near Khe Sanh. In particular, the enemy sought to protect a major supply road that wound through the jungle, initially hidden from spotter planes. In response, Robert's unit moved into the area around Lang Hole near the concealed road, meeting vicious resistance and taking heavy casualties while inflicting significant damage on the enemy forces.[36]

During the night of June 18, the unit had settled into a position near the enemy road, carefully placing claymores and trip wires at strategic intervals. Into the night, the enemy probed the Marine perimeter, looking for weak points. Alerted, the Marines sent up additional flares into the sky to illuminate the area, and in anticipation of an enemy buildup, officers called for heavy artillery. All night, Robert and his colleagues waited tensely under the eerie glow of the flares, which outlined the shadows of the jungle that hid the enemy. By the time morning arrived, the NVA troops had crawled to within 30 feet of the Marine position, concentrating their efforts on the perimeter manned by K Company.[37]

At about 0610, bugles sounded and enemy officers blew whistles as hundreds of NVA soldiers jumped up and rushed headlong toward the American lines. With the support of 82mm mortars and rocket-propelled grenades (RPGs), they punched a hole in the perimeter and streamed in, often fighting in small groups among the Americans. As the NVA tore through the lines, Col. F. L. Bourne dispatched Robert's platoon to meet the enemy. The Marine commanders also called for air and artillery support, including helicopter gunships that relentlessly strafed the NVA. By 0945, the enemy soldiers broke off their attack, only to have three Douglas A-4E Skyhawks pound them with bombs and machine-gun fire as they retreated. By the end, they left behind more than 120 dead.[38]

The Americans also suffered significant losses, with 14 KIA, Robert among them, and 30 wounded in action (WIA). In the midst of the battle, punctuated at times by hand-to-hand combat, Robert had found himself fighting for his life. Somewhere along the way, an enemy soldier shot him in the back.[39] His fellow Marines retrieved his body, along with the bodies of the 13 other Americans who died in the encounter. Like Robert, a number of them hailed from small towns: Carey Johns of Oneonta, Alabama; Albert Taylor of Springville, California; Elwood Owens of Windsor, North Carolina; Ronald Fogard of Battle Lake, Minnesota; and Elmer Faulkner of Greenwood, Delaware.[40] The twenty-two-year-old Marine from Morenci, Arizona, became another casualty in the growing list of Americans dying in Vietnam, joining his four friends who had begun their journey only two years earlier.

Not long after the Marine officer visited Robert's mother to tell her about his death, a message arrived: "Jose Robert Moncayo sustained a gun shot in the body from hostile rifle fire while engaged in action with hostile forces. Remains will be prepared and shipped, accompanied by escort to a funeral home or National cemetery selected by relatives." Leonard Chonan, General, USMC, signed the telegram.[41]

Within a short time, Robert's body returned to Morenci, accompanied by Clive. Like his fallen friends, he initially lay at the Lewallen Funeral Home, where people traveled down the hill from Morenci to visit the

Clive and Robert celebrating graduation from boot camp, September 1966. (Photo courtesy of the Garcia family.)

body and joined others from Clifton to honor the popular Robert in the midst of the hot summer days. The evening before the burial, the family conducted a rosary, and many people attended the solemn service. Sadness gripped the family and his friends, including Clive, who watched over the body at the mortuary.[42]

On Tuesday, July 1, Robert's family and friends gathered at the Holy Cross Catholic Church in old Morenci. All around, there were signs of transformation, as the mine continued to consume the old town, swallowing huge chunks as it expanded. Soon, it would reach the church—but not this day. For many sitting in the pews on that sweltering day, this was the fifth funeral they had attended in ten months for members of the Morenci Nine. Relatives of the living and dead of the group joined Robert's mother and stepfather to honor him, including the Garcias, who watched Clive march to the front of the church in his dress-blue uniform. Many others from the community joined the Moncayos to once more pay tribute to a young man who had died in Vietnam. It had become too common of an experience, and no one could really explain why so many members of the Morenci group had died.[43]

The parish priests performed the Mass, highlighting Robert's service to his country and the sense of the loss caused by the death of such a fine young man. Afterward, the family and community proceeded to the Bunker Hill Cemetery, which sat in the shadow of the fuming smokestack of the smelter. They laid Robert's body into the red clay as the tears of mourners fell to the ground. The unlikely Marine had arrived home as he had feared: in a casket. Standing near the grave, Clive watched the caretakers lower the body into the earth. It was his first experience of personally burying a friend who had joined up with him almost exactly two years earlier. Little did he know that he would return to the same site in eighteen months.[44]

The collective grief that day capped a long three months that saw the loss of three young men from the Morenci Nine; now, five had died within just nine months. Other families in Morenci waited uneasily for the appearance of the military's death angels bearing horrible news, mirroring the experience of families in certain other small communities across the country, such as Beallsville, Ohio; Bardstown, Kentucky; and Empire, Alabama. The year had been a devastating one for the nation, one President Johnson would characterize as a year of "a continuous nightmare."[45] The families of the three Morenci Nine members who died in the first six months of 1968 clearly understood what a year of loss and anguish entailed.

9

Two Friends

Few people in the Morenci Nine had such a close connection as Mike Cranford and Larry West. The self-described kickers had been friends since elementary school, sharing a love of horses, cars, girls, beer, and hell-raising. They would climb through the red clay canyons south of Morenci on horseback or hike through the beautiful aspens and ponderosa pines in the forest north of town. In school, they drove teachers crazy with some of their antics, hanging out in the hallway together and at lunch when not in class. Mike loved joining Larry to work on his '62 Chevy pickup at the local Texaco station. They would ride around in it on the weekends, cruising through town or maybe heading off to shoot rabbits down in the canyons near York, often joined by Joe or others looking for ways to blow off steam. Larry and Mike were great friends and united by a destiny that would stretch halfway around the world into a small corner of South Vietnam by 1968.

In late December 1967, Larry had stood on the deck of the *General Gaffey* and said his good-byes to Leroy, Joe, and Bobby Dale. Like his friends, he walked down the gangplank and jumped in the back of a huge truck, in his case to join a security unit in the Third Marines stationed about 20 miles north of Da Nang. The happy-go-lucky and unassuming kicker from Morenci joined many young men from throughout the country who, like himself, had been sitting in a high school classroom less than nine months earlier dreaming of graduation and girls, not the war in Vietnam. Yet the Vietnamese jungle was their new reality.

Larry West's boot camp portrait. (Photo courtesy of the US Marine Corps.)

Larry found himself in a dangerous area, where he worked hard during the day loading sandbags to pile high on bunkers or digging trenches as the sun beat down on him, draining his energy. At other times, he found himself patrolling along the roads linking US bases or through villages dotting the routes. Though often monotonous, this duty could be hazardous. Within two weeks, he wrote his parents, "Well, I got my ass shot at today." As Larry and his comrades labored building a fortification, an enemy sniper opened up on them, pinning them down for over an hour. "I always wondered what it was like to be shot at," he wrote. "Scared the shit out of me!"[1]

The enemy kept up the pressure on Larry and his fellow Marines. For several evenings, some "old Vic" (a reference to the Vietcong) snuck up near the perimeter and threw rocks at the bunkers to aggravate the Americans. But one night while Larry and his colleagues slept, instead of a rock the "little bastard threw a gernade [*sic*]." The sergeant of the guard happened by just as it landed. Initially, he ignored it, believing another rock had fallen. Then he heard the fuse go off and tried to dive into a bunker, but shrapnel tore through both of his legs. From that point forward, Larry reported, every time he heard a rock hit while on guard duty, "I shot my ass off, so damn dark I could not see what I was shooting at but it was fun shooting anyway."[2]

The death and destruction that he witnessed affected Larry. Often, sniper fire came from a small village near the encampment, and on one occasion, a frustrated Marine returned the fire. In the morning, the commander sent out a patrol to assess the damage. Larry and his comrades found a sixty-year-old man blown away and a young boy hit in the kneecap. Larry helped retrieve the boy, carrying him to a medevac helicopter, and later recalled, "He was so scared I guess he thought we were carrying him off to kill him." His mother scurried along with the Marines and grabbed Larry's arm, "trying to make me turn lose [sic] of that stretcher, crying and screaming bloody murder." "I sure feel sorry for these people," he said, but he stressed that he would have fired also. He concluded that he now understood why the others had let him volunteer to join a patrol checking out the damage in the village that morning, but he added, "I ain't ever going on another one unless they make me."[3]

Such events left Larry angry, and he directed his resentment toward the enemy. He denounced the VC for using the people as shields, going into the villages and the huts and threatening to kill anyone who moved. He wrote his parents, "I just hope I see one of them little bastards because [he's] going to have so many damn holes in him there [sic] going to pick him up in pieces to bury him."[4]

Before long, Larry had an opportunity to exact some revenge—but with nearly dire consequences. His platoon had gone on a patrol, and while crossing a big rice paddy, all hell broke loose when the enemy opened up on the exposed Americans with two 50-caliber machine guns and small-arms fire from a tree line. Without cover, the Marines furiously ran through the water and up the embankments of the fields toward a village about 600 yards away. The enemy pursued the Marines, encircling them and pinning them down for nearly three hours while an officer called in air support and artillery and begged for reinforcements.[5]

The engagement left Larry and some of his comrades not only scared but furious. Several of their leaders had panicked, leaving behind a couple of men and the medic as they scrambled across the open terrain. When the Marines discovered their buddies were missing, they began yelling for them and sending up flares. The medic ultimately showed up and reported that one of the two missing men had died but the other had been injured and needed assistance. They prepared to go after their wounded comrade, but a sergeant ordered them to stand down and wait for reinforcements. Although they were irate, they obeyed. By the time they could move out, the Vietcong had killed the Marine and scattered.[6]

In a letter home, an enraged Larry reported that the sergeant who ordered the delay faced a possible court-martial, and officers charged another sergeant with cowardice in the face of the enemy. The latter had carried the grenade launcher that should have provided cover against the machine guns, but he froze and never fired a round. When the commanding officer questioned him on why he failed to fire, he responded that his weapon had malfunctioned. The incensed officer took the launcher from him and immediately shot three rounds, threw it down, and had him arrested on the spot. "I hope that they kill that chicken shit because one of those guys would still be alive," Larry wrote.[7]

The next day, the Marines went out searching for some payback. They tracked the VC and ultimately killed fifteen of them. During the fighting, Larry wrote, "I got 1 enemy dead in my record book." He saw a VC soldier running through a cane field, disappearing for a short time before reappearing on the other side. Larry waited, then squeezed his trigger and dropped the man, just like he would have shot a rabbit or deer back in Greenlee County. "I killed him then I just kept shooting him. Man, I went crazy. I was pissed off and scared. I guess I just lost my head," he stated. Afterward, his commander ordered him to the rear area to talk to a doctor. "I told him what happened, and he said he didn't want me to think they thought I was crazy, that they just had to confirm things like that or something."[8]

The fighting extracted a heavy toll from Larry in other ways as well. During his first tour, he told Mike and others about one incident that particularly enraged him. While out on a mission with the security team, his group made contact with the enemy. They took some casualties, so they called in a helicopter to take them out. As it landed, the enemy opened up with a ferocious broadside. Larry had begun loading a wounded comrade on the helicopter when its crew panicked, and one of them pushed his wounded friend out of the helicopter as it took off. Larry went ballistic, standing on the ground and pulling out his .45 and emptying the clip as the American ship escaped skyward.[9]

Upon returning from the mission, someone reported the incident. Officers called Larry in and after hearing his side of the story promptly demoted him and fined him more than $200, nearly two months' pay, taking $50 to $75 out of his paycheck until he had cleared the debt. As a result, he was usually broke after buying cigarettes and having a wild night out off base. When Mike asked him later if he had learned anything from the experience, Larry responded: "Yes sir, I learned a lesson. I will be carrying a M60 and I will shoot the mother fucker out of the air next time."[10]

Like many grunts, Larry found that his attitude toward the Vietnamese soured as his frustrations in combat swelled. He became increasingly antagonistic toward all Vietnamese, whether friend or foe, as did many other young Americans in Vietnam.[11] The process of dehumanizing the enemy had begun during boot camp, and Larry became even more distrustful of the Vietnamese once he arrived in country. He commented in one letter that the Vietnamese children "sure are cute, to get so ugly when they get older."[12] Another time, he wrote about buying a camera, commenting, "I'm waiting to come across a dead gook so I can get a picture of the turd."[13] When he had received a plum assignment of Vietnamese language learning school at Da Nang, he wrote, "Now I'll know what the hell these gooks are saying every time they open their mouth."[14]

Larry's prejudices were often evident when he found himself in direct contact with the Vietnamese. After a few months around Da Nang, he had moved north to Dong Ha and joined the Third Battalion of the Ninth Marine Regiment. Assigned to the headquarters battalion, he oversaw a half dozen Vietnamese workers, whom he described as "so damn stupid." It was a relatively easy duty, and he stressed, "I can kick the shit out of them if I want to."[15] Another time, he wrote, "Don't worry about them stupid VC workers. They're so damn scared of us everytime [sic] you point the rifle at them, they don't know whether to shit or fall down on their face." He also enjoyed making them clean out the "shitters" underneath the outhouses. "I been making them haul that shit around funny as hell, but if they don't do it they'd have a Marine doing it. That's a good job for them anyway."[16]

Besides his aggravations in dealing with the Vietnamese, Larry, like many Marines, grew frustrated with the way the political and military leaders waged the war. He complained in late May that the "damn war sure as hell ain't getting any better. I wish the hell they would bomb the shit out of Hanoi. I'm tired of the damn playing around of everybody we got." Ironically, he added, "Oh, well, 7 more months and I am getting the hell out of here, and then don't give a shit what happens."[17]

Larry fought in the north, not far from where Joe would land in June, in some of the most intense combat in the country. He wrote his parents that the enemy often bombarded the base with rockets and mortars: "Tell old Bob & Joe better be damned glad their [sic] down south, these turds up here are professional, they ain't farmers, they got their shit together on how to get to you." He reported that he had a new job humping around the radio and that, even though "them damn gooks look for that," his assignment was "pretty cool . . . cause you're the first one to know when something happens." He also noted that he went wherever the captain did, which "usually ain't where the action is too hot so its [sic] got some advantages."[18]

The heavy fighting along the DMZ continued, and Larry remarked, "Damn boy they sure been trying to get back at us." One day, the NVA pounded the base with 150 rockets, although he noted that only minor injuries occurred, including a major who broke his finger jumping inside a bunker.[19]

In late May, the Marines went on the offensive in Operation Hickory near Con Thien. Larry exclaimed, "Well, I heard some good news, they say that this operation we're on might end the war. Boy, we've been killing people by the thousands. I'm not lying either." He added, "I'm going out again tomorrow. . . . I hope so, damn gooks have just about had it." He also liked the fact that "they been buying us guys all the beer we can drink. Funny as hell everybody is in a good mood because we're killing so many of them little bastards."[20]

Numerous operations followed in the summer of 1967 around Con Thien as the Marines battled heavily armed NVA forces that relied on artillery support from across the border. Larry knew Joe was near, but they never had an opportunity to share some beers and talk about old times. Instead, Larry slogged through the mud, heat, and humidity, never knowing where the enemy might wait in ambush. It was a serious business that further changed the lighthearted teenager into a tough and cynical combat veteran. Other young Marines in Leatherneck Square experienced similar transformations throughout the brutal summer and fall of 1967.

Not everything proved deadly serious during Larry's tour, despite the setting. Like many grunts, he took several R & Rs to various places in South Vietnam and other parts of the region. The hell-raising kicker knew how to have a good time, lamenting that he spent $250—almost his entire savings—on one memorable trip. Still, he admitted, "I had that much fun." He told his parents to tell his younger sister, Bev, not to relay this information to his girlfriend, Lydia, who was "all pissed off about the last time I went. I am not going to tell her anymore, it won't hurt her if she don't [know] nothing about it."[21] He also received some time off to head to Da Nang to study Vietnamese, although he quickly grew tired of the duty because it seemed to make the days crawl by.[22]

Sometimes, even combat provided lighter moments. In late August, for instance, Larry reported, "Today when we got hit this guy came running out of the outhouse, with his pants down and tollet [sic] paper in one hand, yelling yippee loud as heck. He had to run about 50 yds to the trench. Funny as hell. Everybody about died laughing."[23] But such moments proved fleeting, as either boredom or sheer terror dominated the majority of his days, leading Larry to declare in August, "I've only got 4 months left in the damn place," adding, ironically enough, "I hope they don't send my butt back a second time."[24]

Despite being angry and tired through most of his tour, Larry continued performing his duties and completed his thirteen months about the same time that Leroy headed stateside. In early January 1968, like Joe and Leroy before him, he boarded a plane for the long ride home to the United States and his final stop in Morenci. In a matter of days, he left behind hot and damp South Vietnam for cold and dry southeastern Arizona in the middle of winter. It was quite a contrast. And now that he was home, he faced the challenge of adjusting to a world where people did not want to kill him at every turn—so different from the realities of his life over the past thirteen months.

* * *

From the outset, Larry had a very difficult time adjusting. Just like Joe, when he returned to Morenci he found himself feeling disconnected and out of place. Around him, people went on with their everyday lives, even in the midst of the strike. Many seemed oblivious to the fact that a war raged where people like Larry bled and died, as most Americans worried more about what car they drove or what would appear on television that night. His peers in particular could not understand what he had seen or done, especially those dealing with the stress of final exams or their careers. As another veteran observed, "We went to Vietnam as frightened, lonely young men. We came back, alone again, as immigrants to a new world. For the culture we had known dissolved while we were in Vietnam, and the culture of combat we lived in so intensely for a year made us aliens when we returned."[25]

The alienation continued to grow when Larry returned to Camp Pendleton after a couple of weeks of leave. Joe had hunkered down, determined not to do anything that would endanger his ability to stay stateside, but Larry by nature challenged authority and hated the spit-and-polish requirements of garrison duty. Like other combat veterans, he questioned many aspects of the military regimen. Why should he have to keep his uniform in perfect order, when in the field no one really cared as long as you performed your duties? Why did he have to take orders from some sergeant who had never been in combat? What was the purpose of training that did nothing to prepare you for the dangers of real fighting? To Larry and many others just returned from Vietnam, it was all just chicken-shit regulations and routines.[26]

For about six weeks, Larry struggled with being stateside. He finally lost it one day when he clashed with MPs during a jaunt off the base. As he sat in a bar in blue jeans and a shirt, a couple of MPs approached him. After a short discussion, they hauled him back to Camp Pendleton for failing to wear a belt, even though he was in civilian clothes. His friend Mike would later speculate that such actions indicated the Marines wanted to force Larry to return to Vietnam. Ultimately, Larry reached the point where he said, "Piss on state side. I am going back to Viet Nam."[27] The Marines would be willing to grant his wish, for by February 1968 at the height of Tet, they needed replacements for those already lost, especially men who had combat experience.

Other factors appeared to have contributed to Larry's disillusionment with stateside life. Mike reported that Larry had planned to propose to his girlfriend, Lydia Milligan, but that she "dumped his ass. Dear John shit, Lydia Milligan had fired him."[28] The refusal naturally affected his mood, and it clouded his belief in what the future held for him. In Vietnam, at least over the preceding year, he had developed a sense of purpose. Back home, he appeared rudderless. At any rate, in Vietnam, he understood the game and its rules.

Many people tried to dissuade Larry from signing up for a second tour. Ernest Milligan, his brother-in-law, remembered that during a trip to Apache Junction where Larry went to buy a new horse, "I told him that he already had done his duty, but Larry already had made up his mind." Ernest also recalled how Larry "was really the most easygoing guy in the world, just fun to be around. The war changed him a little bit. He seemed sort of lost."[29]

His mother also tried to convince him to stay in the States. She asked him, "Why, Larry, why go back? You've done your part." He responded, "Better me than someone else. I've had experience in fighting. I saw lots of boys die because they didn't know how to protect themselves."[30]

Larry was determined to go back, and nothing would stop him, even when doubts about his own mortality crept in. One night in Morenci before shipping out, he leaned up against a wall at the bowling alley. Coach Friedli approached him and observed that "his eyes [were] blank, his mind a thousand miles away." The coach began talking with him. As they finished their conversation, Larry extended his hand and gripped that of the coach, saying, "It was nice knowing you." The stunned coach simply replied, "What do you mean?" Larry nonchalantly responded, "There's no way. No way for me. I won't be back. I came close to it a number of times."[31]

Larry returned to Vietnam carrying with him the dark shadows of his premonitions. He arrived in country on February 19 and returned to the Da Nang perimeter to join the Third Battalion of the Twenty-Seventh Marines, India Company. As a lance corporal with combat experience, he found himself in the middle of some of the heaviest fighting of the war following the Tet Offensive. It was a dangerous time: the number of Americans dying skyrocketed in February and March 1968, producing some of the highest casualty figures of the conflict.

Almost immediately after getting back to Vietnam, Larry reunited with his best friend from home. One day, while walking across the base to lunch, he saw someone in the distance who looked strangely familiar, even in the midst of the sea of green uniforms. As he approached, Larry started yelling out, "Cranford! Cranford! Cranford, wait up!" Mike turned and scanned the crowd of soldiers before finally spotting his good friend. They hugged each other right there, in the middle of all the commotion of Marines scrambling to and from the mess hall. Larry had not even known Mike had arrived in country, and now they found themselves in the same battalion.[32]

It was like old times as Larry showed Mike around the base at Da Nang and its infamous suburb, Dog Patch, a conglomeration of cardboard shacks that housed makeshift bars and brothels that serviced the large base. Just like back in Morenci, they drank together and enjoyed talking about people and cars and how much they missed home. Over the next couple of months, they hung out often, meeting to drink and reminisce about the good old days of hunting in the northern forests or riding horses down by the corrals south of town.[33] Yet this time, they were not the young boys from Greenlee County without any cares other than graduating from high school. Rather, they were Marines engaged in a life-or-death struggle thousands of miles from home.

For nearly three months, LCpl. Larry West fought in the bloody aftermath of the Tet Offensive. Though bruised by the ferocious American and South Vietnamese counteroffensive, the NVA and VC continued to put pressure on the Americans, and casualties soared on both sides. US commanders furiously counterattacked, ensuring some successes after the initial shock of the enemy operation wore off. Fighting raged in the north around Khe Sanh, in the south around Saigon, and in traditional hot spots near Da Nang where Mike and Larry operated.

Sadly, Larry's premonition about not surviving his second tour came true. On May 17, 1968, India Company moved out with other companies from the Third Battalion of the Twenty-Seventh Marines in Operation Allen Brook. Their objective was the enemy stronghold on Go Noi Island, where intelligence reported that three enemy battalions operated. The "island" actually only existed during the monsoon season, when the swollen Ky Lam, Thu Bon, Ba Ren, and Chiem Son Rivers isolated the relatively flat land from Da Nang Province. In those conditions, Liberty Bridge was the major connection to Go Noi. Located about 15 miles south of Da Nang, the area had historically been dominated by the Vietcong and NVA, providing a safe sanctuary for operations against US and ARVN forces throughout the province. The enemy found that the dense hedges and the tunnels that linked hamlets were good positions from which to inflict punishment on the Americans when they sporadically launched operations throughout the war. The intensity of fighting there led the Americans to nickname the area Dodge City.[34]

In mid-May, India Company had saddled up and flown south toward Go Noi. Then, on May 17, after several days in the field, the men marched in a sweltering heat that reached nearly 120 degrees. Larry's company took the lead in an effort to make contact with the enemy as the officers held other units in reserve, ready to pounce. Just above Route 537, elements of the company came upon a dry riverbed shadowed by a dense wood line near the hamlet of Le Nam. The enemy waited in ambush as the Marines exited some tall grass. As the front group crossed the open ground, the NVA launched a devastating attack from its bunkers and trenches, peppering the advancing troops with heavy fire.[35]

Throughout the unbearable day, the enemy poured down rifle, machine-gun, and mortar fire on the beleaguered India Company. Other Marines desperately tried to reach it, but the terrain and heat stymied their relief efforts. After much delay, a helicopter assault team landed and forced the NVA from the field as the sun set. The heavy fighting claimed more than thirty-nine Marines, including fifteen from India Company. At some point, Larry fell from a gunshot, along with his commanding officer, Capt. Thomas Ralph of the small Texas town of Clifton; two platoon leaders; and Pvt. Robert Burke of the little hamlet of Monticello, Illinois, who posthumously won the Medal of Honor for bravely charging the enemy with his M-60 to protect his comrades.[36] Others who died with Larry were from small towns such as Oroville, California; Pagosa Springs, Colorado; Hanley Hills, Missouri; and Anita, Pennsylvania. In addition, fifty men from India Company suffered wounds on that terrible day, a devastating one for the unit and for many families across the United States.[37]

On May 23, a US government-issue car again made the drive over to Morenci from Phoenix. Anxious parents peered out the windows, breathing a sigh of relief when it passed them by. Of course, not everyone was so lucky. Larry's mother, Ethel, looked out and knew that the two Marines approaching her house likely bore bad news. Expecting the worst, she went into the bedroom and awakened her husband, Martin. They walked toward the front door, bracing themselves. They had already lost another son, Bobby, in an accident when Larry was fourteen, yet nothing could really prepare them for the announcement that came moments later: "We're here to inform you that your son, Larry West, has been killed."[38] As had happened three times in the past ten months for other families of the Morenci Nine, the West family experienced the numbness and despair of losing a loved one in Vietnam. The community joined them in their grieving as news of Larry's death spread quickly.

In Southern California, Joe also heard about Larry. He wanted to attend the services at home, but the Marines initially denied his request for leave. Ethel West, however, put in a special request to have Joe accompany Larry's body to Morenci. After a short period, the Marines relented. Joe met the casket in California and began the long trip by plane to Tucson and then by car for the 160-mile drive to Clifton. He stood by his friend's body at the Lewallen Funeral Home, where three friends had already preceded him, admitting that he felt numb the whole time and that he only went through the motions of the service before heading off to the gravesite in Safford. Joe later told an interviewer, "I lost a friend. I ask today, 'Why didn't he get a chance to grow up?' You always wonder what it would have been like to have him around."[39]

On June 7, 1968, the community once again gathered to remember a fallen hero, this time at the First Southern Baptist Church of Morenci. There, people extolled the sacrifice Larry made for his country. Many then joined the family for the trek over to Safford, where they laid Larry to rest next to his older brother. It was a long, hot, and sad day for the people of Morenci. The family, friends, and community mourned the loss of another young man, this one four months shy of his twentieth birthday. Many

Mike Cranford's boot camp portrait.
(Photo courtesy of the US Marine
Corps.)

began to raise questions about the cluster of deaths among the group of boys who had so faithfully marched off to defend their country against the Communists in Southeast Asia. They asked privately, Why so many dead? Why so many from Morenci? Unfortunately, the deaths among the Morenci Nine had not ended.

With Larry's death in mid-May, only one of the Morenci Nine, Mike Cranford, was in Vietnam, since Clive remained stateside awaiting his turn and Robert would not arrive in country until May 31. Of course, many other young men from Morenci were in the midst of the bloody fighting of Tet and its aftermath. The miners' kids, along with boys from the farms and factories, had continued to provide a steady supply of American soldiers in Vietnam. In this regard, the situation was no different in 1968 than in 1965, when large numbers of American combat troops started landing in Vietnam.

The road to Vietnam had been different for Mike than for his good friend Larry. Right after boot camp, he had separated from the group and headed off to train as a communications expert. During his leave after boot camp, he returned home to marry Joyce in the LDS temple in Thatcher before departing for more training in San Diego. After a short honeymoon, he started RTO School but midway through developed a severe case of strep throat and ended up in the Balboa Naval Hospital. He had to begin all over again after he recovered, and he got through the course the second time. At one point, he saw Larry and Joe, who wanted him to go with them to Tijuana, but the newlywed refused, knowing his bride would not approve. That was the last time he saw his two friends before they boarded the *General Gaffey*.[40]

After completing training, Mike was stationed at Camp Pendleton. Often living in a small apartment just off base with Joyce, he continued training through 1967 and into early 1968, rising to the rank of lance corporal. The often restless Mike endured the monotony of the schedule, knowing he had it good, as, more and more, the visual images of the expanding Vietnam War reached people via the media. Mike also had numerous reminders from letters from friends and also the returning veterans who increasingly populated Camp Pendleton. He really was in no hurry to head overseas.[41]

In early 1968, he found himself off the coast of California participating in maneuvers. Upon returning, he received a seventy-two-hour pass and joined Joyce. He had barely been home after enjoying a nice dinner when Mike heard someone pounding on the front door. The apartment manager had been alerted and began telling all the Marines in his complex to return to base. Mike got a ride back to Camp Pendleton, where he walked into the barracks and found field transport packs laid out and an MP standing by the door to prevent anyone from bolting. He and his fellow Marines had a sense of what was about to transpire, but they waited anxiously for confirmation. Officers soon appeared and told them that they would ship out the following day for Vietnam.[42]

The news sparked a flurry of activity. People scurried about in the barracks, packing their gear, and Mike ran to find a phone to call Joyce. He only had twenty cents and used it at the pay phone, telling her, "I am going to Vietnam, we are leaving in the morning. I gotta get hold of my dad to come and get you and get you back to Morenci." Next, he called his father collect at about 3:00 a.m. and told him, "Get your ass out here. I am going to Vietnam right now. Get Joyce moved home." Within twelve hours, his father arrived in San Diego, having driven through the desert at night to retrieve his daughter-in-law.[43]

The trip proved unnecessary for the moment. For several days, the Marines stayed in place, as everyone hurried up and waited. Restricted to base and bored, Mike and some comrades collected several hundred dollars and passed the cash through the fence to Joyce and his father, who went to town to buy beer, wine, whiskey, and whatever else they could find. The group partied long into the night, many of the young Marines getting stinking drunk. The next morning, Valentine's Day 1968, they moved over to El Toro and stood around in a large hangar.[44] All of a sudden, a special guest appeared—a towering Texan who mounted a hastily constructed stage. With Mike only a few feet away, President Johnson told the men how proud he was of them; as Mike later put it, the president told him "what a good son-of-bitch I was and what a great job I was doing."[45] It was a memorable send-off, for Mike and his friends soon boarded a large plane for the long trip to South Vietnam.

Within twenty-four hours, Mike arrived in the heat and humidity of Da Nang, starting the rite of passage already experienced by many of his friends. As the plane readied to land, the new contingent of Marines waited apprehensively in the belly of the aircraft. A burly first sergeant walked down the line issuing ammunition as they descended during a rocket attack.[46]

"Move, move!" they heard their commanders yelling as the ramp of the plane lowered when they touched ground and stopped taxiing. Explosions punctured the stifling air, sounding like thunder in a monsoon storm back in Greenlee County. The Marines scurried down the ramp with their packs and weapons, running toward the fence line and jumping into trenches. Breathing hard from the forced run to cover, Mike was, he later admitted, "so fucking scared. This was the first time I had ever been out of Arizona, other than to go to California for the service. I had never been anywhere or done anything. I was scared."[47]

He endured a long night on the airport perimeter, listening to planes take off and artillery firing in the distance. He had always been a cocky guy, a kicker who walked with a cowboy swagger, but that attitude dissipated as he found himself in a strange, foreign land thousands of miles from home and confronting an enemy intent on killing him. He looked for friendly faces, but none materialized. All around him were other replacements thrown together by a random selection process, most of them terrified and wanting to be anywhere but in Vietnam. This only enhanced the sense of isolation and confusion he felt.[48]

There was little time to adjust to the new environment. His unit in the Third Battalion of the Twenty-Seventh Marines headed immediately toward Hue, where the troops still battled the last remnants of the VC and NVA there. As they approached, Mike watched black smoke rise in the sky. Overhead, American helicopter gunships made strafing runs on suspected enemy positions in what had been a beautiful old capital, now razed by weeks of heavy fighting that was later immortalized in movies such as *Full Metal Jacket* (1987). He passed war-weary Marines marching by, burned-out buildings destroyed by artillery and bombs, and Vietnamese refugees clogging the road. Fear remained a constant companion, combined with uncertainty over how he would respond when his chance came to engage the enemy.[49]

His unit stayed only a little while around Hue before shipping off to a position in the lush and beautiful area surrounding the Marble Mountains where the enemy had been active for years. A short time in, Mike and his squad went on a night ambush, hoping to catch some unsuspecting enemies in their cross fire. A few veterans integrated with the mostly green FNGs. "I was sitting there," he remembered, "you know you were just totally terrified." Flares occasionally illuminated the area, and mortar rounds popped off as a few tracers flew by as well. Mike settled in for a long night.[50]

At one point during the night, he looked around and found that almost everyone had fallen asleep, exhausted from a full day of slogging along in search of Charlie. Suddenly, in the darkness he saw the silhouettes of five or six enemy troops approaching their position, carrying a large machine gun and RPGs. Petrified, he hesitated, wondering whether to wake up everyone. Instead, he responded by getting on the radio and calling in artillery, rationalizing, "I was a radio operator. I was trained. I had been to school for this. . . . I called it in." Within a short time, shells fell in the general vicinity of the enemy, startling everyone and also bringing an officer scampering over, demanding to know what had happened. Mike owned up to his action. The officer did not appreciate the initiative he had shown as Mike later noted, "I was in a shit load of trouble." His actions led to bad reports that pushed him far down in the rankings in his unit.[51]

Although Mike's early problems intensified his fears and frustrations, life improved when Larry found him in the sea of green at the base camp mess hall. All of a sudden, Mike had a tie to home, and it was his great friend at that. They hung out when possible, drinking and partying late into the night. Mike spent time reading and rereading Joyce's almost daily letters, which kept him updated regarding life back home, including the end of the strike. He integrated into his unit and became more comfortable with his job as his experience increased. It was still a combat zone thousands of miles from home, but like so many others, he adjusted and began focusing on the countdown to the day when he could return home at the end of his thirteen-month tour.[52]

Larry's death on May 17 shredded an intimate tie to home. Ironically, Mike had been scheduled to go out with Larry's unit to Go Noi Island. But as he boarded an amtrac, someone came running down the ranks screaming out several names. He called Mike's name and the names of friends from communication school, including Larry Shoot, Ron Leopold, and George Smith. The runner told them to disembark and jump into some trucks for transfer to the Seventh Marines. Mike never saw Larry again.[53]

While with the Seventh Marines and about three weeks after the transfer, he received a packet of letters from Joyce. He opened the first and learned that Larry had been killed on May 17 during a major operation. Shocked, Mike could not believe what he was reading. He later admitted, "To this day I have told her [Joyce] . . . he is not dead. I always expect to see him . . . but I know he is dead."[54]

Tears flowed often when he thought of Larry. The loss crushed him, much more so than that of Bobby Dale, Stan, or Van. He and Larry had been so close and shared many adventures over the years. The death had a profound, long-term effect on him. He had lost his best friend, whom he had seen only days before. It was hard to process for someone barely out of his teens. The pain of surviving while Larry died would haunt Mike for nearly forty years.[55]

* * *

Though devastated by Larry's death, Mike slogged along in his new outfit, Alpha Company of the First Battalion of the Seventh Marines. During his remaining eleven months in Vietnam, he came very close to joining his five dead friends on several occasions. In one instance, his group went out on an operation riding on top of a large, lumbering amtrac. Carrying his radio and a shotgun because he hated the M-16, Mike sat with his comrades as they traveled down a road surrounded by thick jungle. Suddenly, an RPG ripped into the amtrac, killing the two drivers, blowing off the top of the vehicle, and flinging those riding on top (including Mike) to the ground. Disoriented, Mike jumped up and began firing in the general direction of the enemy as he ran for cover in a ditch. Frantically, he loaded and reloaded the shotgun, shooting at anything that moved in the jungle, although he understood that its short range limited its effectiveness. Still, he felt better doing so. As the short firefight ended, he noticed that the barrel of the shotgun had been damaged beyond repair.[56]

Despite the casualties they took, Mike's unit moved forward toward a hill where the Marines had built a base. Engineers had constructed bunkers stacked high with sandbags and surrounded the encampment with barbed wire. All around, trenches and foxholes dotted the landscape as well as machine-gun and mortar emplacements. It was like a fort in the old West, one right in the middle of Apache territory. But Mike knew that these fortifications provided only limited cover and also invited an enemy response. He and his fellow Marines waited anxiously for an attack.[57]

As darkness fell, the enemy began probing the American lines. Mike stood by his lieutenant, who called in artillery and air strikes. During the heavy fighting that ensued, the young radio operator from Morenci found himself lifted out of his foxhole and slammed face first into the ground by an explosion. He slowly turned over while still holding his rifle and looked skyward toward a surreal night lit by flares and tracers. All around him, he could hear the sound of guns and mortars firing even as the loud blaring of enemy bugles and whistles pierced the battlefield. Eventually, he recovered his senses and survived the night. His unit inflicted heavy casualties on the relentless enemy but also sustained significant losses.[58]

Another type of enemy proved equally relentless—and also almost claimed his life. The heat and humidity wore on all the Americans but especially on those carrying heavy packs or machine guns. Lugging the radio took a toll on Mike. While humping through the bush, he found himself crawling up a hill with the 25-pound radio as well as his own pack and weapon. At some point, the unit took a break, and as Mike leaned back on his radio, he suddenly fell unconscious, the victim of heatstroke. Immediately, his officer called in a helicopter, which whisked him back to Da Nang.[59]

When he awoke the next day, Mike found himself lying in a huge rubber bed filled with ice and water. Barely awake, he heard the Patsy Cline song "Hillbilly Heaven" playing on Armed Forces Vietnam Radio. "I dreamed I was there in Hillbilly Heaven and St. Peter was calling off the rolls," he recalled. "It was Patsy Cline and all of the sudden, I can't remember the guy that sang this song that was playing. I am lying there and I am not awake but it is playing in my mind and I thought I died and went to heaven."[60]

Before long, a Navy attendant began shaking him and asking, "You all right, Marine? You didn't die and you ain't in heaven, you are still in Vietnam." Years later, Mike stated, "To this day I get upset whenever I hear that song." He soon returned to Hill 10, where he assumed light duties, all the while having to "drink water and all that kind of crap."[61]

As with many grunts in Vietnam, Mike grew harder and more callous toward the Vietnamese as his tour continued. He already despised the "gooks" for killing his friends, but the hatred intensified as he moved forward. In one case, while his unit escorted a convoy up Highway 1 a young Vietnamese boy stood in the road and stopped the trucks. A lieutenant approached the boy, who jumped up on a truck and released a grenade that killed them both. Then, the enemy launched a mortar attack that gave Mike his first and only wound of the war, as some shrapnel ripped through his hand, leaving a scar from his thumb to his index finger. Air support ultimately drove away the enemy.[62]

As a result of the attack and other interactions with the Vietnamese, Mike's attitudes changed. He recalled, "The people . . . when I first got there I felt sorry for them. The longer I was there, the harder I got. You could watch a little five-year-old baby walk up to you and the first lieutenant with a grenade [and the child] would turn it loose and hand it to him and kill him. . . . A ninety-year-old woman would do the same."

Just as Mike's tour extracted a heavy toll on him, it also had a dramatic effect on Joyce. As the only married couple among the Morenci Nine, the Cranfords had an extremely difficult time separating, since they had barely shared their first anniversary when the Marines whisked Mike off to Vietnam. Initially, Joyce returned to Morenci to stay with her family. Within a short time, however, she went again to San Clemente, wanting to "be back where she last saw him." She regained her job at a factory making components for Motorola, each day rising early, making the bed, and cleaning up the apartment. She hoped that the routine would make the time pass faster.[63]

Throughout Mike's tour, Joyce battled loneliness and heartache. She had some advantages in San Clemente because Joe and Gina lived nearby, and she had other friends as well, including Mike and Rita Gibson. Rita and Gina joined Joyce at the beach to smoke and hang out under the California sun, often watching the beautiful sunsets to the west where she knew Mike fought thousands of miles away. It was so hard waiting, and like so many Americans at the time, Joyce watched or listened to the news that highlighted the staggering losses of young soldiers in Vietnam. She was keenly worried about her husband, understanding fully that five of his friends had already died in Southeast Asia.[64]

For fourteen months and nine days, she awaited Mike's return, writing him almost daily and treasuring his infrequent letters. One day toward the end of his tour, she decided to sleep in rather than jumping up and starting her daily routine as usual. Of course, that was the day that Mike showed up at the front door. They embraced, so happy to see each other for the first time in so many months. He had survived and now rejoined his high school sweetheart.[65]

Mike and Joyce wasted no time in enjoying the leave that he had received upon finishing his tour. They jumped on a plane to Las Vegas to pick up a car, a '69 Chevelle. An ultimate muscle car, the two-door coupe fit Mike's personality well, looking remarkably similar to the Dodge Charger that later became famous in the television show *Dukes of Hazzard*. After a short stay in Sin City, Mike and Joyce sped across the desert to San Clemente, where they gathered some belongings and then headed for Morenci to celebrate his return home. That he had made it through was no small feat, given when he arrived in Vietnam and the nature of his duty there.[66]

After two weeks at home, Mike and Joyce drove back to Southern California so he could complete his service. By the summer of 1969, the

Marines had begun withdrawing from Vietnam in large numbers. Never one to consider a career in the military, Mike gladly accepted an early discharge when offered it.

As he left Camp Pendleton for the last time in his Chevelle, the head-strong Mike flipped the bird to the Marines standing guard at the gate. Free at last and heading home, he had ended a long and challenging chapter in his life. Unfortunately for him, that episode would be a constant and central source of pain and anguish throughout his life, a defining moment for a young man that shaped the rest of his days.

Joe and Leroy also had accepted discharges. Joe headed to Apache Junction with Gina to work, and Leroy moved home to labor in the mine. With five of the Morenci Nine buried and three out of the service, only Clive Garcia remained in the Marines. Thus far, he had avoided Vietnam, although not by choice. At a point when the Marines began to curtail activities in Vietnam, they would finally honor his request and send him overseas. With a 55 percent death rate among the Nine, the odds seemed to favor his chances of joining his three discharged friends. But only time would tell.

10

Last Man There

In the Pacific Ocean, scenic landscapes—the stuff of postcards—abounded, but few surpassed the beauty of the Cocos, a 100-acre island located a mile off the southern coast of Guam and only a short ferry ride from its city of Merizo. The lush island, with a white-sand beach and crystal-clear, nearly emerald water, evoked visions of what most people thought of as a tropical Pacific paradise. White beach houses dotted the island, and there were stretches of green grass among the palm trees as well as a small wharf for the ferries and sailboats. People flocked over from the big island to enjoy the water sports at the Cocos, and some searched for the silver treasures of the *Neustra Senora del Pilar de Zaragosa y Santiago*, a ship that sank somewhere near Guam during a voyage from Manila to Acapulco in 1690.

In August 1967, Clive Garcia's gunny (gunnery sergeant) called him into his office. His skin further darkened by the Pacific sun, Clive had lost weight after several weeks in the jungle on maneuvers. On entering the office, he stood at attention, his broad shoulders and thick neck hoisting his head high as he looked at his superior, not knowing what the veteran had in store for him. Had he done something wrong? Had someone reported an incident? A young Marine corporal always worried.

"At ease," the gunny told Clive, who relaxed a little but was prepared for a broadside for some as-yet-unknown transgression. But instead, the senior Marine launched into a discussion of Clive's exemplary performance, particularly in the field and on the rifle range. After more praise and congratulations, the gunny asked Clive, "How would you like two weeks of duty on the Cocos?" Every Marine on Guam knew about the island paradise, and without thinking, the boy from arid Arizona

Clive Garcia, Jr.'s, boot camp portrait. (Photo courtesy of the US Marine Corps.)

responded, "Yes, sir." Clive must have walked out of the office with an extra bounce in his step and a smile on his face.

The next day, he packed a few things and headed down to Merizo to jump on the ferry for the short hop over to the small island. As the ship plowed through the relatively calm waters, Clive congregated with civilians and military personnel heading over to take advantage of the beaches and wonderful snorkeling and scuba diving. He followed everyone down the gangplank and headed to the Marine quarters, where he settled in.

The Marine recruiter back in his hometown, Sergeant Peterson, had promised the Morenci boys the opportunity to visit the most beautiful places on earth, and in this case, he had not lied. For two weeks, Clive would enjoy the leisurely duty of heading up a nine-person crew responsible for generators and boats on the Cocos. A typical day started with him sleeping in. He melted into the soft mattress and covered himself with the linen sheets, the sound of the ocean waves striking the beach in the distance nearly drowned out by the oscillating fan blowing a cool breeze on him as he lay in bed. What a contrast this was to the rigors of jungle training, when he slept on hard ground and had only a poncho for shelter.

Instead of immediately jumping up and preparing his quarters when he awoke, Clive slowly rose and slipped on a T-shirt, shorts, and sandals. He took his time making his bed and then washing up. Finally, he headed to breakfast, a hearty meal of real eggs, bacon, and toast, not the prepackaged food he had survived on during the last two weeks on maneuvers. There was no running around to do, no salutes to give. All that lay ahead was a lazy day with few responsibilities other than making sure the Marines and their families enjoyed their time on the beach.

During the day, water sports provided the greatest diversion. Barefoot, Clive ran down to the ocean and jumped into the warm water. Unlike his time in the bush with no showers, he constantly washed off the sand that accumulated from lounging around on the pristine white beach.[1]

Snorkeling was another pleasurable pursuit. It was strangely quiet underwater, absent the sounds of guns firing or Marines yelling and cursing. The waters teemed with ocean life and beautiful colors—an alien world for the young man from the Arizona desert. Only the sudden appearance of a shark from time to time disturbed the tranquility, a dramatic contrast to his life since entering boot camp.[2]

When tired of the water, Clive sailed a 15-foot sailboat around the island, often accompanied by one or more of the beautiful young women who flocked over from Guam for sun and fun. When he stretched out on the sand or lay in a hammock, the ocean serenaded him.[3]

Even when on duty, Clive enjoyed his time on the Cocos. In one letter home, he exclaimed, "This is the life pops." On duty "guarding" the island's magazine, he really had nothing to do other than write letters. And while doing so, he sat next to a case of beer that he occasionally tapped as he munched on potato chips and other goodies. "Every once in a while I'll go kick the juke box," he added, "and the lights go on so I play the juke box all night long and not even pay."[4]

Yet even in the midst of paradise, Clive longed for something more. At times, he looked westward while sitting on the beach, knowing that off in the distance, his buddies in Vietnam fought in the widely expanding war. He thought about Bobby Dale, Leroy, Joe, and Larry as well as friends from his time in Guam. Sitting in the surf watching the sun set while listening to the waves crash against the shore, he could almost see their faces. Deep down, he could not help but wonder when his chance to fight would come. When would he be able to prove himself and do his part?

When would he fulfill his destiny as a warrior? Would the war end before he had his chance?[5]

The two weeks on the island passed quickly. When he departed at the end of the first week of September, he wrote, "I hate leaving this small island. . . . But all good things come to an end before you even secure a beach head hold on them. I guess that's the way my life an' my world will always be."[6] It was a prescient statement.

Of all the Morenci Nine, Clive most wanted to serve in Vietnam and appeared the likeliest of the group to become a career Marine. In fact, Leroy always thought Clive might become the commandant of the corps. However, during the bus ride back to base after the short leave to Morenci in November 1966, Clive knew that he would have to wait for his chance to go to Vietnam. Sitting on the vehicle as it edged its way across the southwestern desert, he looked out the window on the barren landscape, which further depressed him. He longed for the lush green jungles of Vietnam where he could prove himself. He heard his friends talking, knowing that Bobby Dale, Leroy, Joe, and Larry had received their orders for Vietnam. But even in his funk, Clive noticed that everyone sounded much more subdued than when they had made the same bus trip only a few months earlier.

Once back at Camp Pendleton, Clive prepared for his first billet. Most Marines would have been ecstatic at the thought of garrison duty in Hawaii, but all he could think about was that he would not walk up the gangplank of the *General Gaffey* with his four friends. He sulked around, seeing other Marines preparing for war. Bitterly, under his breath, he cursed the Marine Corps for not choosing him to go into combat. Why not him? He was a model warrior, fit and aggressive. Still a teenager, Clive wanted the chance to fight and win glory. He did not understand what some Marines who had already been there knew: combat rarely corresponded with the romantic visions of the movies and novels.

Unlike the three-week, bargain-basement cruise his friends endured on their voyage to Vietnam, Clive would travel to Hawaii by plane. His aircraft, unlike their ship, lacked the putrid smells of vomit and overflowing heads and the anxiety of people nearing combat. Instead, Clive settled into a comfortable seat, his broad shoulders spilling over into his neighbor's space, and a pretty flight attendant came by and asked him what meal he wanted. As he scarfed his food down, he thought about his mother's wonderful tortillas and beans, which he had just enjoyed during his short leave at home. Gazing out the window, he looked down on the blue Pacific Ocean, enjoying it from a far different perspectives than his friends had on the *General Gaffey*. Still, he would have traded places with them in a heartbeat.[7]

When Clive deplaned in Hawaii, the only thing missing was a group of beautiful girls handing out leis, something reserved for the tourists, not Marines. He bounded down the stairs, picked up his gear, and headed off to jump in a truck bound for the base. For the first time in his life, he looked around at mountains covered in green foliage, a lushness that contrasted sharply with the arid landscape around Morenci. The humidity hanging in the air was so unlike the dry atmosphere of home. To most people, this was truly paradise.

But Clive hated Hawaii, especially when homesickness set in. No longer having his family and friends around, he lamented, "Mom & Dad I miss everyone so very, very much I feel like a little hog lost in the woods." More important, he wanted combat like his four friends in Vietnam, not continued training. Exasperated, he complained about being sent "just to rott [sic] in this place. I'm so very angry and disappointed. Here I'm throwing my life away. I'm a soldier a pro fighter."[8]

Christmas came and went, and within two months, Clive was on the move again but not to Vietnam as he had hoped. Instead, he landed duty as an MP on Guam in February 1967. "I'll be getting to Viet-Nam when Leroy, Joe, & Bob Dell [sic] & Larry will be coming home," he grumbled when he informed his brother of his next assignment.[9] However, in many ways, Guam proved a good fit for Clive, despite the fact that Vietnam, though so close geographically, remained so far away.

Initially, Clive found it hard to concentrate on the positive aspects of his new assignment, grousing to his brother that "Guam isn't much of a place, to tell you the truth there's more to be done or to see in a junkyard." He also complained about not having friends and that the local girls only seemed intent on chasing the Marines for their money and luxuries. Cash was tight in the early stages, as he needed to buy additional uniforms and other clothes, so much so that he reported, "I don't even have 15 cents for a coke or a beer for the free movies . . . let alone for smokes."[10]

Building on his success in boot camp and AIT, he continued to impress his commanders. Shortly after arriving, he set a company record on the rifle range with his M-14. He was in his element with the rifle; whether he fired while sitting, standing, or lying prone mattered little. Since he was old enough to remember, he had been a hunter. At the range, he could envision lining up a deer or rabbit in the sight just like he did back home, squeezing the trigger, and sending the projectile flying toward the target. For his exploits, he won $39 from the colonel. He promptly took the money and bought beer for others in his company. He noted that almost everyone got drunk; however, he himself avoided getting falling-down drunk that night. Still, he admitted, "Im' [sic] no saint and at best once every 2 or 3 months I get pretty stinky mainly because of the pressure."[11]

During his duty on Guam, he found his way into the field for additional jungle training, often for weeks at a time. At one point, he reported having a thick beard and long hair and smelling horrible from his days in the bush. His complexion darkened from the sun, to the point where he said he looked "like some kind of black man with hair" on his face. At the same time, he lamented, "*I only wish it was for real and I was doing the job I long to have.*"[12]

Though sometimes preoccupied with the death of his friends, including Bobby Dale and his island friend, Todd, who "got blowed away by 50 caliber," Clive had duties that helped take his mind off such tragedies.[13] His work as an MP often provided challenges. In August 1967, he complained bitterly about all the race riots sweeping the base, lamenting the fact that everyone appeared to want to follow the examples being set back home.[14]

In another case, he dealt with a recalcitrant Marine named Williams who received extra punishment duty from a staff sergeant. Accordingly, Clive constructed some "shit" detail for him. "Follow me," he ordered Williams. The Marine refused and responded, "Fuck off!" Clive loudly repeated the order, "Follow me!" Suddenly, the wiry Williams spun around and smashed his fist into Clive's face. Momentarily stunned, Clive responded instinctively, his legendary temper exploding in full force. He grabbed Williams's shirt and then "[let] fly a couple of 190 lbs. worth of fists." The fusillade subsided when Clive literally picked Williams off the ground and carried him like a sack of potatoes to the brig, where he served ten days for striking an NCO and refusing to obey a direct order.[15]

Clive standing in front of his squad at the base on Guam. (Photo courtesy of the Garcia family.)

Not all of Clive's duties required him to use his training as an MP, but hand-to-hand combat training sometimes did come in handy. Though he had originally hesitated to date local women, Clive ultimately decided to play the field. At one point, despite claiming to be an ugly jarhead himself, he crowed about dating "the cream of the crop."[16] One in particular caught his eye, a young woman named Vicky. When she returned stateside, he wrote to his folks that he was glad she had gone, "since I was really getting all worked up over her." He concluded that he did not want to lose his freedom, as he figured that "the Corps is all you really need any way."[17]

Even with his amorous pursuits, Clive remained extremely homesick. Isolated partly by his rank, which he obtained at an early age, and probably due to his ethnicity, he complained often of feeling lonely. Midway through his tour on Guam and on the anniversary of his departure from Morenci, he sat down and listed his friends who had been transferred or killed, including Yack, P. J., Hunt, and Simmons. In a letter home, he declared, "I'll never make a friend again. It hurts to [sic] much when you have to say good bye."[18] Though he eventually did make new friends, he always remained leery of creating bonds that were too deep.

Despite the personal struggles, Clive continued to excel as a Marine, receiving a promotion to lance corporal only ten months after joining. As a reward, he received special recognition when his commanders selected him to serve as a member of the USMC Presidential Honor Platoon Guard when President Johnson visited Guam in March 1967.[19] Clive guarded the president during his stay on Guam, only leaving him when he entered a building where special Marine security guards waited. He and others marveled at the size of the tall Texan and most likely stared at his large, floppy ears. Undoubtedly, the president took some pride in seeing a tough-looking Mexican American among his escorts, remembering his days in south Texas when he taught at a predominantly Mexican American school. The hours on this guard duty were long, "but it's an honor to be chosen," Clive proudly reported to his parents.[20]

Being a member of the president's special honor guard was a highlight of Clive's tour on Guam, which ended soon after. As his time wound down, he reflected on his frustrations and anger. In April, he wrote that when he attended his friend Mike's wedding, for the first time in a long while he "felt human and not like an animal." He acknowledged that he felt distant from others and admitted to forgetting how to act well in company. "But I hope I never . . . feel this way again. When you forget how to be happy its [sic] like beig [sic] dead."[21]

The problem centered on his "hatred" for the entire world and the situation that had taken away his good friends, including Bobby Dale and Stan. Lamenting their loss, he said, "I'll never really understand why it had to be them the better men that died," but he promised that he would stop fighting everyone who did not wear Marine green, try to live his life to the fullest, and remember that an eternal plan existed for him and his friends.[22]

Finally, in June 1968, Clive boarded a plane for the long flight from Guam to Camp Pendleton. Upon arriving stateside, the colder Southern California climate affected his tropically thinned blood, so much so that he admitted to needing to learn to wear Skivvies again. He transferred to the Fifth Marines, Fifth Recon, reporting, "Let me tell you there [sic] guys should all be in a nut house. The're [sic] all crazy. . . . I fit in perfectly." He drew the unit emblem for his parents, a skull with knives crossed behind it; to the left was written SILENT, on the top SWIFT, and on the right DEADLY.[23]

Clive enjoyed the new pace and the challenges he faced, writing that he loved changing from garrison duty to the roughest and toughest outfit within the Marine Corps. "It feels good to feel like a man again," he said. Days were long, full of time in the classroom, doing intense physical training, and learning advanced fighting techniques and tactics. Still, he had time to eat three squares a day and get enough sleep, all the while enjoying the beautiful Southern California weather. The new duty also allowed him to reconnect with several comrades from training and Guam. All of this heartened him, and his attitude improved dramatically; the morose feelings subsided in the California sunshine.[24]

Although the training intensified, Clive enjoyed it. He loved Southern California, telling his family that he felt so much better not being boxed in on a small island surrounded by the ocean. Nonetheless, he still spent a lot of time in the water, noting, "Of the 13 days of [sic] been here I've spent 10 days in the water." One day, he found himself in a speedboat that took his group out 3 miles and dropped them off to swim back. Floating in the ocean, the shoreline looking like it was a thousand miles away, he thought to himself that he was about to drown or die of hypothermia, but he started swimming and ultimately arrived back on dry land. They also worked off submarines and speedboats, leading him to brag that one day he would become "either . . . a perfect frogman or one heck of a cold big fish." He talked about his hopes to make it to jump school and about the future and emphasized how much he loved his career choice. "Its [sic] rough and the rougher it gets the more I like it."[25]

A sad event interrupted Clive's training. In mid-June, he received orders to depart camp. His unenviable task, one of his most difficult ever, was to escort the body of his friend Robert Moncayo back to Morenci for burial. Upon arriving in a huge warehouse, he found others gathered to escort the many bodies there to their final resting places, spread throughout the country—from small towns such as Viborg, South Dakota, and Amburgey, Kentucky, to huge cities such as Chicago.[26] Young men from all over Arizona, including Superior, Ajo, Tumacocori, Window Rock, and Tonalea, had passed this way in that deadly month of June 1968.[27]

In the large, imposing warehouse, everyone quietly stood near the government-issue steel caskets loaded with the bodies of friends and comrades. Clive looked down on the closed casket next to him, knowing that inside lay one of his buddies, the fifth one of the original nine from Morenci. There would be no parties at the local hall as they had originally planned but a burial in the shadow of the smokestack. Anger mixed with sadness for Clive that day. His blood boiled with hatred for those who had killed his friend, but his mood swung to sadness when he thought about Robert's family members and how they must be dealing with his loss. It would prove an extremely difficult week.[28]

Clive flew with the body to Phoenix, where they transferred to a hearse for the four-hour drive to Clifton and the mortuary. The flight and the long car ride gave him more time to think about his own mortality and his continued frustrations with being the only one of the nine not to have made it to the fighting in Vietnam. He seethed at the idea he had not done his part yet, especially in the face of the earlier deaths of Van and Larry. As they made the trip up Highway 666 toward Clifton, he relaxed a bit at seeing the rustic red rock beauty of Greenlee County, but he never lost sight of the fact that in the back of the vehicle lay his friend.

Once home, he took many turns standing beside Robert as he lay in the mortuary on Chase Creek. People stopped by to view the body, particularly during shift changes at the mine. He greeted many old friends who trekked down the hill to Clifton, but the death dampened the pleasure that came with his short stay at home and the home-cooked meals prepared by his mother. He walked along the meandering creek cutting through the small town during breaks from guarding his friend's body, having a lot of time to think. He paused in the shade of the large trees overhanging the creek, caught up in thoughts of revenge. Why Robert, one of the nicest people Clive had ever known? Why not him? Why did God make such choices? When would he get his chance to fight?

Finally, on a hot day in late June, Clive awoke and prepared to put on his dress-blue uniform. Meticulously, he pressed his pants and wiped off any lint, and then he dressed himself in the small bedroom in the company house on Gila Street. As he finished combing his hair, he stared in the mirror at a young man who had aged quite a bit in the nearly two years since he took the bus to boot camp. He had written earlier, "I feel as though I've lived a century."[29] And yet he had not followed his friends into combat, something that Robert's death reminded him of on a deep personal level.

He took the short ride up the highway to the Holy Cross Catholic Church, on the hill overlooking central Morenci. The heat of the Arizona summer caused everyone to sweat profusely as the priest eulogized Robert. But that day, it was tears more than sweat that darkened the red clay after the funeral procession made its way down toward the Bunker Hill Cemetery. In the shadow of the smokestack that loomed to the north and below Tent City, a large group gathered at the gravesite, where a hole had been dug; a green artificial turf had been laid around the hole, standing out among the rocks and red clay ground. Little did Clive know on that summer day at the cemetery that he would return to almost the exact spot only eighteen months later.

The ceremony was an especially sobering experience for Clive. He had encountered loss before, beginning with Bobby Dale, Stan, Van, and Larry and continuing with the deaths of several friends from boot camp and Guam. But this death hit closest to home, as he actually experienced the final act of burial. He looked down as they finished lowering Robert's casket into the red clay. The government-issue gray coffin contained the body of his friend of many years, a fellow Mexican American whose family toiled in the mines and lived in the segregated camp just like his. The coffin reminded him that he would never see his comrade again; now, only the memories of a thousand small things from school, church, and special events remained. It was painful on so many levels for the young Marine—and worse still for Robert's family.

After the funeral, Clive spent some time with his own family before reporting back to California. His folks took photos of him in his dress blues standing next to his mother in the front yard of their home on Gila Street. Julia looked so sad as Clive put his arm around her. On the back of one photo, with the towering smelter smokestack in the background, Clive wrote his mother, "Your eyes are swollen, you've cried too much mama. Life itself really isn't that bad. We only have a few sad moments. And all we can do is accept and live with reality."[30]

Such words hardly comforted Julia. She had always worried about her son, like any mother would, and the death of Robert exacerbated her fears. Even before Clive had returned home with Robert's body, she had written him a long and heartfelt letter expressing her anguish. She remembered

Clive and Julia in front of their home on Gila Street during Clive's visit to accompany the body of Robert Moncayo, June 1968. (Photo courtesy of the Garcia family.)

knowing the exact date—June 23—when Robert's mother had received news of her son's death, right after Mass. She wrote Clive about how much she loved Robert and how he always visited them when he had leave. "I'm always making tortillas when I get such news & therefore they come out a little saltier," she told her son, adding, "Tears are so hard to hold back."[31]

In relation to her own son, she expressed her insecurities about his military service, especially as she, along with many Americans, watched news of the incredible death and destruction in Vietnam in 1968. She admitted that she prayed hard that he never had to go to Vietnam, apologizing for her selfishness, saying, "I want you to face facts. Out of the family of 9 what percentage have we welcomed back? Alive?" She concluded, "I try so hard to be the marine among the best but I can't. I'm a lousy, sentimental one. . . . Guess battles are not or ever were won by sentiment. This is a price I must pay for loving my son so dearly, so hard & selfishly. . . . I pray God keeps you safe."[32]

His mother's words added to Clive's ambivalence as he returned to California. He continued to prepare for Vietnam, telling his brother Danny that he had to go because "I must do my part or I just as well as spit on their graves."[33] Meanwhile, back on base, Clive appeared to return to normal. In mid-July, he wrote his parents that while overseas, he had been all work and no play, but now, "come Friday I make the scene with some of the finest and darkest taned [sic] blondes there is. All sorts of good times. . . . Too bad the girls can't be California girls. Their'ld [sic] be all kinds of good whoopy going on." He could not wait until September when he finally would have enough money to buy a car.[34]

The Marines allowed him little time to grieve for Robert or enjoy the California summer season before sending him to his next assignment at Army Ranger School. For sixty days, starting in late July in the heat of the southern summer, Clive endured sleep and food deprivation and intense training sessions at Fort Benning, in the mountains of Georgia, and finally in the swamps of Florida. Many started the course, but on average only one out of four finished the first time around. Clive recognized the honor the Marines bestowed on him by allowing him to participate in some of the most intense, grueling training in the US military.

The taxing regimen began almost immediately upon arrival at Fort Benning, where he entered the First Platoon, Class 2-69, Third Ranger Company. A short time into the training, Clive wrote his parents that he had already dropped quite a bit of weight despite the fact that he had three square meals a day and ate like ten men. For days, he went without bathing, all the while being deprived of sleep, although he told his parents that things had changed, as "now were [sic] in the bush and we get more sleep." He signed off by saying that "I've never felt better in all my life" and that he planned to "[get] in my bag for the greatest thing yet since girls, sleep."[35]

The intense training gave Clive opportunities to hone his skills. One day, he stood on top of a 3,800-foot mountain whose name he could not pronounce, peering over one particular 280-foot sheer cliff that scared him senseless when he looked down. During an exercise, he rappelled down the cliff while a comrade rode on his back. About 60 feet down, his feet slipped, and both of the men flipped upside down. "Boy, was I ever so scared. I held on to that rope with . . . a death lock and that's one heck of [a] lock. Coming down a cliff upside down is some fun." He concluded, "Boy do I ever enjoy myself here."[36]

Clive spent a lot of his time in Ranger school in the field. For instance, before he headed out to Florida, his group went on a six-day patrol that covered 50 miles in harsh terrain. "It wouldn't be so bad," he reported, "if one could eat but for 6 days all we have is 2 c-rations." During the patrol, he carried either a machine gun or a PRC 25 radio. Straining under the weight of the equipment, he climbed steep inclines, all the while trying to stay awake. In the daytime, he constantly wiped the sweat from his face, but he and his comrades shivered at night from the cold. Such conditions exacted a significant toll. Clive especially complained about the hunger. "I had a sandwich a while ago and my stomach still hurts because I'm still hungry but I'm to [sic] full to take more in."[37]

After finishing the rigorous training—including time in the swamps of Florida among snakes, mosquitoes, and alligators—Clive graduated with his group in mid-September 1968. Old family movies show him sometime before the graduation with his Army buddies as they horsed around in a mock enemy village in the Georgia countryside.[38] Clive looked healthy, despite losing nearly thirty pounds. He soon proudly donned his black beret and the uniform patch signifying that he had finished Army Ranger School. He wrote his parents, "I'm just thank ful [sic] I could [finish] the army school of hell because now I have my life insurance for the NAM."[39]

After graduating, Clive flew back to Camp Pendleton and more training in the fall of 1968, all the while awaiting his orders for Vietnam so that he could earn the respect associated with combat. His hard work continued to pay dividends: in February 1969, he received his promotion to sergeant at the ripe old age of twenty-one. He admitted that it sounded strange to be called "Sarge GAR" but added that he was very proud.[40]

He filled his time in California with more training and administrative duties. His company commander at Pendleton, Capt. Curtis Frisbie, stressed that Clive had no equal "in our company or in our battalion [and] had everything it took to be a good Marine—the leadership, the drive, the ambition and in uniform he was the epitome of what you think of when they think of a Marine." He described Clive as a good instructor who always stuck up for his men, no matter what they did. Though Clive lacked combat experience, Captain Frisbie characterized him as "so proficient in his work that no one would ever have been able to tell it," as evidenced by his rapid rise in the Marines. Finally, he acknowledged that Clive often spoke about going to Vietnam because "he felt that he ought to go do what he considered his duty."[41]

On the weekends, Clive headed into town in his newly purchased car. The young, stout, broad-shouldered, and handsome Marine sometimes donned a black wig so that the girls would not automatically shy away from him because they recognized his regulation haircut.[42] He would later wear the wig again as he stood outside the dealership where he had bought his car and held a sign protesting the bad vehicles that the dealer sold to Marines. In a short time, his long-coveted car had turned into a money pit, requiring frequent repairs.[43]

He also found time to spend with several family members who lived in Southern California, including his cousin Maxine. She remembered him coming to her house and sleeping on the couch. He always told the family never to touch him in sleep, warning he could not be responsible for how he would respond. He also talked about killing the "gooks" and about how he could not trust people, especially those gooks—something she found out of the ordinary for Clive. Obviously, his attitudes had been conditioned by conversations with colleagues who had returned from Vietnam talking about the difficulties of identifying the enemy and about horrible incidents of young and old caught in the cross fire of the war.[44]

Clive remained optimistic, but he also planned for the future should he ship out to Vietnam, as the deaths of his friends hung over him. He had told his mother that if anything happened to him, there would be enough money from his insurance to cover the funeral, and the rest, he said, should help fund the education of his baby sister, Kathy.[45]

In March 1969, six months before Clive shipped out to Vietnam, the *Eastern Arizona Courier* in Safford ran a long story on the Morenci Nine and the five who had died in combat in Southeast Asia. Highlighting the story of how the group joined up together, the author emphasized that time would not heal all wounds and that "Joe, Mike, Clive, and David [Leroy] will never forget their departed buddies." At future high school reunions of the class of 1966, the reporter prophesied, "inadvertently a name will slip. A painful silence will follow and scores of classmates will feel a void in the pit of their stomachs."[46]

Despite the seriousness of his job and the prospect that he would be heading to Vietnam at any moment, Clive enjoyed his time in Southern California, and during one of his jaunts, his life changed dramatically. He met a young woman named Susie Hibbard, a blue-eyed, blonde Californian with a contagious laugh that often ended with a snort. Just out of high school in her hometown of Costa Mesa, not far from the ocean of Huntington and Newport Beaches, she worked for the phone company. She met the young Marine at a dance in San Diego, and they fell in love. A whirlwind romance ensued, and by late 1968, they announced their engagement.[47]

The future suddenly looked different for the couple, and they made plans for a wedding in the summer of 1969. However, they decided to put it off when Clive learned about his impending deployment to Vietnam. He did not want to chance leaving behind a young widow.[48]

Instead, they made the long trip to Morenci in July, where they basked in the glow of their newly found love and the genuine excitement shared by the Garcia family. Clive's parents showered them with early wedding gifts, including a blender and dishes, and Clive proudly showed everyone Susie's engagement ring. The Marine sergeant traversed his old stomping grounds, from the bowling alley to the football field, regaling his teenage girlfriend with stories about his life before they met. He also enjoyed introducing the pretty Californian to everyone in Morenci. The company town was quite a contrast to her large, urban Southern California hometown, but she enjoyed meeting the family and Clive's friends.[49]

While staying with the family in their small home, Clive and Susie kept a secret to themselves—that the Marines finally had honored his long-standing request for deployment to Vietnam. He received that assignment even though the Marine Corps had started withdrawing most of its troops in 1969. In fact, the numbers would plummet to only fifty thousand by the end of the year, and the withdrawal would be completed by the summer of 1971.[50]

Like many others who preceded him, Clive obeyed his orders, even as more and more young American males had started deserting or fleeing northward to Canada to escape the draft.[51] He understood that a Marine sergeant needed combat experience, and he wanted to contribute as his friends had done. To be sure, he had listened to Joe when they met at Camp Pendleton: "You're crazy. You're not missing a thing; don't do it."[52] And he thought a lot about leaving Susie and his family and facing the specter of death like his Morenci friends had. But when the time came, he marched off as any good Marine would do.

Before that moment came, however, he and his fiancée, holding dreams of a future together, traveled back to Southern California and waited for the terrible day of separation. Millions had shared this experience, of course, but for Clive and Susie, young love exacerbated feelings and apprehensions. They had only recently found each other, and now the military planned to ship one of them off to a combat zone. Clive later told his parents, "I found her crying so many times and she'ld [sic] smile always but her eyes [filled with fear and trepidation] I could tell her cause [it] was mine also."[53] As they waited, they talked about life after Vietnam while enjoying dinners, cuddling on the couch, or taking long walks. They shared the worries that came with having a loved one heading to combat—apprehensions about Clive dying or returning home severely disabled. Nothing could banish their feelings of dread regarding the forthcoming thirteen months, absolutely nothing.

Finally, the day arrived when they traveled to the airport and Clive boarded the plane for the long trip to Vietnam. Susie tried to put on a brave face, but her tears soon flowed over the impending departure of her fiancé. Thirteen months, they rationalized, was not such a long time, and yet for them, as for many young people, it seemed like an eternity. No matter what, they would never have that time again to be together.

Over the next day, Clive slumped in his seat on the airplane as it made its way across the Pacific, loaded with new replacements. Occasionally, he looked out at the never-ending blue ocean below and thought about leaving Susie, his family, the loss of his friends, and the challenges that lay ahead. It was a very long day.[54]

*   *   *

Like many of his friends who preceded him, Clive stepped off the plane within a day of leaving everything that he had known, touching down on the alien Vietnamese soil on August 27, 1969. Fortunately for him, his training in Guam and Hawaii had prepared him for the heat and humidity, so he was better able to cope with the climate than most. Yet he had been in Southern California for more than a year, an area that looked more like his beloved home in Greenlee County (albeit with tons of houses and a dense smog) than the humid green jungle areas and rice paddies of South Vietnam. And no matter what training a Marine received, until he arrived in Vietnam he could not truly understand the feeling of walking off a plane into a moist blast oven and into a foreign land in the middle of a war.

Almost immediately, Clive sat down and wrote a long letter to his parents to apologize for not telling them about his deployment to Vietnam when he and Susie visited. "[The reason] I didn't tell you I was leaving for the Nam was to make my time at home as pleasnt [sic] as I could," he said. He worried especially about Julia and his young sister, Kathy, fearing that they would have cried the entire time and dampened the visit. "I didn't ever lie to you," he added, "but I never told you all of the story or where I was to go."[55] He also asked his parents to check in with Susie, praising her for being so brave and loving but pleading, "Keep in touch with her at least now she can share our lonliness [sic]."[56]

Though concerned about his family, Clive had to turn his attention to the task at hand. He ended up being stationed on Hill 37 in Happy Valley, ironically in the Arizona Territory. He bragged about his colleagues and their fighting spirit and dedication but lamented not being able to use his special Ranger or Recon training. His accommodations were spartan, a 4-foot-wide, 6-foot-long, and 4-foot-high bunker surrounded by sandbags. Flies and mosquitoes swarmed the area, and the smells of cow dung and the jungle filled his nostrils. Nonetheless, he reported, "I've been lucky no colds and my head doesn't hurt. And believe it or not I haven't had the shits once yet."[57]

Base camp provided some luxuries, including cold soft drinks and a cot to sleep on, but Clive often headed into the bush on patrols with his men. They suffered through the seemingly constant rain of the monsoon season, sometimes so heavy they could see only a few feet ahead. It drenched everyone and never allowed a grunt to dry out, so different from the climate back home in the desert or in Southern California. The men trudged through mud and up slippery slopes, sitting and lying down on the drenched earth to rest, all the while searching for an elusive enemy. Even while enduring such aggravations, Clive philosophically observed, "Sure it all sucks but don't all wars and its [sic] weird & delayed so much for Sue & I but at least now I can live with myself."[58]

The frustrations he experienced sometimes manifested themselves in intemperate actions. One morning, after the platoon had been on 100 percent alert all night safeguarding a bridge, the tired grunts collapsed on the floor of a tent in the shadow of the structure that they had been assigned to protect. Suddenly, Clive entered and started barking orders for them to wake up and move out. Exhausted, they responded slowly, so he began kicking them to speed up the process. One grunt observed, "I guess Garcia believed that a Sgt in the corps had to be feared, not necessarily loved. . . . I didn't care much for him after that."[59] Such actions, when combined with his rank, age, and race, further alienated Clive from many people, and loneliness remained a constant companion for him in Vietnam.

At the end of September, a tragic event shaped Clive's destiny. Many times as a platoon sergeant, he had ordered people out on patrols, but on one horrible day, a group of his men hit a mine while riding on an amtrac. Five died instantly, likely blown apart by the antitank ordnance. The first major loss of soldiers under his command haunted Clive, and soon thereafter, he requested a change in duty to that of a squad leader heading a "killer team" to search for the "gooks" who had murdered his comrades.[60] He admitted that he hated the bush and that he wanted to be home with Susie, wishing that he had "refused the order for NAM." Still, he praised his troops and their willingness to follow him, noting that at least now he could sleep at night knowing he had done his part. "Now if my eternal Father will only forgive me for what I have done & are [sic] responsible for having happened," he said.[61]

His loneliness undermined his ability to deal with this tragedy and another that involved the killing of a Vietnamese child during a firefight.

Clive posing for a photo while at base camp in South Vietnam in fall 1969. (Photo courtesy of the Garcia family.)

The death of the child bothered him a great deal, and he had nightmares about all the killing around him. He carried the guilt deeply, conditioned partly by his devout Catholic upbringing. At night especially, he thought about his dead men, closing his eyes and seeing their faces. And when he slept, images of the dead child worked their way into his dreams. He tried to forget and longed for an ability to transport himself back in time to when his men and the child lived, but he never mastered the art of time travel. He prayed to God for forgiveness, but the pain lingered and never fully dissipated.[62]

Even while he was dealing with the anguish and guilt, always lurking in the background was a desire to put his Special Forces training to good use. In late October, an Army general requested his services for Recon duty possibly in Cambodia and Laos. Excited, Clive bragged that he would probably earn gold wings for going to jump school and that he would be in the heart of the enemy territory where only the hardiest souls ventured to slog it out with the NVA—far away from civilians and the chance to ever see children die. He asked his parents to send him his black Ranger beret and his pin inscribed with "Rangers Lead the Way," calling the opportunity that awaited him a dream come true and a reward for all his hard work and sacrifice. "All the long lonely & hard life I led to learn how to be a recon man wont [sic] go to waist [sic]," he wrote.[63]

But three months into his tour, Clive continued to serve on the front lines, and the promise of moving into Recon never materialized. Though he had traveled to the rear for some R & R and additional training, for the most part he had stayed near the fighting. He found time to write home, focusing on issues such as sending one dozen long-stemmed red roses to Susie on her birthday, November 6. He asked his mom to deliver the message: "Lo que te quiero mi vida," telling his parents that though Susie understood only a few phrases of Spanish, she knew what those words meant because he often sang the refrain to her while stateside.[64] He also told them that he and Susie planned to meet in Hawaii in January for his midtour R & R break.[65]

Clive never made it to his rendezvous with Susie. In his last letter to his parents, he stated, "I'm getting short . . . about 200 more days."[66] Five days later, on November 26, just two days after he and his men celebrated Thanksgiving, Clive went on a mission that he likely could have delegated to someone else. During the patrol in a driving rainstorm, the point man discovered a wire extending across a path with a 250-lb ordnance at the end, ready to explode if some unknowing Marine tripped it. Following procedure, Clive straddled the wire and let his men pass. Once his troops moved out of harm's way, he decided to defuse the bomb, although protocol typically called for a C-4 explosive charge to blow up a booby trap. Nonetheless, Clive stayed, along with his radioman, Bill Merrill, and began the process. Somehow, something went terribly wrong, and an explosion ripped the jungle, killing both men.[67]

The death of the two young soldiers devastated the platoon. Soon after, Clive's commander, 1st Lt. Dave D. Miller, wrote Julia Garcia about her son's death. He emphasized, "His death was just one of those things that happens over here all too often, but which is something we must deal and live with." He praised Clive as a soldier and a leader and told Julia, "Your

218   *Chapter Ten*

son died honorably, as an American & as a Marine, something you can be very proud of."[68]

Within a few days, a government-issue car drove through Clifton and started up the steep switchback toward Morenci. Everyone knew the drill, and many people held their breath as it climbed the incline and entered the outskirts of town. People with sons in the military prayed that the vehicle would not stop in front of their homes. They exhaled sighs of relief when the car passed, but dread filled them nonetheless, for they knew someone in town was about to receive devastating news. This time, the car turned left and away from the main part of the dying old center of Morenci, the one being buried under tons of rocks.

It headed into the Mexican American part of town, an area dotted by rows of white houses with short chain-link fences surrounding the yards. Down the hill about a quarter of a mile, it passed near Bunker Hill Cemetery, where Robert Moncayo lay. More people watched as it slowly went down Gila Street and stopped in front of the Garcia home. Julia watched the car pull up, and she went outside to greet the men about to pass through her gate. Knowing the worst but hoping for some kind of miracle, she told the Marines, "Please tell me that you are not looking for 90 Gila Street." The expressions on the faces of the men answered her implicit question. Her eldest son was dead. Tears began to flow down her face and onto the ground, and they would rarely stop over the next few weeks.[69]

11

The Long Trip Home
The Journey of Sgt. Clive Garcia, Jr.

Clive Garcia, Jr., had made the trip from Phoenix to Morenci on a number of occasions. This time, on a cool December day in 1969, his uncle, Angel Zepeda, a Navy corpsman also serving in Vietnam, accompanied him. Angel had joined Clive when the Marine's body arrived in the United States from South Vietnam aboard a government plane. Then they flew to Phoenix. At the airport, they entered a big black car and settled in for the four-hour drive home.

The car left Phoenix Sky Harbor Airport and headed out University Street for the trip to Morenci. The Gila River lay to their north, the same river that snaked through the length of the state to Clive's beloved Greenlee County before branching off to become the San Francisco River. Before long, they entered the countryside of small farms and orange groves that surrounded Tempe and then Mesa. In 1969, these towns were still relatively small communities. On this day, large fields of corn, alfalfa, and cotton along with orange groves bracketed the highway, not the small mobile-home parks, long rows of cookie-cutter homes, and endless strip malls that arose later when hundreds of thousands of midwesterners invaded the Valley of the Sun.

Finally, Clive and Angel left the valley, passing in the shadows of the imposing red rock Superstition Springs Mountains that rose several thousand feet into the air to the north. In all directions, the saguaros stood like tall sentinels watching over the desert floor, some having arms rising upward as if offering praise to an unseen deity. The car climbed over the 2,651-foot Gonzales Pass and descended into Superior, a mining town of several thousand people. Much like in Morenci, smelter and mining operations dotted the landscape. The war also had taken a significant toll in this town: six of its young men—Roy Dorsett, Eugene Fritz, Manuel Mendoza, Luis Romero, Manuel Ybarra, and Ray Jones—had all died in Vietnam, the last just two months earlier, on October 14, 1969.[1]

Rising out of Superior, the car headed into the high hills of the Apache Leap Mountains, where legend claimed that the US Cavalry trapped a band of Apache warriors who chose to ride their horses off the bluffs rather than surrender. Upon hearing of their deaths, the story went, their loved ones reportedly cried, but before the tears reached the ground, they turned to black translucent stones. These stones were later sold as good luck souvenirs. A steep canyon boxed in the road, made more passable by the Queen Creek Tunnel. As darkness engulfed the car when it went through the tunnel, some motorists hit their horn to hear the echo, mainly to thrill their young passengers. The driver's hands gripped the steering wheel tightly that day.

Curves and narrow roads dominated the drive through the canyon from Superior to Miami. Large oak trees rose up along the sides of the red hills, and toward the top of the canyon walls, rocks balanced precariously on one another, looking as if they could easily spill on the road. Finally, the highway descended into Miami, the site of the huge Phelps Dodge mine and processing plant where laborers toiled day and night. Over the years, hundreds of young men had left Miami and its sister cities, Claypool and Globe, for the military. And as in Morenci, a number of them had returned in caskets. Miami had lost one young man, José González, in Vietnam, and Globe had suffered five deaths up to that date, Andrew Lee, Andrew Deal, Fernando Quintero, Paul Sánchez, and Philip Tompkins. Another, Dennis Gilliland, would die in combat in 1971.[2]

Past Globe, the land flattened as the black car entered the San Carlos Apache Reservation. Unlike today, no modern casino existed just a few miles outside the town. Instead, the car entered one of the poorest regions of Arizona. Scrub brush and cacti covered terrain with few natural resources such as copper. Poverty and unemployment plagued the reservation, accompanied by problems of alcoholism and crime.

Clive and his entourage also passed not far from the home of Sam Ybarra, an Apache who had fought in Vietnam with the infamous Tiger Force. When Ybarra's best friend from high school, Kenneth Green, died in Vietnam, he went over the edge. He became a cold-blooded killer, even decapitating a young baby. Ultimately, his behavior led to a dishonorable discharge for insubordination. He returned home, became an alcoholic trying to forget the past, and ballooned to 300 pounds before disease ravaged his body. He died in 1982 at thirty-six, having wasted away to less than 100 pounds while holding on to a dream of returning to Vietnam to redeem himself.[3] Others across the reservation dealt with the ghosts of Vietnam as well, although rarely in such terrible fashion.

The boring drive through the reservation lasted more than an hour, the only real change in the land being the disappearance of the saguaros halfway through the trip. Then Clive and Angel passed through the small town of Bylas, a community of run-down houses and trash-strewn roads. Finally, they reached the little community of Fort Thomas, leaving the reservation, and entered the Gila Valley, where Mormon farmers had created a vibrant agricultural community in the shadow of Mount Graham. Before long, they passed through the twin communities of Thatcher and Safford. These farming and cattle towns had more stores, government buildings, and other amenities than most of the mining and reservation towns.

Thatcher and Safford also had taken many fewer casualties than their counterparts in surrounding areas. The larger of the two, Safford, had only lost two people in Vietnam, Michael Dunagan and Walter Foote, and another man, James Thomas, had been reported missing in action in April 1968.[4] Like many agricultural communities in eastern Arizona, such as Show Low, Pinetop, and Eager, both Safford and Thatcher had been more successful than the mining towns in avoiding the grim reaper.

Finally, Clive and Angel made their way eastward out of Safford, going several miles before turning north on Highway 666 and starting their final 40 miles to Clifton. The two-lane highway carried them out of the valley and into rolling hills dotted with scrub brush, ocotillo, and cacti, at last reaching the three-way intersection where they would turn left and travel a few more miles into Clifton, known throughout the area as Morenci's rival.

This day, they did not make their way up the mountain and to the Garcia home at 90 Gila Street in Morenci. Instead, they passed down the streets of Clifton, ones lined with garlands and Christmas candles and store windows that featured nativity scenes and advertisements for holiday specials. The year before, the miners' strike had dampened the mood in town. But this year, everyone had gone back to work, and the smelter pumped out plumes of smoke, indicating that things had returned to normal and that everyone could enjoy the holidays.

Though a festive mood enveloped the town, the men in the car seemed oblivious to it as they stopped at the Lewallen Funeral Home, where only eighteen months before, Clive had stood guard beside Robert Moncayo's body. This day, Angel exited the car, went inside the building, and returned with people to help carry Clive's casket inside. As had happened five times before for the Morenci Nine, the men stood at the end of the black hearse and received a gray coffin containing the lifeless body of another casualty of Vietnam. Up the hill, the heartsick Garcias had waited for this day for more than a week. Instead of being aglow with the happiness of the Christmas season, the small house on Gila Street was overwhelmed by sadness. Families in hundreds of homes across the country experienced the same feelings of bereavement that holiday season.

When the news of Clive's death arrived, family members descended on Morenci to grieve, so many that Clive's brothers Danny and Marty moved to the houses of other relatives in order to make room for the visitors. Julia cooked and hosted everyone, all the while dealing with her own grief. To some people, Clive, Sr., appeared to be in shock, unable to process the loss of the son who bore his name. The normally vibrant and animated father retreated into himself. He had seen death before in the jungles of the South Pacific and had lost close family members in World War II, but nothing could ever prepare a father for the loss of his child. It felt like a kick in the stomach that took away a person's breath and left a tightness in the chest that never fully dissipated.[5]

Clive's body lay in the funeral home down the hill and across the bridge in Clifton. Angel took the first duty of guarding the body as close family members began visiting. When Danny arrived and looked at his brother in the open casket, several things struck him. Some of Clive's body parts appeared to be missing, including a shoulder, and the mortician had mistakenly parted Clive's hair on the wrong side and left his mustache poorly trimmed.[6]

Many others traveled down the mountain to view the body, and long lines soon developed, especially as shifts at the mine turned over. For the sixth time, the people of the community dealt collectively with the death of a member of the Morenci Nine. The pain just continued for most, and more and more families feared additional visits by the Marines and Army to inform them of the loss of another Wildcat.

But unlike the earlier deaths, Clive's passing brought national attention to Morenci. The controversy over Vietnam had heightened in the months since Robert's funeral in June 1968, and the national media arrived to tell the story of the losses suffered in this small mining town and their impact on the families and community. *Time* magazine, ABC News, the *Los Angeles Times*, the *Arizona Republic*, and other news outlets dispatched reporters to cover the funeral that took place on Tuesday, December 9. Morenci momentarily became a focus of a nation struggling to deal with the divisive conflict and its far-reaching effects.

Dark-gray clouds, barely rising above the peaks and the smokestack of the smelter, descended on Morenci the day the community gathered to pay its final respects to the fallen warrior. That cold and dreary day, a light rain fell on arriving mourners, more than 250 people who crammed into the Holy Cross Catholic Church. Only a year and a half earlier, the wooden, light green-and-white structure had been the setting for Robert's funeral. But this time, volunteers had placed plastic over the empty window frames as PD prepared to move the church down the hill as it buried old Morenci to make way for a bigger mine.

Several Marines and others, including Angel, had taken their seats near the altar as people arrived. Many stood in the aisles as Julia and Clive, Sr., walked slowly to the front, joined by Susie. Clive's little sister, Kathy, his princess, proceeded down the aisle holding the hand of one of her other brothers. A large figure of Christ on the crucifix, flanked by statues of Joseph and Mary, stood above the gray coffin draped with an American flag. Father Cornelius McGrenra, the popular Irish-born priest, led the service, which emphasized Clive's commitment to his community and country. Tears flowed, even among some of the stoic miners, as people mourned their loss in the church that soon became only a memory, buried under tons of rocks.[7]

A young Kathy Garcia walks the aisle near the casket of her brother Clive. (Photo reprinted with permission of the Arizona Republic.*)*

Julia Garcia and Susie Hannah Hibbard (Clive's fiancée) at Clive's funeral. (Photo reprinted with permission of the Arizona Republic.*)*

Once the Mass ended, many of the mourners made the short trip down the mountain to the Bunker Hill Cemetery, where Clive had stood just months earlier as the caretaker lowered Robert into the red clay. In the shadow of the always billowing smokestack, Father McGrenra recited the ancient words of the dead, "Man, who is born of woman, is of few days and full of sorrow."[8]

The family sat on cold, folding metal chairs, jumping a bit when a Marine Corps color guard fired three volleys, the sound of the guns echoing through the canyons to the north and across the plains to the south. As the memorial ended, a Marine handed Julia the folded flag and pronounced: "We present this flag to you in recognition of your son who gave his life in the defense of the United States of America." An observer noted that Julia "cuddled it in her arms like a baby."[9]

As the crowd prepared to disperse, Julia rose slowly and whispered through the glass over Clive's face, "Thank you for being my son, my son. Oh, my dear boy, thank you so much." One reporter wrote, "And so

Clive's casket before it was laid into the ground, December 1968. (Photo reprinted with permission of the Arizona Republic.*)*

Sgt. Garcia, U.S. Marine Corps, was laid to rest in the rocky, red earth he loved so well." The same writer concluded, "Morenci, in keeping with the sad rainy day, cried collectively with the Garcia family. For Morenci . . . had gone through the ordeal before."[10]

While some mingled under the dark, low-hanging clouds as evening approached and darkness enveloped the town, the large crowd began to head to their cars to return home, where they would deal with their grief in their own ways. The collective sense of community dissipated as people turned inward, conditioned to loss by the deaths of the young soldiers who had preceded Clive. One observer recorded: "In the growing gloom, with the lowering clouds, the hanging smelter smoke and steam from the slag dump combining to mask the raw earth, the mourners' cars climbed the winding road from the cemetery."[11] They headed home, and many of the miners went right back to work in the pit or smelter, which rarely stopped producing copper, even in the face of tragedy.

*   *   *

The next day, Julia, her face still swollen from crying, sat down with a reporter and recalled that Clive had told her that if he died, "he would be brought home by a grunt, by someone who loved him, 'a grunt, Mom, a grunt like me.'" As Susie helped prepare coffee in the small kitchen of the home on Gila Street, Julia stressed, "Clive was a magnificent young man. They all were. Such beautiful young men." Her attention wavered, and she apologized, "I go back to those moments when he was here, sitting in that chair," referring to the seat occupied by the reporter. "I close my eyes, and I see them [the young men], sitting around the table, quibbling among themselves like little kids." She concluded, "I thank God for lending him to me. I had him so long, 22 years, and now God wants him back."[12]

She told another reporter, from the *Tucson Daily Star,* "I believe Almighty God did what he did, and we accept it. I pray that no more will die, and I most certainly wish the war could end." Yet she stressed, "As our boys died, I used to feel that it was such a waste, but I no longer feel that it was a waste. I lost my son, and he gave of himself, and this could not have been a waste."[13] This became a common refrain among many in the community, especially the family members.

In the immediate aftermath of the funeral, the media continued to spotlight Morenci. Stories in the *Arizona Republic* concentrated on various people in the town. One mentioned how Ethel West had attended Clive's funeral and then gone to the home of another woman who had a son serving in the Marines in Vietnam. She stated:

> The mother was hysterical, just sitting there waiting her turn. . . . I don't know what the President would say about it, but I think those Morenci boys now in Vietnam should come home if they want to. . . . It doesn't seem right that such a small town should give so much. Oh, I know that the people haven't groaned about it. They don't like it, but they accept it and go along like before. But I feel they've just had enough.[14]

Others expressed the fatigue the community felt in the wake of the losses. A *Los Angeles Times* reporter commented, "The people, like those in any small town, share an equal capacity for love, hate, frustration, gossip, success, failure and despair. But they believe now they have had their share of despair."[15] One Morenci resident, Tom McWilliams, told the reporter, "It's just like this town has been the butt of a twisted joke. The bodies just keep coming in—one at a time."[16]

Though they were of course devastated by the deaths the war caused, many in the community underscored their disdain for those who opposed it. Mrs. Alton Whitmer, Van's mother, remained defiant. She expressed animosity toward the war protestors, some of whom had tried to exploit the deaths of the Morenci boys. "My boy died honorably, and I have no reason to be ashamed of him. One woman told me that I'd be happy if my son were a hippie and dope addict because he'd still be alive." She retorted, "No. If I had a son like that I'd crawl in a hole and pull it in after me. These boys were the cream of the crop. The best."[17]

Others echoed her disgust for the antiwar movement, particularly the long-haired hippies. One resident told a reporter, "We're a hawk community pretty much. We feel, 'do it right or don't do it.'" Another said that "one or two hippies [lived] around here" but not many more, and a young waitress emphasized that "we don't get them and we don't want them."[18] Leroy Cisneros stressed the United States had a mission to complete in Southeast Asia. "He believes that the U.S. should be in Vietnam," the reporter wrote, "and he has no regrets about the part he played in a cause he supports. Yet, in talking with this brave young man who escaped from the jaws of hell to return home, the usual arguments over Vietnam seem somehow unimportant, even irrelevant."[19]

The high school principal, Paul Lemons, built on the theme of patriotism in the community. "Our town is a little more—I don't know whether the word is patriotic or what—but we haven't had any demonstrations or anything else as a result of this."[20]

Many people in the growing antiwar movement, mainly in San Francisco or Los Angeles or the larger cities in Arizona including Tucson, would question why no protest or real resentment existed in Morenci, especially since the community had sacrificed so much for a system that often favored the giant corporation at the expense of the workers and their families. Yet in Morenci, antiwar talk constituted heresy. In a similar way, Mexican Americans in the community refused to identify with the burgeoning Chicano movement developing throughout the West because of its perceived radicalism. Morenci remained an insular community, with patriotism as a cornerstone. Change occurred gradually in such towns, and in December 1969, turning against the war, except to question why it could not be won, put someone in the minority.

Perhaps equally as important to the mind-set of the people in Morenci, to question the war diminished the immense sacrifice made by their fallen soldiers, as well as the danger faced by hundreds of others fighting in Vietnam. Admitting that anything less than victory was acceptable or characterizing the conflict as impractical or immoral, as argued by various antiwar groups, was an acknowledgment that the loss of the six Morenci men—and tens of thousands of others from across the country—had been in vain, to say nothing of the millions of lives affected by the devastation of the fighting in Southeast Asia. Thus, the people of Morenci, largely isolated from the rest of the country, rarely asked the hard questions. They may have done so behind closed doors, but community standards and peer pressure reduced public displays of discontent and disillusionment.

On December 18, in the aftermath of Clive's death, people across the United States heard the story of Morenci in a piece featured on ABC News. In the lead-in, anchorman Frank Reynolds highlighted that 85 Americans had died in the past week in Vietnam, 15 fewer than one week earlier. He also observed that new casualty figures demonstrated the continued decline in the American commitment in Vietnam, noting that in the previous year through December 15, a total of 14,271 Americans had died, compared to only 9,213 through the same date in 1969. "So in terms of the index that is really the most important," he added, "there has been a change for the better."[21]

Then a photo of a crouching, sleeveless grunt moving forward cautiously with an M-16 in hand appeared, superimposed on a map of Vietnam, with the words *Morenci, Arizona* running in large letters underneath. Reynolds observed, "But for those who have suffered a personal loss in this war, the figures are of no consolation [and] in some communities, Vietnam has claimed an unusually high number of young men."[22]

Dick Shoemaker, a young reporter with large, black-rimmed glasses, took over the story at that point, noting his location in Morenci, a small community of six thousand in southeastern Arizona. The first image to appear featured a vast, panoramic picture of the barren countryside of Morenci, with the huge smelter and tall smokestack standing in the foreground. Shoemaker stated, "A few years ago, nine young boys from the local high school joined the Marines. They went to war together and six never came back." He focused on those who had died, underscoring the athleticism of Bobby Dale and Stan and the fact that Morenci boys loved playing football. The senior pictures of Robert, Van, and Larry appeared as he outlined how each had died in combat in Vietnam.[23]

The broadcast concentrated, however, on "the last to die, Clive Garcia." The segment opened with the final family photo of the Garcia family, showing Clive dressed in his khaki Marine uniform, smiling and looking very young. Then Shoemaker remarked, "His mother believes there was a meaning to her son's death." The camera showed Julia, wearing dark-rimmed glasses and sitting in a big white chair in the small living room of the family's home. In the background sat the 8" × 10" photo of Clive taken at the end of boot camp, revealing a stern-faced Marine in dress blues. In front of it lay a folded triangle of flag wrapped in plastic, with only the white stars visible on the dark-blue background—the flag that was presented to Julia at her son's funeral.[24]

The interview opened with Julia speaking slowly but firmly: "He died for, for this cause. This cause of freedom. This democracy of ours that you and I may think as we please. And speak as we may." The photographer pulled back and focused on the picture of Clive and the flag as she added, "And it will be hard, it will be very hard, very, very hard," talking about the future. Then, as the photographer took a close-up of Julia, her eyes looking down and away from the camera, she emphasized: "The waiting was hard. It took many days, the waiting for his body to come. But it will be very hard, you know, I know it will be harder, especially when the clothes come. When his belongings come. When the spring comes and he was to marry this young lady." Julia, her faced twisted with pain, became more visibly upset, and Shoemaker said in the background, "I don't want to put you into too much." As the segment ended, the photographer pulled back again as Julia began crying.[25]

The visuals then broke to Clive's gravesite at the Bunker Hill Cemetery, still surrounded by flowers and several small American flags. Shoemaker, standing in front of the grave, stated, "[Julia's] son is buried here. The last young man from Morenci, Arizona to die in Vietnam." "Mrs. Garcia," he added, "has two more sons and she says that if they want to join the

Marines, and if they want to go to Vietnam, she won't stop them." He signed off, "Dick Shoemaker, ABC News, Morenci, Arizona."[26]

For the Garcias, the televised piece left a bitter taste in the mouth, for they believed their story had been overly politicized. Julia stressed that in the filming, which lasted more than two hours, she talked at length about the commitment of her son and that during the interview, she only cried briefly. Yet in the story that appeared on television, the emphasis was on the sadness and loss, not the celebration of Clive's life and his sacrifice. As a result, the family members requested that local authorities block other reporters from approaching them.[27]

Soon after, *Time* ran its 1970 "Man of the Year" edition, dedicated to "Mr. and Mrs. Middle America." It contained a small feature story entitled "Semper Fidelis: The Marines of Morenci," which told the story of nine youngsters who "led some of the scrappiest high school football and basketball teams," enjoyed "roaring beer busts," and "rode horses along the Coronado Trail [and] stalked deer in the Apache National Forest." It described how they joined the Marine Corps as a group and how they banded together to demand that Joe be allowed to retake a service-aptitude test. "Beneath their careless courage," the story went on, "six of the nine harbored a premonition, a vision of a future that they could accept calmly."[28]

The *Time* reporter observed, "There is understandable weariness, but no bitterness" in Morenci, although many families with sons in Vietnam worried, "Who's next." He noted that Leroy thought little about the war except when he saw news reports but that he believed it was "best to try to stop Communism there before it gets closer to home." "That kind of unquestioning patriotism," the reporter added, "persists among Morenci's tough-minded mining families." The story concluded with a comment from Julia Garcia: "I used to feel that it was such a waste. But I no longer feel that way. I lost my son, and he gave of himself, and this could not have been a waste."[29]

In the end, one *Arizona Republic* editorial writer, Edwin McDowell, summed up the feelings of many in the community when he wrote, "Morenci will withstand the pain and suffering." He quoted Coach Friedli, who asserted, "This is too tough a community to be broken. Bent, perhaps, even stretched out of shape. But not broken." McDowell astutely observed that "men who have spent a lifetime of working 26 straight days before getting two days off—are not devoid of emotion or inured to tragedy. But they have learned to cope with setbacks better than most of us."[30]

The Garcia family continued to struggle with Clive's death. In the aftermath, they received his Purple Heart, a seemingly superfluous piece of metal and cloth. The Republic of Vietnam also bestowed on him posthumously the Military Merit Medal and the Gallantry with Palm with a special citation noting that Clive had been "a serviceman of courage and rare self-sacrifice" in "aiding the Armed Forces of the Republic of Vietnam to repel the Red wave undermining South Vietnam and Southeast Asia."[31] Of course, no medals or commendations could fill the void caused by the death of such a vibrant young man.

Heartfelt letters arrived at the Garcia home, including one from LCpl. Carl E. Wells of Clive's Third Platoon of India Company. He wrote, "Your son was one that could nor will never [sic] be forgotten. You'd [sic] might say he was one in a million." The young soldier added that Clive had been a nice guy whom he enjoyed serving under during the short time they fought together in Vietnam: "He was the kind of man we enveyed [sic] and try to be like. God bless you for bringing up such a wonderful guy."[32]

Ethel West sent a note soon after asking their forgiveness for her failure to visit after Clive's death. She explained that her husband was on the night shift and that "we just seem [sic] not to be able to get there." At the funeral, she added, "it was so bad and cold we desided [sic] not to bother you." She said that she did not know Clive as well as some of the others but that "I told my family I thought Clive was the proudest Marine I had ever known." Empathetically, she added: "I know your sorrow as well as four other families at Morenci know them. We will always keep our fond memories of your fine son in our heart & mind."[33]

With less than three weeks until Christmas, the last of the Morenci Nine to die in Vietnam had returned home. No great joy existed in the Garcia house that holiday, though the season was one the family had enjoyed immensely over the years. Even the Christmas tree crowding the small living room and the decorations on the walls could not lift their spirits. The loss of the eldest son tore a hole in the heart of the family, a wound that would never fully heal. As sadness descended on the small town of Morenci that December, it settled in particular on a little white house on Gila Street.

Nearly fifty thousand American families shared the experience of waking up on Christmas Day 1969 and not having a son, a brother, a husband, a cousin sitting there enjoying the festive time. More would die, nearly ten thousand more, over the following five years before the United States completely extricated itself from Vietnam and the North Vietnamese and Vietcong emerged victorious. As a consequence, families in every corner of the United States would miss their fallen loved ones on holidays forever after. And Memorial Day would now have a special meaning for them all.

12

Life after Deaths

Dealing with the Absence
of Loved Ones

On December 23, 1969, student journalists released the latest edition of the Morenci High newspaper, *The Wildcat*. Stories appeared on white 8" × 14" paper with dark-black print, obviously run off on a mimeograph machine. At the top of the page, there was a dove overlaid with the words Peace on Earth. Underneath that was a story about the senior class president, Kelly O'Neill, being honored by the Rotarians and an announcement on the "Christmas through the Ages" program being presented by the MHS Music Department, directed by Jan Goodner.[1]

At the bottom of the page, the tone of the material became more serious, running under the headline "'WHY, OH WHY?' FIRST THERE WERE NINE, NOW THREE." Bobby Dale's younger brother, Ken Draper, authored this story and wrote, "With the ink hardly dry on their MHS Diploma, eight graduates of the Class of '66 and one from the Class of '64, boarded a bus on July 4, 1966 and headed for San Diego to begin their Marine Corps training." He talked about how the Marines' promotion of the "buddy system" proved to be the "motivating factor" for the nine young men who "wanted to be Marines over anything else."[2]

Ken observed that they all achieved that goal and that all eventually headed to Vietnam. He noted that his brother, Bobby Dale, died first, in August 1967, followed soon after by Stan, shot by a sniper. Then came Robert (a mistake) and the others and finally Clive, buried only two weeks earlier, "the latest victim . . . of the original nine." He underscored

234

that "the incredible fate of the six young men, representing the cream of Morenci's youth, has stunned the school and the community."[3]

The remaining three had returned home—Mike and Leroy working for PD and Joe for the General Motors Proving Grounds in Apache Junction. Ken stated, "Life continues to go on both in the community and the school. There are no antiwar posters or demonstrations in the town." Instead, the community celebrated a successful football season and a basketball team that had its eyes on the playoffs.[4]

However, the young reporter, who knew firsthand the sense of loss, concluded his article by pointing out that Morenci's soldiers in Vietnam had a death rate six times higher than the national average. He observed that "the young men of Morenci know how to die for their country and their parents accept this with sincerity and dedication. They believe Almighty God did what he did and accept it." Nonetheless, he stated, "they pray that this dreadful war with all of its suffering will end soon." Underneath the final line, the paper included a poem from a friend entitled "The Brave Young Lads," with a picture of the Marine emblem on one side and an American flag on the other.[5]

The deaths of the six Marines had far-reaching and lasting effects on families, friends, and the community at large. It changed the dynamics of all nine families, including those of the three Marines who returned home. The deaths made some question why Morenci had to pay such a heavy price for such an unpopular war, one winding down with American troops starting to withdraw by early 1970. Others worried that their own sons would die next, for many of the mining camp's young people continued to serve in Vietnam. In Morenci and other insular communities across the United States, the consequences of the war in Southeast Asia persisted for decades, as did the struggle to find meaning in the divisive conflict.

The deaths had some tangible and immediate effects as well. One young man from Greenlee County, for instance, found that the deaths affected the local draft board's decisions. In August 1969, even before Clive died, this man had received a letter to appear before the draft committee. He arrived at its headquarters at Virgil Waters's Mobil station in Clifton and explained that he had a family and a job. In response, Waters replied, "We've given enough blood from our draft board. I think we can lose your file for six months." The young man escaped the draft net, although he carried some guilt for having done so.[6] Over time, such stories began to fade as the draft calls subsided and ultimately halted with the implementation of an all-volunteer military in 1973.[7]

The end of the war corresponded with a waning interest in the story of the Morenci Nine. And at last, the Marine and Army officers bearing bad news stopped arriving in town. Relieved and exhausted, the community retreated into its own grief and eventually moved on with the mundane activities of everyday life. In the meantime, people adjusted to the slow death of old Morenci under the rubble of tons of rocks and the rebirth of the new town built down the hill a couple of miles.

Like Morenci, the country as a whole tried to move on. As distinguished historian George Herring observed, the nation "experienced a self-conscious, collective amnesia" in regard to the war.[8] This occurred because many Americans wanted to put an end to that divisive chapter in US history and to stop the riots in the streets. They also wanted to heal the divisions between families and look forward, not back. As a consequence, soldiers returning from Vietnam, unlike the World War II veterans, were by and large treated as pariahs. Few communities hosted parades or built memorials or even acknowledged the sacrifices of their countrymen who had fought in Vietnam.

In Morenci, the people dealt with their grief individually or within small units. They did not rush to erect memorials to the returning Vietnam veterans like those often constructed for World War II troops. In many cases, even the older generation of veterans treated their Vietnam counterparts with contempt, originally denying them membership in certain groups, a process exacerbated by the substantial generation gap that had developed between fathers and sons.

Over time, some wounds healed, and people opened up more as the country and community gradually came to terms with the issues of the Vietnam veterans. Yet the ghosts of the war haunted the red rock terrain around Ward Canyon Cemetery and Bunker Hill Cemetery, in the shadow of the still fuming smokestack.

Of course, a fallen soldier's family and friends bore the heaviest burden. Each holiday, often the worst of times for the family, there was an empty seat in the small living or dining room of the white company house. As one Morenci native put it, it was reminiscent of the famous song from the

Broadway production of *Les Miserables* entitled "Empty Chairs at Empty Tables," whose lyrics read, in part: "There's a grief that can't be spoken. / There's a pain goes on and on. / Now my friends are dead and gone."[9]

Families gradually removed the belongings of the dead, although they would occasionally come across stray items that had been overlooked in drawers or closets. It was hard to let go of the physical remnants, and it proved impossible to erase recollections. Years passed and memories faded but never disappeared, and some family members found themselves crying over random thoughts that entered their consciousness years afterward—even a smell or sound could trigger memories of a fallen son, brother, or husband.

For some family members, especially the younger siblings, the loss of their loved ones in such a violent manner was translated into action. In the Garcia family, Martin, Clive's youngest brother, seemed determined to join the Marine Corps and follow in the footsteps of the brother whose gallantry and sacrifice he worshipped. Julia Garcia desperately wanted to protect her son, so she approached Martin's history teacher, William Senne, and begged him to persuade the youngest Garcia male not to join—but to no avail.[10] Martin drove the two and a half hours to the Marine recruiters' office in Globe, intent on signing up. But since he was underage, the Marine on duty called his parents, who refused to sign the waiver needed for enlistment. Ultimately, the war wound down and dampened Martin's drive to join the military, but he found another form of service as a policeman in Tucson.[11]

Other younger brothers coped with the loss of their elder siblings in various ways. Sam King followed Stan into the service, but he developed a series of health problems and died at a relatively young age from cancer. Robert's brother, Bobby Mesa, found it very difficult to deal with the loss of his brother and often landed in trouble with authorities.[12] In other cases, younger siblings found themselves having to fill a void in the family, as happened in the Draper family where the strain of Bobby Dale's death helped destroy the parents' marriage.[13] In all instances, the younger men in particular found it hard to fill the shoes of their immortalized siblings, who earned a larger-than-life reputation in the community, one that only grew with time.

The sadness and pain stayed for all of those left behind, including female siblings such as Larry's sister, Patsy. As one reporter observed nearly three decades later, "The death of her brother, Larry West, still weighs so heavily on Patsy Milligan that she can't bear to dredge up the memories."[14] Others, among them Clive's younger sister Kathy, missed their brothers so much that they dealt with the grief of the loss for many years, a heartache that never completely dissipated.

One of Larry West's close family members, though not related by blood, struggled with his loss even into the early 1990s. Brother-in-law Ernest Milligan remembered that he helped Larry secure his first job at Foster Simms's Texaco Station. And right before Larry shipped out for Southeast Asia for the second time, Ernest recalled, "I tried to talk him out of going [back to Vietnam]. I told him that he already had done his duty." For years thereafter, Ernest was troubled: "I still keep wondering if I had just kept at him or maybe been more persuasive that I might have changed his mind."[15]

Close friends of the six who died also missed their buddies greatly, and some had to deal with that grief even as they coped with their own experiences in Vietnam. One of Stan's good friends was Vietnam veteran Gerald Hunt, who emphasized that "the deaths really affected us" and remembered that he often dreamed about Stan wandering around old Morenci.[16] Another classmate, Army veteran Larry Kenan, talked about the loss of the six Marines and recalled how their absence created a quietness within his circle of friends and the community. He thought about them frequently, always regretting not being able to say good-bye to them. Even forty years later, he still visited the gravesites of Stan and Bobby Dale at the Ward Canyon Cemetery, taking time to clean the sites of weeds and debris and talking to them about the town and especially the current football season.[17]

Other friends from the community observed that the memories of the six who died lingered for years. Nearly twenty-five years after the last death, one classmate, Wanda Ruedas, told a reporter, "Morenci still struggles with its war burden . . . and the really terrible thing is that those boys were the nice ones, the ones everybody wanted to be around, the guys you remembered."[18]

The burdens borne by the three members of the Morenci Nine who returned home were unlike any others. Leroy, Joe, and Mike completed their enlistments and immediately gravitated back to Arizona and eventually Morenci. Of the three, Leroy outwardly appeared to handle the adjustment to civilian life most easily, with few acute manifestations of problems. After his tour in Vietnam, he had been stationed in security in Yuma, where, he acknowledged, the Marines took very good care of Recon veterans. Several times, they asked him to return to Vietnam, offering a promotion for doing so, but he refused, partly because he knew how lucky he had been during his first tour. He bided his time in Yuma, only about 300 miles from home, and in 1969, he headed back to Morenci.[19]

He stayed there for a year, working a variety of jobs with PD, and then left to go back to Yuma, where he met his future wife, Gloria. Eventually, he returned home to work for PD once more. Always, the war and the loss of his friends haunted him. At times, he admitted to drinking a lot to dull the pain, and he found himself in fights when someone dared question his decision to join the Marines. Loud noises made him jump, and he occasionally woke up during the night screaming, having dreamed of being in the far-off jungles of Vietnam with bullets flying overhead and grenades exploding close by. In his free time, he spent many hours traveling around to play softball, enjoying the camaraderie with his buddies but often at the expense of his family.[20]

The deaths of his friends and the nightmares of Vietnam extracted a toll on his marriage and other relationships. In addition, he endured a tragedy that only exacerbated the problems he had in dealing with Vietnam. While visiting family in California, Leroy's wife asked him to watch his young daughter, Roxanne. For a moment, he turned his attention elsewhere, and the child somehow got into the swimming pool and drowned. His wife had a terribly hard time dealing with the death of their daughter. And Leroy, who admitted that he was "not the greatest dad in the world," found self-pity and anger surfaced often in him after that, which only brought on more drinking and fighting.[21]

Ultimately, the miners' strike forced him out of Morenci in 1983. When PD laid him off, he left the town for the last time and returned to Yuma, where he worked at the Operations and Maintenance Division of the Artillery Systems Test Branch at the Marine Corps Proving Grounds. Around that time, Gloria issued an ultimatum: she would leave if he did not change his ways. Leroy later stated, "One day it hit me" that his wife was right. He eventually sought help from mental health professionals, who had begun to see new patients returning from the Gulf War.[22]

The family settled into life in Yuma, and things improved for Leroy, as he had found a measure of peace with the help of the doctors. Though still shaped by the Vietnam experience—his big truck had a license plate reading "Mornci 9" and his Corvette had "Recon" on its plate—he had moved away from the daily reminders in his hometown.

Still, Vietnam haunted Leroy when events brought back the memories, as happened when his oldest son served in the Gulf War. His emotions strengthened further during the Iraq War that started in 2003. He drew parallels between Vietnam and the conflict in the Middle East and felt strongly that "we shouldn't be there in the first place" and that President George W. Bush "lied about it." He hated that there were "no front lines" and that the Iraqis "don't help themselves." The bitterness clearly intensified as the war escalated and more people died, including some who had been stationed at the Marine base in Yuma.[23]

But even as the war in Iraq dragged on, Leroy moved forward. In 2005, he retired from his job at the Marine Corps Proving Grounds and spent more time at his home, only a few blocks off the main street of Avenue A heading into the heart of Yuma. He devoted many hours to caring for his six grandchildren and enjoyed fishing and building wood projects. He battled a variety of health issues but kept a good attitude and always proved a friendly interviewee for anyone showing an interest in the story of the Morenci Nine. Keeping alive the memories of his fallen brothers, from Morenci and elsewhere, remained his goal. "I don't want them to be forgotten because they sacrificed their lives," he told one reporter. "Those guys have been dead for 30 years but not in mind. I want my kids to at least know that Bobby Draper, their dad's best friend, died in Vietnam for a good reason."[24]

Even up until the last few months of his life, Leroy sought to preserve those memories and to remind people of the sacrifices that had been made. In one of his final public appearances, on November 11, 2011, he proudly joined other veterans at American Legion Post 19 to celebrate their service. He wore a black jacket with a large Marine emblem on the back, with "Vietnam" printed in bold gold letters above the emblem and "1st Recon" below. On his left chest, he had his "Combat Veteran: U.S. Marine Corps" patch, and on his upper sleeves, he wore two other emblems: "Vietnam Veterans Memorial, 1982–2007: 25 Years of Honor" and "Brothers Forever: Fallen but Not Forgotten." The latter depicted a soldier holding an M-16 and kneeling in front of a rifle with the bayonet in the ground topped by a helmet; in the foreground was a cross. He mingled with other Vietnam veterans in the group, many of whom received special recognition that day.[25]

At one point, a reporter approached Leroy to question him about his experiences in Vietnam. She asked him about his return home after serving in Southeast Asia, and he complained about people insulting him and his friends. "You lose a lot of friends, they died for the country and what they believed in. . . . For somebody to call them dumb or whatever for serving this war or going to Vietnam . . . that hurts."[26] Even forty years later, the memories of what happened and how people treated him and his comrades were open wounds.

The November 11 interview was the last one that he completed. On March 27, 2012, he passed away at his home, surrounded by his family.[27] He suffered from a rare disease that destroyed his kidneys. Only a week earlier, Joe had traveled to the Veterans Administration (VA) hospital in Tucson and visited with his friend, posing at the bedside for a photo with Leroy.[28] A few days later, Leroy went home to Yuma and into hospice care.

His funeral took place on April 2 at the St. Rose of Lima Catholic Church in Safford. Earlier, his body had made the long journey from Yuma to southeastern Arizona, and along the way, a group of Vietnam veterans on motorcycles joined the car transporting his remains. With their escort, Leroy made his last trek back to the area where he had spent most of his early life.

Hundreds of people gathered for his funeral, many of them coming down from Morenci and Clifton to honor the fallen hero. Joe made the 160-mile trip from Glendale to be a pallbearer for his friend, the two linked by forty-six years of history as members of a legendary group. At one point, Joe stood in front of a huge Marine Corps banner that had been signed by Leroy's friends to honor him for his service. Wearing a dark-black shirt with a bright gold-and-silver Marine insignia on his left chest as well as a Vietnam Veteran hat, Joe stood proudly to honor his friend.[29]

At the Safford Cemetery, Leroy's final resting place, other Vietnam veterans helped Joe carry their longtime friend, including Oscar and Manny Urrea, Jimmy Martinez, Juan Aparicio, and Rick Aparicio.[30] In the shadow of Mount Graham, his family laid Leroy to rest not too far from Van and Larry, who had been buried forty-four years earlier. The continuities in the history of these men escaped very few.

Like Leroy, Joe struggled with the memories of the war and especially the loss of his friends. Though he originally headed to Apache Junction, a small town just outside Phoenix, he ultimately returned with his wife, Gina, to Morenci, where he worked as a mechanic for PD. They began a family and settled into the community just like other family members and friends, among them Mike Cranford, whom Joe spent time with doing many things, including hunting for turkeys and deer. The two men typically avoided talking about the old times, as the memories of Vietnam haunted them both.[31]

Early on, Joe tried dealing with the grief and anger by utilizing Navajo rituals to assist in the reintegration process for life beyond combat. After returning from Vietnam, he wanted to reverse the process of going to war with an Enemy Way Ceremony, designed to help ease the tension and fear caused by battle. Along with Gina, he traveled to the Navajo Reservation in northeastern Arizona. Gina stayed outside the structure as required while Joe, on the orders of a medicine man, discarded his clothes and put on new ones, a sign of the change. During the rite, which featured chants and songs, the elders told him that in the future, he would accomplish fine things and that everything he would see would be good.[32] Though therapeutic, the ceremony could not fully erase the memories of Vietnam.

Despite his often quiet external demeanor, deep down Joe battled the demons of having seen good men die, their corpses stacked like cords of logs in the back of trucks. The fact that he himself had almost been blown apart and had experienced other near brushes with death further added to the problem. A great deal of restlessness accompanied his life, and he admitted to sometimes having a lousy attitude that led him to drink too much and get into fights at the local bars, following the pattern of many Vietnam veterans. He never talked about his feelings and mostly tried to block out the horrors of Vietnam.[33] The experience had a noticeable effect nonetheless, for as his sister Mary observed, he appeared more withdrawn after the war and did not seem to care as much about his life or culture.[34]

The loss of his friends added to the burden. Daily reminders of them existed in the small town, from the horse stables in the south to familiar haunts that had not been buried under the expanded mine, such as the houses of Clive and Stan. Other physical cues appeared as well, including the presence of many of the parents and brothers and sisters of his fallen friends. Joe admitted that when he saw them, he never knew what to say, and as a result, he often tried to get away from them as fast as possible. Each time, the encounters reminded him that things had changed for the worse and never would be the same as in those carefree days before Vietnam.[35]

The effects of the deaths of his friends sometimes manifested themselves in violent outbursts. For example, at the family house in Tent City, Joe suddenly flew into a rage, having a flashback. He grabbed a knife and threatened everyone, all the while screaming that they had killed his friends. Ultimately, he settled down but not before terrifying his family.[36] Still, like so many other Vietnam veterans, he resisted seeking help and remained isolated in dealing with the grief—grief that endured but thankfully abated over time.

Unfortunately, lots of Vietnam veterans across the nation shared Joe's experience and attitude, often with more tragic results. Large numbers of them refused to get assistance in part because they feared being identified with the negative stereotypes already ascribed to them by popular culture and society, such as baby killers, drug addicts, and crazed criminals.

Living in a small town and within a culture imbued with particularly strong masculine concepts of work and life, Vietnam veterans like Joe fought hard not to be identified with such ugly stereotypes and to avoid the perception of not being able to handle their experiences. The troubles Joe and others faced were only compounded by the fact that many World War II veterans, including the code talkers, had been idolized after they returned home, and few showed outward manifestations of their own struggles with combat experiences (other than heavy drinking). With little support, many Vietnam veterans simply turned inward and tried to mask their problems, all the while carrying guilt for the emotional turmoil that bedeviled them.

Joe eventually left Morenci and the constant reminders of the mining camp after the brutal 1983 strike. He settled in Glendale, Arizona, where he worked for a trucking company for more than twenty years before retiring. He raised a family and, like many Vietnam veterans, continued to deal with the memories of his service. In the early 1990s, he lost Gina to cancer, but he eventually remarried and continued his life not too far from the Arizona Cardinals' massive stadium, which has hosted Super Bowls.

Ultimately, at the urging of Mike and another veteran, Richard Adair, he sought assistance from the VA for his previously undiagnosed post-traumatic stress disorder (PTSD) and filed all the requisite paperwork, although he faced significant obstacles in the process. He had hesitated to do so initially because he believed that, in his words, "once I started receiving compensation . . . something would happen to me."[37] Throughout, Joe remained close to Mike and returned to his hometown each hunting season to spend time with his friend. Yet the loss of Larry and the others left a void in his life that would never be filled. In this and myriad other ways, he would find that a decision he and his buddies made as carefree teenagers would affect him every day of his life.

Like many others who served on the front lines in Southeast Asia, Joe and Leroy struggled with memories of the war for decades. But Mike's battle with the ghosts of Vietnam was even more intense. He returned home to Morenci in 1969, riding in his brand-new Chevelle with Joyce at his side, and started to work for PD, joining many other Vietnam veterans starting their lives anew in the same way that their fathers had after 1945. But almost immediately, tragedy struck. Mike had replaced his love of riding horses with a passion for motorcycles, and while riding one day, a drunk driver cut in front of him and laid him out, severely damaging his leg. For two years, he wrestled with the injury, the insurance company, and disability claims.[38]

Out of work in his early twenties, he fought to find himself. He and Joyce moved to Phoenix, where he planned to attend Mesa Community College. However, that plan never came to fruition, for Mike reinjured his leg. While turkey hunting, he ran down the road after a prize, and the metal plate in his leg broke loose. The resulting wound required more surgery and took a long time to heal. For the rest of his life, he limped a little, and his knee and ankle always swelled when he stood too long.[39]

Eventually, Mike and Joyce returned to Morenci to be closer to friends and family, which was a good move in many ways, especially with the addition of their sons—Clint in 1971 and Tyrel in 1973. Mike rejoined

PD. At times, he found himself laboring alongside Larry's father, and he later stated that they became friends but that "we never really talked about Larry. That was something we didn't talk about."[40] Often, he dreamed about Larry, believing that somehow he was alive and would show up to go hunting and partying with their friends, just like they did before Vietnam. Even thirty years later, he reiterated that he believed "to this day . . . he is not dead. I always expect to see him."[41]

Working closely with Larry's father and being in Morenci with other family members of his fallen comrades exacerbated the survivor's guilt that developed in Mike, something experienced by many other Vietnam veterans. Mike, Joe, and Leroy echoed the sentiments expressed by one Vietnam survivor regarding the guilt that plagued him: "Guilt for surviving. Guilt for not saving someone. Guilt for being saved."[42] Yet another Marine veteran stressed that "those demons diminish with time but never go away."[43]

The burden seemed to weigh more heavily on Mike than on many others, leading him to constantly brood on imponderable questions. What explained why six of the friends with whom he had marched to war had died and he had not? Why had he won the lottery to return home alive when other good people like Larry had not? The guilt hung over him like a dark cloud throughout most of his life.

Mike struggled with other issues as well in the years after Vietnam. Life never proved easy, and the horrible strike in 1983 caused him a great deal of angst. Like most of his fellow union members, he left his job to join the picket lines on that fateful midnight of July 1, 1983. He refused to cross the lines even when others in the community and scabs recruited from mining towns elsewhere began doing so. Later, he underscored the fact that "we wouldn't let one of the group fall out [in Vietnam]. And that's where it all starts. That's where your unionism goes back to."[44]

The strike lasted longer than the Cranford family could tolerate financially, especially with two young boys in school. Mike and Joyce retreated to a small place they owned in the picturesque little town of Alpine, 60 miles to the north of Morenci along Highway 666. Amid mountains rising more than 8,000 feet, with beautiful stands of pine and aspen trees and streams teeming with trout, the Cranford family struggled to make ends meet. Everyone worked as Mike concentrated on a split-rail fence business, and Joyce labored as a housekeeper at a local inn.

After school, Clint and Tyrel also chipped in to help the family meet its financial obligations.[45]

In Alpine, Mike also found time to work with some fellow Vietnam veterans who grappled with the pain resulting from their time in the service. Occasionally, he gathered them up to go out and talk about their experiences, all the while dealing with his own internal demons. Yet he focused more on the others than on himself at that time, and he never sought the psychological counseling that some around him thought he needed as he increasingly confronted his memories of Vietnam.[46]

Finally, the family returned to the Morenci-Clifton area in 1989 when Mike went back into the mine. This time, however, he refused to live in the company town. Instead, he and Joyce bought a small house and property near York in the Apache Grove area, just southeast of Morenci. At work, he remained bitter about the scabs who had crossed the picket lines and emasculated the union, allowing PD to emerge victorious and severely constrict workers' rights. The anger only fueled the underlying frustrations and animosity spawned by his experiences in Vietnam and the tragedies that occurred afterward.[47]

Over the years, Mike became more and more vocal about the war and its effects. In a 1993 interview, he complained, "Vietnam was a lower middle class war. If you had money, you went to college. I didn't go because I wanted to. I went because I was too stupid to know better." He added:

> Back then I could have told you the make and model of every car going down the road and what was under the hood and the stats of all the cheerleaders, but I didn't even know what a Vietnam was. I wasn't even sure who was the president. The fartherest any of us had ever been was Lordsburg and maybe Phoenix. And we're going off to fight for democracy? . . . We were small town kids who didn't know any better.[48]

The memories continued to haunt him. One reporter who interviewed him in the early 1990s noted that for Mike, "a quarter century later . . . it's still as vivid as yesterday." After hearing Mike talk about his combat experience when the enemy crept up on his position and the officers called in artillery strikes right on them, the reporter wrote: "He might have trouble recalling exactly how yesterday unfolded. But the memories

Cranford holds of a place and time where no drama had to be invented and the fear was real and constant and where the thrill of surviving through another day was just as intense, are bound to him forever." Of his combat experience, Mike simply remarked: "I don't guess I've ever been scared since Vietnam. After that, something like an overdue bill or a speeding ticket just doesn't quite get you all worried."[49]

His survivor's guilt continued to manifest itself for many years, even intensifying as he aged. The feelings often deepened when efforts occurred to memorialize him and his eight friends. In August 2002, a crowd of more than two hundred people gathered for a ceremony to commemorate the erecting of the Wall of Honor, a wooden board constructed by Vietnam veteran Daniel Robles to hang at the American Legion Hall in Clifton. The wall memorialized the seventy-seven men from Greenlee County who had died in combat during the nation's wars.[50]

A reading of the men's names followed the presentation of the colors and singing of the national anthem and "America the Beautiful." Different people read from a list of those who died in World War I, World War II, and Korea. Then Mike rose to represent the Vietnam veterans, with Leroy standing nearby. Wearing jeans, a black T-shirt, and a bright bandana on his head, he began to speak. Though he had only a few names to recite, he struggled, his voice breaking several times. He had to stop and gather himself before continuing to deliver the names of his close friends as well as acquaintances from Greenlee County who had died in Southeast Asia. As a Clifton Vietnam veteran observed, "Man, that had to be rough for Mike, really rough. I don't think I could have done it."[51] Mike completed the arduous task, but the pain persisted.

In reality, beyond the survivor's guilt, Mike suffered from undiagnosed PTSD for much of his life after Vietnam. He had all the classic symptoms, which only magnified over the years. Health care professionals had struggled with defining PTSD and its symptoms before Vietnam, using terms such as *shell shock* to diagnose people unable to process or cope with combat trauma. Countless veterans had dealt with the problem before Vietnam, among them World War II hero Audie Murphy, whose illness went undiagnosed and untreated for years.[52] Many other World War II and Korean veterans grappled with the jolts experienced in combat, yet assistance often proved difficult to obtain for various reasons. All too often, sufferers simply self-medicated with alcohol and drugs.[53]

The response to a catastrophic experience such as combat frequently included a hostile and mistrustful attitude toward the outside world, depression, and anxiety, which in turn led to withdrawal from society and estrangement from families and friends. Chronic health problems related to stress and alcohol and drug abuse often developed as well. Many veterans experienced varying degrees of PTSD, with the severity typically depending on the intensity of their own experiences and their psychological profiles. Though the exact numbers suffering from PTSD due to their experiences in Southeast Asia remain unknown because other psychiatric problems intermeshed with it, several hundred thousand Vietnam veterans likely dealt with—and continue to deal with—the disorder.[54]

Mike had all the classic symptoms of PTSD. His wife emphasized that he remained suspicious of others and felt like he was "losing his mind most of the time." He really hated being around people, and crowds especially distressed him. Some observers characterized his demeanor as antisocial, and he compounded the problem by telling people exactly what he thought of them. He slept most of his life with a pistol under the mattress, and everyone in the family knew never to directly wake him. Instead, they turned on the lights and turned off the fan in the room and then gently talked to him. They never touched him when sleeping for fear of how he would respond.[55]

The PTSD worsened as he aged. Joyce stressed that her husband was "so sweet, loving, and caring" but that his "attitude just changed. It came on gradually until the final five years. Then just bang."[56] He never became violent, but he did drink a lot, which eased the pain somewhat and allowed him to gloss over the anger and the hurt.

He also found some comfort in riding his bike, one of his true passions. He had bought a wrecked 1984 Harley Softail motorcycle from someone in Sedona. Mike had it rebuilt, calling it *perra negra* (black bitch). Often, when he needed to escape from the realities of his work and the pressures of his life, he jumped on it and rode all over the county, sometimes taking off into the mountains to the north and heading into New Mexico.[57] Looking like the hard-rocker Ted Nugent and at times sporting a blond ponytail, he mounted the black motorcycle and listened to music by groups such as the Doors and Iron Butterfly. On the bike, Mike escaped the memories and pressures that originated when he was a young man in the jungles of Vietnam, a distant and alien world far from his beloved Greenlee County.

Despite the obvious signs that something was wrong, Mike remained in denial. In large part, he found himself entrapped in the masculine myth that plagued many men. One author explained, "Men, especially the machine men of the military, are not supposed to be helpless, depressed, or unable to handle life. The masculine mystique causes the ostracism of men who ask for help, who experience fright, horror, and worst of all, who have become dependent on people or the government." "After all," he concluded, "real men pull themselves up by their bootstraps and don't go 'crybabying' about jitters or bad dreams."[58]

To show weakness somehow undermined a man's perception of himself (especially if he was from a working-class background) and sometimes even diminished him in the eyes of the community. Though much had changed in American society in the 1960s and 1970s, the culture in which Mike lived had in many ways remained the same. World War II veterans at times proved to be the harshest critics of the Vietnam returnees, adding to the poor treatment most of them had received when they arrived home. One prime example was the powerful chair of the House Committee on Veterans' Affairs, Olin "Tiger" Teague (D-TX). Although a decorated World War II veteran, Teague at one point said of the Vietnam veterans: "How can you little wimps be sick? A tour of duty lasted only twelve months. In World War II, soldiers fought in the war for years. How can you be traumatized?"[59]

Such attitudes led many Vietnam veterans, Mike included, to defer seeking assistance. And when these attitudes combined with community standards dictating how "real men" should behave, it was incredibly hard for veterans like Mike to even acknowledge their need for help, let alone seek it out. As late as 2001, Mike continued to deny having PTSD and actually condemned those suffering with it, despite the manifestations of his own illness that were so obvious to those around him. When Robert O'Malley, the first Marine to receive the Medal of Honor in Vietnam, gave a speech in Clifton, Mike congregated with a group of people outside the hall. As they talked about a variety of subjects, one of them heard him comment, "Fuck all this PTSD shit. They need to pull themselves up by the bootstraps."[60]

Mike continued to function, although he became more and more distant and disconnected as time went by. Many manifestations of the PTSD evolved. Nearly thirty years after the death of his friends, he had a tattoo of "Morenci 9" inscribed on his arm, and he planned to put six crosses up that arm, from his wrist to his shoulder. In each, he wanted the name of one of his six buddies who died in Vietnam. Thus, in large black crosses on his body, he would memorialize his friends. The tattoos would be a constant reminder to himself, his family and acquaintances, and anyone else he encountered, for if the crosses prompted questions from the uninformed, he gladly told them the story of the Morenci Nine. Around Greenlee County, Mike ensured that the losses incurred decades earlier were never forgotten.[61]

The disengagement continued. Mike traveled to a tattoo parlor once again. This time, he had the artist inscribe across his forehead "AMIIGAF." He liked for people to query him on what it meant—to which he simply responded, "Ask Me If I Give A Fuck."[62] Such an attitude caused him problems with authority figures, and some in the community avoided the aging Vietnam veteran, whom they frequently observed zipping through Clifton and Morenci on his black Harley.

Finally, after years of being pressed to do so and after watching other Vietnam vets whom he respected precede him, Mike sought medical assistance in 2004. He traveled 100 miles to the Veterans Administration hospital in Tucson. The doctors almost immediately diagnosed him with a severe case of PTSD and declared him 70 percent PTSD and 30 percent unemployable.[63]

He took the disability payments and immediately quit PD and began doing a series of odd jobs, including prospecting in the mountains around his home in York. Now he could go where and when he wanted without encountering the everyday stresses he had known for so long. He at last had the flexibility to avoid people unless he sought out their company. Meanwhile, the doctors helped him with his issues, with both counseling and medications. Mike had taken a significant step toward a better life and out of the darkness created by the PTSD.

Sadly, just as things seemed to be improving, Mike's life took another tragic turn as he neared his sixtieth birthday. On the night of February 12,

2007, he began experiencing pain in his chest. He first thought it was the acid reflux that he had been battling and took the medicine prescribed by the doctor. The pain, however, only worsened, and he screamed in agony as it traveled down his arm. Joyce frantically called for help, and the emergency services dispatched a helicopter to retrieve Mike. It landed right on the highway and airlifted him to the hospital in Safford. But when he arrived, the doctors pronounced him dead, the victim of a massive coronary.[64]

Three days later, on a cold Tuesday morning, several hundred people packed the funeral home in Safford for his service. The self-described Jack Mormon had not wanted a traditional religious ceremony and had outlined very simple plans for his funeral.[65] After a short time in Safford, the party of more than three hundred started the procession to the cemetery in Franklin. Many of the leather-clad bikers jumped on their Harleys and rode through the streets of staid Safford, with American flags strapped to the backs of some of the bikes, furling in the cool morning air during the 45-mile trip to Franklin. The loud roar of the motorcycles upset the area's normal tranquility as they sped out of town on Highway 70 and across the wind-swept plains.

Hundreds of people on motorcycles and in pickups traveled behind Mike's body, which lay in a simple pine box in the back of a white pickup. His precious "perra negra" Harley followed in the bed of a gray truck. They only slowed down in Duncan, where a number of people lined the street to pay their respects and others at the local restaurant, Ol Joes', watched curiously as the long line of bikes and other vehicles flowed through the town. A couple more miles down Highway 70, the group finally arrived at the Franklin Cemetery, not too far from the New Mexico border.

At the gravesite, the group pulled up with the music of Steppenwolf's "Born to Be Wild" blaring. The classic song with its emphasis on the search for adventure and hell-raising in many ways summed up Mike's personal philosophy. His friends chose it to set the tone for the march to his final resting place.

As the music blasted, the funeral participants climbed off their motorcycles and out of their cars and trucks and proceeded to the gravesite. Several of Mike's friends, all but one clad in leather, took the coffin and moved to the hole in the ground; there, someone took an American flag and draped it across the pine box while a Marine Corps

Joyce Cranford, flanked by her sons, accepting a flag at Mike Cranford's funeral in February 2007. (Photo courtesy of Walter Mares and the Copper Era.*)*

flag unfurled in the foreground. Joyce and the family took their places, and in the large crowd, Leroy, wearing a white vest and a black sweatshirt with a bright-red "USMC" on the chest, stood next to a stoic Joe, who was wearing his heavy black leather jacket and dark glasses. For forty-one years, the three men had been linked by the fateful decision they made in March 1966.[66]

Mark Vallejo, close friend of Mike and Joyce, presided over the funeral. A color guard from American Legion Post 28 in Clifton provided a rifle salute while Jacob Herrera played "Taps." The reporter covering the event commented that Herrera's rendition "drew audible sobs from the crowd." Robert Dellis, with the Marine Corps League in Casa Grande and a member of the Ira Hayes American Legion Post in Sacaton, presented Joyce with a Native American Medal of Honor to recognize Mike and his service, both during and after Vietnam. Then a fellow Vietnam veteran and commander of Post 28, Abe Muñoz, presented the folded flag that had draped the casket to Joyce. To that point, she had been composed, but as she took the triangular flag and pressed it against her face, she began crying.[67]

The casket descended into the ground, and the mourners started passing by the grave for the last time. As they did so, a leather-clad friend threw a copy of *Biker* magazine on top of the pine box. "In case you get bored and need something to read," he told his fallen friend. Another colleague tossed in a can of Bud Light and remarked, "In case you get thirsty, Mike." Tears flowed, even from some of those who looked like they feared nothing.

Slowly, the crowd dispersed, and the bikers and kickers returned up Highways 70 and 75 from Duncan to Clifton and Morenci or Safford or other destinations, heading home to deal with their grief. A number of Mike's fellow bikers held back at the gravesite for a while and then moved toward their motorcycles. Once mounted, one man yelled out, "Fire 'em up!" All the Harleys started in unison, and for more than a minute, the nearly deafening sound of engines revving vibrated across the normally tranquil countryside surrounding the cemetery. It was the final salute for Mike.[68]

It had been thirty-eight years since the last member of the Morenci Nine had passed away during the war. The first six had died of wounds suffered in combat in Vietnam. So, too, did Mike, although he died slowly from what he experienced in Southeast Asia and from the guilt associated with surviving the war. His friends remained forever frozen in time, captured in memories as young men barely beyond their teens. Mike, by contrast, had grown older and had dealt with the ghosts of Vietnam on a daily basis throughout his life.

Other factors contributed to his death, including his chain smoking and hard drinking, but Mike's premature demise had its roots in the exotic land so far away from Greenlee County. Like many tens of thousands of other Vietnam veterans who succumbed early to suicide, depression, Agent Orange, and heart failure attributable to the stress of living, Mike died too young. No memorial exists for these casualties of Vietnam, although some people have argued for one. Even though he lived forty more years than his friends, Mike really never had the life that he would have had without Vietnam. The conflict in Southeast Asia killed him slowly and daily with the horrors he witnessed and the survivor's guilt he carried.

In the end, with all the tragedies experienced by individuals, families, and the community, the story of perseverance in the face of adversity may constitute the greatest component of the Morenci narrative. Everyone lost a piece of himself or herself when a loved one died, whether in the war or nearly forty years later. The conflict in Southeast Asia exacted a huge toll on Morenci, far exceeding that suffered by most communities in the United States. Yet life continued in the small town despite the severe strain put on it. The citizens of Morenci showed a remarkable resilience, particularly those townspeople directly affected by the deaths.

People coped with the sorrow and loss in many ways, both public and private, as grief had many manifestations. And as the concluding chapter will show, one highly significant aspect of this was the way in which people chose to remember the sacrifice and its meaning for the community and the nation.

13

Remembering the Fallen

Community, Memory, and the Nine

On May 26, 2007, a warm Saturday morning, the loud sounds of motorcycles resonated against the red rock hills that surrounded the road leading out of Clifton to Ward Canyon. Arizona Rangers, volunteers dressed in their traditional khaki uniforms, blocked the thoroughfare and directed traffic. More than a hundred people, many on motorcycles, roared down the asphalt. Some had American flags on the backs of their cycles, waving in the hot desert wind of the Memorial Day weekend.[1]

Some in the caravan had traveled more than 160 miles from Phoenix, starting before dawn in Mesa at the Applebee's at Gilbert and Baseline Roads. They picked up more riders in Globe and Safford before making the final leg of the trip to Clifton, a journey of nearly four hours from start to finish. As their numbers grew, so did the stares of the passersby heading toward Phoenix for the holiday weekend. In small towns such as Superior, Miami, and Thatcher, people also marveled at the strange sight, which looked more like a scene from *Easy Rider* than the normal parade of trucks and tractors that plied the roads on a typical Saturday morning.

The group of black leather–clad bikers, many with long gray hair flowing in the wind, joined people exiting their large Ford and Chevy pickups to the sounds of the Doors' "LA Woman" playing loudly on a stereo. One by one, they parked and dismounted, most of the men in their late fifties and early sixties, with a significant number of Mexican Americans and Native Americans in the group. They joined others who gathered at the bottom of a steep trail for the processional, including a small group of fresh-faced Reserve Officers' Training Corps (ROTC) recruits dressed in green uniforms, readying to serve as an honor guard.

The assembled crowd took some time before beginning the climb to the memorial on top of Mares Bluff. The local paper had warned beforehand, "Anyone with a heart condition or respiratory ailment should not attempt the climb."[2] A few people started the long, steep trek but almost immediately turned back. The majority, among them the young cadets in the shined black boots as well as a couple of very fit World War II veterans in their eighties, marched forward. As they progressed, their feet slipped in the small rocks and shifting dirt amid the ocotillos and scrub brushes, making the going challenging for many.

Sometime before the main group of bikers arrived, another band of people marched up the bluff. Bobby Dale's father, Robert Draper, Sr., now in his seventies but in remarkably good shape, led the way. He easily traversed the narrow path, quickly moving toward the crest. A few veterans of the Iraq War from Clifton and Morenci and their family members joined him, arriving first at the top of the bluff.

The Mares Bluff Veterans Memorial was the brainchild of Steve Guzzo, a Vietnam veteran from Clifton who could have passed for the brother of Tommy Chong (of Cheech and Chong fame), complete with a long ponytail and intense, dark eyes. One night, Steve dreamed that God transported and then suspended him above the ultimate site for the memorial. There, he received instructions on how to build a line of dog tags strung underneath poles hoisting the flags of the various branches of the US military, with an American flag nearer the edge of the bluff.[3]

Consequently, the memorial had strong religious symbolism. Up the hill from the flags, a stand housed a Bible and a log book where people could leave their reflections. Etched on a small plaque was the inscription from John 15:13, "No greater love does a man have than he would lay down his life for another." Steve also felt compelled to create signposts, like the stations of the cross, along the steep path up the bluff, inscribed with the names of the dead from the various wars in which the veterans of Greenlee County fought. Guzzo envisioned the memorial as a place of healing for everyone in the community.[4]

This particular day, many of the veterans and their families and friends scaled the rugged path, with the young ROTC members bringing up the rear. Sweating profusely underneath their jackets, their boots becoming dusted with the red clay, these youngsters took their positions with rifles in hand just up the hill overlooking the memorial. A diverse group of people gathered at various points around the memorial. They waited for stragglers to reach the top, which had been no small task for some standing there at that point.

A simple ceremony followed. The niece of Lori Piestewa, the Hopi Indian who had died in Iraq in the early stages of the Iraq War, sang the national anthem. After a few short speeches, several men, including Mike Cranford's two sons, Ty and Clint, walked to the poles to help raise the flags of each of the branches of the US military. Then, someone rang a bell that had been taken from one of the old churches and dragged to the site. The sounds echoed through the canyons surrounding the bluff, as did the rifle shots fired by the honor guard to end the ceremony. It was a solemn event that clearly marked the holiday's focus on honoring those who had fought and died for their country.

Once the observance ended, people began to disperse and congregate again at a park in Clifton for a meal and speeches commemorating Memorial Day. A few lingered on the bluff, admiring the beautiful view. Others remained behind to look at the thousands of dog tags strung underneath the flags, including those of local veterans as well as celebrities who had served such as Elvis Presley, Jimi Hendrix, and John McCain. However, the first ones on the line, starting from the left, bore the names of Larry West; Clive Garcia, Jr.; Stan King; Bobby Dale Draper; Van Whitmer; and Robert Moncayo.

In Greenlee County, the Morenci Nine (particularly those who had died) played a significant role in any remembrance of the service of veterans. It may have been nearly forty years since the first of the nine Marines had died, but their story remained fresh in the minds of many in the county. The sacrifices made by the Morenci Nine, both living and dead, had evolved into a larger-than-life story that became a cornerstone of the community's consciousness and, to a degree, part of the regional and even the national story of the Vietnam War.

The memorialization of Vietnam veterans, including the Morenci Nine, played out within a very different context than that of their fathers and uncles who fought in World War II. In 1945, the troops returned home as a large collective group and exuded the joy and confidence of a victorious force serving a just cause. Across the country, communities organized parades and erected monuments to honor them. The federal government heaped benefits on them, including the immensely popular GI Bill. A national narrative celebrated the triumph of the Americans over the fascists, while often glossing over the immense losses that occurred and the challenges faced by many returnees, including those of color and the severely wounded.[5]

World War II veterans were wildly popular and soon dominated all the veterans' organizations. In the political arena, veterans such as Dwight Eisenhower and John F. Kennedy parlayed heroic service into electoral success. Throughout society, especially as the Cold War intensified, people increasingly heralded the triumph of the World War II veterans, holding them up as role models. Popular culture reinforced the perceptions, with actors such as John Wayne, Clark Gable, Jimmy Stewart, and Gregory Peck depicting valiant wartime figures.[6] As a result, millions of men and women occupied a special place in society for their service and sacrifices, especially in the public realm.[7]

In contrast, Vietnam veterans received few parades or monuments and generally felt isolated within society. This reflected the country's mood as the United States began large-scale withdrawals from Vietnam in 1970, culminating in the fall of Saigon in April 1975. After years of division and protests, the American people wanted to close the book on a sad chapter in the nation's history. Consequently, Vietnam veterans in essence became invisible, apart from the negative stereotypes assigned to them and also perpetuated in movies and on television.[8] As one distinguished historian has noted, the country developed a "self-conscious, collective amnesia" regarding the war and those who fought it.[9]

The death of Clive Garcia had brought national attention to Morenci, but interest in the story faded quickly. Morenci shared the nation's war weariness and struggled under the weight of the heavy sacrifice paid by the community. Even veterans groups such as the American Legion and the Veterans of Foreign Wars in Greenlee County grappled with how Vietnam veterans fit into their organizations, a problem exacerbated by the generation gap that developed between the World War II and Vietnam veterans.[10] This dislocation happened in many communities across the country.

*   *   *

Thus, the memorialization of the Vietnam veteran for the first decade and a half after Clive's death took place almost exclusively in the personal, rather than the public, sphere. Few Americans, including those in Greenlee County, publicly challenged the standard negative narrative of the war, and so the private efforts of the soldiers and their families and friends became the cornerstone of remembrance. Most refused to let the memories wane, but at the heart of their efforts to remember their veterans was the idea of the sacrifice that caused so much sorrow—instead of the triumphalism of the World War II generation—even as the nation searched for some meaning in the Vietnam experience.

Family members became the crucible for sustaining and protecting the memory of the young men of the Morenci Nine, particularly those who died. Instinctively, many had become disillusioned with the news coverage after Clive's death. They believed the media politicized the deaths of their Marines with an antiwar slant. For years, parents and family members worried about how their sons and their sacrifices would be portrayed by those outside the community.[11]

As a result, when a Hollywood producer showed up in Morenci in 1970 and talked about making a movie, most family members decided against it, wanting instead to deal with the grief at hand. The same thing occurred in the 1980s when a reporter and Safford native, Don Hoffman, sought to write the story. This time, several families resisted, and the Garcias even considered hiring legal counsel to stop the process. Hoffman made some progress but eventually dropped the project due to the lack of cooperation.[12]

Some of the most vigilant guardians of memory regarding the dead members of the Morenci Nine were close relatives, who naturally possessed an intimate knowledge of the habits and histories of their sons and brothers before joining the Marines. Certain friends had long-term relationships with these young men, but few approximated those of the parents or siblings, particularly since many of the families had younger sons and daughters who walked in the shadow of their legendary brothers.

In many cases, family members preserved physical reminders of their loved ones. Stan's family followed his instructions and for a long time kept his toiletries and clothes where he had left them.[13] The West and Draper families collected the belongings of their fallen sons, including letters, medals, and photos, keeping them in safe places.[14] Parents and siblings refused to part with the tangible reminders of their loved ones, determined to hold onto the memories despite the pain that often accompanied the mementos.

Individual actions also sustained the memories of the dead. An early example was Kenneth Draper's school newspaper article, which appeared after Clive's death and chronicled the sacrifices of his brother, Bobby Dale, and the other members of the Morenci Nine.[15] Martin Garcia's relentless attempts to join the Marine Corps demonstrated his commitment to carry on his brother's legacy by following in his footsteps. In other instances, the continued respect and love felt for the lost loved ones were manifested in long-term actions, such as Danny Garcia caring for the graves of Clive and Robert in Bunker Hill Cemetery around each Memorial Day or Clive's birthday on September 17.[16] These small but powerful symbolic acts helped sustain the memory of the fallen on the personal level.

Maintaining the memories on a personal level often went beyond archiving physical belongings or performing commemorative actions and encompassed common psychological acts of remembering the dead. Though a normal coping mechanism would have been to suppress the painful losses, most family members fought such an impulse and remembered their loved ones in different ways. The poetic statement of one family that lost a son in Vietnam highlighted how many people felt:

When the evening shades are falling
And we are sitting all alone
In our hearts there comes a longing
If he only could come home[17]

As the distinguished author Gabriel García Márquez observes, "The memory of the heart eliminates the bad and magnifies the good; thanks to this artifice, we are able to bear the past."[18]

The memories of the good times that circulated within families regarding those violently ripped from their midst proved extremely important. The Memorial Day statement of a family whose son died in Korea encapsulated the feelings of many others who lost sons in combat: "Nothing can ever take away the love a heart holds dear. Remembrances keep him near."[19] Preserving memories became a way to deal with the deaths, a form of healing. With the absence of a collective public effort after Vietnam to deal with the war and the huge psychological trauma experienced by the nation, the small acts of memory that allowed for some measure of personal healing became even more crucial, especially for those who lost family members in Southeast Asia.

Remembrance unfolded in multiple ways. It could be as random as a thought or maybe a conversation during a meal, as when people talked about Stan getting in a fight with some Clifton boys or when family members relived the big game where Bobby Dale returned a fumble for a touchdown only to have the score negated.[20] Relatives retold tales about Clive and his brothers trying to trap animals along the river and the disappointment they felt at finding a skunk instead of the legendary tiger they sought.[21] In most cases, the memories of the dead remained firmly implanted in the recollections of the living, and many were passed on to young people who may not have known their uncles or cousins.

Legends grew over time about those who died, and though sadness usually followed, the act of talking about them helped somewhat in the long healing process for those left behind. Forty years after his brother died, Martin Garcia noted, "A month does not go by without my other brother and me speaking of and remembering him." The context was important, as he watched people around him deal with new losses. "I feel for all those younger siblings who have lost their older idols to wars in Iraq and Afghanistan in these modern times. Even after they return home, let us never forget the impact each and every one [who] served in the military made in our lives."[22]

But sustaining the memories also carried a cost. For instance, as the twentieth anniversary of Clive's death neared, Julia Garcia wrote a letter to Martin expressing that "because I am human & weak I most certainly remember & at times still grieve." However, she added, "my grief is not as painful for the dead as it is for the living." "I hurt so much to see what the conflict of Viet Nam has done to you," she lamented. "So many lives have been marred. I am sorry yours has to be one of them. Sorry because it's so unfair that someone like you has to suffer so much." She continued, "I have been able to cope with hurts . . . & with God's grace accept death because I have the hope which the resurrected Christ has given to us."[23]

The pain of the loss was substantial, even years later, and the living struggled mightily. War most closely affected those who fought it, but its reach extended well beyond to families, friends, and communities across the nation.

Most family members—including aunts and uncles, cousins, and nieces and nephews—had their own special memories of the fallen, which they sometimes shared. Time would help heal the wounds, although a tinge of sadness always existed. And over time, reflections focused as much on the good as on the bad, the positive rather than the loss. Almost always, people remembered the great potential of the young men and what might have been had they lived. In those memories, the dead never aged one more day, even as the people holding them moved forward.

Beyond the families, Joe, Mike, and Leroy carried the strongest memories of their fallen friends, and they worked to sustain them. Several had been friends with their lost buddies since grade school, sharing time in school hallways, sweating under the hot August sun during football practices, and hunting and fishing together. They also had some of the most recent shared experiences, having taken the oath of allegiance together, supported each other in boot camp, climbed hills together during advanced training, and in some cases even partied together in Vietnam. These memories of their comrades helped them process the losses as well as come to terms with their own service.

Nonetheless, difficult memories sometimes flooded the minds of the survivors. Mike recalled being with Larry right before he went on a mission and lost his life. Leroy remembered being passed out in a trench with Bobby Dale at Camp Reasoner, just before he died in an ambush. Joe would think about escorting Larry on his final trip home, reflecting on the images of his friend's lifeless body in his coffin. They had a bond to the dead as well as to each other, the legendary Morenci Nine who had paid such a high price during the Vietnam War. It often proved a heavy burden to carry.

Just like the family members, the three survivors talked about their friends and kept photos and additional mementos of their fallen comrades. Furthermore, their mere presence served as a constant reminder of the Morenci Nine. In essence, they constituted walking memorials to the group of teenaged boys who became forever intertwined that fateful day in March 1966 when they decided to join the Marines.

Their status as survivors and the constant reminders significantly affected Joe, Leroy, and Mike. Questions arose for them. Why had they been so lucky? Why had they survived when their friends had not? How could they face the family members of those who had not come home? Across the country, many veterans dealt with such questions, but these three had a unique identity tied to their friends due to their personal closeness and the notoriety of their particular story. The pressure built over time, especially for Mike, who struggled with survivor's guilt.

In the end, the survivors became a critical source of remembrance, especially as witnesses to the story. "I don't want them to be forgotten because they sacrificed their lives," Leroy told one reporter. He emphasized that even though his friends had died years ago, they remained in his thoughts. In particular, he wanted people to understand that his friends had made the ultimate sacrifice for a good cause.[24] The latter sentiment carries great significance. Survivors and family members wanted people to know that the fallen soldiers had not died in vain. Further, they wanted to challenge others never to forget to honor those who had paid the ultimate price. For many years, this remained a central focus in sustaining the memory of the Nine.

The community also served as a depository of the memories of the Nine, especially close friends and former mentors. The fact that Morenci was a close-knit community aided the process, and many shared the feeling expressed by one high school friend, Larry Aker, who commented about his lost comrades, "They're not gone as long as you say their names."[25] Though it was hard to do so, people would talk about their missing friends at special events, such as high school reunions. These remembrances sustained their legacies and served as a reminder of the sacrifices the community had made in the defense of the nation. This was especially significant because few people in the town debated the outcome of the war publicly, choosing instead to place the losses in a narrative that maintained that those who died had unflinchingly answered the call of their country.[26]

Just like family members, friends also performed small acts for those who died. These might be relatively mundane acts, such as Larry Kenan traveling to several gravesites to clean them and then talk to the lost friend about that year's Morenci football team. Or they might be simple but lasting acts, such as members of the class of 1964 giving a plaque honoring Stan to his parents, inscribed with the words "In Memoriam Lance Cpl. Bradford Stanley King. Killed in Action November 6, 1967 in Vietnam. Class of 1964." The King family placed the plaque in the high school trophy case only a few years after his death, where it remained for students to view.[27]

Many former mentors also played a role in the remembrance process. William Senne, a local high school history teacher, frequently told his students about the Morenci Nine, and over the years, he joined other teachers in having their students do research on the topic. One of these students, Oscar Baca, even wrote a prize-winning paper on the Nine for the Arizona Historical Convention in 2004.[28] The mentors' efforts would continue for many years as the story became a pivotal part of the historical consciousness of the community. Furthermore, it was a reminder to subsequent generations of their duty to serve, despite the horrific costs inflicted on the families and the community.

The memories carried by friends and members of the community extended beyond Morenci. Like so many rural areas across the United States since the 1970s, Greenlee County lost large numbers of people, especially after the 1983 strike. Some headed to other mining towns; many retired in Safford and in Graham County. Others sought more stable employment in larger towns, such as Phoenix and Tucson, that boomed in the 1980s and 1990s. They also spread throughout the West into California, Oregon, Utah, Idaho, and Montana, settling in Los Angeles, San Diego, and other densely populated cities.

As they left, they carried the memories of their community, with its rich history of labor strife and seemingly larger-than-life tales. Their remembrance of the Morenci Nine transferred to friends, coworkers, and children in their new homes. People took pride in where they came from as they moved into new lives in different areas, and they told the stories of their community, allowing the Morenci Nine narrative to seep into the regional consciousness.

Personal memories about the Morenci Nine had to suffice because few public commemorations occurred. Although the families, friends, and associates of more than fifty-eight thousand people across the United States dealt with the individual losses of Vietnam, in Morenci, a large part of the central narrative revolved around the Nine. The clustering of the deaths made their story more exceptional. Several communities in Arizona and elsewhere in the country lost similar numbers, and some of these towns were even smaller than Morenci. But because the Nine joined up together and also because they lived in the relatively distinctive setting of a mining camp, their story was unique. The fact that their deaths touched so many members of the community had long-term consequences for the ways in which the Vietnam War was remembered in Greenlee County when the process of memorialization became more fashionable in the mid-1980s.

The efforts had some therapeutic effects, for personal remembrance was a coping mechanism that ultimately assisted the healing process. Sustaining the memories of the fallen allowed people to hold on to the positive and eventually suppress the negative aspects of the loss, albeit never fully. Ultimately, pride in the commitment of those who served during the divisive conflict increasingly blended with the anguish people felt. In time, the memorialization became centered on the sacrifices that were made and on honoring those who died.

Finally, retaining remembrances in the private realm allowed people to protect the memories of their sons, brothers, and friends. Vietnam veterans had no grand narrative like the World War II one, where triumph usually trumped—or at least masked—sadness. Therefore, families and friends fashioned their own account, focusing on the sorrow and the search for meaning in the sacrifices. That allowed them to prevent the appropriation and misuse of the memories by those with political agendas, whether they were activists in the antiwar movement or hawks who sought to extol the constructed virtue of the crusade in Vietnam to promote their own aggressive foreign policy agenda in the 1980s.

It is easier to look at national and community commemoration efforts, for they usually create permanent structures to honor the dead—visible markers shared by the collective citizenry. But private manifestations are enduring, albeit constantly in flux because they lack the permanency of a monument or other structures. Also, they are more difficult to observe. But in the case of the Morenci Nine, the personal manifestations of loss forcefully sustained the memory of individuals and became the foundation of remembrance for the town and, to a degree, for the region and even the nation relating to the Vietnam War.

The Morenci example corresponded closely with the national story of remembrance of the Vietnam soldier for the first decade after the war ended. Memories resided primarily in the private realm and focused on sorrow as well as feelings of neglect and betrayal. After the mid-1980s, however, changes occurred. Sorrow remained central to the narrative, but more and more, an effort to heal evolved. The story of the Morenci Nine, along with many others across the country, played a part in redefining the discourse.

The memorialization of the Vietnam soldiers differed significantly from earlier manifestations. After the American Revolution, the Civil War, and World War II, civic leaders quickly erected memorials to those who fought as well as those who died.[29] However, starting with Korea and especially during the long, tumultuous struggle in Vietnam, Americans sought to forget, not glorify, the conflicts in the public realm.[30] Though some memorialization efforts occurred for Vietnam in the 1970s, such as the dedication of the Vietnam Veterans Peace and Brotherhood Chapel in 1971 just outside Taos, New Mexico, they paled in comparison to those after World War II.[31] The early efforts of the post-Vietnam era, much like the private ones, centered more on loss than on creating a grand narrative of triumph comparable to that crafted after forces returned home in 1945.

Meanwhile, Vietnam veterans fought to overcome the prejudices and negative stereotypes permeating American society in the 1970s. The most significant struggle involved the efforts by veterans to build a national Vietnam memorial on the Washington Mall in the 1980s. The project was the creation of Vietnam veteran Jan Scruggs. After watching the movie *Deer Hunter*, Scruggs experienced flashbacks, seeing the faces of his fallen comrades. "The names, the names," he lamented. "No one remembers their names." He told how he emerged from his traumatic experience wanting to build a memorial that would "have the names of everyone killed."[32]

For more than three years, Scruggs and his comrades raised money to construct the memorial while simultaneously lobbying Congress to allocate a site for it on the National Lawn near the Lincoln Memorial.[33] Eventually, they succeeded, and a twenty-one-year-old Yale University undergraduate, Maya Lin, designed a wall built into the ground in the shape of an elongated V, with the names of the service members who died in the conflict embedded in the dark-black granite. To personalize the experience, the polished stone reflected the image of the person viewing the names. Lin emphasized that her design left it "up to each individual to resolve or come to terms with this loss. For death is in the end a personal and private matter and the area containing this within the memorial is a quiet place, meant for personal reflection and private reckoning."[34]

Despite some criticisms that led to the addition of a statue and a flagpole, the official unveiling of the memorial occurred on November 12, 1982.[35] Overall, people responded quite favorably. For some, it became a place of healing, especially for family members, friends, and comrades in arms.[36] One Marine stressed: "I think the Vietnam Memorial has been a great thing for the Vietnam veterans. It's really focused people's attention on Vietnam veterans in a respectful way. . . . I think it's helped us 100 percent."[37]

Historian Kristin Ann Hass aptly summarizes the effect of the memorial: "The Wall elicits a physical response. It has inspired visitors to represent their own grief, loss, rage, and despair." Over time, people began leaving memorabilia, including letters, medals, and teddy bears. "Contributing their private representations to public space," Hass explains, "they cross the boundary between the private and public, the nation and the citizen, powerfully claiming the memorial as their own."[38] The memorial, still one of the most visited sites in Washington, led to a flurry of activity because veterans from World War II and Korea sought their own memorials after 1982. It also shaped the design of many future memorials, including those built to honor Vietnam veterans in other locations.

In addition, the memorial provided the Vietnam veterans with a renewed sense of purpose that allowed them to claim a place of respect in the country. Long-delayed parades followed in cities such as Houston and Chicago. And on May 7, 1985, more than twenty-five thousand Vietnam veterans marched in New York City's "Canyon of Heroes," passing by more than a million people who showered them with 468 tons of ticker tape.[39] The unveiling of the wall, combined with other activities, inspired the veterans and their families to build other memorials at state and local levels, sparking a new pride in their contributions to the nation that would be expressed in many different venues, among them Greenlee County.

*   *   *

At the Vietnam Memorial, the Morenci Nine constitute only a small portion of the more than fifty-eight thousand names engraved into the black granite. Yet for people from Greenlee County, they represent a permanent reminder of the sacrifice made by their community, a story that became interwoven with the narrative of other towns that also paid a heavy price during Vietnam.

When people go to the memorial, they often search through a couple of the large books located at both ends of the structure, ones listing all the names on the wall. For people interested in the Morenci story, the search carries them to the following parts of the wall (though the search process is made harder by the fact that Clifton is listed as Stan's hometown):

Bobby Dale Draper	Panel 24E, Line 66
Stan King	Panel 29E, Line 32
Van Whitmer	Panel 49E, Line 48
Larry West	Panel 62E, Line 4
Jose (Robert) Moncayo	Panel 56W, Line 26
Clive Garcia	Panel 16W, Line 124

Many people from Morenci have never had the opportunity to visit Washington, DC, because of the significant costs associated with traveling there, but some have witnessed firsthand the power of the monument. They included Clive Garcia's younger sister, Kathy, who made the journey in June 1986. While attending a conference in Baltimore, she joined a colleague on a hot and humid Friday for the short trip to the memorial. After a long, circuitous excursion along the intricate Washington freeway system, they arrived at the mall.[40]

The journey was a hard one for Kathy, who had been so close to the brother who called her his "princess." "As we walked along the long reflection pond," she remembered, "I started to shake and I had a hard time catching my breath, then my legs were shaking so bad a couple of times I grabbed my friend's arm." When her coworker asked if she really wanted to continue, Kathy replied affirmatively. By the time she reached the book of names used to locate the fallen, she recalled, "I was full blown hyperventilating. All I can say is it's a good thing that the book had a glass

Kathy Garcia Windsor at the Vietnam Wall in Washington, DC, in 1986.
(Photo courtesy of Kathy Garcia Windsor.)

cover because I was crying so bad, my tears [were] falling on the glass." As she looked through the index, she thought, "all these names." She found Clive's name and began rubbing it with her finger, crying hard.[41]

A long walk followed, down to where she located Clive's name toward the middle of the memorial. As they passed the other panels, "all these names" kept flooding her mind. She stopped in front of panel 16W. "Then my eyes locked on his name and my knees buckled a little and the sobbing was uncontrollable. Lots of people all around but I didn't care. . . . I squatted down and rubbed my finger over his name." After a while, she made a rubbing of his name and took lots of pictures. As she walked away, she looked back down the long wall with all the flowers and other things people had left in tribute, again thinking, "all those names."[42]

The architect of the wall, Maya Lin, clearly achieved her goal of creating a quiet, personal space for people like Kathy, whose emotional journey in 1986 was replicated by many others who have visited the site over the years. More people from Greenlee County followed, including Penny King and Oscar Urrea, the latter traveling in a motorcycle caravan to pay homage to his fallen comrades as well as those missing in action.[43] More wanted to make the trip as well, for the wall became a shrine to visit for the Vietnam generation. Mike even made plans to travel with his sons on their motorcycles for a cross-country trip. However, he passed away before he could make the journey.[44]

People who visited the wall often took the time to make rubbings of names and snap pictures. They carried back the memories of the wall and morphed them onto other sites honoring Vietnam veterans. Furthermore, some returned with a commitment to create their own memorials, sites that they could visit more often. The freeing of the country to honor the Vietnam veterans, both living and dead, symbolized by the wall, was an important step in the healing of a generation of warriors scarred by their experiences. Much more remained to be done, as evidenced by the continued battles survivors waged with issues related to Agent Orange poisoning and PTSD, but it was a start. And as the memorialization moved out of the private and increasingly entered the public realm, a new set of tensions arose.

The Vietnam Memorial became iconic, and within a short time the Vietnam Veterans Memorial Fund (VVMF) commissioned the Moving

Wall, a scale model of the original that could be transported across the country. Its supporters recognized that many people could not afford trips to Washington, DC, and they decided to make the powerful memorial available to as many people as possible.

The Moving Wall traversed the country for nearly thirty years. It visited Arizona several times, but it did not reach southeastern Arizona until 2008. The VFW Auxiliary in Thatcher—with financial support from the Freeport-McMoran Company (which had bought out Phelps Dodge) and the cities of Safford, Thatcher, and Pima—hosted the week-long event in early April. The 370-foot-long wall, 8 feet high at the center, had thirty-five black-granite panels. A four-person team accompanied it, in part to set it up and in part to serve as guides to help visitors locate their loved ones or friends. As one of the organizers of the 2008 event, Charlotte Reynolds, remarked, "The main focus is to provide the whole community a chance to honor, respect and remember those who have paid the ultimate price for our freedom."[45]

The Morenci Nine figured prominently in the ceremony. A limousine transported Clive and Julia Garcia from their small trailer house just outside Safford to the New Mexico line, where they greeted the large trucks transporting the wall and then led them to the temporary site. Leroy traveled from Yuma to participate, taking time to pose for a picture with Julia.[46] Several people gave speeches, and others, including Steve Guzzo, played music that honored the friends from Morenci and Clifton who had fought and died in Vietnam. One veteran noted, "It's wonderful that the sponsors thought it was worthwhile and I appreciate it."[47]

Technological advances also brought different renditions of the wall to people in Greenlee County. With the information revolution in the 1990s, several online versions of the wall appeared. Volunteers devoted countless hours to put the names of those who died in Vietnam where people could contribute their own memories. They listed units, dates of birth and death, hometowns, and the locations on the real wall where the names appeared. On the digital versions, viewers could post their condolences and memories, and some even allowed people to make a virtual rubbing that could be printed.

One well-done example, the Vietnam Veterans Memorial—The Wall, features the Morenci Nine prominently.[48] Under the section "Names of the Wall," the Morenci story appears along with stories of other small towns and entities that made similar sacrifices, such as Beallsville, Ohio (population 475), which had six young men die in Vietnam, and Thomas Edison High School in Philadelphia, which lost fifty-four. The Morenci story on this site borrows heavily from the 1970 *Time* magazine article, including this description of the nine boys before they joined the Marines: "They led some of the scrappiest high school football and basketball teams that the little Arizona copper town of Morenci (pop. 5,058) had ever known and cheered." Ultimately, the story highlighted the fact that "only 3 returned home." It also listed all six who died and how they perished, although it made some mistakes, such as claiming the enemy wiped out Robert's entire platoon.[49]

Friends and family often left messages on the individual pages of the fallen soldiers. Bobby Dale's friend Rick Melton wrote: "Bobby, was a great friend" who "loved his family. . . . Bobby was like a brother to me. Wish he was still here with us." He concluded, "Just want him to know I've missed him a great deal and want to thank him and the rest for giving me and my family the freedom we have. Bobby, I know your life here on this earth was short but I thank you and the Good Lord for the times we had. May God bless you!!!"[50]

The Internet changed the nature of memorials by making the information accessible to more people and creating virtual communities that often spread across the globe. Though lacking the emotional power of the real wall, with the names of more than fifty-eight thousand Americans engraved in black stone, the online versions offer people a chance to research the fallen, to leave messages, and to interact with others. As the medium becomes more sophisticated, it will continue to assist in sustaining the memories and disseminating information about the Morenci Nine, as well as the stories of other communities that suffered so much.[51]

Local efforts at publicly memorializing the Vietnam soldiers, the Morenci Nine included, followed on the heels of the national memorial. Time had allowed communities to heal, at least in part, from the open wounds caused by the losses they sustained. Furthermore, a change in the old guard in the veterans' community occurred, for the Vietnam veterans increasingly became leaders in local organizations such as the American

Legion. As many reached their fifties and sixties, they devoted more time to organizing and promoting acts of remembrance.

Nonetheless, challenges would surface in the efforts to remember the service and sacrifice of the Vietnam veteran. As historian John Bodnar notes, "The shaping of a past worthy of public commemoration in the present is contested and involves a struggle for supremacy between advocates of various political ideas and sentiments."[52] The challenges unfolded on many levels, including the national one because some leaders, among them President Ronald Reagan, tried to reframe the war as a noble cause. Many Vietnam veterans resisted such efforts, arguing that they demeaned the sense of loss and undercut the healing process. They also feared such representations were smokescreens for Reagan's efforts to involve the United States in new adventures in the jungles of El Salvador and Nicaragua.[53]

Challenges also existed on the local level. How would Greenlee County commemorate its Vietnam veterans, in particular those who lost their lives in Southeast Asia? Who would be included? How would they be memorialized? What would be emphasized—sorrow and healing or renewed pride? What role would race play in terms of who received attention? How would the events since the war shape the discourse of memory? Each of these questions had already played out to a degree in discussions related to the wall in Washington, DC, but debates at many levels, including the local, continued throughout the thirty-year period after the unveiling of the national memorial.

Slowly, public manifestations commemorating the sacrifice of the Morenci Nine arose. Remembering them became a fundamental part of honoring the service of all the Vietnam veterans from Greenlee County. The community remembrances embodied the major components of the Vietnam narrative for many people in the mining towns of Arizona and industrial centers across the country, such as sorrow, a desire for healing, and the demographics of the community. Though the Morenci story continued to percolate in the private realm, it also became a greater part of the public discourse.

Beyond the local level, newspapers helped keep the story alive in the public consciousness. Retrospectives, such as the tribute to the living and dead members of the Morenci Nine that ran in the *Mesa Tribune* on Veterans Day 1993, often appeared around patriotic holidays and reached large audiences. Another piece, covering nearly two full pages, emerged several years later in the Memorial Day 2000 edition of the *Arizona Republic*, featuring Mike, Joe, and Leroy. Both articles were extensive accounts and reached a sizable number of readers in the Phoenix metropolitan area, where many people originally from Morenci lived. The reports also educated others about the Morenci Nine, introducing their story to the numerous transplants from the Midwest and the West Coast who had flooded the Valley of the Sun after the end of the war.[54]

Even with such publicity, it still took a while before a permanent memorial to the Morenci Nine appeared. And when it did, in 1998, organizers placed it near Morenci High School, not the old three-story building that the young men attended but the modern one down the hill not far from Clive's home on Gila Street. In late February 1998, the American Legion requested permission from the Morenci Unified School District's governing board to erect a monument holding a plaque dedicated to the Morenci Nine. District Superintendent David Woodall reported that people had suggested placing it near the main entrance to the high school.[55]

The plans to construct the monument went forward with the financial assistance of PD. Finally, on July 4, 1998, the organizers officially dedicated the memorial; the day marked the thirty-second anniversary of the Morenci Nine boarding a bus for boot camp. Family members of the group—including representatives of the Garcia, Moncayo, King, and Draper clans—joined Leroy and Mike outside the high school near the flagpole that many young people passed each day. More than a hundred spectators attended, among them Maj. Ruben Garcia, who arrived in town to represent the Marine Corps at the event.[56]

Before the formal ceremony, people circled around the memorial to view the 4-foot-high pedestal constructed from local materials, including the turquoise-colored rock sometimes found in the riverbeds. Recessed into the front side was a plaque with the words "In Honor of 'The Marines From Morenci' Class of 1966." Underneath, organizers had listed the name and rank of each of the nine Marines, starting from the first who died in the war and concluding with the three who came home. Small crosses placed to the left side of their inscriptions signified the dead.[57]

On an overcast day with high, thin clouds shielding the sun, the ceremony began. The participants watched members of an honor guard from the American Legion post line up, dressed in short-sleeve white shirts, dark pants, and blue berets. They were mostly Mexican American veterans, who now composed a large segment of the organization. Once notified to start, they raised the American flag as the crowd of spectators looked on. Then they stepped back several yards behind the memorial and stood at attention with their rifles in hand.[58]

Several speakers moved forward to talk about the memorial. At one point, organizers asked Leroy to speak. Dressed in black jeans and a gray polo shirt with a black collar and wearing a large belt buckle and cowboy boots along with a red Marine baseball hat, he slowly advanced to stand near the monument. Not a physically imposing figure and by nature relatively reserved, he started his address by thanking everyone responsible for the memorial to his friends, focusing on those who died during the Vietnam War. Then he choked up and could not go on, so Mike joined him. Wearing blue jeans with a big belt buckle and boots, Mike stood out in his bright turquoise western shirt, black cowboy hat, and dark aviator glasses. He continued to thank everyone for coming and honoring in particular his friends who had not made it home. Many in the crowd that day were brought to tears.[59]

Once the speakers concluded their remarks, the honor guard smartly stood and fired a salute. A bugler played "Taps," the haunting sound sweeping the community; perhaps some of the notes even reached the Bunker Hill Cemetery where Robert and Clive lay side by side. With that, the solemn occasion—an important occasion not only for the Morenci Nine but also for other Vietnam veterans—came to an end. People milled around taking pictures, among them the parents of the soldiers as well as Mike and Leroy. They soon dispersed to take part in the Fourth of July events that brought together young and old in the community to celebrate the nation's birthday and remember those who had played a role in defending America.

The memorial at the entrance to the high school represented the first permanent effort to remember the Morenci Nine. The people who chose to locate it near the front door of the school consciously placed it where future soldiers would pass. This tied into the community's pride in being a conduit for troops in the US armed forces. A small percentage of

Morenci's teenagers had hopes of attending college, but military recruiters still found many willing volunteers, just as they had in 1966. The military remained an attractive alternative for men (and, by this time, women) who wanted to find a career outside the boom-and-bust mining industry. Thus, the Morenci Nine became a fundamental part of the lore of sacrifice and service for young people in the mining camp.

Many efforts, local and distant, big and small, continued to commemorate the service of the Morenci Nine. Stories about the Nine appeared in the *Copper Era* and *Eastern Arizona Courier,* and other memorials incorporated the Morenci Nine as well, among them the Mares Bluff Veterans Memorial, a large wall commemorating those killed in action in all wars at the American Legion Hall in Clifton, and a relief near the bell tower at Eastern Arizona College in Thatcher.[60]

One poignant act of remembrance developed in California when a memorial arose around a 160-year-old live oak tree in an empty field just outside Banning and Beaumont, on the outskirts of Los Angeles. During the Gulf War, someone had tied a huge yellow ribbon around the tree and placed an American flag in front of it. Before long, more flags appeared, and people began leaving letters and photos of loved ones serving in the conflict. For years, local people maintained this informal monument.[61]

When the Iraq War started in 2003, the site took on new meaning. More flags appeared as well as small white crosses honoring the dead. One day, Fred Knight, a dentist in nearby Cherry Valley and a native of Safford who had played football against some of the Morenci Nine, paid a visit to the site. He noticed that a large white cross honoring the Morenci Nine had appeared near the back of the memorial and next to a fence. "Who put it there is unknown," Knight later said, but he noted both his excitement and his surprise at finding it, adding that it brought back many memories of home. No matter how it materialized and became a prominent part of the display, it highlighted a war long over and a community far removed from the Southern California landscape.[62]

Additional efforts to memorialize the Morenci Nine continued for years. The account became a fundamental part of local history and increasingly that of the region. On Memorial Day in 2007, the *Arizona Republic* ran a piece entitled "5 Memories of Arizonans Who Gave Their Lives for Their Country." The first story listed was "The Marines of Morenci,"[63] demonstrating just how far remembrance of the Morenci Nine had seeped into the consciousness of the state.

*   *   *

Some fundamental questions remain. Why were the Morenci Nine so important to the community (and even the region)? And why was so much energy expended in acts of remembrance? There are a number of explanations, such as the fact that honoring Vietnam veterans became more fashionable after the Gulf War and even more so after the initiation of the Iraq War in 2003, which reinvigorated a warrior culture.[64] This development built on the efforts made by veterans during the 1980s to secure their rightful place in the veterans' pantheon, so in large part, it reflected broader national trends.

However, several local dimensions added to the story of the Morenci Nine. One related to the fact that the community needed to heal not only from the war but also from the added trauma of loss when PD buried the original town under tons of rocks as the mine expanded. The area where everyone had gone to high school, to sports events, to church, and to special events disappeared over time, consumed by the mine. The houses of people such as Clive Garcia survived, as did the cemetery, but the physical plant embedded with so many memories became a different landscape, which meant that people could only sustain memories through pictures and mental images that faded with time. Therefore, stories related to old Morenci became valuable assets to those trying to hold on to the past.

The devastating 1983 strike was another trauma that pushed people to try to find meaning in their lives vis-à-vis the country as a whole. The betrayal of the workers by the state government and by coworkers and neighbors who crossed the picket lines brought great frustration. Many Vietnam veterans, albeit not all, stood strong, Mike, Leroy, and Joe included, but what about the workers who took their jobs and never put their lives on the line for their country when asked? What about the government that suddenly sent in the Arizona National Guard, dressed in riot gear and armed with tear gas, to drive the workers away from the picket lines? The obvious treachery angered Mike and others. In part, the story of the Morenci Nine became a way for Joe, Leroy, Mike, and others who served in the military to craft their own narrative about their place in the community and juxtapose it against the selfish and cowardly actions of Phelps Dodge.

Deep down, a sense of pride also developed regarding the service and sacrifice of the Morenci Nine and other veterans. Many in Morenci held a fundamental belief in the superiority of small-town life and the idea that the hardworking miners represented the true values of America. Context was key. Like many Americans watching their televisions in the late 1960s and into the early 1970s, people in Greenlee County had been repulsed by the anti-Americanism of the long-haired, shabbily dressed, disrespectful hippies and college students they saw on the nightly news at antiwar rallies. Reactively, they longed to emphasize how they themselves represented a truer America, one based on hard work, respect for others, and devotion to God and country. At a time when they felt that the country had changed, they fought back by pointing out their sacrifices on behalf of the nation.

Finally, the memorialization also raised the stature of Morenci in the eyes of its neighbors. Much like communities rally around their sports teams as a source of pride, Morenci could note that its young men had made the ultimate sacrifice for their country at a higher rate than their peers in similar towns. This belief remained a cornerstone of the community's consciousness and highlighted the patriotism of Morenci, both inside and outside the mining camp. It also played nicely into the social constructions of masculinity in Morenci's self-perception as a camp of tough and dedicated patriots willing to answer the nation's call. Even though many people continued to grieve privately, the pride associated with the service of the Morenci Nine underscored the community's commitment to more public acts designed to illuminate the sacrifices.

But there was also some contestation in the process of public remembrance. Though most Vietnam veterans recognized the value of the Morenci Nine story in terms of highlighting the contributions made by all the veterans who served in Southeast Asia, a certain understandable ambivalence emerged. Some believed that concentrating on the Morenci Nine diminished the value of the service and sacrifices of others, especially other individuals from the area who had lost their lives in Vietnam.

The construction of the Mares Bluff Memorial and the Wall of Honor at the local American Legion Hall reflected the tensions that evolved. Vietnam veterans took the lead in constructing them, and though they acknowledged the importance of the Morenci Nine, they folded the story into a larger narrative about those who fought and died from Greenlee

County. In a newspaper article in late 2011, Steve Guzzo expressed the feelings of some regarding those who served in Vietnam, telling a reporter, "What brought it home, what made the impact, was the Morenci Nine," but, he added, "we can't forget our other people, either."[65]

Music written by local veterans also reflected ambivalence about concentrating too much on the Morenci Nine. In 2001, a high school classmate, Russ Gillespie (class of 1965), put out an album consisting of several songs, including "Boys in Vietnam." Though the lyrics focused on his experience as a Navy veteran who returned to an ungrateful country, the song also described how he wandered around after high school but found, when he returned home, "all my friends gone to Vietnam." Gillespie emphasized that "I didn't want to go but couldn't stay," so he ended up in Vietnam himself. One of the stanzas observes, "Heard all about my friends' demise in a letter from home. / Seems they all got killed one day in a place on a map you cannot find. / Oh, the article was splendid and the funerals they say was grand, / a tribute to all the boys in Vietnam."[66]

The exploits of the Morenci Nine clearly shaped Gillespie's viewpoint, as he later told a reporter that he was close to the group and those who died. Yet he also stressed that he knew others who fell in Vietnam, such as Ronald Gene White from Morenci and Joe Salinas and Eddie Lopez from Clifton. And though he acknowledged he did not know the boys from Duncan who lost their lives in Vietnam, Manuel Thomas Montoya and William Niel Wilson, he dedicated the song to them as well as to his Morenci buddies.[67]

Like many veterans from the area, Gillespie tried to find some meaning in the loss of not only his own high school friends but also others.[68] The concern sometimes expressed by veterans about the heavy focus on the Morenci Nine is understandable. Even Joe Sorrelman feared the prospect of their story somehow mattering more than others.[69]

In truth, all memories about the Vietnam veterans, both those who lived and those who died, matter. As young men, most made hard choices about service, and they endured significant challenges in training and combat. However, the story of the Morenci Nine provides an insight into the lives of everyone who served in Southeast Asia, and it will continue to do so: if anything, it amplifies the service and sacrifice of all Vietnam veterans.

*   *   *

Remembrance of the Morenci Nine has not been a static process, and it remains prone to influence by outside forces, including time and changes in the nation's perceptions about its military prowess. With the story increasingly part of both the local and the regional consciousness relating to veterans, it will for years to come be central to the narrative of the Vietnam War for those who fought.

Across the country since the end of the war, small communities have shared the challenges of Morenci in dealing with their sorrow and anguish. Morenci also has a great deal in common with other small towns such as St. Ignatius, Montana, and War, West Virginia, that lost a disproportionate number of young men in comparison to other American towns and cities during the Vietnam War. Their process of remembrance undoubtedly bore a striking resemblance to that of Morenci. In the initial stages, individuals remained the primary depositories of the memories, with public remembrances becoming more common after the 1980s. It was often a painful process but one that over time brought some healing and closure. Still, for many, the wounds will never fully close.

Epilogue

Even today, the Morenci Nine are a prominent part of the historical consciousness of the Southwest. As recently as November 2011, a newspaper article in the *Arizona Daily Star* addressed the lives and deaths of the nine Marines.[1] The ongoing loss of life in Afghanistan and reports about the lingering effects of military service on American soldiers in that country and in Iraq have kept such stories in the limelight. More and more, people have looked to the experience of the Vietnam veterans for insights into what today's young men and women must deal with in relation to their service in the Middle East.

Meanwhile, Morenci continues to hold on tightly to the memories of the group. On April 26, 2012, teachers and students gathered at the high school for a Morenci Nine memorial dedication ceremony at the Fine Arts and Scholarship Fundraising Night, which featured pencil portraits of the Nine by Ashley Cronister. Others provided rubbings from the Vietnam War Memorial in Washington, DC, and the Traveling Vietnam Memorial Wall. The organizers reproduced the 1970 *Time* article for those who did not know the story well. The wall of etchings and portraits included the following lines:

We pledge to remember all veterans including the Morenci Nine
Your unquestioning patriotism of which you represented
We dedicate this memorial to the nine Marines who once walked our
    halls
Tears of pride well in our eyes as we honor you.

The event was a big success, and though it was not the only feature, the Morenci Nine exhibition received a great deal of attention.[2]

The interest in the topic will likely persist in the near future. New manifestations to honor the Morenci Nine have evolved; Oscar Urrea, for instance, has plans for a memorial in Clifton that will prominently feature them. A Safford T-shirt shop, Trophies 'n Tees, has produced a series of shirts honoring the Nine. And even this book to a large degree continues the memorialization of the friends who made the fateful decision in March 1966 to join the Marine Corps. The story has become a central element in the community's and even the region's consciousness in defining patriotism. But it is also a story of devastating consequences. As a result, some see the story as an example of unfailing patriotism, whereas others see it as a cautionary tale. Debates revolving around such interpretations will remain unsettled, and people will take their own lessons from the account.

The story of the Morenci Nine was replicated in many ways across the United States during the Vietnam War. Though it was unique in terms of how the group joined up together and in the clustering of deaths that ensued, the Morenci Nine narrative is an American tale for the Vietnam generation. The Nine marched off to war, rarely questioning their leaders. By contrast, millions of other young men actively avoided the war through all means available. The people of Morenci never publicly debated their duty. But in many of the large urban centers, people rose up throughout the war to challenge the assumptions of the political leaders. The story fits well into the multitude of narratives that existed and persisted even into the postwar era, when the memories were still contested.

The story also goes beyond the Vietnam War and has universal applications, ones that often cross national lines and chronological periods. Consequently, the story is timeless. The memories and how they are constructed matter. We can hope that more people will focus on similar memories from other sources, particularly before the Vietnam generation passes. It took many years for people to capture the stories of World War II. Retaining the accounts of the Vietnam veterans as well as those of soldiers from the most recent conflicts in Iraq and Afghanistan should become a priority for all who want to keep such invaluable memories from disappearing.

Notes

Introduction: A Small Town and the Vietnam War

1. Jonathan D. Rosenblum, *Copper Crucible: How the Arizona Miners' Strike of 1983 Recast Labor-Management Relations in America*, 2nd ed. (Ithaca, NY: Cornell University Press, 1998), 46–80.

2. Ibid., 83.

3. Ibid., 82.

4. Ibid., 134–137.

5. Christian G. Appy, *Working-Class War: American Combat Soldiers & Vietnam* (Chapel Hill: University of North Carolina Press, 1993), 11–43; James Ebert, *A Life in a Year: The American Infantryman in Vietnam* (New York: Presidio Press, 2004).

6. Jim Wilson, *The Sons of Bardstown: 25 Years of Vietnam in an American Town* (New York: Crown, 1994).

7. Appy, *Working-Class War*, 14.

8. *Philadelphia Inquirer*, May 26, 1989.

9. Kyle Longley, *The Sparrow and the Hawk: Costa Rica and the United States during the Rise of José Figueres, 1942–1957* (Tuscaloosa: University of Alabama Press, 1997); Kyle Longley, *Senator Albert Gore, Sr.: Tennessee Maverick* (Baton Rouge: Louisiana State University Press, 2004).

10. Karl Jacoby, *Shadows at Dawn: A Borderlands Massacre and the Violence of History* (New York: Penguin Press, 2008), 3–4.

11. Donald A. Ritchie, *Doing Oral History* (New York: Twayne Publishers, 1995), 6–17.

Chapter 1. Life in a Small Town

1. The whole narrative of the first section of this chapter relies exclusively on Linda Gordon's *Great Arizona Orphan Abduction* (Cambridge, MA: Harvard University Press, 1999).

2. *The Supreme Court Reporter: Cases Argued and Determined in the United States Supreme Court—December 1906–July 1907* (St. Paul, MN: West Publishing, 1907), 53.

3. Barbara Kingsolver, *Animal Dreams* (New York: HarperCollins, 1990), 19.

4. Sandra Day O'Connor and H. Alan Day, *Lazy B* (New York: Modern Library, 2005).

5. The best study of the topic is Ted Cogut and Bill Conger, *History of Arizona's Clifton-Morenci Mining District—A Personal Approach*, vol. 1, *The Underground Days* (Thatcher, AZ: Mining History, 1999). Other good works on the topic include: Robert Glass Cleland, *A History of Phelps Dodge, 1834–1950* (New York: Alfred A. Knopf, 1952), 75–113; Marshall Trimble, *Arizona: A Cavalcade of History* (Tucson, AZ: Treasure Chest Publications, 1989), 131–133; Thomas Sheridan, *Arizona: A History* (Tucson: University of Arizona Press, 1995), 165–166.

6. Carlos A. Schwantes, *Vision and Enterprise: Exploring the History of Phelps Dodge Corporation* (Tucson: University of Arizona Press, 2000), 63–68.

7. Gordon, *Great Arizona Orphan Abduction,* 172.

8. Ronald C. Brown, *Hard-Rock Miners: The Intermountain West, 1860–1920* (College Station: Texas A&M University Press, 1979), 24–26; Samuel Truett, *Fugitive Landscapes: The Forgotten History of the U.S.-Mexico Borderlands* (New Haven, CT: Yale University Press, 2006).

9. For more on mining camps in the West as well as the East, see Eric L. Clements, *After the Boom in Tombstone and Jerome, Arizona: Decline in Western Resource Towns* (Reno: University of Nevada Press, 2003); Duane A. Smith, *Rocky Mountain Mining Camps: The Urban Frontier* (Bloomington: Indiana University Press, 1967); Ronald D. Eller, *Miners, Millhands, and Mountaineers: Industrialization of the Appalachian South, 1880–1930* (Knoxville: University of Tennessee Press, 1982), 161–198; Crandall A. Shifflett, *Coal Towns: Life, Work, and Culture in Company Towns of Southern Appalachia, 1880–1960* (Knoxville: University of Tennessee Press, 1991).

10. "Morenci," *Arizona Highways* (January 1946): 23.

11. *Arizona Republic,* February 19, 1999.

12. As cited in Gordon, *Great Arizona Orphan Abduction,* 35.

13. Interview by the author with Armando Ramirez, July 31, 2003, Tempe, AZ.

14. Schwantes, *Vision and Enterprise,* 236.

15. This song related to the coal-mining industry in West Virginia and Kentucky but seemed most appropriate for the Western mines also. For the lyrics, see Tennessee Ernie Ford, "Sixteen Tons," 1955, accessed November 9, 2011, http://www.cowboy lyrics.com/lyrics/classic-country/sixteen-tons---tennessee-ernie-ford-14930.html.

16. Interview by the author with Ernest Calderón, September 25, 2002, Phoenix, AZ.

17. For more on the topic, see David Robertson, *Hard As the Rock Itself: Place and Identity in the American Mining Town* (Boulder: University Press of Colorado, 2006).

18. For more on the topic, see James W. Byrkit, *Forging the Copper Collar: Arizona's Labor-Management War of 1901–1921* (Tucson: University of Arizona Press, 1982), 28–29; Jonathan D. Rosenblum, *Copper Crucible: How the Arizona Miners' Strike of 1983 Recast Labor-Management Relations in America*, 2nd ed. (Ithaca, NY: ILR Press, 1998), 20–21.

19. For more on the Ludlow Massacre, see Scott Martelle, *Blood Passion: The Ludlow Massacre and Class War in the American West* (New Brunswick, NJ: Rutgers University Press, 2008); George S. McGovern, *The Great Coalfield War* (Boulder: University Press of Colorado, 1996); Thomas G. Andrews, *Killing for Coal: America's Deadliest Labor War* (Cambridge, MA: Harvard University Press, 2008).

20. Quote is from Rosenblum, *Copper Crucible*, 23. The best book on the clash is James R. Kluger, *The Clifton-Morenci Strike: Labor Difficulty in Arizona, 1915–1916* (Tucson: University of Arizona Press, 1970); also see Rosenblum, *Copper Crucible*, 22–25. Another good work on labor relations from the period is Betsy Jameson, *All That Glitters: Class, Conflict, and Community in Cripple Creek* (Urbana: University of Illinois Press, 1998).

21. Rosenblum, *Copper Crucible*, 31–37.

22. Rodolfo Acuna, *Occupied America: A History of Chicanos*, 6th ed. (New York: Longman, 2006); Vicki Ruiz, *Out of the Shadows: Mexican Women in Twentieth-Century America* (New York: Oxford University Press, 1998); Katherine Benton-Cohen, *Borderline Americans: Racial Division and Labor War in the Arizona Borderlands* (Cambridge, MA: Harvard University Press, 2009); Manuel G. Gonzales, *Mexicanos: A History of Mexicans in the United States* (Bloomington: Indiana University Press, 2000).

23. For more on the topic, see the work of a person raised in Morenci, Elena Díaz Björkquist, *Suffer Smoke* (Houston, TX: Arte Público Press, 1996).

24. Calderón interview.

25. Interview by the author with Paula Rhoads, March 7, 2003, Scottsdale, AZ.

26. Tim O'Brien, *If I Die in a Combat Zone: Box Me Up and Ship Me Home* (New York: Laurel, 1987), 27.

27. For more on the culture of Cold War America in the 1950s, see Elaine Tyler May, *Homeward Bound: American Families in the Cold War Era*, 2nd rev. ed. (New York: Basic Books, 2008); Stephen Whitfield, *The Culture of the Cold War*, 2nd ed. (Baltimore, MD: Johns Hopkins University Press, 1996).

28. James J. Lorence, *The Suppression of Salt of the Earth: How Hollywood, Big Labor, and Politicians Blacklisted a Movie in the American Cold War* (Albuquerque: University

of New Mexico Press, 1999); Ellen Baker, *On Strike and on Film: Mexican American Families and Blacklisted Filmmaker in Cold War America* (Chapel Hill: University of North Carolina Press, 2007).

Chapter 2. Semper Fi Boys

1. Interview by the author with Leroy Cisneros, June 5, 2007, Yuma, AZ.

2. Interview by the author with Robert Draper, Sr., April 22, 2004, York, AZ.

3. Interview by the author with Larry Kenan, February 11, 2004, Mesa, AZ.

4. Telephone interview by the author with Gerald Hunt, January 12, 2005. Hunt and King had been best friends since they started kindergarten together.

5. *Copper Era,* November 19, 1965.

6. Jack McLean, *Loon: A Marine Story* (New York: Ballantine Books, 2009), 21.

7. Interview by the author with Mike Cranford, May 23, 2003, York, AZ; interview by the author with Joe Sorrelman, July 20, 2003, Glendale, AZ.

8. Sorrelman interview.

9. *Los Angeles Times,* December 11, 1969.

10. Kenan interview.

11. Interview by author with Alma "Penny" King, April 24, 2004, Safford, AZ.

12. Ibid.

13. Ibid.

14. Office of Institutional Research and Evaluation, University of Arizona, "The University of Arizona Enrollment History," accessed May 13, 2007, http://oire.arizona .edu/files/Student_Demo/enrollment_old_current.pdf.

15. Hunt telephone interview.

16. Ibid.; telephone interview by the author with Robert Martinez (Stan's classmate at Morenci High School and also the University of Arizona), May 30, 2012.

17. Telephone interview by the author with Carol Navarette, November 22, 2004.

18. Interview by the author with Oscar Urrea, January 30, 2004, Mesa, AZ; interview by the author with Leroy Cisneros, August 19, 2001, Yuma, AZ.

19. Urrea interview.

20. Interview by the author with Elena Sanchez, May 23, 2003, York, AZ.

21. Urrea interview.

22. Ibid.

23. Cisneros interview, August 19, 2001.

24. Urrea interview.

25. Interview by the author with Armando Rameriz, July 31, 2003, Tempe, AZ.

26. Cisneros interview, August 19, 2001.

27. Cisneros interview, June 5, 2007.

28. Draper interview.

29. Interview by the author with Julia Garcia, April 23, 2004, Safford, AZ.

30. Interview by the author with Danny Garcia, April 23, 2004, Safford, AZ.

31. Interview by the author with Julia and Clive Garcia, Sr., April 23, 2004, Safford, AZ.

32. Kenan interview.

33. Donald W. Hoffman, "A Few Good Men: The True Story of the Morenci Marines," book proposal, 1989, 10 (proposal provided by Joe Sorrelman to the author; copy in possession of the author). Hoffman started research on a book on the Morenci Nine in the late 1980s but quit after encountering strong opposition from several families. He conducted a number of interviews with family members and friends as well as Cranford and Sorrelman before stopping the process.

34. Cisneros interview, August 12, 2001.

35. Interview by the author with Mary Morgan (née Sorrelman), May 11, 2005, Safford, AZ.

36. Sorrelman interview.

37. Ibid.; M. Cranford interview.

38. Urrea interview.

39. Sorrelman interview.

40. Sandra Day O'Connor, with H. Alan Day, *Lazy B* (New York: Modern Library, 2005).

41. M. Cranford interview.

42. Ibid.

43. Ibid.

44. Sorrelman interview.

45. Kenan interview.

46. Draper interview.

47. Ibid.

48. Ibid.

49. Kenan interview.

50. Draper interview.

51. Kenan interview.

52. Hoffman, "A Few Good Men," 19.

53. Interview by the author with Joyce Cranford, November 10, 2007, Clifton, AZ.

54. I have outlined this in great detail in my book *Grunts: The American Combat Soldier in Vietnam* (Armonk, NY: M. E. Sharpe, 2008). Other works that provide a good comparison and contrast include: Ron Kovic, *Born on the Fourth of July* (New York: Pocket Books, 1976); Bob Kerrey, *When I Was a Young Man: A Memoir* (New York: Harcourt, 2002); W. D. Ehrhart, *Vietnam-Perkasie: A Combat Marine Memoir* (Jefferson, NC: McFarland, 1983); Philip Caputo, *A Rumor of War* (New York: Holt, 1977); Phil Ball, *Ghosts and Shadows: A Marine in Vietnam, 1968–1969* (Jefferson, NC: McFarland, 1998); Robert Peterson, *Rites of Passage: Odyssey of a Grunt* (New York: Ballantine Books, 1997); William E. Merritt, *Where the Rivers Run Backward* (Athens: University of Georgia Press, 1989).

55. Sorrelman interview.

56. Hoffman, "A Few Good Men," 16–17.

57. Cisneros interview, June 5, 2007.

58. .M. Cranford interview.

59. Ibid.

60. Ibid.

61. Others with Morenci ties also would die in Vietnam, but the clustering of deaths within the group made the story stand out.

Chapter 3. The Creation of a Warrior in Cold War America

1. Tim O'Brien, *If I Die in a Combat Zone: Box Me Up and Ship Me Home* (New York: Laurel, 1987), 27.

2. Jack McLean, *Loon: A Marine Story* (New York: Ballantine Books, 2009), 208.

3. James W. Davis, Jr., and Kenneth M. Dolbeare, *Little Groups of Neighbors: The Selective Service System* (Chicago: Markham Publishing, 1968), v.

4. Ibid., 33.

5. Interview by the author with Oscar Urrea, January 30, 2004, Mesa, AZ.

6. Ibid.

7. Donald W. Hoffman, "A Few Good Men: The True Story of the Morenci Marines," book proposal, 1989, 23 (proposal provided by Joe Sorrelman to the author; copy in possession of the author).

8. Interview by the author with Mike Cranford, May 23, 2003, York, AZ.

9. George Q. Flynn, *The Draft, 1940–1973* (Lawrence: University Press of Kansas, 1993), 171.

10. Davis and Dolbeare, *Little Groups of Neighbors*, 13.

11. Phil Ball, *Ghosts and Shadows: A Marine in Vietnam* (Jefferson, NC: McFarland, 1998), 5.

12. Mark Baker, *Nam: The Vietnam War in the Words of the Soldiers Who Fought There* (New York: Berkley Books, 1981), 30.

13. Interview by the author with Joe Sorrelman, July 20, 2003, Glendale, AZ.

14. *Eastern Arizona Courier*, March 26, 1969.

15. Loren Baritz, *Backfire: A History of How American Culture Led Us into Vietnam and Made Us Fight the Way We Did*, 2nd ed. (Baltimore, MD: Johns Hopkins University Press, 1998), 14.

16. O'Brien, *If I Die in a Combat Zone*, 27.

17. *Arizona Republic*, April 30, 2000.

18. A good work on the matter is Robert D. Dean, *Imperial Brotherhood: Gender and the Making of Cold War Foreign Policy* (Amherst: University of Massachusetts Press, 2001).

19. Graham Dawson, *Soldier Heroes: British Adventure, Empire and the Imaging of Masculinities* (New York: Routledge, 1994), 1, 22–23.

20. This was especially true through 1967 when deferments started ending for college graduates and then later with the imposition of a lottery system. See Christian Appy, *Working Class War: American Combat Soldiers and Vietnam* (Chapel Hill: University of North Carolina Press, 1993); James Ebert, *A Life in a Year: The American Infantryman in Vietnam* (New York: Presidio Press, 2004).

21. A good essay that highlights the issues of military service and the mining industry during World War II is Matthew Brasso, "Man-Power: Montana Copper Workers, State Authority, and the (Re)drafting of Manhood during World War II," in Brasso, Laura McCall, and Dee Garceau, eds., *Across the Great Divide: Cultures of Manhood in the American West* (New York: Routledge, 2001), 185–210.

22. Baker, *Nam*, 28.

23. E. Anthony Rotundo, *American Manhood: Transformations of Masculinity from the Revolution to the Modern Era* (New York: Basic Books, 1993), 234–235.

24. Interview by the author with Clive Garcia, Sr., April 23, 2004, Safford, AZ.

25. Cranford interview.

26. A total of 5,950 Phelps Dodge employees from throughout company operations served in the US military during World War II, with more than 100 dying. See Carlos A. Schwantes, *Vision & Enterprise: Exploring the History of Phelps Dodge Corporation* (Tucson: University of Arizona Press, 2000), 217.

27. Sorrelman interview.

28. Urrea interview.

29. Interview by the author with Steve Guzzo, May 23, 2003, Clifton, AZ.

30. Interview by the author with George Vasquez, April 23, 2004, Morenci, AZ.

31. Urrea interview. There were sometimes problems with the veterans and their impact on young men in the community. James Jones wrote that as memories of war's unpleasantness faded, "we old men can in all good conscience sit over our beers at the American Legion on Friday nights and recall with affection moments of terror thirty years before. Thus we are able to tell the youngsters that it wasn't really so bad." See Jones, *WWII: A Chronicle of Soldiering* (New York: Ballantine Books, 1976), 6.

32. Tom Magedanz interview in *South Dakotans in Vietnam: Excerpts from the South Dakota Vietnam Veterans Oral History Project—Pierre Area* (Pierre, SD: State Publishing, 1986), 3.

33. Marc Feigen Fasteau, *The Male Machine* (New York: McGraw-Hill, 1974), 101–114; Rotundo, *American Manhood*, 239–244.

34. Fasteau, *Male Machine*, 101.

35. Telephone interview by author with Art Montez, April 3, 2009.

36. Interview by the author with Leroy Cisneros, August 19, 2001, Yuma, AZ.

37. Urrea interview.

38. Rotundo, *American Manhood*, 258.

39. Ibid.

40. Robert Peterson, *The Boy Scouts: An American Adventure* (New York: American Heritage, 1984), 250.

41. Jay Mechling, *On My Honor: Boy Scouts and the Making of American Youth* (Chicago: University of Chicago Press, 2001), 128–129.

42. Interview by the author with Robert Clinton Draper, April 22, 2004, York, AZ.

43. Urrea interview.

44. Vasquez interview.

45. Michael Kimmel, *Manhood in America: A Cultural History* (New York: Free Press, 1996), 267–269; Fasteau, *Male Machine*, 163–165.

46. Dean, *Imperial Brotherhood*, 169–199.

47. Telephone interview of Martin Brady by Richard Verrone, June 25, 2003, Vietnam Archive Oral History Project, Texas Tech University, Lubbock, TX, 6.

48. Philip Caputo, *A Rumor of War* (New York: Henry Holt, 1977), xiv.

49. Frank J. Wetta and Stephen J. Curley, *Celluloid Wars: A Guide to Film and the American Experience of War* (Westport, CT: Greenwood Press, 1992), 157–183.

50. Ron Kovic, *Born on the Fourth of July* (New York: Pocket Books, 1976), 55.

51. This was covered in a chapter entitled "The Images of the Marines and John Wayne," in Lawrence H. Suid, *Guts and Glory: The Making of the American*

Military Image in Film, rev. ed. (Lexington: University of Kentucky Press, 2002), 116–135.

52. Sorrelman interview.

53. Aaron O'Connell, *Underdogs: The Making of the Modern Marine Corps* (Cambridge, MA: Harvard University Press, 2012).

54. Telephone interview by the author with Gerald Hunt, January 12, 2005.

55. *Los Angeles Times*, December 11, 1969.

56. Charley Trujillo, ed., *Soldados: Chicanos in Vietnam* (San Jose, CA: Chusma House, 1990), vii; George Mariscal, ed., *Aztlán and Vietnam: Chicano and Chicana Experiences of the War* (Berkeley: University of California Press, 1999), 3; Ruben Treviso, "Hispanics and the Vietnam War," in Harrison E. Salisbury, ed., *Vietnam Reconsidered: Lessons from a War* (New York: Harper & Row, 1984), 184–186.

57. Cited in Trujillo, *Soldados*, i.

58. Baker, *Nam*, 35.

59. Charley Trujillo, "It Sure As Hell Wasn't 'English Only' in Vietnam," in Christian Appy, ed., *Patriots: The Vietnam War Remembered from All Sides* (New York: Penguin, 2004), 367.

60. A good discussion of the topic exists in Steven Rosales, "Double Victory: Mexican American G.I.'s and the Post-war Struggle for Civil Rights," paper presented at the Pacific Coast Branch of the American Historical Society, August 2009, Albuquerque, NM, 5–6.

61. Jonathan D. Rosenblum, *Copper Crucible: How the Arizona Miners' Strike of 1983 Recast Labor-Management Relations in America*, 2nd ed. (Ithaca, NY: Cornell University Press, 1998), 33–34. Deep down, there was also the need to prove one's Americanness, beyond race, relative to the unionism that certain powerful forces portrayed as un-American during the 1950s and 1960s.

62. Good books on the topic of Native Americans and military service, including those who served in World War II and were the fathers and uncles of the Vietnam veterans, are: William C. Meadows, *Kiowa, Apache, and Comanche Military Societies: Enduring Veterans, 1800 to the Present* (Austin: University of Texas Press, 1990); Cynthia H. Enloe, *Ethnic Soldiers: State Security in Divided Societies* (Athens: University of Georgia Press, 1980); Kenneth W. Townsend, *World War II and the American Indian* (Albuquerque: University of New Mexico Press, 2000); Jere Bishop Franco, *Crossing the Pond: The Native American Effort in World War II* (Denton: University of North Texas Press, 1999).

63. Tom Holm, *Strong Hearts, Wounded Souls: Native American Veterans of the Vietnam War* (Austin: University of Texas Press, 1996), 11.

64. Ibid., 118.

65. Tom Roubideaux interview in *South Dakotans in Vietnam: Excerpts from the South Dakota Vietnam Veterans Oral History Project—Pierre Area* (Pierre, SD: State Publishing, 1986), 62.

66. Doris Paul, *The Navajo Code Talkers* (Pittsburgh, PA: Dorrance Publishing, 1998); Sally McClain, *Navajo Weapon: The Navajo Code Talkers* (Tucson, AZ: Rio Nuevo Publishers, 2002); Kenji Kawano, *Warriors: Navajo Code Talkers* (Flagstaff, AZ: Northland Publishing, 2002); Deanne Durrett, *Unsung Heroes of World War II: The Story of the Navajo Code Talkers* (Lincoln, NE: Bison Books, 2009).

67. For more on the topic of religion and the Cold War, see William Inboden, *Religion and American Foreign Policy, 1945–1960* (New York: Cambridge University Press, 2008); Andrew Preston, *Sword of the Spirit, Shield of Faith: Religion in American War and Diplomacy* (New York: Alfred A. Knopf, 2012), 440–573.

68. Joseph G. Morgan, *The Vietnam Lobby: The American Friends of Vietnam, 1955–1975* (Chapel Hill: University of North Carolina Press, 1997); Seth Jacobs, *The Miracle Man in Vietnam: Ngo Dinh Diem, Religion, Race, and US Intervention in Southeast Asia* (Durham, NC: Duke University Press, 2005); Patrick McNamara, *A Catholic Cold War: Edmund A. Walsh, SJ, and the Politics of American Anticommunism* (Bronx, NY: Fordham University Press, 2005).

69. As cited in William D. Miscamble, "Francis Cardinal Spellman and 'Spellman's War,'" in David L. Anderson, ed., *The Human Tradition in the Vietnam Era* (Wilmington, DE: Scholarly Resources, 2000), 17.

70. For more on the opposition within the church to the war, see Shawn Francis Peters, *The Catonsville Nine: A Story of Faith and Resistance in the Vietnam War* (New York: Oxford University Press, 2012); James Carroll, *An American Requiem: God, My Father, and the War That Came between Us* (New York: Mariner Books, 1997); Murray Poiner and Jim O'Grady, *Disarmed and Dangerous: The Radical Life and Times of Daniel and Philip Berrigan, Brothers in Religious Faith and Civil Disobedience* (Boulder, CO: Westview Press, 1998).

71. Lewis B. Puller, Jr., *Fortunate Son: The Autobiography of Lewis B. Puller, Jr.* (New York: Bantam, 1993), 25.

72. For a good study of the topic, see Anne C. Loveland, *American Evangelicals and the US Military, 1942–1993* (Baton Rouge: Louisiana State University Press, 1997).

73. Daniel K. Williams, *God's Own Party: The Making of the Christian Right* (New York: Oxford University Press, 2010), 79.

74. Gregory A. Prince and William Robert Wright, *David O. McKay and the Rise of Modern Mormonism* (Salt Lake City: University of Utah Press, 2005); Mary Jane

Woodger, "A Latter-day Saint Servicemen's Response to Their Church Leaders' Counsel during the Vietnam War," paper presented at the Center for Studies of New Religions Conference, June 20–23, 2002, Salt Lake City and Provo, UT, http://www.cesnur.org/2002/slc/woodger.htm; Gary Schwendiman and Knud Larsen, "The Vietnam War through the Eyes of a Mormon Subculture," *Dialogue: A Journal of Mormon Thought* (Autumn 1968): 152–162; Eugene England, "The Tragedy of Vietnam and the Responsibility of Mormons," *Dialogue: A Journal of Mormon Thought* (Winter 1967): 71–90.

75. Daniel J. Combs, "Official LDS Anticommunism, 1901–1972" (Master's thesis, Brigham Young University, 2005); John L. Sorenson, "Vietnam: Just a War, or a Just War?" *Dialogue: A Journal of Mormon Thought* (Winter 1967): 93–103.

76. For an interesting review of Benson's view on the Vietnam War, see "The Vietnam War," with an introduction by John Wayne, n.d., http://www.youtube.com/watch?v=ZLbu-mgKgiM.

Chapter 4. Eight Weeks in Hell and Beyond

1. Interview by the author with Leroy Cisneros, June 6, 2007, Yuma, AZ.

2. Ibid.

3. The exact language has been reconstructed from oral histories as well as memoirs from Marines, both those in Training Platoon 1055 and others who landed in San Diego and at Parris Island during the Vietnam War era. There are remarkable similarities in the memories and in the language used by the drill instructors.

4. W. D. Ehrhart, *Vietnam-Perkasie: A Combat Marine Memoir* (Jefferson, NC: McFarland, 1983), 12.

5. Interview by the author with Michael Cranford, May 23, 2003, York, AZ; interview by the author with Joe Sorrelman, August 21, 2003, Glendale, AZ. For a good overview of the experience of boot camp, see US Department of Defense, "Your First 80 Days," film, 1966, accessed November 3, 2011, http://www.youtube.com/watch?v=nSa96KakIZw.

6. Telephone interview of Michael Bradbury by Richard Burks Verrone, September 15, 2003, Vietnam Archive Oral History Project, Texas Tech University, Lubbock, TX [hereafter cited as Texas Tech Vietnam Oral History Project], 6.

7. "First Phone Call," Marine Parents, accessed March 16, 2012, http://www.recruitparents.com/bootcamp/first-phone.asp.

8. Bradbury telephone interview.

9. Ray Hildreth and Charles W. Sasser, *Hill 488* (New York: Pocket Books, 2003), 7.

10. E-mail from Fred Wingfield (member of Platoon 1055) to Thomas Pierson (member of Platoon 1055), forwarded to the author, January 19, 2008.

11. John Corbett, *West Dickens Avenue: A Marine at Khe Sanh* (New York: Ballantine Books, 2003), 8.

12. Jack McLean, *Loon: A Marine Story* (New York: Presidio Press, 2009), 16–17.

13. Philip Caputo, *Rumor of War* (New York: Owl Books, 1977), 18–19.

14. E-mail from Thomas Pierson to the author, January 15, 2008.

15. David Parks, *GI Diary* (Washington, DC: Howard University Press, 1984), 14.

16. As quoted in James Ebert, *A Life in a Year: The American Infantryman in Vietnam, 1965–1972* (Novato, CA: Presidio Press, 1993), 38.

17. McLean, *Loon,* 16.

18. Kyle Longley, *Grunts: The American Combat Soldier in Vietnam* (Armonk, NY: M. E. Sharpe, 2008), 44.

19. E. Michael Helms, *The Proud Bastard* (New York: Pocket Books, 1990), 9.

20. Letters from Clive Garcia, Jr., to his parents, Julia and Clive Garcia, Sr., July 11, 1966, and July 13, 1966, San Diego, CA, personal possessions of Garcia family, copies held by the author [hereafter cited as Letters of Clive Garcia].

21. Wingfield e-mail.

22. Ibid.

23. Letter from Thomas Pierson to the author, January 14, 2008.

24. Garcia letter, July 13, 1966.

25. Cisneros interview.

26. Pierson letter.

27. E-mail from Thomas Pierson to the author, January 12, 2008.

28. Letter from Clive Garcia, Jr., to his parents, Julia and Clive Garcia, Sr., July 24, 1966, San Diego, CA, Letters of Clive Garcia.

29. Peter Barnes, *Pawns: The Plight of the Citizen-Soldier* (New York: Alfred A. Knopf, 1972), 74–76.

30. Letter from Clive Garcia, Jr., to his parents, Julia and Clive Garcia, Sr., August 15, 1966, San Diego, CA, Letters of Clive Garcia.

31. Telephone interview of David Crawley by Steve Maxner, February 27, 2001, Texas Tech Vietnam Oral History Project, 10.

32. Cisneros interview.

33. Pierson e-mail, January 12, 2008.

34. Garcia letter, August 15, 1966.

35. Letter from Clive Garcia, Jr., to his parents, Julia and Clive Garcia, Sr., August 24, 1966, San Diego, CA, Letters of Clive Garcia.

36. Ibid.

37. Interview by the author with Joe Sorrelman, July 20, 2003, Glendale, AZ.

38. Letter from Clive Garcia, Jr., to his parents, Julia and Clive Garcia, Sr., August 22, 1966, San Diego, CA, Letters of Clive Garcia.

39. Garcia letter, August 15, 1966.

40. Sorrelman interview, July 20, 2003.

41. Ibid.

42. Cranford interview.

43. Sorrelman interview, July 20, 2003.

44. Cranford interview.

45. Pierson letter.

46. Sorrelman interview, July 20, 2003.

47. Cisneros interview.

48. Interview by the author with Julia Garcia, April 23, 2004, Safford, AZ.

49. William U. Tant interview in James R. Wilson, *Landing Zones: Southern Veterans Remember Vietnam* (Durham, NC: Duke University Press, 1990), 46.

50. As cited in Tom Holm, *Strong Hearts, Wounded Souls: Native American Veterans of the Vietnam War* (Austin: University of Texas Press, 1996), 127.

51. Cranford interview.

52. Cisneros interview.

53. Crawley telephone interview, 15.

54. Clive Garcia, Jr., to his parents, Julia and Clive Garcia, Sr., September 21, 1966, San Diego, CA, Letters of Clive Garcia.

55. Clive Garcia, Jr., to his parents, Julia and Clive Garcia, Sr., September 27, 1966, San Diego, CA, Letters of Clive Garcia.

56. George Herring, *America's Longest War: The United States and Vietnam, 1950–1975*, 4th ed. (New York: McGraw-Hill, 2003), 181.

57. Interview by the author with Clive and Julia Garcia, April 23, 2004, Safford, AZ.

58. Ibid.

Chapter 5. The First Wave Hits Vietnam

1. Interview by the author with Leroy Cisneros, June 5, 2007, Yuma, AZ.

2. Only a week later, an Army infantryman, David Parks, began the voyage on the USS *Patch*. His letters highlight an experience very similar to that of the Morenci boys. See Parks, *GI Diary* (Washington, DC: Howard University Press, 1984), 45–49.

3. Cisneros interview, June 5, 2007.

4. Ibid.

5. Letter from Bobby Dale Draper to his parents, December 18, 1966, South Vietnam, personal possessions of Draper family, copies held by the author [hereafter cited as Letters of Bobby Dale Draper].

6. Cisneros interview, June 5, 2007.

7. Ibid.

8. Ibid.

9. Ibid.

10. Interview by the author with Joe Sorrelman, July 20, 2003, Glendale, AZ.

11. Telephone interview by the author with Col. Tim Geraghty (First Recon veteran, Vietnam), August 2, 2010.

12. Sorrelman interview.

13. Cisneros interview, June 5, 2007.

14. Ray Hildreth and Charles W. Sasser, *Hill 488* (New York: Pocket Books, 2003), 28.

15. Ches Schneider, *From Classrooms to Claymores: A Teacher at War in Vietnam* (New York: Ivy Books, 1999), 18.

16. Interview by the author with Leroy Cisneros, January 27, 2011, Yuma, AZ.

17. Cisneros interview, June 5, 2007.

18. Cisneros interview, January 27, 2011.

19. Ibid.

20. Ibid.

21. As cited in Hill and Sasser, *Hill 488*, 40.

22. As cited in Michael C. Hodgins, *Reluctant Warrior: A Marine's True Story of Duty and Heroism in Vietnam* (New York: Ballantine Books, 1996), 46.

23. Cisneros interview, January 27, 2011.

24. Cisneros interview, June 5, 2007.

25. Cisneros interview, January 2 , 2011.

26. Ibid.

27. Cisneros interview, June 5, 2007.

28. Ibid.

29. Cisneros interview, January 27, 2011.

30. As cited in Hill and Sasser, *Hill 488*, 47.

31. Cisneros interview, January 27, 2011.

32. Ibid.

33. Ibid.

34. Cisneros interview, June 5, 2007.

35. Cisneros interview, January 27, 2011.

36. Ibid.

37. Cisneros interview, June 5, 2007.

38. Cisneros interview, January 27, 2011.

39. For examples of experiences with snakes, see interview of Robert Wrinn by Wayne Johnson, Lexington, Kentucky, May 12 and 19, 1989, University of Kentucky Oral History Program, University of Kentucky, Lexington, 11; Robert Peterson, *Rites of Passage: Odyssey of a Grunt* (New York: Ballantine Books, 1997), 324.

40. For more about dealing with the insects, mosquitoes, and leeches, see Col. Chester B. McCoid II to his wife, Dorothy, August 12, 1966, in Bill Adler, *Letters from Vietnam* (New York: Ballantine Books, 2003), 104; Frederick Downs to his wife, November 5, 1967, in Bernard Edelman, *Dear America: Letters Home from Vietnam* (New York: W. W. Norton, 1985), 60; Larry Holguin, "Marine," in Charley Trujillo, ed., *Soldados: Chicanos in Vietnam* (San Jose, CA: Chusma House, 1990), 80; John Talbott, in Harry Maurer, ed., *Strange Ground: An Oral History of Americans in Vietnam, 1945–1975* (New York: Da Capo Press, 1998), 274; Tom Magedanz interview in *South Dakotans in Vietnam: Excerpts from the South Dakota Vietnam Veterans Oral History Project, Pierre Area* (Pierre, SD: State Publishing, 1986), 15; "Gilberto, US Army— Corporal E4, 11th Armored Division, August 1966–January 1967," in Lea Ybarra, ed., *Vietnam Veteranos: Chicanos Recall the War* (Austin: University of Texas Press, 2004), 19–20.

41. Cisneros interview, June 5, 2007.

42. Cisneros interview, January 27, 2011.

43. Cisneros interview, June 5, 2007.

44. Cisneros interview, January 27, 2011.

45. Cisneros interview, June 5, 2007.

46. Ibid.

47. Cisneros interview, January 27, 2011.

48. Interview by the author with Leroy Cisneros, August 19, 2001, Yuma, AZ.

49. Cisneros interview, June 5, 2007.

50. Cisneros interview, January 27, 2011.

51. Ibid.

52. Ibid.

53. Ibid.

54. *Arizona Republic,* April 30, 2000.

55. Cisneros interview, January 27, 2011.

56. Ibid.

57. Ibid.

58. Ibid.

59. Ibid.

60. Ibid.

61. Ibid.

62. Cisneros interview, June 5, 2007.

63. Cisneros interview, August 19, 2001.

64. Cisneros interview, June 5, 2007.

65. US Marine Corps, Command Chronology, 1st Recon Battalion, May 1, 1967, to May 31, 1967, United States Marine Corps Archive, Quantico, VA, 148.

66. Ibid.

67. Cisneros interview, June 5, 2007.

68. US Marine Corps, Command Chronology.

69. Cisneros interview, August 19, 2001.

70. Cisneros interview, June 5, 2007.

71. Cisneros interview, January 27, 2011.

72. Ibid.

73. Ibid.

74. Ibid.

75. Cisneros interview, June 5, 2007.

76. Cisneros interview, January 27, 2011.

77. Ibid. Others shared similar experiences or made observations about those on their way home from Vietnam. For more examples, see telephone interview of Gary Smith by Stephen Maxner, December 4, 2003, Vietnam Archive Oral History Project, Texas Tech University, Lubbock, 76; Larry Gates interview, in *South Dakotans in Vietnam*, 63; Charles Gadd, *Line Doggie: Foot Soldier in Vietnam* (Novato, CA: Presidio Press, 1987), 184–187; Micki Voisard, "Civilian Airline Flight Attendant," in Keith Walker, ed., *A Piece of My Heart: The Stories of 26 American Women Who Served in Vietnam* (Novato, CA: Presidio Press, 1985), 233–234.

78. Cisneros interview, January 27, 2011.

79. Cisneros interview, June 5, 2007.

80. Cisneros interview, January 27, 2011.

81. Ibid.

82. Cisneros interview, June 5, 2007.

83. Ibid.

84. Cisneros interview, January 27, 2011.

85. Ibid.

86. Ibid.

87. Ibid.

88. Edwin McDowell, "Close-Knit Community of Morenci Sags under Weight of Vietnam Casualties," *Arizona Republic*, n.d., Morenci Public Library, Morenci, AZ.

89. Cisneros interview, June 5, 2007.

Chapter 6. The Miraculous Journey

1. The ceremony had several purposes, including preparing women for childbirth. Navajo Ceremonials, "Blessingway," http://www.hanksville.org/voyage/navajo/BlessingWay.php.

2. Interview by the author with Joe Sorrelman, May 2, 2011, Glendale, AZ.

3. Robert Peterson, *Rites of Passage: Odyssey of a Grunt* (New York: Ballantine Books, 1997), 9.

4. Sorrelman interview, May 2, 2011.

5. Ibid.

6. For more on the early operations of Chu Lai, see Otto Lehrack, *The First Battle—Operation Starlite and the Beginning of the Blood Debt in Vietnam* (New York: Ballantine Books, 2006).

7. Interview by the author with Joe Sorrelman, July 20, 2003, Glendale, AZ.

8. Interview by the author with Joe Sorrelman, April 18, 2012, Glendale, AZ.

9. Sorrelman interview, May 2, 2011.

10. Sorrelman interview, July 20, 2003.

11. Sorrelman interview, May 2, 2011.

12. Ibid.

13. Ibid.

14. James P. Coan, *Con Thien: The Hill of Angels* (Tuscaloosa: University of Alabama Press, 2004), 1–2.

15. Ibid., 50–59.

16. Ibid.

17. Sorrelman interview, April 18, 2012.

18. Sorrelman interview, May 2, 2011.

19. Sorrelman interview, July 20, 2003.

20. Ibid.

21. Interview of V. Dean Quillet by Terry L. Birdwhistell and George Herring, Louisville, Kentucky, March 18, 1985, University of Kentucky Oral History Program, University of Kentucky, Lexington, 5.

22. Edward F. Murphy, *Semper Fi Vietnam: From Da Nang to the DMZ, Marine Corps Campaigns, 1965–1975* (Novato, CA: Presidio Press, 1997), 132–143.

23. Ibid.

24. Sorrelman interview, April 18, 2012.

25. Ibid.

26. For more on the fighting around Con Thien in 1967 from a personal perspective, see William L. Buchanan, *Full Circle: A Marine Rifle Company in Vietnam* (San Francisco: Baylaurel Press, 2003), 15–43.

27. Sorrelman interview, April 18, 2012.

28. Ibid.

29. Ibid.

30. Sorrelman interview, July 20, 2003.

31. Ibid.

32. *Arizona Republic,* April 30, 2000.

33. Sorrelman interview, April 18, 2012.

34. *Arizona Republic,* April 30, 2000.

35. Ibid.

36. Sorrelman interview, April 18, 2012.

37. Sorrelman interview, July 20, 2003.

38. Ibid.

39. Ibid.

40. Sorrelman interview, April 18, 2012.

41. Sorrelman interview, May 2, 2011.

42. *Mesa Tribune,* November 11, 1993.

43. Sorrelman interview, April 18, 2012.

44. Ibid.

45. Donald W. Hoffman, "A Few Good Men: The True Story of the Morenci Marines," book proposal, 1989, 31 (proposal provided by Joe Sorrelman to the author; copy in possession of the author).

46. Sorrelman interview, July 20, 2003.

47. Ibid.

48. *Mesa Tribune,* November 11, 1993.

49. Sorrelman interview, April 18, 2012.

50. Don Oberdorfer, *Tet! The Turning Point in the Vietnam War* (Baltimore, MD: Johns Hopkins University Press, 2001); Keith Nolan, *Battle for Saigon, Tet 1968* (Novato, CA: Presidio Press, 2002); James R. Arnold, *Tet Offensive 1968: Turning Point in Vietnam* (Westport, CT: Praeger Press, 2004).

51. Sorrelman interview, July 20, 2003.

Chapter 7. The Grim Reaper Descends

1. Jonathan D. Rosenblum, *Copper Crucible: How the Arizona Miners' Strike of 1983 Recast Labor-Management Relations in America,* 2nd ed. (Ithaca, NY: Cornell University Press, 1998), 37–38.

2. Ibid., 40–41. Joe Sorrelman's father had retired from the company only a few months earlier and moved home to New Mexico. The Whitmer family also had left Morenci, locating in Safford.

3. The White House watched the strike closely, recognizing its possible effects on the economy and the war effort. In late August, Undersecretary of Labor James Reynolds briefed President Johnson on the matter, noting that "thus far can report no prospect of settlement in the immediate future." Memorandum for the President by Under Secretary of Labor James Reynolds, August 26, 1967, Legislative Background Collection, Report of Situations and Its Impact, 9/7/67–9/21/67, Box 1, Lyndon Baines Johnson Library, Austin, TX [hereafter cited as LBJ Library].

4. Rosenblum, *Copper Crucible*, 39–40.

5. Ibid., 41–42.

6. Interview by the author with Robert Clinton Draper, April 22, 2004, York, AZ.

7. Interview by the author with Leroy Cisneros, August 19, 2001, Yuma, AZ.

8. Letter from Clive Garcia, Jr., to his parents, Julia and Clive Garcia, Sr., December 6, 1967, Guam, personal possessions of Garcia family, copies held by the author [hereafter cited as Letters of Clive Garcia].

9. Letter from Bobby Dale Draper to his parents, December 28, 1966, South Vietnam, personal possessions of Draper family, copies held by the author [hereafter cited as Letters of Bobby Dale Draper].

10. Letter from Bobby Dale Draper to his parents, January 12, 1967, South Vietnam, Letters of Bobby Dale Draper.

11. Ibid.

12. Letter from Bobby Dale Draper to his parents, January 17, 1967, South Vietnam, Letters of Bobby Dale Draper.

13. Letter from Bobby Dale Draper to his parents, January 19, 1967, South Vietnam, Letters of Bobby Dale Draper.

14. Draper letter, January 12, 1967.

15. Letter from Bobby Dale Draper to his parents, February 22, 1967, South Vietnam, Letters of Bobby Dale Draper.

16. Letter from Bobby Dale Draper to his parents, March 17, 1967, South Vietnam, Letters of Bobby Dale Draper.

17. Letter from Bobby Dale Draper to his parents, March 2, 1967, South Vietnam, Letters of Bobby Dale Draper.

18. Letter from Bobby Dale Draper to his parents, April 13, 1967, South Vietnam, Letters of Bobby Dale Draper.

19. Ibid.

20. Letter from Bobby Dale Draper to his parents, July 5, 1967, South Vietnam, Letters of Bobby Dale Draper.

21. Letter from Bobby Dale Draper to his parents, July 8, 1967, South Vietnam, Letters of Bobby Dale Draper.

22. Letter from Bobby Dale Draper to his parents, February 18, 1967, South Vietnam, Letters of Bobby Dale Draper.

23. Cisneros interview, August 19, 2001.

24. *Mesa Tribune*, November 11, 1993.

25. Cisneros interview, August 19, 2001.

26. Interview by the author with Leroy Cisneros, June 5, 2007, Yuma, AZ.

27. US Marine Corps, Command Chronology, August 1, 1967, to August 31, 1967, United States Marine Corps Archive, Quantico, VA, 12–13.

28. Ibid.

29. Donald W. Hoffman, "A Few Good Men: The True Story of the Morenci Marines," book proposal, 1989, 14 (proposal provided by Joe Sorrelman to the author; copy in possession of the author). Joe Sorrelman later ran into a member of Bobby Dale's Golf Company who reported that the commanders at first did not believe the report of heavy action because no one had been hit in the area before. Once they dispatched a reaction force, it was too late. Interview by the author with Joe Sorrelman, April 18, 2012, Glendale, AZ.

30. US Marine Corps, Command Chronology.

31. Harry Spiller, *Death Angel: A Vietnam Memoir of a Bearer of Death Messages to Families* (Jefferson, NC: McFarland, 1992), 166–167.

32. Interview by the author with William H. Gibson, July 23, 2009, Austin, TX. Gibson became the recruiting officer for Arizona in March 1966. He retained that position until December 1967. Several times, he supplemented the work of the Marine Corps inspector and instructor due to the heavy demands.

33. Hoffman, "A Few Good Men," 15.

34. Draper interview.

35. Ibid.

36. *Copper Era*, August 16, 1967.

37. Ibid.

38. Draper interview.

39. *Copper Era,* August 16, 1967.

40. Ibid.

41. Ibid.

42. Lyndon B. Johnson to Robert C. Draper, August 14, 1967, Papers of Lyndon B. Johnson, NS-Defense, ND 9-2-2 Dr-Drhz, Box 73, LBJ Library.

43. American War Library, "Vietnam War Death and Casualties by Month," August 1967, accessed May 31, 2012, http://www.americanwarlibrary.com/vietnam /vwc24.htm.

44. Interview by the author with Mike Cranford, May 23, 2003, York, AZ.

45. *Arizona Republic,* April 30, 2000.

46. Interview by the author with Leroy Cisneros, June 6, 2007, Yuma, AZ.

47. Letter from Larry West to his parents, September 4, 1967, Papers of Larry West (copies provided by Don Hoffman from original research).

48. Letter from Clive Garcia, Jr., to his parents, Julia and Clive Garcia, Sr., September 8, 1967, Guam, Letters of Clive Garcia.

49. Ibid.

50. *Copper Era,* October 18, 1967.

51. For an example, see "Devoll Active in Operation Wheeler," *Copper Era,* November 15, 1967.

52. Interview by the author with Alma "Penny" King, April 24, 2004, Safford, AZ.

53. Ibid.

54. E-mail from Gerald Hunt to the author, May 30, 2012.

55. *Arizona Republic,* December 11, 1969.

56. James R. Ebert, *A Life in a Year: The American Infantryman in Vietnam, 1965–1972* (Novato, CA: Presidio Press, 1993), 1–2.

57. Interview of V. Dean Quillett by Terry L. Birdwhistell and George Herring, Louisville, Kentucky, March 18, 1985, University of Kentucky Oral History Program, University of Kentucky, Lexington, KY, 5.

58. Robert Peterson, *Rites of Passage: Odyssey of a Grunt* (New York: Ballantine Books, 1997), 9.

59. Ches Schneider, *From Classrooms to Claymores: A Teacher at War in Vietnam* (New York: Ivy Books, 1997), 18.

60. King interview.

61. Gary L. Telfer and Lane Rogers, with V. Keith Fleming, *U.S. Marines in Vietnam: Fighting the North Vietnamese, 1967* (Washington DC: History and Museum Division Headquarters, US Marine Corps, 1984), 120.

62. Ibid., 120–121.

63. Ibid.

64. Ibid., 121–122.

65. US Marine Corps, Command Chronology, 2nd Battalion, 5th Marines, "Combat Operations After Action Report," November 1, 1967, to November 30, 1967, United States Marine Corps Archive, Quantico, VA, 8.

66. King interview.

67. Ibid.

68. *Copper Era*, November 22, 1967.

69. Ibid.

70. Ibid.

71. Ibid.

72. Ibid.

73. Drew Gilpin Faust, *This Republic of Suffering: Death and the American Civil War* (New York: Alfred A. Knopf, 2008), 6–17.

74. *Copper Era*, November 22, 1967.

75. Ibid.

76. King interview.

77. Ibid.

78. *Eastern Arizona Courier*, March 26, 1969.

79. King interview.

Chapter 8. The Death Angel Returns

1. Melvin Small, *Antiwarriors: The Vietnam War and the Battle for America's Hearts and Minds* (Lanham, MD: Scholarly Resources, 2002), 39–94.

2. As cited in Edward F. Murphy, *Semper Fi Vietnam: From Danang to the DMZ—Marine Corps Campaigns, 1965–1975* (San Francisco: Presidio Press, 1997), 148.

3. As cited in Robert Dallek, *Flawed Giant: Lyndon Johnson and His Times, 1961–1973* (New York: Oxford University Press, 1998), 500.

4. George Herring, *LBJ and Vietnam: A Different Kind of War* (Austin: University of Texas Press, 1994), 140–148.

5. For more on the battle, see Robert Pisor, *The End of the Line: The Siege of Khe Sanh* (New York: W. W. Norton, 2002); Gordon Rottman, *Khe Sanh, 1967–1968: Marines Battle for Vietnam's Vital Hilltop Base* (New York: Osprey, 2005); Ronald Drez and Douglas Brinkley, *Voices of Courage: The Battle for Khe Sanh, Vietnam* (New York:

Bullfinch, 2005); John Corbett, *West Dickens Avenue: A Marine at Khe Sanh* (New York: Ballantine Books, 2003).

6. Irving Bernstein, *Guns or Butter: The Presidency of Lyndon Johnson* (New York: Oxford University Press, 1996), 474.

7. Walter LaFeber, *The Deadly Bet: LBJ, Vietnam, and the 1968 Election* (Lanham, MD: Rowman & Littlefield, 2005), 25–26.

8. Don Oberdorfer, *Tet! The Turning Point in the Vietnam War*, updated and rev. ed. (Baltimore, MD: Johns Hopkins University Press, 2001), 116–235.

9. Charles E. Neu, *America's Lost War: Vietnam: 1945–1975* (Wheeling, IL: Harlan-Davidson, 2005), 134.

10. Dallek, *Flawed Giant*, 506.

11. Neu, *America's Lost War*, 132–136.

12. *Copper Era*, November 29, 1967.

13. *Copper Era*, February 7, 1968.

14. Paul Fannin to Lyndon Johnson, February 1, 1968, White House Central Files Collection—EX LA 6/Copper 8/1/67–12/5/67, letter and memos, Box 24, Lyndon Baines Johnson Library, Austin, TX [hereafter cited as LBJ Library].

15. Frank Swobado, Memorandum on Special Mediation, January 24, 1967, Legislative Background Collection, Report of Situations and Its Impact, 10/3/67–2/26/68, Box 1, LBJ Library; *Copper Era*, January 31, 1968.

16. Memorandum of Meeting of the President, February 29, 1968, January 24, 1967, Legislative Background Collection, Meeting of Smith, Trowbridge et al., Box 1, LBJ Library.

17. President Lyndon Johnson to I. W. Abel, P. L. Siemiller, Gordon Freeman, Paul Jennings, Walter Ruether, R. D. Bradford, C. Jay Parkinson, Frank Milliken, and Robert Page, March 1, 1968, White House Central Files Collection—EX LA 6/Copper 8/1/67–12/5/67, letter and memos, Box 24, LBJ Library.

18. As cited in Jonathan D. Rosenblum, *Copper Crucible: How the Arizona Miners' Strike of 1983 Recast Labor-Management Relations in America*, 2nd ed. (Ithaca, NY: Cornell University Press, 1998), 42.

19. *Copper Era*, March 20, 1968; Carlos A. Schwantes, *Vision and Enterprise: Exploring the History of Phelps Dodge Corporation* (Tucson: University of Arizona Press, 2000), 308.

20. Irwin Unger and Debi Unger, *LBJ: A Life* (New York: John Wiley and Sons, 1999), 459.

21. *Arizona Republic*, December 11, 1969.

22. Ibid.

23. The Virtual Wall at the Vietnam Veterans Memorial, "Full Profile for Alfred Whitmer," accessed June 24, 2012, http://www.virtualwall.org/dw/WhitmerAV01a.htm.

24. Report of Casualty, "Whitmer, Alfred Van," reported on April 17, 1968, CG First Marine Division, Marine Corps Archives, Quantico, VA.

25. *Copper Era,* April 24, 1968.

26. Donald W. Hoffman, "A Few Good Men: The True Story of the Morenci Marines," book proposal, 1989, 21 (proposal provided by Joe Sorrelman to the author; copy in possession of the author).

27. Anonymous, http://woodburygazette.com/remember-the-heroes-p917-1.htm.

28. The Virtual Wall at the Vietnam Veterans Memorial, "Full Profile for Jose Roberto Moncayo," accessed June 24, 2012, http://www.virtualwall.org/dm/Moncayo JR01a.htm.

29. Letter from Robert Moncayo to Carol Figueroa, November 22, 1967, personal copy provided by Carol Figueroa to the author.

30. Letter from Robert Moncayo to Carol Figueroa, September 13, 1967, personal copy provided by Carol Figueroa to the author.

31. *Arizona Republic,* December 11, 1969.

32. Interview by the author with Elena Sánchez, May 23, 2003, York, AZ.

33. Letter from Robert Moncayo to Carol Figueroa, June 3, 1968, personal copy provided by Carol Figueroa to the author.

34. *Eastern Arizona Courier,* June 1968, n.d., Morenci Public Library, Morenci, AZ.

35. Ibid.

36. Jack Shulimson et al., *U.S. Marines in Vietnam: The Defining Year 1968* (Washington, DC: History and Museum Division, Headquarters, USMC, 1997), 322–324.

37. US Marines Corps, Command Chronology of the 3rd Battalion, 4th Marines, June 1968, Marine Corps Archives, Quantico, VA, 21–22.

38. Ibid.

39. Ibid.

40. While treating Marines in the landing zone after the battle, a Navy corpsman entered into his log: "Moncayo, J. R., Cpl. Service #2269659. KIA, Gun Shot Wound, Back." Letter from C. D. Pickard to the author, September 3, 2006.

41. *Eastern Arizona Courier,* June 1968.

42. *Copper Era,* July 3, 1968.

43. Ibid.

44. Ibid.

45. Lyndon Baines Johnson, *The Vantage Point: Perspectives of the Presidency, 1963–1969* (New York: Holt, Rinehart and Winston, 1971), 533.

Chapter 9. Two Friends

1. Letter from Larry West to his parents, January 8, 1967, personal papers of Larry West, copies provided by Don Hoffman [hereafter cited as Papers of Larry West].

2. Ibid.

3. Letter from Larry West to his parents, January 10, 1967, Papers of Larry West.

4. Ibid.

5. Letter from Larry West to his parents, January 24, 1967, Papers of Larry West.

6. Ibid.

7. Ibid.

8. Ibid.

9. Interview by the author with Mike Cranford, May 23, 2003, York, AZ.

10. Ibid.

11. Others shared Larry's disdain for the Vietnamese. Examples are found in John Dabonka to his parents, December 23, 1966, in Bernard Edelman, *Dear America: Letters Home from Vietnam* (New York: W. W. Norton, 1985), 54; John Magedanz interview in *South Dakotans in Vietnam: Excerpts from the South Dakota Vietnam Veterans Oral History Project, Pierre Area* (Pierre, SD: State Publishing, 1986), 47; letter from Bruce McInnes to his mother, July 20, 1969, in Edelman, *Dear America*, 111; Marion Lee Kemper to Marion Levy, August 12, 1966, in Edelman, *Dear America*, 113–114; Bobby Mueller interview in Kim Willenson, ed., *The Bad War: An Oral History of the Vietnam War* (New York: NAL Books, 1987), 111–112; Leroy TeCube, *Year in Nam: A Native American Soldier's Story* (Lincoln: University of Nebraska Press, 1999), xii.

12. Letter from Larry West to his parents, March 4, 1967, Papers of Larry West.

13. Letter from Larry West to his parents, May 7, 1967, Papers of Larry West.

14. Letter from Larry West to his parents, June 24, 1967, Papers of Larry West.

15. West letter, May 7, 1967.

16. Letter from Larry West to his parents, May 18, 1967, Papers of Larry West.

17. Letter from Larry West to his parents, May 27, 1967, Papers of Larry West.

18. Letter from Larry West to his parents, May 11, 1967, Papers of Larry West.

19. Letter from Larry West to his parents, May 24, 1967, Papers of Larry West. He emphasized in the same letter that "damn news reporters exaaterate [*sic*] the hell out of things. They must be damn scared when the shit hits the fan."

20. Ibid.

21. West letter, May 27, 1967.

22. Letter from Larry West to his parents, June 28, 1967, Papers of Larry West.

23. Letter from Larry West to his parents, August 24, 1967, Papers of Larry West.

24. Ibid.

25. William Jayne, "Immigrants from the Combat Zone," in A. D. Horne, ed., *Wounded Generation: America after Vietnam* (Englewood Cliffs, NJ: Prentice Hall, 1981), 161.

26. Another marine, Richard Ensminger, complained about being home: "I didn't feel comfortable going outside a military base. Somehow, I felt I wasn't wanted in American society. . . . I was getting tired of the petty-spit-shined mentality of the stateside marines." After a year, he volunteered to return to Vietnam. "I think I wanted another in Vietnam to help keep marines from getting killed." See Ensminger, "Blowing Rock, North Carolina, Marine Forward Observer," in James R. Wilson, ed., *Landing Zones: Southern Veterans Remember Vietnam* (Durham, NC: Duke University Press, 1990), 29.

27. M. Cranford interview.

28. Ibid.

29. *Mesa Tribune,* November 11, 1993.

30. *Arizona Republic,* December 11, 1969.

31. Ibid. Friedli later told a reporter that it was "just a flat statement. And, when he went back there on his second tour, he went fast. But that's the way these guys were. You tell them they have to die for their country, and they'd do it. Not just fanaticism. They really believed it."

32. M. Cranford interview.

33. Ibid.

34. Jack Shulimson, Leonard A. Blasiol, Charles R. Smith, and David A. Dawson, *U.S. Marines in Vietnam: The Defining Years, 1968* (Washington, DC: History and Museums Division, Headquarters, US Marine Corps, 1997), 328–329.

35. Ibid., 331–335.

36. Edward F. Murphy, *Vietnam Medal of Honor Heroes* (Novato, CA: Presidio Press, 2005), 142–143.

37. Shulimson et al., *U.S. Marines in Vietnam,* 331–335; US Marine Corps, Command Chronology, 3rd Battalion, 27th Marines, 1st Marine Division, May 1, 1968, to May 31, 1968, Operation Allen Brook After Action Report, June 5, 1968, United States Marine Corps Archive, Quantico, VA, 3–5.

38. Donald W. Hoffman, "A Few Good Men: The True Story of the Morenci

Marines," book proposal, 1989, 25–26 (proposal provided by Joe Sorrelman to the author; copy in possession of the author).

39. *Arizona Republic*, April 30, 2000.

40. M. Cranford interview.

41. Ibid.

42. Ibid.

43. Ibid.

44. Interview by the author with Joyce Cranford, November 11, 2007, Clifton, AZ.

45. M. Cranford interview.

46. Ibid.

47. Ibid.

48. Ibid.

49. Ibid.

50. Ibid.

51. Ibid.

52. Ibid.

53. Ibid.

54. Ibid.

55. Ibid.

56. Ibid.

57. Ibid.

58. Ibid.

59. Ibid.

60. Ibid.

61. Ibid.

62. Ibid.

63. J. Cranford interview.

64. Ibid.

65. Ibid.

66. Ibid.

Chapter 10. Last Man There

1. A series of letters outline the road leading to his R & R on the Cocos and his short visit. See letter from Clive Garcia, Jr., to his parents, Julia and Clive Garcia, Sr., August 23, 1967, Guam, personal possessions of the Garcia family, copies held by the author

[hereafter cited as Letters of Clive Garcia]; letter from Clive Garcia, Jr., to his parents, Julia and Clive Garcia, Sr., September 8, 1967, Guam, Letters of Clive Garcia.

2. Garcia letter, August 23, 1967; Garcia letter, September 8, 1967.

3. Garcia letter, August 23, 1967; Garcia letter, September 8, 1967.

4. Garcia letter, August 23, 1967; Garcia letter, September 8, 1967.

5. Garcia letter, August 23, 1967; Garcia letter, September 8, 1967.

6. Garcia letter, August 23, 1967; Garcia letter, September 8, 1967.

7. Letter from Clive Garcia, Jr., to his parents, Julia and Clive Garcia, Sr., December 6, 1966, Hawaii and California, Letters of Clive Garcia.

8. Ibid.

9. Letter from Clive Garcia, Jr., to his brother Danny Garcia, February 13, 1967, Guam, Letters of Clive Garcia.

10. Ibid.

11. Letter from Clive Garcia, Jr., to his parents, Julia and Clive Garcia, Sr., July 4, 1967, Guam, Letters of Clive Garcia.

12. Letter from Clive Garcia, Jr., to his parents, Julia and Clive Garcia, Sr., July 11, 1967, Guam, Letters of Clive Garcia (emphasis in original).

13. Garcia letter, July 4, 1967.

14. Garcia letter, August 23, 1967; Garcia letter, September 8, 1967.

15. Letter from Clive Garcia, Jr., to his parents, Julia and Clive Garcia, Sr., October 12, 1967, Guam, Letters of Clive Garcia.

16. Letter from Clive Garcia, Jr., to his parents, Julia and Clive Garcia, Sr., September 5, 1967, Guam, Letters of Clive Garcia.

17. Letter from Clive Garcia, Jr., to his parents, Julia and Clive Garcia, Sr., December 6, 1967, Guam, Letters of Clive Garcia.

18. Garcia letter, July 4, 1967.

19. Letter from Clive Garcia, Jr., to his parents, Julia and Clive Garcia, Sr., March 20, 1967, Guam, Letters of Clive Garcia.

20. Ibid.

21. Letter from Clive Garcia, Jr., to his parents, Julia and Clive Garcia, Sr., April 8, 1968, Guam, Letters of Clive Garcia.

22. Ibid.

23. Letter from Clive Garcia, Jr., to Julia and Clive Garcia, Sr., June 9, 1968, Camp Pendleton, personal letters of Clive Garcia, Jr., copy in possession of author.

24. Letter from Clive Garcia, Jr., to Julia and Clive Garcia, Sr., June 12, 1968, Camp Pendleton, personal letters of Clive Garcia, Jr., copy in possession of author.

25. Letter from Clive Garcia, Jr., to Julia and Clive Garcia, Sr., June 20, 1968, Camp Pendleton, personal letters of Clive Garcia, Jr., copy in possession of author.

26. For a listing of the people who died on the same day as Robert Moncayo, see Vietnam Veterans Memorial Fund, The Virtual Wall, accessed January 3, 2007, http://www.vvmf.org/index.cfm?SectionID=110&SearchResult=true&FieldName=Casul_Date&FieldValue=06%2F18%2F1968.

27. U.S. Military Personnel Who Died (Including Missing and Captured Declared Dead) As a Result of the Vietnam Conflict, 1957–1995, National Archives, accessed January 3, 2007, http://www.archives.gov/research/vietnam-war/casualty-lists/az-alpha.html.

28. Mark Hatfield, "Body Escort," in Stanley W. Beesley, ed., *Vietnam: The Heartland Remembers* (Norman: University of Oklahoma Press, 1987), 18.

29. Letter from Clive Garcia, Jr., to his brother Danny Garcia, April 17, 1967, Guam, Letters of Clive Garcia.

30. Photo in personal possession of Julia and Clive Garcia, Sr., copy with the author.

31. Letter from Julia Garcia to Clive Garcia, Jr., June 24, 1968, Morenci, AZ, Letters of Clive Garcia.

32. Ibid.

33. Interview by the author with Danny Garcia, September 18, 2005, Benson, AZ.

34. Letter from Clive Garcia, Jr., to Julia and Clive Garcia, Sr., July 14, 1968, Camp Pendleton, personal letters of Clive Garcia, Jr., copy in possession of author.

35. Letter from Clive Garcia, Jr., to his parents, Julia and Clive Garcia, Sr., August 3, 1968, Fort Benning, GA, Letters of Clive Garcia.

36. Letter from Clive Garcia, Jr., to his parents, Julia and Clive Garcia, Sr., August 23, 1968, Fort Benning, GA, Letters of Clive Garcia.

37. Ibid.; letter from Clive Garcia, Jr., to his parents, Julia and Clive Garcia, Sr., August 30, 1968, Elgin Air Force Base, FL, Letters of Clive Garcia.

38. Garcia family home movies, copy in possession of the author. Clive wrote his father, the Army veteran, "Dad with due respect to the army after this school no body [sic] better say any thing [sic] against it." Letter from Clive Garcia, Jr., to his parents, Julia and Clive Garcia, Sr., September 14, 1968, Fort Benning, GA, Letters of Clive Garcia.

39. Garcia letter, September 14, 1968.

40. Letter from Clive Garcia, Jr., to his parents, Julia and Clive Garcia, Sr., February 26, 1969, Camp Pendleton, CA, Letters of Clive Garcia.

41. Letter from Curt Frisbie to Julia Garcia, January 21, 1970, San Antonio, TX, Letters of Clive Garcia.

42. Interview by the author with Cobe Montoya (Clive's cousin), September 18, 2005, Benson, AZ.

43. D. Garcia interview.

44. Interview by the author with Maxine Alvidez, September 18, 2005, Benson, AZ.

45. Interview by the author with Julia Garcia, April 23, 2004, Safford, AZ.

46. *Eastern Arizona Courier,* March 26, 1969.

47. D. Garcia interview.

48. Letter from Clive Garcia, Jr., to his parents, Julia and Clive Garcia, Sr., November 21, 1969, South Vietnam, Letters of Clive Garcia.

49. Ibid.

50. Charles R. Smith, *U.S. Marines in Vietnam: High Mobility and Standdown, 1969* (Washington, DC: History and Museum Division, Headquarters, US Marine Corps, 1988); Allen R. Millett, *Semper Fidelis: The History of the United States Marine Corps,* rev. ed. (New York: Free Press, 1991), 594–596.

51. For more on the breakdown of discipline and support for the war among the military, see G. David Curry, *Sunshine Patriots: Punishment and the Vietnam Offender* (South Bend, IN: University of Notre Dame Press, 1985); Dick Perrin, with Tim McCarthy, *GI Resister: The Story of How One American Soldier and His Family Fought the War in Vietnam* (Victoria, British Columbia, Canada: Trafford Press, 2001); David Cortright, *Soldiers in Revolt: GI Resistance during the Vietnam War* (New York: Doubleday, 1975).

52. Donald W. Hoffman, "A Few Good Men: The True Story of the Morenci Marines," book proposal, 1989, 8 (proposal provided by Joe Sorrelman to the author; copy in possession of the author).

53. Letter from Clive Garcia, Jr., to his parents, Julia and Clive Garcia, Sr., date unknown, late August–early September 1969, South Vietnam, Letters of Clive Garcia.

54. Ibid.

55. Ibid.

56. Ibid.

57. Letter from Clive Garcia, Jr., to his parents, Julia and Clive Garcia, Sr., September 7, 1969, South Vietnam, Letters of Clive Garcia.

58. Letter from Clive Garcia, Jr., to his parents, Julia and Clive Garcia, Sr., September 12, 1969, South Vietnam, Letters of Clive Garcia.

59. E-mail from Rex Weigel to the author, July 10, 2007.

60. Letter from Clive Garcia, Jr., to his parents, Julia and Clive Garcia, Sr., October 17, 1969, South Vietnam, Letters of Clive Garcia.

61. Letter from Clive Garcia, Jr., to his parents, Julia and Clive Garcia, Sr., October 9, 1969, South Vietnam, Letters of Clive Garcia; Garcia letter, October 17, 1969.

62. Garcia letter, October 9, 1969.

63. Letter from Clive Garcia, Jr., to his parents, Julia and Clive Garcia, Sr., October 21, 1969, South Vietnam, Letters of Clive Garcia.

64. Garcia letter, October 9, 1969.

65. Letter from Clive Garcia, Jr., to his parents, Julia and Clive Garcia, Sr., October 20, 1969, South Vietnam, Letters of Clive Garcia.

66. Garcia letter, November 21, 1969.

67. Weigel e-mail.

68. Letter from Lt. Dave Miller to Julia Garcia, February 7, 1970, South Vietnam, Letters of Clive Garcia. Another story about Clive's death was related later. In the late 1980s, one of Clive's comrades, Vic Delp, contacted the family. During Clive's time in Vietnam, Vic had exchanged letters with Danny Garcia, but the letters stopped after Danny asked him point blank how Clive had died. When Vic got in touch with the family years later, he told Danny that he had some demons he needed to exorcise, one of which related to the fact that he had not responded to Danny's letter in 1970. He went on to tell Danny that Clive's patrol had actually gone into Laos, which is where they were when the enemy booby trap exploded. Bill Merrill was killed instantly, he said, but Clive lingered, though he was badly hurt. The team called in a medevac helicopter, but commanders refused the request because officially US troops did not operate in Laos. The team was several kilometers from the border, and Vic carried the wounded Clive as he sought desperately to reach an extrication point. Unfortunately, according to Vic, Clive died in his arms along the way. E-mail from Danny Garcia to the author, August 30, 2004.

69. J. Garcia interview.

Chapter 11. The Long Trip Home

1. "State-Level Fatal Casualty Lists for the Vietnam War," Arizona, National Archives of the United States, accessed July 10, 2012, http://www.archives.gov /research/military/vietnam-war/casualty-lists/az-alpha.pdf.

2. Ibid.

3. Michael Sallah and Mitch Weiss, *Tiger Force: A True Story of Men and War* (New York: Little, Brown, 2006), 312–313.

4. "State-Level Fatal Casualty Lists."

5. Interview by the author with Danny Garcia, September 18, 2005, Benson, AZ.

6. Ibid.

7. *Arizona Republic*, December 11, 1969.

8. Ibid.

9. Ibid.

10. Ibid.

11. Ibid.

12. Ibid.

13. *Tucson Daily Star,* December 10, 1969.

14. *Arizona Republic,* December 11, 1969.

15. *Los Angeles Times,* December 11, 1969.

16. Ibid.

17. *Arizona Republic,* December 11, 1969.

18. *Tucson Daily Citizen,* December 10, 1969.

19. Edwin McDowell, "Close-Knit Community of Morenci Sags under Weight of Vietnam Casualties," *Arizona Republic,* n.d., Morenci Public Library, Morenci, AZ.

20. *Los Angeles Times,* December 11, 1969.

21. Frank Reynolds and Dick Shoemaker, "Vietnam/Casualties/Arizona," ABC News, December 18, 1969, Television News Archive, Vanderbilt University, Nashville, TN.

22. Ibid.

23. Ibid.

24. Ibid.

25. Ibid.

26. Ibid.

27. Interview by the author with Julia Garcia, April 23, 2004, Safford, AZ.

28. "Semper Fidelis: The Marines of Morenci," *Time,* January 5, 1970, 43–44.

29. Ibid.

30. McDowell, "Close-Knit Community of Morenci."

31. Letter from Nguyen Van Thieu, President of the Republic of Vietnam, to the Garcia family, March 11, 1970, personal possessions of Garcia family, copies held by the author [hereafter cited as Letters of Clive Garcia].

32. Letter from Carl Wells to Julia and Clive Garcia, Sr., undated, South Vietnam, Letters of Clive Garcia.

33. Letter from Mrs. Martin West to Julia and Clive Garcia, Sr., December 14, 1969, Morenci, AZ, Letters of Clive Garcia.

Chapter 12. *Life after Deaths*

1. Kenneth Draper, "'Why, Oh Why?' First There Were Nine, Now Three . . . ," *The Wildcat* (Morenci High School), December 23, 1969, 1.

2. Ibid.

3. Ibid., 3.

4. Ibid.

5. Ibid.

6. E-mail to the author, June 26, 2006. The correspondent asked for anonymity.

7. For a good discussion on the end of the draft, see Beth Bailey, *America's Army: Making the All Volunteer Force* (Cambridge, MA: Harvard University Press, 2009).

8. George Herring, *America's Longest War: The United States and Vietnam, 1950–1975* (New York: McGraw-Hill, 2002), 347.

9. "Empty Chairs at Empty Tables," Lyrics on Demand website, accessed February 23, 2009, http://www.lyricsondemand.com/soundtracks/l/lesmiserableslyrics/emptychairs atemptytableslyrics.html.

10. Interview by the author with William Senne, November 12, 2004, Morenci, AZ.

11. Interview by the author with Julia Garcia, April 23, 2004, Safford, AZ.

12. Interview by the author with Oscar Urrea, January 30, 2004, Mesa, AZ.

13. Interview by the author with Robert Clinton Draper, April 22, 2004, York, AZ.

14. *Mesa Tribune,* November 11, 1993.

15. Ibid.

16. Telephone interview by the author with Gerald Hunt, January 12, 2005.

17. Interview by the author with Larry Kenan, February 11, 2004, Mesa, AZ.

18. *Mesa Tribune,* November 11, 1993.

19. Interview by the author with Leroy Cisneros, June 5, 2007, Yuma, AZ.

20. Ibid.

21. Ibid.

22. Ibid.

23. Ibid.

24. *Arizona Republic,* April 30, 2000.

25. Stephanie Sanchez, "Vietnam War Veteran in Yuma Shares His War Experience," KSWT News (Yuma/El Centro), November 11, 2011, http://www.kswt. com/story/16020809/vietnam-war-veterans-in-yuma-share-their-war-experience? clienttype=printable.

26. Ibid.

27. "Obituary for David Leroy Cisneros," YumaSun.com, March 28, 2012, http://www.legacy.com/obituaries/yumasun/obituary.aspx?n=david-leroy -cisneros&pid=156739070.

28. Interview by the author with Joe Sorrelman, April 18, 2012, Glendale, AZ.

29. *Eastern Arizona Courier,* April 1, 2012. Friends posted a picture of Joe on the Morenci Facebook page.

30. *Eastern Arizona Courier,* April 1, 2012.

31. Interview by the author with Joe Sorrelman, July 20, 2003, Glendale, AZ.

32. Donald W. Hoffman, "A Few Good Men: The True Story of the Morenci Marines," book proposal, 1989, 31 (proposal provided by Joe Sorrelman to the author; copy in possession of the author).

33. Sorrelman interview, July 20, 2003.

34. Interview by the author with Mary Morgan, May 11, 2005, Safford, AZ.

35. Sorrelman interview, July 20, 2003.

36. Morgan interview.

37. Sorrelman interview, April 18, 2012.

38. Interview by the author with Joyce Cranford, November 11, 2007, Clifton, AZ.

39. Ibid.

40. Interview by the author with Mike Cranford, May 23, 2003, York, AZ.

41. Ibid.

42. Jack Estes, "A Vietnam Survivor's Guilt," *San Diego Union Tribune,* August 22, 2010. More on the topic can be found in Chuck Dean, *Nam Vet: Making Peace with Your Past* (N.p.: CreateSpace, 2012); James McGarrity, *Checkpoint One-Four: A Vietnam Veteran's Chronicle of Survivor's Guilt, Posttraumatic Stress Disorder and Mending the Invisible Wound,* 2nd ed. (published by the author, 2009).

43. E-mail from Col. Tim Geraghty to the author, June 24, 2012.

44. As quoted in Jonathan D. Rosenblum, *Copper Crucible: How the Arizona Miners' Strike of 1983 Recast Labor-Management in America,* 2nd ed. (Ithaca, NY: Cornell University Press, 1998), 82.

45. J. Cranford interview.

46. Ibid.

47. M. Cranford interview.

48. *Mesa Tribune,* November 11, 1993.

49. Ibid.

50. *Eastern Arizona Courier,* August 14, 2002.

51. Ibid.

52. By the 1960s, Murphy had become a leading spokesman on the issues of "battle fatigue" and "shell shock" for many veterans. For more on Murphy, see Charles Whiting, *Hero: The Life and Death of Audie Murphy* (Chelsea, MI: Scarborough House, 1990); Peggy Cervantes, *American Hero: The Audie Murphy Story* (Greensboro, NC: Avisson Press, 2005).

53. Mark D. Van Ells, *To Hear Only Thunder Again: America's World War II Veterans Come Home* (New York: Lexington Books, 2001); Thomas Childers, *Soldier from*

the War Returning: The Greatest Generation's Troubled Homecoming from World War II (Boston: Houghton Mifflin Harcourt, 2009); Robert Saxe, *Settling Down: World War II Veterans' Challenge to the Postwar Consensus* (New York: Palgrave Macmillan, 2007); Randy Horsak, *Cross in the Background* (Bloomington, IN: Westbow Press, 2010); Carol Schultz Vento, *The Hidden Legacy of World War II: A Daughter's Journey of Discovery* (Camp Hill, PA: Sundbury Press, 2011).

54. Jonathan Shay, *Achilles in Vietnam: Combat Trauma and the Undoing of Character* (New York: Scribner, 1994), xx, 169; Ronald J. Glasser, *Wounded: Vietnam to Iraq* (New York: George Braziller, 2006), 95; Patience H. C. Mason, *Recovering from the War: A Guide to All Veterans, Family Members, Friends and Therapists* (High Springs, FL: Patience Press, 1998), 221–267. For the changing tactics of dealing with PTSD, see Ben Shephard, *A War of Nerves: Soldiers and Psychiatrists in the Twentieth Century* (Cambridge, MA: Harvard University Press, 2000), 389–396.

55. J. Cranford interview.

56. Ibid.

57. Ibid.

58. Andrew Kimbrell, *The Masculine Mystique: The Politics of Masculinity* (New York: Ballantine Books, 1995), 255.

59. Robert Schulzinger, *A Time for Peace: The Legacy of the Vietnam War* (New York: Oxford University Press, 2006), 81.

60. Interview by the author with Walter Mares, May 22, 2003, Clifton, AZ.

61. J. Cranford interview.

62. M. Cranford interview.

63. J. Cranford interview.

64. Ibid.

65. The term *Jack Mormon* refers to those who are Mormon in name only. Such individuals did not participate in the ritual or everyday life of the Mormon community.

66. *Copper Era*, February 21, 2007.

67. Ibid.

68. Ibid.

Chapter 13. Remembering the Fallen

1. The author attended the event, and the memory stems from his own observations as well as those of his colleague at Arizona State University, Ed Escobar.

2. *Eastern Arizona Courier*, May 9, 2007.

3. Interview by the author with Steve Guzzo, May 23, 2003, Clifton, AZ. The region fundamentally shaped the memorial. It reflected the West's individualism, ruggedness, and isolation. All these characteristics were manifested in the structure and location of the memorial on Mares Bluff.

4. Guzzo interview.

5. John Bodnar, *The "Good War" in American Memory* (Baltimore, MD: Johns Hopkins University Press, 2010), 60–129. A good example of those facing challenges is found in Linda Tamura's *Nisei Soldiers Break Their Silence: Coming Home to Hood River* (Seattle: University of Washington Press, 2012).

6. This is covered in the chapter titled "The Images of the Marines and John Wayne," in Lawrence H. Suid, *Guts and Glory: The Making of the American Military Image in Film*, rev. ed. (Lexington: University of Kentucky Press, 2002), 117–135; Frank J. Wetta and Stephen J. Curley, *Celluloid Wars: A Guide to Film and the American Experience of War* (Westport, CT: Greenwood Press, 1992), 157–183.

7. Bodnar, *"Good War" in American Memory*, 130–165.

8. Patrick Hagopian, *The Vietnam War in American Memory: Veterans, Memorials, and the Politics of Healing* (Amherst: University of Massachusetts Press, 2009), 65–67.

9. George Herring, *America's Longest War: The United States and Vietnam, 1950–1975*, 4th ed. (New York: McGraw-Hill, 2002), 347.

10. Guzzo interview.

11. Interview by the author with Julia Garcia, April 23, 2004, Safford, AZ.

12. Ibid.

13. Interview by the author with Alma "Penny" King, April 24, 2004, Safford, AZ.

14. Numerous examples of such materials have been viewed and reproduced by the author, who has possession of many of the letters and photos.

15. Kenneth Draper, "'Why, Oh Why?' First There Were Nine, Now Three . . . ," *The Wildcat* (Morenci High School), December 23, 1969, 1, 3.

16. E-mail from Daniel Garcia to the author, June 22, 2012.

17. John Bodnar, *Remaking America: Public Memory, Commemoration, and Patriotism in the Twentieth Century* (Princeton, NJ: Princeton University Press, 1992), 91.

18. Quote found at Spanish Quotes Presents, http://www.spanish-learning-corner.com/spanish-quotes-marquez.html.

19. As cited in Bodnar, *Remaking America*, 39.

20. King interview; interview by the author with Robert Clinton Draper, April 22, 2004, York, AZ.

21. Nikki Windsor (niece of Clive Garcia) posted on the Vietnam Virtual Wall, May 22, 2006, accessed July 7, 2012, http://www.virtualwall.org/dg/GarciaCx01a.htm.

22. Comments by Martin Garcia in response to story by Whitney Phillips, "'Morenci Nine' Brought Home," November 11, 2011, *Arizona Daily Star*, accessed November 22, 2011, http://dynamic.azstarnet.com/comments/viewcommentsnew .php?id=/news/local/morenci-nine-brought-war-home/article_cc5888ec-cc42-50b9 -808b-12c4b27d6b07.html&h='Morenci%20Nine'%20brought%20war%20home.

23. Letter from Julia Garcia to Martin Garcia, October 29, 1989, personal possessions of Garcia family, copies held by the author [hereafter cited as Letters of Clive Garcia].

24. *Arizona Republic*, April 30, 2000.

25. As cited in Oscar Baca, "The Morenci Nine: An Encounter with the Vietnam War," paper prepared for National History Day by a Morenci High School student, accessed June 20, 2009, http://www.nhdarizona.org/SRHP016-PDF1.pdf.

26. Interview by the author with Manny Urrea, July 10, 2012, Tempe, AZ.

27. *Copper Era*, November 6, 1968.

28. Interview by the author with William Senne, November 9, 2003, Morenci, AZ.

29. For good works on the topic, see Michael Kammen, *Mystic Chords of Memory: The Transformation of Tradition in American Culture* (New York: Alfred A. Knopf, 1991); David Waldstreicher, *In the Midst of Perpetual Fetes: The Making of American Nationalism, 1776–1820* (Chapel Hill: University of North Carolina Press, 1997); James Mayo, *War Memorials as Political Landscape: The American Experience and Beyond* (New York: Praeger, 1988).

30. For more on the topic of Korea, see James Kerin, Jr., "The Korean War in American Memory" (Ph.D. diss., University of Pennsylvania, 1994); Philip West and Suh Ji-moon, eds., *Remembering the "Forgotten War": The Korean War through Literature and Art* (Armonk, NY: M. E. Sharpe, 2001); Paul M. Edwards, *To Acknowledge a War: The Korean War in American Memory* (Westport, CT: Greenwood Press, 2000).

31. The chapel, dedicated in 1971, honored the memory of Lt. Victor Westphall III, who died in 1968 in Vietnam. His family took the insurance money and built the chapel, which his father stressed was to ensure that his son's death would "become a symbol that will arouse all mankind and bring a rejection of the principles which defile, debase, and destroy the youth of the world." Cited in Robert Schulzinger, *A Time for Peace: The Legacy of the Vietnam War* (New York: Oxford University Press, 2006), 104. For more on the subject, also see Victor Westphall, *David's Story: A Casualty of Vietnam* (Springer, NM: Center for the Advancement of Human Dignity, 1981).

32. Jan C. Scruggs and Joel L. Swerdlow, *To Heal a Nation: The Vietnam Veterans Memorial* (New York: Harper & Row, 1985), 7. Scruggs had outlined plans to create a national memorial a couple of years earlier in a publication, but this story carried

a lot of weight as a slew of films followed *The Deer Hunter* on the war and changed perceptions of the service. See Hagopian, *Vietnam War in American Memory*, 81.

33. Schulzinger, *Time for Peace*, 96.

34. Ibid., 98.

35. Bodnar, *Remaking America*, 6.

36. Kristin Hass, *Carried to the Wall: American Memory and the Vietnam Veterans Memorial* (Berkeley: University of California Press, 1998), 20–21.

37. Tom Magedanz interview in *South Dakotans in Vietnam: Excerpts from the South Dakota Vietnam Veterans Oral History Project—Pierre Area* (Pierre, SD: State Publishing, 1986), 72.

38. Hass, *Carried to the Wall*, 21.

39. *Los Angeles Times*, May 7, 1985.

40. E-mail from Kathy Windsor Garcia to the author, July 4, 2012.

41. Ibid.

42. Ibid.

43. Interview by the author with Oscar Urrea, July 10, 2012, Tempe, AZ.

44. E-mail from Joyce Cranford to the author, June 22, 2012.

45. *Eastern Arizona Courier*, December 2, 2007.

46. D. Garcia e-mail.

47. *Eastern Arizona Courier*, March 30, 2008.

48. There are a couple such constructions, including the official one of the Vietnam Veterans Memorial Foundation at http://www.virtualwall.org/, and others, including VietnamWall.org at http://www.vietnamwall.org/, which allows for a printable virtual rubbing of the wall.

49. "Names on the Wall," The Vietnam Veterans Memorial, The Wall—USA, http://thewall-usa.com/names.asp.

50. "Robert Dale Draper," The Virtual Wall, Vietnam Memorial, http://www .virtualwall.org/dd/DraperRD01a.htm.

51. Alison Landsberg, *Prosthetic Memory: The Transformation of American Remembrance in the Age of Mass Culture* (New York: Columbia University Press, 2004), 153–155.

52. Bodnar, *Remaking America*, 13.

53. Hagopian, *Vietnam War in American Memory*, 81.

54. *Mesa Tribune*, November 11, 1993; *Arizona Republic*, April 30, 2000.

55. "Legion Plans Memorial at Morenci High School," *Copper Era*, n.d., Letters of Clive Garcia. The proposal caught some people off guard, including the families of the Morenci Nine. Julia Garcia wrote a letter to Dr. Woodall, noting, "None of the

parents of the young men have ever been contacted" about the memorial. Officials from the school district and people in the community, among them those associated with the American Legion, worked to assuage the family's concerns, and the planning for the memorial went forward. Letter of Julia Garcia to David Woodall, February 22, 1998, personal possessions of Garcia family, copies held by the author.

56. *Copper Era*, July 8, 1998.

57. Photos of the dedication were provided by Kathy Windsor Garcia. They constitute the materials used to construct the event. E-mail from Kathy Windsor Garcia to the author, June 24, 2012.

58. Ibid.

59. J. Cranford e-mail.

60. *Eastern Arizona Courier*, August 14, 2002; *Eastern Arizona Courier*, May 3, 2003; *Eastern Arizona Courier*, September 5, 2007.

61. *Eastern Arizona Courier*, June 14, 2006.

62. Ibid.

63. *Arizona Republic*, May 28, 2007.

64. For a good study on the topic, see Andrew Bacevich, *The New American Militarism: How Americans Are Seduced by War* (New York: Oxford University Press, 2006).

65. Whitney Phillips, "Decades after Vietnam, Community Preserves Memory of Morenci Nine," KTAR.com, November 10, 2011, accessed May 25, 2012, http://stage4.ktar.com/61469574/Decades-after-Vietnam-community-preserves-memory-of-Morenci-Nine/.

66. Russ Gillespie, "Boys in Vietnam," in the album *Women Are Trouble*, Rusty Nail Records, Clifton, AZ, 2002. Also see Steve Guzzo's song "You Know Not What They See: True Story of a Viet-Nam Vet," Road Rash Studios, Clifton, AZ, 2008.

67. *Eastern Arizona Courier*, November 6, 2001.

68. Interview by the author with Russ Gillespie, November 24, 2003, Safford, AZ.

69. Interview by the author with Joe Sorrelman, July 20, 2003, Glendale, AZ.

Epilogue

1. *Arizona Daily Star*, November 11, 2011.

2. Morenci High School Dedication Handout, Fine Arts and Scholarship Fundraising, April 26, 2012, http://morenci.k12.az.us/Morenci%20Nine%20Dedication%20Handout.pdf.

Bibliography

Personal Interviews by the Author

Alvidez, Maxine, September 18, 2005, Benson, AZ
Boyd, Col. Ed, May 14, 2004, Mesa, AZ
Calderón, Ernest, September 25, 2002, Phoenix, AZ
Cisneros, Leroy, August 19, 2001, Yuma, AZ; June 5, 2007, Yuma, AZ; January 27, 2011, Yuma, AZ
Cranford, Joyce, November 11, 2007, Clifton, AZ
Cranford, Mike, May 23, 2003, York, AZ
Draper, Robert, Sr., April 22, 2004, York, AZ
Garcia, Clive, Sr., April 23, 2004, Safford, AZ
Garcia, Danny, April 23, 2004, Safford, AZ; September 18, 2005, Benson, AZ
Garcia, Julia, April 23, 2004, Safford, AZ
Gibson, William H., July 23, 2009, Austin, TX
Gillespie, Russ, November 24, 2003, Safford, AZ
Guzzo, Steve, May 23, 2003, Clifton, AZ
Kenan, Larry, February 11, 2004, Mesa, AZ
King, Alma "Penny," April 24, 2004, Safford, AZ
Mares, Walter, May 22, 2003, Clifton, AZ
Montoya, Cobe, September 18, 2005, Benson, AZ
Morgan, Mary (Sorrelman), May 11, 2005, Safford, AZ
Ramirez, Armando, July 31, 2003, Tempe, AZ
Rhoads, Paula, March 7, 2003, Scottsdale, AZ
Sanchez, Elena, May 23, 2003, York, AZ
Senne, William, November 12, 2004, Morenci, AZ
Sorrelman, Joe, July 20, 2003, Glendale, AZ; April 18, 2012, Glendale, AZ
Urrea, Manny, July 10, 2012, Tempe, AZ
Urrea, Oscar, January 30, 2004, Mesa, AZ; July 10, 2012, Tempe, AZ
Vasquez, George, April 23, 2004, Morenci, AZ

Telephone Interviews by the Author

Geraghty, Tim, August 2, 2010
Hunt, Gerald, January 12, 2005
Martinez, Robert, May 30, 2012
Montez, Art, April 3, 2009
Navarette, Carol, November 22, 2004

E-mails to the Author

Cranford, Joyce, June 22, 2012
Garcia, Daniel, August 30, 2004; June 22, 2012
Geraghty, Tim, June 24, 2012
Hunt, Gerald, May 30, 2012
Pierson, Thomas, January 15, 2008
Weigel, Rex, July 10, 2007
Windsor Garcia, Kathy, July 4, 2012
Wingfield, Fred, January 19, 2008

Letters to the Author

Pickard, Corpsman C. D., September 3, 2006

Private Letter Collections

Draper, Robert Dale (1966–1967)
Figueroa, Carol (1968)
Garcia, Clive, Jr. (1966–1969)
West, Larry (1967)

Memoirs

Ball, Phil. *Ghosts and Shadows: A Marine in Vietnam, 1968–1969*. Jefferson, NC: McFarland, 1998.

Buchanan, William L. *Full Circle: A Marine Rifle Company in Vietnam*. San Francisco: Baylaurel Press, 2003.

Caputo, Philip. *A Rumor of War*. New York: Holt, 1977.

Corbett, John. *West Dickens Avenue: A Marine at Khe Sanh*. New York: Ballantine Books, 2003.

Ehrhart, W. D. *Vietnam-Perkasie: A Combat Marine Memoir*. Jefferson, NC: McFarland, 1983.

Gadd, Charles. *Line Doggie: Foot Soldier in Vietnam*. Novato, CA: Presidio Press, 1987.

Helms, E. Michael. *The Proud Bastard*. New York: Pocket Books, 1990.

Hodgins, Michael C. *Reluctant Warrior: A Marine's True Story of Duty and Heroism in Vietnam*. New York: Ballantine Books, 1996.

Johnson, Lyndon Baines. *The Vantage Point: Perspectives of the Presidency, 1963–1969*. New York: Holt, Rinehart and Winston, 1971.

Kerrey, Bob. *When I Was a Young Man: A Memoir*. New York: Harcourt, 2002.

Kovic, Ron. *Born on the Fourth of July*. New York: Pocket Books, 1976.

McLean, Jack. *Loon: A Marine Story*. New York: Ballantine Books, 2009.

Merritt, William E. *Where the Rivers Run Backward*. Athens: University of Georgia Press, 1989.

O'Brien, Tim. *If I Die in a Combat Zone: Box Me Up and Ship Me Home*. New York: Laurel, 1987.

Parks, David. *GI Diary*. Washington, DC: Howard University Press, 1984.

Peterson, Robert. *Rites of Passage: Odyssey of a Grunt*. New York: Ballantine Books, 1997.

Puller, Lewis B., Jr. *Fortunate Son: The Autobiography of Lewis B. Puller, Jr.* New York: Bantam, 1993.

Schneider, Ches. *From Classrooms to Claymores: A Teacher at War in Vietnam*. New York: Ivy Books, 1999.

Spiller, Harry. *Death Angel: A Vietnam Memoir of a Bearer of Death Messages to Families*. Jefferson, NC: McFarland, 1992.

TeCube, Leroy. *Year in Nam: A Native American Soldier's Story*. Lincoln: University of Nebraska Press, 1999.

Oral History Collections

Appy, Christian, ed. *Patriots: The Vietnam War Remembered from All Sides*. New York: Penguin, 2004.

Charley Trujillo

Baker, Mark. *Nam: The Vietnam War in the Words of the Soldiers Who Fought There*. New York: Berkley Books, 1981.

Beesley, Stanley W., ed. *Vietnam: The Heartland Remembers*. Norman: University of Oklahoma Press, 1987.
  Mark Hatfield

Drez, Ronald, and Douglas Brinkley. *Voices of Courage: The Battle for Khe Sanh, Vietnam*. New York: Bullfinch, 2005.

Horne, A. D., ed. *Wounded Generation: America after Vietnam*. Englewood Cliffs, NJ: Prentice Hall, 1981.
  William Jayne

Maurer, Harry, ed. *Strange Ground: An Oral History of Americans in Vietnam, 1945–1975*. New York: Da Capo Press, 1998.
  John Talbott

South Dakotans in Vietnam: Excerpts from the South Dakota Vietnam Veterans Oral History Project—Pierre Area. Pierre, SD: State Publishing, 1986.
  Larry Gates
  Tom Magedanz
  Tom Roubideaux

Trujillo, Charley, ed. *Soldados: Chicanos in Vietnam*. San Jose, CA: Chusma House, 1990.

University of Kentucky Oral History Program. University of Kentucky. Lexington, KY.
  V. Dean Quillt
  Robert Wrinn

Vietnam Archive Oral History Project. Texas Tech University. Lubbock, TX.
  Michael Bradbury
  Martin Brady
  David Crawley
  Gary Smith

Walker, Keith., ed. *A Piece of My Heart: The Stories of 26 American Women Who Served in Vietnam*. Novato, CA: Presidio Press, 1985.
  Micki Voisard

Willenson, Kim, ed. *The Bad War: An Oral History of the Vietnam War*. New York: NAL Books, 1987.
  Bobby Mueller

Wilson, James R. *Landing Zones: Southern Veterans Remember Vietnam*. Durham, NC: Duke University Press, 1990.

Richard Ensminger

William U. Tant

Ybarra, Lea., ed. *Vietnam Veteranos: Chicanos Recall the War.* Austin: University of Texas Press, 2004.

Gilberto, US Army—Corporal, E4, 11th Armored Division

Government Documents

Lyndon B. Johnson Library. Austin, TX

Legislative Background Collection

Papers of Lyndon B. Johnson

White House Central Files

National Archives of the United States. "State-Level Fatal Casualty Lists for the Vietnam War," Arizona. http://www.archives.gov/research/military/vietnam-war/casualty-lists/az-alpha.pdf.

Shulimson, Jack, et al. *U.S. Marines in Vietnam: The Defining Year 1968.* Washington, DC: History and Museum Division Headquarters, USMC, 1997.

Smith, Charles R. *U.S. Marines in Vietnam: High Mobility and Standdown, 1969.* Washington, DC: History and Museum Division, Headquarters, USMC, 1988.

Telfer, Gary L., and Lane Rogers, with V. Keith Fleming. *U.S. Marines in Vietnam: Fighting the North Vietnamese, 1967.* Washington, DC: History and Museum Division Headquarters, USMC, 1984.

US Marine Corps. Command Chronology. 1st Recon Battalion. May 1, 1967, to May 31, 1967. Marine Corps Archives, Quantico, VA.

———. Command Chronology. 2nd Battalion, 5th Marines. August 1, 1967, to August 31, 1967. Marine Corps Archives, Quantico, VA.

———. Command Chronology. 2nd Battalion, 5th Marines. November 1, 1967, to November 30, 1967. Marine Corps Archives, Quantico, VA.

———. Command Chronology. 3rd Battalion, 4th Marines. June 1968. Marine Corps Archives, Quantico, VA.

———. Command Chronology. 3rd Battalion, 27th Marines, 1st Marine Division. May 1, 1968, to May 31, 1968. Marine Corps Archives, Quantico, VA.

———. Report of Casualty. "Whitmer, Alfred Van," reported on April 17, 1968. CG First Marine Division. Marine Corps Archives, Quantico, VA.

Book Proposals

Hoffman, Donald W. "A Few Good Men: The True Story of the Morenci Marines."
1989.

Books

Acuna, Rodolfo. *Occupied America: A History of Chicanos*. 6th ed. New York:
Longman, 2006.

Adler, Bill. *Letters from Vietnam*. New York: Ballantine Books, 2003.

Andrews, Thomas G. *Killing for Coal: America's Deadliest Labor War*. Cambridge, MA:
Harvard University Press, 2008.

Appy, Christian. *Working Class War: American Combat Soldiers and Vietnam*. Chapel
Hill: University of North Carolina Press, 1993.

Arnold, James R. *Tet Offensive 1968: Turning Point in Vietnam*. Westport, CT: Praeger
Press, 2004.

Bacevich, Andrew. *The New American Militarism: How Americans Are Seduced by
War*. New York: Oxford University Press, 2006.

Bailey, Beth. *America's Army: Making the All Volunteer Force*. Cambridge, MA:
Harvard University Press, 2009.

Baker, Ellen. *On Strike and on Film: Mexican American Families and Blacklisted
Filmmakers in Cold War America*. Chapel Hill: University of North Carolina Press,
2007.

Baritz, Loren. *Backfire: A History of How American Culture Led Us into Vietnam and
Made Us Fight the Way We Did*. 2nd ed. Baltimore, MD: Johns Hopkins University
Press, 1998.

Barnes, Peter. *Pawns: The Plight of the Citizen-Soldier*. New York: Alfred A. Knopf,
1972.

Benton-Cohen, Katherine. *Borderline Americans: Racial Division and Labor War in the
Arizona Borderlands*. Cambridge, MA: Harvard University Press, 2009.

Bernstein, Irving. *Guns or Butter: The Presidency of Lyndon Johnson*. New York: Oxford
University Press, 1996.

Bodnar, John. *The "Good War" in American Memory*. Baltimore, MD: Johns Hopkins
University Press, 2010.

———. *Remaking America: Public Memory, Commemoration, and Patriotism in the
Twentieth Century*. Princeton, NJ: Princeton University Press, 1992.

Brown, Ronald C. *Hard-Rock Miners: The Intermountain West, 1860–1920*. College Station: Texas A&M University Press, 1979.

Byrkit, James W. *Forging the Copper Collar: Arizona's Labor-Management War of 1901–1921*. Tucson: University of Arizona Press, 1982.

Carroll, James. *An American Requiem: God, My Father, and the War That Came between Us*. New York: Mariner Books, 1997.

Cervantes, Peggy. *American Hero: The Audie Murphy Story*. Greensboro, NC: Avisson Press, 2005.

Childers, Thomas. *Soldier from the War Returning: The Greatest Generation's Troubled Homecoming from World War II*. Boston: Houghton Mifflin Harcourt, 2009.

Cleland, Robert Glass. *A History of Phelps Dodge, 1834–1950*. New York: Alfred A. Knopf, 1952.

Coan, James P. *Con Thien: The Hill of Angels*. Tuscaloosa: University of Alabama Press, 2004.

Cogut, Ted, and Bill Conger. *History of Arizona's Clifton-Morenci Mining District—A Personal Approach*. Vol. 1, *The Underground Days*. Thatcher, AZ: Mining History Press, 1999.

Cortright, David. *Soldiers in Revolt: GI Resistance during the Vietnam War*. New York: Doubleday, 1975.

Curry, G. David. *Sunshine Patriots: Punishment and the Vietnam Offender*. South Bend, IN: University of Notre Dame Press, 1985.

Dallek, Robert. *Flawed Giant: Lyndon Johnson and His Times, 1961–1973*. New York: Oxford University Press, 1998.

Davis, James W., Sr., and Kenneth M. Dolbeare. *Little Groups of Neighbors: The Selective Service System*. Chicago: Markham Publishing, 1968.

Dawson, Graham. *Soldier Heroes: British Adventure, Empire and the Imaging of Masculinities*. New York: Routledge, 1994.

Dean, Chuck. *Nam Vet: Making Peace with Your Past*. N.p.: CreateSpace, 2012.

Dean, Robert D. *Imperial Brotherhood: Gender and the Making of Cold War Foreign Policy*. Amherst: University of Massachusetts Press, 2001.

Díaz Björkquist, Elena. *Suffer Smoke*. Houston: Arte Público Press, 1996.

Durrett, Deanne. *Unsung Heroes of World War II: The Story of the Navajo Code Talkers*. Lincoln, NE: Bison Books, 2009.

Ebert, James. *A Life in a Year: The American Infantryman in Vietnam*. New York: Presidio Press, 2004.

Edelman, Bernard. *Dear America: Letters Home from Vietnam*. New York: W. W. Norton, 1985.

Edwards, Paul M. *To Acknowledge a War: The Korean War in American Memory.* Westport, CT: Greenwood Press, 2000.

Eller, Ronald D. *Miners, Millhands, and Mountaineers: Industrialization of the Appalachian South, 1880–1930.* Knoxville: University of Tennessee Press, 1982.

Enloe, Cynthia H. *Ethnic Soldiers: State Security in Divided Societies.* Athens: University of Georgia Press, 1980.

Fasteau, Marc Feigen. *The Male Machine.* New York: McGraw-Hill, 1974.

Faust, Drew Gilpin. *This Republic of Suffering: Death and the American Civil War.* New York: Alfred A. Knopf, 2008.

Flynn, George Q. *The Draft, 1940–1973.* Lawrence: University Press of Kansas, 1993.

Franco, Jere Bishop. *Crossing the Pond: The Native American Effort in World War II.* Denton: University of North Texas Press, 1999.

Glasser, Ronald J. *Wounded: Vietnam to Iraq.* New York: George Braziller, 2006.

Gonzales, Manuel G. *Mexicanos: A History of Mexicans in the United States.* Bloomington: Indiana University Press, 2000.

Gordon, Linda. *The Great Arizona Orphan Abduction.* Cambridge, MA: Harvard University Press, 1999.

Hagopian, Patrick. *The Vietnam War in American Memory: Veterans, Memorials, and the Politics of Healing.* Amherst: University of Massachusetts Press, 2009.

Hass, Kristin. *Carried to the Wall: American Memory and the Vietnam Veterans Memorial.* Berkeley: University of California Press, 1998.

Herring, George. *America's Longest War: The United States and Vietnam, 1950–1975.* 4th ed. New York: McGraw-Hill, 2003.

———. *LBJ and Vietnam: A Different Kind of War.* Austin: University of Texas Press, 1994.

Hildreth, Ray, and Charles W. Sasser. *Hill 488.* New York: Pocket Books, 2003.

Holm, Tom. *Strong Hearts, Wounded Souls: Native American Veterans of the Vietnam War.* Austin: University of Texas Press, 1996.

Horsak, Randy. *Cross in the Background.* Bloomington, IN: Westbow Press, 2010.

Inboden, William. *Religion and American Foreign Policy, 1945–1960.* New York: Cambridge University Press, 2008.

Jacobs, Seth. *The Miracle Man in Vietnam: Ngo Dinh Diem, Religion, Race, and U.S. Intervention in Southeast Asia.* Durham, NC: Duke University Press, 2005.

Jameson, Betsy. *All That Glitters: Class, Conflict, and Community in Cripple Creek.* Urbana: University of Illinois Press, 1998.

Jones, James. *WWII: A Chronicle of Soldiering.* New York: Ballantine Books, 1976.

Kawano, Kenji. *Warriors: Navajo Code Talkers.* Flagstaff, AZ: Northland Publishing, 2002.

Kimbrell, Andrew. *The Masculine Mystique: The Politics of Masculinity*. New York: Ballantine Books, 1995.

Kimmel, Michael. *Manhood in America: A Cultural History*. New York: Free Press, 1996.

Kingsolver, Barbara. *Animal Dreams*. New York: HarperCollins, 1990.

Kluger, James R. *The Clifton-Morenci Strike: Labor Difficulty in Arizona, 1915–1916*. Tucson: University of Arizona Press, 1970.

LaFeber, Walter. *The Deadly Bet: LBJ, Vietnam, and the 1968 Election*. Lanham, MD: Rowman & Littlefield, 2005.

Landsberg, Alison. *Prosthetic Memory: The Transformation of American Remembrance in the Age of Mass Culture*. New York: Columbia University Press, 2004.

Lehrack, Otto. *The First Battle—Operation Starlite and the Beginning of the Blood Debt in Vietnam*. New York: Ballantine Books, 2006.

Longley, Kyle. *Grunts: The American Combat Soldier in Vietnam*. Armonk, NY: M. E. Sharpe, 2008.

Lorence, James J. *The Suppression of Salt of the Earth: How Hollywood, Big Labor, and Politicians Blacklisted a Movie in the American Cold War*. Albuquerque: University of New Mexico Press, 1999.

Loveland, Anne C. *American Evangelicals and the U.S. Military, 1942–1993*. Baton Rouge: Louisiana State University Press, 1997.

Mariscal, George, ed. *Aztlán and Vietnam: Chicano and Chicana Experiences of the War*. Berkeley: University of California Press, 1999.

Martelle, Scott. *Blood Passion: The Ludlow Massacre and Class War in the American West*. New Brunswick, NJ: Rutgers University Press, 2008.

Mason, Patience H. C. *Recovering from the War: A Guide to All Veterans, Family Members, Friends and Therapists*. High Springs, FL: Patience Press, 1998.

Mayo, James. *War Memorials As Political Landscape: The American Experience and Beyond*. New York: Praeger, 1988.

McClain, Sally. *Navajo Weapon: The Navajo Code Talkers*. Tucson, AZ: Rio Nuevo Publishers, 2002.

McGarrity, James. *Checkpoint One-Four: A Vietnam Veteran's Chronicle of Survivor's Guilt, Posttraumatic Stress Disorder and Mending the Invisible Wound*. 2nd ed. Self-published, 2009.

McGovern, George S. *The Great Coalfield War*. Boulder: University Press of Colorado, 1996.

McNamara, Patrick. *A Catholic Cold War: Edmund A. Walsh, S. J., and the Politics of American Anticommunism*. Bronx, NY: Fordham University Press, 2005.

Millett, Allen R. *Semper Fidelis: The History of the United States Marine Corps*. Rev. ed. New York: Free Press, 1991.

Meadows, William C. *Kiowa, Apache, and Comanche Military Societies: Enduring Veterans, 1800 to the Present*. Austin: University of Texas Press, 1990.

Mechling, Jay. *On My Honor: Boy Scouts and the Making of American Youth*. Chicago: University of Chicago Press, 2001.

Morgan, Joseph G. *The Vietnam Lobby: The American Friends of Vietnam, 1955–1975*. Chapel Hill: University of North Carolina Press, 1997.

Murphy, Edward F. *Semper Fi Vietnam: From Da Nang to the DMZ, Marine Corps Campaigns, 1965–1975*. Novato, CA: Presidio Press, 1997.

———. *Vietnam Medal of Honor Heroes*. Novato, CA: Presidio Press, 2005.

Neu, Charles E. *America's Lost War: Vietnam: 1945–1975*. Wheeling, IL: Harlan-Davidson, 2005.

Nolan, Keith. *Battle for Saigon: Tet 1968*. Novato, CA: Presidio Press, 2002.

Oberdorfer, Don. *Tet! The Turning Point in the Vietnam War*. Baltimore, MD: Johns Hopkins University Press, 2001.

O'Connell, Aaron. *Underdogs: The Making of the Modern Marine Corps*. Cambridge, MA: Harvard University Press, 2012.

O'Connor, Sandra Day, and H. Alan Day. *Lazy B*. New York: Modern Library, 2005.

Paul, Doris. *The Navajo Code Talkers*. Pittsburgh, PA: Dorrance Publishing, 1998.

Perrin, Dick, with Tim McCarthy. *GI Resister: The Story of How One American Soldier and His Family Fought the War in Vietnam*. Victoria, British Columbia, Canada: Trafford Press, 2001.

Peters, Shawn Francis. *The Catonsville Nine: A Story of Faith and Resistance in the Vietnam War*. New York: Oxford University Press, 2012.

Peterson, Robert. *The Boy Scouts: An American Adventure*. New York: American Heritage, 1984.

Pisor, Robert. *The End of the Line: The Siege of Khe Sanh*. New York: W. W. Norton, 2002.

Poiner, Murray, and Jim O'Grady. *Disarmed and Dangerous: The Radical Life and Times of Daniel and Philip Berrigan, Brothers in Religious Faith and Civil Disobedience*. Boulder, CO: Westview Press, 1998.

Preston, Andrew. *Sword of the Spirit, Shield of Faith: Religion in American War and Diplomacy*. New York: Alfred A. Knopf, 2012.

Prince, Gregory A., and William Robert Wright. *David O. McKay and the Rise of Modern Mormonism*. Salt Lake City: University of Utah Press, 2005.

Robertson, David. *Hard As the Rock Itself: Place and Identity in the American Mining Town*. Boulder: University Press of Colorado, 2006.

Rosenblum, Jonathan D. *Copper Crucible: How the Arizona Miners' Strike of 1983 Recast Labor-Management Relations in America*. 2nd ed. Ithaca, NY: ILR Press, 1998.

Rottman, Gordon. *Khe Sanh, 1967–1968: Marines Battle for Vietnam's Vital Hilltop Base*. New York: Osprey, 2005.

Rotundo, E. Anthony. *American Manhood: Transformations of Masculinity from the Revolution to the Modern Era*. New York: Basic Books, 1993.

Ruiz, Vicki. *Out of the Shadows: Mexican Women in Twentieth-Century America*. New York: Oxford University Press, 1998.

Saxe, Robert. *Settling Down: World War II Veterans' Challenge to the Postwar Consensus*. New York: Palgrave Macmillan, 2007.

Schultz Vento, Carol. *The Hidden Legacy of World War II: A Daughter's Journey of Discovery*. Camp Hill, PA: Sundbury Press, 2011.

Schulzinger, Robert. *A Time for Peace: The Legacy of the Vietnam War*. New York: Oxford University Press, 2006.

Schwantes, Carlos A. *Vision and Enterprise: Exploring the History of Phelps Dodge Corporation*. Tucson: University of Arizona Press, 2000.

Scruggs, Jan C., and Joel L. Swerdlow. *To Heal a Nation: The Vietnam Veterans Memorial*. New York: Harper & Row, 1985.

Shay, Jonathan. *Achilles in Vietnam: Combat Trauma and the Undoing of Character*. New York: Scribner, 1994.

Shephard, Ben. *A War of Nerves: Soldiers and Psychiatrists in the Twentieth Century*. Cambridge, MA: Harvard University Press, 2000.

Sheridan, Thomas. *Arizona: A History*. Tucson: University of Arizona Press, 1995.

Shifflett, Crandall A. *Coal Towns: Life, Work, and Culture in Company Towns of Southern Appalachia, 1880–1960*. Knoxville: University of Tennessee Press, 1991.

Small, Melvin. *Antiwarriors: The Vietnam War and the Battle for America's Hearts and Minds*. Lanham, MD: Scholarly Resources, 2002.

Smith, Duane A. *Rocky Mountain Mining Camps: The Urban Frontier*. Bloomington: Indiana University Press, 1967.

Sturken, Marita. *Tangled Memories: The Vietnam War, the AIDS Epidemic, and the Politics of Remembrance*. Berkeley: University of California Press, 1997.

Suid, Lawrence H. *Guts and Glory: The Making of the American Military Image in Film*. Rev. ed. Lexington: University of Kentucky Press, 2002.

Tamura, Linda. *Nisei Soldiers Break Their Silence: Coming Home to Hood River*. Seattle: University of Washington Press, 2012.

Townsend, Kenneth W. *World War II and the American Indian*. Albuquerque: University of New Mexico Press, 2000.

Trimble, Marshall. *Arizona: A Cavalcade of History*. Tucson, AZ: Treasure Chest Publications, 1989.

Truett, Samuel. *Fugitive Landscapes: The Forgotten History of the U.S.-Mexico Borderlands*. New Haven, CT: Yale University Press, 2006.

Tyler May, Elaine. *Homeward Bound: American Families in the Cold War Era*. 2nd rev. ed. New York: Basic Books, 2008.

Unger, Irwin, and Debi Unger. *LBJ: A Life*. New York: John Wiley and Sons, 1999.

Van Ells, Mark D. *To Hear Only Thunder Again: America's World War II Veterans Come Home*. New York: Lexington Books, 2001.

Waldstreicher, David. *In the Midst of Perpetual Fetes: The Making of American Nationalism, 1776–1820*. Chapel Hill: University of North Carolina Press, 1997.

West, Philip, and Suh Ji-moon, eds. *Remembering the "Forgotten War": The Korean War through Literature and Art*. Armonk, NY: M. E. Sharpe, 2001.

Westphall, Victor. *David's Story: A Casualty of Vietnam*. Springer, NM: Center for the Advancement of Human Dignity, 1981.

Wetta, Frank J., and Stephen J. Curley. *Celluloid Wars: A Guide to Film and the American Experience of War*. Westport, CT: Greenwood Press, 1992.

Whitfield, Stephen. *The Culture of the Cold War*. 2nd ed. Baltimore, MD: Johns Hopkins University Press, 1996.

Whiting, Charles. *Hero: The Life and Death of Audie Murphy*. Chelsea, MI: Scarborough House, 1990.

Williams, Daniel K. *God's Own Party: The Making of the Christian Right*. New York: Oxford University Press, 2010.

Articles and Essays

Baca, Oscar. "The Morenci Nine: An Encounter with the Vietnam War." Paper prepared for National History Day by a Morenci High School student. http://www.nhdarizona.org/SRHP016-PDF1.pdf.

Brasso, Matthew. "Man-Power: Montana Copper Workers, State Authority, and the (Re)drafting of Manhood during World War II." In Matthew Brasso, Laura McCall, and Dee Garceau, eds., *Across the Great Divide: Cultures of Manhood in the American West*. New York: Routledge, 2001, pp. 185–210.

Combs, Daniel J. "Official LDS Anticommunism, 1901–1972." Master's thesis, Brigham Young University, 2005.

Draper, Kenneth. "'Why, Oh Why?' First There Were Nine, Now Three. . . ." *The Wildcat*. Morenci High School. December 23, 1969, p. 1.

England, Eugene. "The Tragedy of Vietnam and the Responsibility of Mormons." *Dialogue: A Journal of Mormon Thought* (Winter 1967): 71–90.

Kerin, James, Jr. "The Korean War in American Memory." Ph.D. diss., University of Pennsylvania, 1994.

Miscamble, William D. "Francis Cardinal Spellman and 'Spellman's War.'" In David L. Anderson, ed., *The Human Tradition in the Vietnam Era*. Wilmington, DE: Scholarly Resources, 2000, p. 17.

"Morenci." *Arizona Highways* (January 1946): 23.

Phillips, Whitney. "Decades after Vietnam, Community Preserves Memory of Morenci Nine." KTAR.com, November 10, 2011. http://stage4.ktar.com/6/1469574/Decades -after-Vietnam-community-preserves-memory-of-Morenci-Nine/.

Schwendiman, Gary, and Knud Larsen. "The Vietnam War through the Eyes of a Mormon Subculture." *Dialogue: A Journal of Mormon Thought* (Autumn 1968): 152–162.

"Semper Fidelis: The Marines of Morenci." *Time*, January 5, 1970, pp. 43–44.

Sorenson, John L. "Vietnam: Just a War, or a Just War?" *Dialogue: A Journal of Mormon Thought* (Winter 1967): 93–103.

Treviso, Ruben. "Hispanics and the Vietnam War." In Harrison E. Salisbury, ed., *Vietnam Reconsidered: Lessons from a War*. New York: Harper & Row, 1984.

Woodger, Mary Jane. "A Latter-day Saint Servicemen's Response to Their Church Leaders' Counsel during the Vietnam War." Paper presented at the Center for Studies of New Religions Conference, June 20–23, 2002. Salt Lake City and Provo, UT. http://www.cesnur.org/2002/slc/woodger.htm.

Newspapers

Arizona Republic
Copper Era
Eastern Arizona Courier
Los Angeles Times
Mesa Tribune
Philadelphia Inquirer
San Diego Union Tribune
Tucson Daily Citizen
The Wildcat (Morenci High School)
Yuma Sun

Television and Music

Gillespie, Russ. "Boys in Vietnam." In the album *Women Are Trouble*. Rusty Nail Records. Clifton, AZ. 2002.

Guzzo, Steve. "You Know Not What They See: True Story of a Viet-Nam Vet." Road Rash Studios. Clifton, AZ. 2008.

Reynolds, Frank, and Dick Shoemaker. "Vietnam/Casualties/Arizona." ABC News. December 18, 1969. Television News Archive, Vanderbilt University, Nashville, TN.

Sanchez, Stephanie. "Vietnam War Veteran in Yuma Shares His War Experience." KSWT News (Yuma/El Centro). November 11, 2011. http://www.kswt.com/story/16020809/vietnam-war-veterans-in-yuma-share-their-war-experience?clienttype=printable.

Index